STUDIES IN
IMPERIALISM

general editor John M. MacKenz

When the 'Studies in Imperialism' series was founded more than ＿..y years ago, emphasis was laid upon the conviction that 'imperialism as a cultural phenomenon had as significant an effect on the dominant as on the subordinate societies'. With more than sixty books published, this remains the prime concern of the series. Cross-disciplinary work has indeed appeared covering the full spectrum of cultural phenomena, as well as examining aspects of gender and sex, frontiers and law, science and the environment, language and literature, migration and patriotic societies, and much else. Moreover, the series has always wished to present comparative work on European and American imperialism, and particularly welcomes the submission of books in these areas. The fascination with imperialism, in all its aspects, shows no sign of abating, and this series will continue to lead the way in encouraging the widest possible range of studies in the field. 'Studies in Imperialism' is fully organic in its development, always seeking to be at the cutting edge, responding to the latest interests of scholars and the needs of this ever-expanding area of scholarship.

Gender, crime and empire

Manchester University Press

Gender, crime and empire

**CONVICTS, SETTLERS AND THE STATE IN
EARLY COLONIAL AUSTRALIA**

Kirsty Reid

Manchester University Press
Manchester and New York
distributed exclusively in the USA by Palgrave

Published by Manchester University Press
Oxford Road, Manchester M13 9NR, UK
and Room 400, 175 Fifth Avenue, New York, NY 10010, USA
www.manchesteruniversitypress.co.uk

Distributed in the United States exclusively by
Palgrave Macmillan, 175 Fifth Avenue,
New York, NY 10010, USA

Distributed in Canada exclusively by
UBC Press, University of British Columbia, 2029 West Mall,
Vancouver, BC, Canada V6T 1Z2

British Library Cataloguing-in-Publication Data is available

Library of Congress Cataloging-in-Publication Data is available

ISBN 978 0 7190 6699 3 paperback

First published by Manchester University Press in hardback 2007

This paperback edition first published 2012

The publisher has no responsibility for the persistence or accuracy of URLs for any external or third-party internet websites referred to in this book, and does not guarantee that any content on such websites is, or will remain, accurate or appropriate.

Printed by Lightning Source

CONTENTS

[v]

GENERAL EDITOR'S INTRODUCTION

There is no better illustration of the interlocking of metropole and empire than the phenomenon of convict transportation. Ridding Great Britain of what were perceived to be criminal undesirables (despite the low level of many of their offences in modern terms) created a circular system embracing the 'founding' and then the 'developing' of distant colonies. 'Mother country' was purged as the colony was promoted. Yet, as Kirsty Reid demonstrates, transportation and development ultimately became mutually incompatible. Emerging colonies embraced economic and social, administrative and intellectual forces that rendered the apparent advantage of unfree labour unappealing. This book examines in new and exciting terms the manner in which this happened.

Reid analyses in some detail both the literal and metaphorical ways in which the concept of the 'family' was manipulated in theorising about transportation, in policy changes associated with it, and ultimately in its demise. If transportation disrupted the micro family of the convict, it cleansed the macro family of the nation. Yet the transportee could be reformed and redeemed through a new colonial family, again at both micro and macro levels. Suitably improved, he or she could be permitted to be reunited with or to re-form a new personal family. When this seemed to make the punishment too soft, the notion of a re-formed (and reformed) family was turned into a more distant objective. But eventually this emphasis on the familial became self-defeating. Free colonists saw themselves as having created a different sort of colonial family. For them, continuing transportation and the presence of convicts in their midst constituted a pollutant that served to disrupt the opportunity to create a new moral and civilised colonial order. All of this was closely bound up with the treatment of the bodies of the transported: the signs and symbols of their unfree, quasi slave status, their garments, chains, floggings and other inhumane treatment. And here the treatment of women as well as of men was key.

Through the relatively long history of transportation, we are able to chart the major shifts in criminological and social theory, in sexual mores (for example in the behaviour of governors and others in positions of power), in capitalist and commercial practices, and in religious and administrative concepts between the eighteenth and nineteenth centuries. The abolition of the slave trade and of the institution of slavery strongly influenced the attack upon transportation. Evangelicalism, humanitarianism and philosophic radicalism all contributed to the major assault mounted upon transportation as an instrument of imperial authority. Moreover, this assault represented a form of what has been called (in the history of science) 'the moving metropolis'. Colony and metropole were once again interlocked, with the initiatives often coming from the so-called periphery. In the era of the assault upon transportation, such initiatives were promoted by polemics that were larded with outraged and almost certainly overstated versions of moral turpitude.

While charting all of these important developments, Reid uses Van Diemen's Land (Tasmania) as a key focus that offers insights into other colonial developments. She also never loses sight of the individual convict. Many real people figure in this account and through their aspirations and desires for 'normal' relations and family life, both men and women reveal themselves to be very different from the members of a hopeless criminal underclass, which held the historical stage for too long. Moreover, there is an environmental sub-text here. Transportation colonies started out as remote and barbarous places, thoroughly alien in their landscapes, climate, vegetation and indigenous peoples. Paradoxically convicts helped to tame this image, through working on the land, through creating infrastructures, even through the paintings some of them produced. Within a few decades, Van Diemen's Land in particular came to be seen as an ideal Eden, a land of 'beauty and bounty', as Reid calls it, wholly unsuited to the polluting stream of convict transportation. The convicts had served to transform the image into one in which they had no place.

John M. MacKenzie

ILLUSTRATIONS

[ix]

ACKNOWLEDGEMENTS

My interest in colonial history began as an undergraduate at the University of Edinburgh when I was lucky enough to be taught by an energetic team of historians working on a range of different societies and periods who were willing to teach students how to interrogate the history of empire in a genuinely comparative perspective. My thanks for this go, in particular, to Paul Bailey, Crispin Bates, Ian Duffield, Paul Nugent and Nigel Worden. As a postgraduate student at the University of Edinburgh I benefited immeasurably from the intellectual scrutiny and guidance, as well as the warm support, of Ian Duffield and Stana Nenadic. My doctoral thesis on female convicts was much the better for their help and assistance. I was also extremely lucky, both during this time and in the years since, to be able to exchange ideas with a lively bunch of my then fellow postgraduate students, many of whom were working on convict transportation and most of whom were writing histories of Australia, and these include Clare Anderson, James Bradley, Hamish Maxwell-Stewart, Tamsin O'Connor and Tina Picton Phillipps.

I would also like to thank the following for providing financial support over the years: the British Academy, the Carnegie Trust for the Universities of Scotland, the University of Bristol, and the Tasmanian Institute for Conservation and Convict Studies for the award of a Margaret Scott Fellowship. Thanks also to the archivists and librarians of the following institutions for all their help and advice: the Archives Office of Tasmania, Bristol University Library and especially Sheena Carter and the staff of the inter-library loan department, the British Library, the National Library of Australia, Rhodes House Library in Oxford, the State Library of New South Wales, the State Library of Tasmania and the University of Tasmania Library and archives. Two institutions in Tasmania have been particularly generous in providing me with much-needed time and space to write: Jane Franklin College of the University of Tasmania and the School of English, Journalism and European Languages, also of the University of Tasmania. Special thanks for all her encouragement and support are due to Lucy Frost of the University of Tasmania.

Since leaving Edinburgh, I have been lucky enough to find a home within a really fine department of history at the University of Bristol. Thanks to all my colleagues for creating a friendly and principled culture in which to teach and research history. Special mention for their friendship and support over this time goes to Josie McLellan, Chris McLeod, Philip Richardson, Brendan Smith, Richard Sheldon, James Thompson and Ian Wei. Thanks also to my undergraduate students, and particularly to those who have taken part in my 'Convicts' special subject seminar over the last few years and who, by provoking lots of lively debates, have helped to keep me stimulated and on my toes.

Thanks for all their friendship and support more generally to: Alison Alexander, Jocelyn Alexander, Andrew Anderson, Paolo di Martino, Grant

ACKNOWLEDGEMENTS

Clark, Anne Lemon, David Meredith, Peter MacFie, Peter McGahan, Elinor and Svatya Morrisby, Deborah Oxley, James and Trish Parker, Marc Stears, Mark Thomas, Sue Marsden, and Caroline and Richard Williams. Thanks also to Harry Dickinson of the University of Edinburgh and to Marian Quartly of Monash University, Melbourne.

My special thanks and deep-seated gratitude are due, in particular, to Robert Bickers, Stella Moss and Peter von Staden for their friendship, patience and much valued support.

I have been lucky enough both during the time I worked on my doctoral thesis and on this book to have acquired a second family in Australia. My deepest thanks and love for this go to Joan and Basil Yule, to Russell Wilson and, of course, the gorgeous Meg. A grand debt is due, in particular, to my sister Fiona, a fellow spirit and a much-loved friend.

Last but most certainly not least, I could not have asked for better, more supportive or caring parents. This book is for them, with all my love, for without whom . . .

Kirsty Reid

ABBREVIATIONS

AOT	Archives Office of Tasmania
BPP	British Parliamentary Papers
CO	Colonial Office
CON	Convict Department
CSO	Colonial Secretary's Office
GO	Governor's Office
HO	Home Office
HRA	*Historical Records of Australia*
LC	lower courts, Van Diemen's Land
ML	Mitchell Library, State Library of New South Wales
MM	miscellaneous microfilms
MS	manuscript source
NA	National Archives, Kew, London
NLA	National Library of Australia
NS	non-state records
NSW	New South Wales
POL	Police Office records
RS	Royal Society of Tasmania archives, University of Tasmania
SC	Supreme Court, Van Diemen's Land
TP	Tasmanian Papers, Mitchell Library, State Library of New South Wales
VDL	Van Diemen's Land

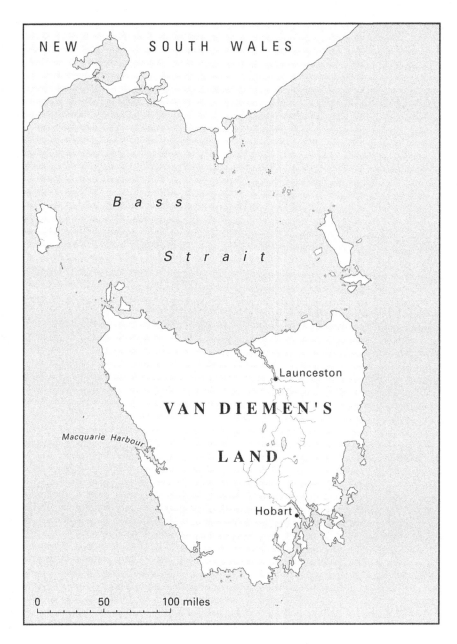

Anon, 'Map of Van Diemen's Land, 1825'
Reproduced courtesy of the National Library of Australia, Canberra

Introduction

On 20 March 1845, Harriet Bowtle wrote to the Governor. She was, she informed him, eager to go home. The 'Daughter of a respectable soldier officer', she explained that her father's early death had 'caursed a great donfall in is unfourtuenate famerly'. This was the case not least for Harriet herself who, in 1831, had been transported to Van Diemen's Land for the theft of a cloak, under a sentence of seven years. Desperate to end her 'unhapy exile', she explained that her family 'wishes me home once more to end My poor ... life with my beloved sisters and brothers' but that she was 'two poor to pay my passage'. As a result, she observed, 'without your excelenecy intersead to government to send Me home ... I must Remane hear for life'. This, she commented, was her second letter to the Governor for she had sent a similar appeal about a month before. She had, however, 'not receaved any answer' and, she remarked, 'I cannot think it hass ever fell into your Hands for I cannot think for one Moment any gentelman could Read my unfortunate Naritive without an Hartfelt feeling – no one that is a father and a Cristan'. 'I pray', she concluded, your Honer will condesind to send an unhapy woman an answar'; 'it will be a great chariety to a fellow creature'. When it came, Governor John Eardley Wilmot's reply was not what Harriet had wanted. 'The Governor', the Colonial Secretary noted briefly on the file, 'has no power to grant this request – refused'.[1]

Harriet's petition serves as a compelling reminder of the painful and fragmenting effects that convict transportation had upon tens of thousands of families. In the half-century between 1803 and 1852, approximately 67,888 men and 12,116 women were transported to the British penal colony of Van Diemen's Land (now Tasmania, Australia), one part of a much larger flow of around 163,000 convicts deported to the Australian colonies between the late eighteenth and the mid-nineteenth centuries.[2] In common with many of these others, the 'unhapy' nature of Harriet's 'exile' was integrally bound up with the loss of home. Her determination to see her siblings again before she died spoke to the ways in which her sense of self was interwoven with family. In this, Harriet was certainly far from alone. The 'state of depression and agony they are in' upon their arrival in the colony, Governor George Arthur noted of the female convicts in the late 1830s, 'is scarcely to be described'. He could, he observed, 'conceive of no punishment greater than for a woman to be separated from her husband and children and placed on board a transport to be conveyed to a country 16,000 or 17,000 miles off'.[3]

There is much to suggest that convict men suffered similarly. In a letter to his wife written on the eve of his departure from England, convict Peter Withers noted that, although he was destined eventually to regain his freedom in the colony, still 'I am shure I shall never be hapy except I can have the plesur of ending my days with you and My dear Children for I don't think ever a man Loved a woman so well as I lovs you'. His 'Hart', he informed her, 'was almost broken to think I must ... lave you behind o my dear What shall I do I am all most destracted for the thoughts of parting from you whom i do Love so dear belive me My dear it Cuts me even to the hart'.[4] At Macquarie Harbour, a remote site of secondary transportation and extreme punishment on the colony's far west coast, some of the men clearly harboured similar thoughts and dreams. On a visit there in the mid-1850s, some two decades after its abandonment as a penal settlement, colonist Henry Button was still able to find signs of the convict past in the ruins and remains. Almost all the 'cell doors and frames' had the 'names or initials' of convicts 'cut or written with pencil or charcoal', and in several of the old cells he came across a number of 'very fairly executed drawings of cottages with enclosing gardens', probably 'the work of unfortunates', he concluded, 'who beguiled their sorrowful solitude by reproducing fading scenes of happiness and comparative innocence'.[5]

Contemporaries were well aware of the emotional dislocation and pain caused to convicts by exile – indeed, many of them regarded it as one of *the* most central components of the terror and dread instilled by transportation, and they argued that it should therefore be stepped up wherever possible by, for example, accelerating the speed at which men and women were removed to the ships and by expediting, if not altogether abolishing, the space and time in which convicts and their families took their farewells.[6] Historians, by contrast, have been relatively slow to consider the personal and emotional meanings of exile to convicts. Those who do research on the family in nineteenth-century Britain continue to be informed by the belief that working-

[2]

class relationships were overwhelmingly governed by material concerns and thus by ties of instrumentalism rather than love and affection, while historical accounts of the early Australian colonies have long been dominated by the idea that convicts, by virtue of their criminal status, were profoundly anti-familial in outlook and nature.[7]

As late as the 1970s, some historians were still arguing, in a largely uncritical reworking of these nineteenth-century discourses of class and criminality, that the convicts were overwhelmingly rootless individuals: the vagrants and wanderers of nineteenth-century society, the uncivilised nomadic tribes of Britain's urban slums.[8] Although these views have been systematically undermined by a series of important works on the history of crime, and by detailed empirical studies of the origins of the convicts, some historians continue to pursue this kind of logic.[9] The 'nomadic' nature of the criminal class, Alastair Davidson (for example) concludes, resulted in the 'absence of social attachments' and a failure to 'see the advantage of a steady job'. These 'propensities', he remarks, forced the early Australian state to engage in the 'regular checking' of convicts in order 'to see that they were learning constant work habits and settling down into orderly sexual relations'.[10] Despite the tenacity of these kinds of views, a string of more recent works has, by examining a rich and imaginative range of written archives and material artefacts (including love tokens, tattoos, petitions, letters and domestic possessions), begun to establish and explore both the complex meanings of home to convicts and the pain caused to many of them by family separation.[11]

Negative views of convict personal, sexual and gender relations were long founded on the ways in which both contemporary observers and successive waves of historians had constructed, or rather demonised, the convict women. Female convicts, the 1812 Select Committee on Transportation concluded in a fairly representative example of these sorts of views, were 'of the most abandoned description' and 'in many instances' likely only 'to whet and to encourage the vices of the men'.[12] These kinds of ideas acquired a certain truth status in the course of the twentieth century, and during the 1950s and 1960s in particular, when several of the leading historians of Australia reworked them in order to produce their own, often profoundly derogatory, accounts of the women. Female convicts, Lloyd Robson (for example) declared, were 'not the sort of women to attract men into marriage'.[13] Even if their contemporaries had 'exaggerated', A.G.L. Shaw similarly concluded, 'the picture [the female convicts] presented is a singularly unattractive one'.[14]

In the decades since, historians of women and gender have done much to deconstruct and demolish these old 'damned whore' myths and they have, in the process, produced a range of powerful critiques. Feminist historians have played an especially important role and, in particular, the path-breaking studies produced, in the mid-1970s, by Miriam Dixson and Anne Summers.[15] Writing against the backdrop of the contemporary women's movement, Dixson and Summers were keen to explore the historical roots of female oppression, and both of them traced the gender inequalities that beset Australia to its founding moments. In Dixson's view, lower-class men, and convicts in particular, had been the key instruments of that oppression. Transferring their own sense of powerlessness, frustration and anger on to their female counterparts, they allegedly transformed the convict women into 'the victims of victims . . . a kind of universal outcast group for most classes in penal society'.[16] For Summers, the women's oppression was more systemic in origin. Female convicts, she concluded, were sent to fulfil an almost wholly sexual and reproductive logic: to provide male colonists – convicts and free – with wives and sexual partners. For women, the convict system consequently comprised 'transportation plus enforced whoredom' and, for at least the first half century, Summers argued, this experience was extended by widespread female unemployment, forcing women to support themselves either through marriage or through prostitution.[17] 'As a distinct minority in a barbaric environment', Summers concluded, 'the women had little option but to accede to being assigned to male settlers, guards and other convicts . . . The best a woman could do was to find a man and live with him, thus gaining herself some kind of protection from uninvited sexual abuse'.[18]

Despite substantial modification and considerable further research, these models continue to exert a major influence over our understanding of gender and sexual relations in early colonial Australia. Sexual exploitation and domestic violence are, for example, both considered to have been peculiarly widespread. Female convicts, a range of historians have concluded, had severely limited options in colonial society and endured widespread abuse and discrimination. Many studies have consequently focused on the ways in which the women supported one another, creating their own cultures of protest and resistance, and on the shared moments and acts of mutual solidarity that enabled them to survive. Others have stressed the women's alleged tendency to seek refuge from the male-dominated culture of the outside world in state-run institutions like the female houses of correction. And, following Summers, others still have argued that some women sought a refuge and an escape in the home, marrying ex-convict and other colonial men in a largely instrumentalist bid for protection.[19]

These studies have done much to extend and enrich our understanding of early colonial society, not least by reminding us that the

[4]

family is as much a site of power and conflict as a space for mutual support, love or affection. The singular focus upon female convicts has, however, had a number of distorting effects upon historical understandings of convict men, and thus, in turn, I would suggest, of the women. First, male–female convict relations are too often read through a wholly negative lens. Sexual and gendered violence on the part of convict men appears almost ubiquitous, with the result that the men tend to figure as almost universally coercive partners, bad husbands and neglectful fathers. Conflict and difference between the men and the women have thus become the main, and sometimes the only, dynamics driving our analyses of gender and convict life. Convict men, in turn, continue to carry a remarkable amount of blame for the oppression of women in early colonial society and, in turn, for the establishment and prevalence of an ostensibly profoundly misogynistic culture. Thus, echoing Dixson, one historian has recently argued that 'the fact that the early non-Aboriginal population was mainly male, combined with the generally lower-class background of most convict settlers and convict status itself, provides an inauspicious beginning for gender relations'.[20] Narratives of male convict brutality have thus tended to displace the older 1960s' emphases on female convict depravity, many of them ironically informed by the same, often class-bound, sources that feminist and gender historians had – when it came to analysing the women – done so much to dissect and deconstruct.

Second, apart from a handful of important and notable exceptions, male convict sexualities and bodies, their ideas about gender and the ways in which, for example, notions of masculinity and of family informed both their sense of self *and* the opinions and strategies of those in power remain unexplored.[21] One result of this is that it is the female convict alone who is considered to have been the target for discourses of bodily pollution and gendered disorder and thus as having what one historian describes as 'a sexed body'.[22] The extent to which notions of gender and sexuality also operated as discourses of difference and domination as regards male convicts has consequently tended to be obscured. Yet, there is much to suggest that ideas about the bodily and sexual disorder of male convicts, and anxieties about their manliness, were major and mounting concerns. Indeed, by the mid to late 1830s, these fears about the men were increasingly moving to centre stage. As chapters five and six explore, the main focus of the growing liberal and humanitarian critiques of the penal colonies in these years, and of the campaign waged by colonial abolitionists during the 1840s and early 1850s, was not the female convict body, which at times rarely got a mention, but rather the reputedly disordered, deviant and polluting nature of convict masculinities and

[5]

male sexualities. These concerns were, in turn, interwoven with debates about settler masculinity and with criticisms of the gendered and sexual nature of state power.

Third, male convicts are considered – largely by virtue of their sex – to have enjoyed a preferential relationship with the male elite and so, in turn, with the state. Early colonial society is deemed to have been characterised by a particular configuration between public and private, a relationship seemingly based upon patriarchal collusion. This was an explicit part of the analysis put forward by Summers – the state, she argued, was an 'imperial whoremaster', intent on supplying convict women as sexual commodities to satisfy the needs of early colonial men.[23] The idea that a set of overlapping male interests overrode distinctions of class and power to shape state action in distinctly patriarchal ways continues, albeit in modified forms, to inform our analyses. Thus Marian Quartly, for example, argues that convict women 'could choose between serving the government and serving a convict "husband" – or less commonly, an officer master – though it remains a moot point whether convict women themselves actually did the choosing, or whether it was done for them by men'. 'The state', she proceeds to argue, 'gladly passed the control of "uncontrollable" women to husbands'.[24] 'New South Wales and Van Diemen's Land', historians Kay Saunders and Raymond Evans similarly remark, were:

> formed in accordance with a patriarchal paradigm which allowed men to monopolise the public sphere and rule at home, while casting women into the proscribed roles of repetitive reproducers, unpaid child-rearers and houseworkers. . . . the state disciplined recalcitrant convict women with punitive internment and passed others over to the control of their 'chosen' husbands . . . A patriarchal (and later capitalistic) public order was therefore to be guaranteed by the establishment of a patriarchal private one.[25]

Although acknowledging that differences such as race and class meant that men 'did not all benefit equally', still Saunders and Evans conclude that 'most men' nevertheless 'benefited to some degree from patriarchal advantage'.[26] In these types of account, convict men appear not only as the beneficiaries of state patriarchy and as the chief instruments of female convict oppression but also, and ironically given their own coerced and bonded status, as the women's jailors.

Many of the existing accounts of convict gender relations continue to be informed, albeit often implicitly, by a conceptual framework which owes much to second-wave feminist theory and which has not only influenced our understanding of the early Australian colonies but also, at times, of the inter-relationships between gender and empire more broadly. Developed by Western feminists in the late 1960s and early 1970s, these models stress the parallels between the condition of women and that of other oppressed groups, and with Black people and the colonised, in particular. In the work of Summers, this model was directly and explicitly deployed. 'When the British invaded the continent of Australia', she writes, 'they did more than colonise a continent and its Aboriginal inhabitants. They also colonised an entire sex – the female sex'.[27] Others have made similar remarks: Quartly, for example, has contended that 'no revision . . . can overturn Summers' understanding of women convicts as a "colonised sex" brought to Australia for the reproductive purposes (whether licit or illicit) of men they were expected to obey'.[28]

As historians have become increasingly sensitive to the importance of recognising and exploring difference between women, this earlier model has been interrogated and critiqued. In an article exploring the methodological and conceptual challenges of writing gendered interpretations of Aboriginal history, Ann Curthoys urges historians to reject the use of an 'analogy of colonial invasion, exploitation and dispossession . . . to describe the experience of white women' on the grounds that it has, too often, helped to construct and sustain 'the historical innocence of women'. The model deployed by Summers and others, Curthoys comments, 'blunts and undermines the possibility of recognising that white women were themselves colonisers, part of the invading society which dispossessed and exploited Aboriginal women and men'.[29] A similar recognition of the problems of writing gender history using this older (women equal colonisation, men equal power) model has also increasingly informed historical understandings of the inter-relationships between gender and empire more broadly. 'The ambiguity of white women's position as the subordinate sex within the master race' has consequently come to 'reside', one historian notes, 'at the core of the debate about gender and colonial historiography'.[30]

As their 'racial privileges in colonial society' have been more fully acknowledged and explored, white women in the empire have thus been increasingly reconfigured as 'the inferior sex within the superior race'.[31] However, as these emphases upon the idea that all whites were members of the 'master race' reveal, much less attention has to date been paid to the equally complex and dynamic inter-relationships between gender and class, and thus to the often marked differences *between* white women and to the ways in which social status and class authority placed some white women in positions of power over some white men. While anxieties about the destabilising presence of 'poor whites' were expressed in other colonial contexts, notions of

[7]

social difference were of particular importance in the nineteenth-century British 'white settler' societies where the emphasis upon the re-planting and re-settling of a socially hierarchical metropolitan order, as well as the exploitation of white labour by white middle-class settlers, tended to place class difference and even conflict between Britons much more closely towards the centre of the imperial project.[32] Nowhere was this perhaps more true than in the early penal colonies where settlers, male *and* female, enjoyed a growing authority over an unfree, and increasingly coerced, convict labour force.

A central aim of this book is, therefore, to ask what happens to our understandings of gender and power in the convict colonies when we let class back into the account. In doing so, this study seeks to explore the idea that the pursuit of various familial and domestic orders and the deployment of discourses of gender and sexuality were designed not simply with a view to the confinement and control of convict women but also as mechanisms for the material and ideological subjugation and domination of the men. In pursuing this agenda, this study endeavours to pay close attention to the late Kay Daniels's advice that historians of the convict colonies should place an understanding of change over time at the heart of their accounts.[33] Transportation to the eastern Australian colonies of New South Wales and Van Diemen's Land continued for almost seven decades. The convict system changed substantially, and on several occasions, during this period, partly as a result of the development of new ideas about penal reform in Britain but also as the offshoot of an increasingly complex and dynamic colonial social order. Daniels's admonition equally serves as a reminder of the need for historians to recognise and pay attention to specificities of place. Historians have too often tended to generalise about convict experiences on the basis of an analysis of New South Wales alone. Although there were close parallels and important overlaps between these two societies, not least because they were subject to similar orders from London, there were also important differences in, for example, colonial social and economic structures and the staffing and composition of the state. This study focuses upon Van Diemen's Land – where almost half the convicts exiled to eastern Australia were, after all, sent – in the half century between its establishment in 1803–4 and the abolition of convict transportation to the colony in 1852.

Close attention to change over time and to place also forces us to go beyond a purely discursive analysis to consider the ways in which ideas interacted – never in a mono-dimensional or socially or economically determinist way but always in a dynamic, mutually constitutive and multi-directional fashion – with material structures and practices.

A tendency to focus solely upon ideas, or discourses – although evident in a wide range of scholarship – has been particularly marked in the development of gender history over the last few decades. This approach has had particular consequences for historians of gender and colonialism: as Padma Anagol notes of India, problems tend to 'arise with studies informed by post-structuralism where the focus is on . . . discourse rather than the female subject'. If women 'are to be studied merely as 'representations' or as a 'site' for the play of dominant discourses', then, she argues, 'we are in danger of erasing them completely from history'.[34] Her warning might be applied with equal force to convicts – men as well as women – given that they were, after all, repeatedly forced in their own lifetimes to seek out ways of living with, adapting to, resisting and evading the processes of being made subject to discourse.

Attention to who said what, where and when is equally crucial if we are to develop a fuller understanding of the dynamics of historical change. An overly exclusive focus upon discourse tends, by contrast, to produce a timeless and static analysis. Thus, if we see 'identity', for example, as one historian of convict women has done, as something which is 'shaped' purely 'through language and through perceptions of the other', it is difficult for us to explain why it shifts over time and the ways in which, in different material circumstances and contexts, one set of ideas can, for example, mutate from being a discourse of power to a vehicle for dissent.[35] Harriet Bowtle's words remind us of exactly this point, revealing, as they do, the ways in which ideas can, at times, serve to reaffirm power and yet simultaneously to hint at critiques of it. Her appeal was, on the one hand, to a model of masculine authority that was properly paternalistic and humane, and her petition might thus be read as a sign of her acceptance of this set of idealised colonial power relations. At the same time, however, Bowtle's petition reveals the potential for these kinds of idealisations to provide the less powerful both with the means to make claims of those in power and to construct critiques of them. Thus, Eardley Wilmot's failure to reply to Bowtle's first petition appears to have opened up a momentary space for dissent: 'no one', Harriet asserts, 'that is a father and a Cristan', no 'gentelman' that is, could fail to be moved by her 'unfortunate Naritive'.[36] Her sentiments almost certainly meant subtly different things to different audiences, in different spaces and places.

The tensions in Bowtle's petition between the potential for a particular masculine model – based upon an image of the governing classes as paternalistic, charitable and humane – to legitimise and sanction authority and the ways in which these kinds of gendered ideals might also serve, in other hands and contexts, to undermine and even challenge power played themselves out on numerous occasions and in a wide range of ways over the first half century of European settlement in Van Diemen's Land. As both Marian Quartly and Alan Atkinson have so clearly established, during its first years the British colonisation of Australia was characterised by a commitment to the establishment of a particular type of gendered social order in which the family and the household figured both as a model for state power and as a means for convict moral redemption and rehabilitation.[37] Patriarchal power – in the historical sense of the rule of the father – lay at the heart of this. Stress was therefore placed upon the idea that a good governor ought to strive to be the father of his people. At the same time, the convict household was to be designed in such a way as to mirror the arrangements of the public sphere by being placed under the rule of an individual father.

Chapters one and two explore the ways in which these ideas informed the attempts to construct a hierarchical and gendered social order in the new settlements of Van Diemen's Land, the reasons why this foundered and the ways in which these same notions of masculine authority came to inform critiques of the powerful and the wealthy. Colonised nearly two decades after the First Fleet had arrived at Botany Bay, and at a time when the socio-economic, political and cultural realities of these earlier mainland settlements were already shifting, an attachment to the patriarchal familial ideal as a model of authority, and to the notion of the male convict-turned-virtuous-yeoman-farmer which went with it, was nevertheless also evident in early Van Diemen's Land. Partly for these reasons, David Collins, the first Governor at Hobart, endeavoured to fashion himself as a father figure. His attempts to create a patriarchal gender order were, however, to fall foul both of the material realities of the early settlements in Van Diemen's Land and of the actions of a number of key individuals, including, in particular, the machinations and corruption of much of the officer class. Against this backdrop, patriarchal models of authority became as much a medium of protest as a channel for power.

Chapter two examines the ways in which a host of similar tensions began systematically to rework the relationships between state and society during the 1810s and early 1820s as growing numbers of free settlers began to arrive – committed to domestic and familial ideals of their own and armed with notions of their moral ascendancy over convicts – and as the British state began to demand the greater subjugation and punishment of those it had transported. The consequent re-forging of the colonial state and the restructuring of settler society were mutually constitutive processes – on the one hand, driven by the state's commitment to its own moral purification and heightened government attempts to intervene and regulate society and, on the other hand, by mounting settler criticism of an older mode of governorial authority. Private conduct became ever more central to public power as a moralised masculinity was increasingly delineated as the only legitimate basis of authority, whether of state rule over the colony or of settler rule over the convicts.

Chapters three and four examine the shifting content and meanings of the convict family and household form. As chapter three establishes, during the first years of settlement convicts were channelled into their own households and encouraged to marry and rear families. These priorities reflected the state's commitment to the fashioning of a particular form of patriarchal authority and order. If there was a point at which the interests of state power and that of the individual heads of household overlapped, then it was during these years when convict women, in particular, were directed towards the family. As Quartly and others have suggested, however, the results of this regime were complex – pushing women towards the household on the one hand, but providing them with particular privileges and exemptions on the other. The scarcity of women in these years combined with their central contribution to household labour may, others have argued, also have created spaces for degrees of female independence.[38]

The fact that Van Diemen's Land was settled later than New South Wales meant that the commitment to this early familial and domestic regime was, however, foreshortened there. Even as Collins and the convicts on board HMS *Calcutta* were disembarking at the Derwent, attempts were being made by the governor-generals in Sydney to curb the independence of convicts and to place greater restraints, in particular, upon their ability to live in their own households. These shifts, as we will see in chapter three, although frequently focused upon the control of women, were nevertheless also integrally bound up with a series of broader attempts to subjugate labour. They came to their logical conclusion during the 1820s and 1830s, when, as chapter four considers, convicts were systematically re-ordered as a coerced colonial labour force and redirected from their own households into the homes of free settlers, there to work without wages. Chapter four explores the ways in which the family form was reconceived in these years as a mechanism of discipline and authority both through the development of the idea that settler households provided naturalised sites for the refashioning and control of convicts and in the growing state attempts to keep convict men and women apart and to circumscribe, regulate and govern their rights to form households and families of their own. Just as the earlier socio-economic order had been linked

[11]

to the promotion of a particular family form, so too the shift to greater servitude was accompanied by the forcible and fairly systematic reconfiguration of the convict private sphere. Against this backdrop, attempts by convicts to enjoy sexual liaisons and to form partnerships and families as and when they chose were increasingly rendered matters of class conflict and contestation.

Chapters five and six examine the ways in which these gendered practices and ideas played themselves out on a bigger, and more global, stage, particularly as a series of liberal and humanitarian critiques of the Australian colonies began to be more fully developed during the 1830s and 1840s. These critiques were partially bound up with the development of new ideas about empire. Throughout the eighteenth century, as Atkinson has established, the practice of exile had partly been legitimised by the idea that colonial settlements formed separate and discrete communities. The idea that transportation represented the necessary amputation of diseased or criminal limbs from the body politic was consequently reinforced by the belief that convicts could be removed from British society and safely replanted elsewhere.[39] Shifting conceptions of imperial authority, as well as a rapidly transforming geography of empire, began to undermine the idea of colonies as places that were separate and apart. By the early to mid-nineteenth century, and not least with the growing and increasingly centralised power of the Colonial Office, the empire was beginning to be reconceived as a unitary state and as a global or imperial body politic. It was partly against this backdrop that growing doubts began to be expressed about the efficacy, as well as the legitimacy, of convict transportation. This occurred at two key levels. First, contemporaries became increasingly convinced that what happened in one part of the empire, or imperial body politic, would inevitably have repercussions throughout the whole. Second, and partly as a consequence, the removal of convict bodies to the colonies no longer promised to have the same quarantining and sanitising effects.

During the 1830s, critics raised two major concerns, in particular. First, convict slavery was seen as alien and antithetical to British traditions, and as fostering the radical demoralisation not only of convicts but also of the colonial population as a whole. Slavery was considered the inverse of a properly ordered and idealised manly self-rule: under its impact, male convicts were deemed to be descending into a state of moral dissolution and even sexual savagery. Second, and related to this, the moral character of settlers was equally condemned – partly because of their reputed role as slave-masters and partly because of the system of state 'tyranny' that was associated with the convict colonies. Major doubts were consequently raised about their continued membership of the nation. Transportation was blamed, in particular, for the production of a profoundly unnatural society, in which men vastly outnumbered women and in which family ties and domestic order were deviant and disordered. In the Australian colonies, critics declared, Britain was giving birth to an alien nation. In place of the existing system, reformers sought to re-fashion the male convict, in particular, into a self-regulating, disciplined and independent wage-labourer. At the same time, they also appealed to a different vision of family, not only as a more moral ideal for colonists to pursue but also as a naturalised model for a liberal and self-governing empire. During the 1840s and 1850s, as colonists themselves became increasingly opposed to transportation, a home-grown abolitionist movement endeavoured to build upon, and re-work, some of these themes. In doing so, it raised the spectre of the widespread addiction of male convicts, in particular, to 'unnatural' sexual practices, thus fostering a major moral panic about the threat of sodomy and child-rape. These critiques were deployed, in turn, against the imperial and colonial states, as colonists denounced the existing system of imperial rule as a polluting, demoralising and profoundly de-civilising force and as a product of a deviant and disordered 'fatherhood'. Like the reformers of the 1830s, colonial campaigners would once again turn to idealised notions of fatherhood and family in order to assert their own capacity for, and inalienable rights to, self-government and to demand the systematic reconfiguration of imperial rule and the abolition of convict transportation.

Notes

1 Petition of Harriet Bowtle, AOT CSO 19/8, pp. 258–9. Harriet was transported on the *America* under the name of Mary Hornet, arriving in Van Diemen's Land in May 1831. She explained on her arrival that her proper name was Harriet Hornet. In 1834, she married ex-convict William Bowtle at Longford, in northern Van Diemen's Land. They appear to have had at least one child together – a son William born at Launceston in 1838. It is unclear – both from Harriet's petition and the surviving records – what happened to this colonial family but Harriet's petition in 1845 was only for her own passage to England. Her husband William left the colony in February 1853 for Melbourne, possibly heading for the gold fields. Harriet's original transportation records reveal that she also had one child and a husband in London at the time of her conviction. AOT CON 40/5, POL 220/3, p. 76. My thanks go to Robyn Eastley, Senior Archivist at the AOT, for confirming this information.
2 Charles Bateson, *The Convict Ships, 1788–1868* (Sydney: A.H. & A.W. Reed, 1974), pp. 381–94.
3 George Arthur, 'Select Committee on Transportation', *BPP* XIX (518), 1837, pp. 292, 312.
4 Peter Withers, Gosport, England, 6 April 1831, AOT NS 887/1.
5 Henry Button, *Flotsam and jetsam: floating fragments of life in England and Tasmania, an autobiographical sketch with an outline of the introduction of responsible government* (Launceston: A.W. Birchall & Sons, 1909), p. 230.

6   See, for example: Sir Matthew Barrington, 'Second Report from the Select Committee on Transportation', *BPP* XVII (296), 1856, pp. 62–3 where he describes the policies he adopted in Ireland during the 1830s. Arthur had similar views about speed of deportation. See Arthur, *BPP* XIX (518), 1837, pp. 289, 305.

7   For an overview of the historical literature on the family in nineteenth-century Britain see Michael Anderson, *Approaches to the history of the western family, 1500–1914* (Cambridge: Cambridge University Press, 1995).

8   M.B. Schedvin and C.B. Schedvin, 'The nomadic tribes of urban Britain: a prelude to Botany Bay', *Historical Studies: Australia & New Zealand*, 18:7 (1978–79), pp. 254–76.

9   Over the last few decades, a series of important studies has systematically demolished the idea that crime was the product of a distinctly separate and innately deviant 'criminal class'. See, in particular: David Philips, *Crime and authority in Victorian England* (London: Croom Helm, 1977) and George Rude, *Criminal and victim: crime and society in early nineteenth-century England* (Oxford: Clarendon Press, Oxford, 1985). Studies of the convicts themselves have reinforced these findings, leading historians to conclude that convicts were overwhelmingly drawn from the British and Irish working class. See in particular: S. Nicholas (ed.), *Convict Workers: reinterpreting Australia's past* (Cambridge: Cambridge University Press, 1988) and Deborah Oxley, *Convict maids: the forced migration of women to Australia* (Cambridge: Cambridge University Press, 1996).

10 Alastair Davidson, *The invisible state: the formation of the Australian state, 1788–1901* (Cambridge: Cambridge University Press, 1991), pp. 31–2, 35.

11 See in particular: Michele Field and Timothy Millett (eds), *Convict love tokens: the leaden hearts the convicts left behind* (Kent Town, South Australia: Wakefield Press, 1998); Lucy Frost and Hamish Maxwell-Stewart (eds), *Chain letters: narrating convict lives* (Carlton, Victoria: Melbourne University Press, 2001); Grace Karskens, *The Rocks: Life in early Sydney* (Melbourne: Melbourne University Press, 1997); David Kent, 'Decorative bodies: the significance of convicts' tattoos', *Journal of Australian Studies*, 53 (1997), pp. 78–88; David Kent and Norma Townsend, *Convicts of the Eleanor: protest in rural England, new lives in Australia* (London: Merlin, 2001); and Ian Duffield and Hamish Maxwell-Stewart, 'Skin deep devotions: religious tattoos and convict transportation to Australia', in Jane Caplan (ed.), *Written on the body: the tattoo in European and American history* (London: Reaktion, 2000), pp. 118–35. Portia Robinson's work on convict women as family women, and her use of non-textual materials like gravestones, in particular, was an important precursor to some of this work: Portia Robinson, *The women of Botany Bay* (Sydney: Macquarie Library, 1989).

12 'Report of the Select Committee on Transportation', *BPP* II (341), 1812, p. 12.

13 Lloyd Robson, *The convict settlers of Australia* (London: Cambridge University Press, 1965), p. 142.

14 A.G.L. Shaw, *Convicts and the colonies* (London: Faber & Faber, 1971), p. 164.

15 Miriam Dixson, *The Real Matilda: woman and identity in Australia, 1788–1975* (Ringwood, Victoria: Penguin, 1976); Anne Summers, *Damned whores and God's police: the colonization of women in Australia* (Ringwood, Victoria: Penguin, 1975). A number of other studies were also important in shifting the agenda, in particular, the early work of Kay Daniels and that of Michael Sturma. See Kay Daniels (ed.), *So much hard work: women and prostitution in Australian history* (Sydney: Fontana, 1984); and Michael Sturma, 'Eye of the beholder: the stereotype of women convicts', *Labour History*, 34 (1978), pp. 3–10.

16 Dixson, *Real Matilda*, pp. 123–4, 127.

17 Summers, *Damned Whores*, p. 270.

18 *Ibid.*, p. 24.

19 See, for example: Joy Damousi, *Depraved and disorderly: female convicts, sexuality and gender in colonial Australia* (Cambridge: Cambridge University Press, 1997); Kay Daniels, 'The flash mob: rebellion, rough culture and sexuality in the Female Factories of Van Diemen's Land', *Australian Feminist Studies*, 18 (1993),

pp. 133–50; Annette Salt, *These outcast women: the Parramatta Female Factory, 1821–1848* (Sydney: Hale & Ironmonger, 1984).

20 Gordon Carmichael, 'So many children: colonial and post-colonial demographic patterns', in Kay Saunders and Raymond Evans (eds), *Gender relations in Australia. Domination and negotiation* (Sydney: Harcourt Brace Jovanovich, 1994), p. 107.

21 The key exception to date is the work by Raymond Evans and Bill Thorpe. See: Raymond Evans and Bill Thorpe, 'The last days of Moreton Bay: power, sexuality and the misrule of law', *Journal of Australian Studies*, 53 (1997), pp. 59–77; Raymond Evans and Bill Thorpe, 'Commanding men: masculinities and the convict system', *Journal of Australian Studies*, 56 (1998), pp. 17–34. Kent and Maxwell-Stewart's work on tattoos has also helped to bring male convict bodies into the discussion. See: Kent, 'Decorative bodies'; Duffield and Maxwell-Stewart, 'Skin-deep devotions'. Three recent doctoral theses have also broken significant new ground in this area: Bruce Hindmarsh, 'Yoked to the plough: male convict labour, culture and resistance in rural Van Diemen's Land, 1820–40' (PhD dissertation, University of Edinburgh, 2002), especially chapter seven; Christina Picton Phillipps, 'Convicts, communication and authority: Britain and New South Wales, 1810–1830' (PhD dissertation, University of Edinburgh, 2002); and Catie Gilchrist, 'Male convict sexuality in the penal colonies of Australia, 1820–1850' (PhD dissertation, University of Sydney, 2004).

22 Damousi, *Depraved*, p. 43.

23 Summers, *Damned whores*, p. 270.

24 Marian Aveling (now Quartly), 'Bending the bars: convict women and the state', in Saunders and Evans, *Gender relations*, p. 150.

25 Kay Saunders and Raymond Evans, 'Gender and reproductive relations', in Saunders and Evans, *Gender relations*, p. 100.

26 *Ibid.*, p. 102.

27 Summers, *Damned Whores*, pp. 197–8.

28 Marian Aveling (now Quartly), 'Imagining New South Wales as a gendered society, 1783–1821', *Australian Historical Studies*, 25:98 (1992), p. 3.

29 Ann Curthoys, 'Identity crisis: colonialism, nation and gender in Australian history', *Gender & History*, 5:2 (1993), pp. 173–4. Despite her seeming re-affirmation of the model put forward by Summers, Quartly is also attuned to the dangers and weaknesses of the 'women equals colonisation' model. Thus, in the same article in which she concludes that no revision will overturn the core conclusions made by Summers, she nevertheless also observes that the model deployed by Summers is 'clearly insufficient and – in the light of what we understand about the colonisation of black women as opposed to the treatment of white migrant females – quite dubious'; see Aveling (now Quartly), 'Bending', p. 145.

30 Frances Gouda, 'Nyonyas on the colonial divide: white women in the Dutch East Indies, 1900–1942', *Gender & History*, 5:3 (1993), p. 318.

31 Clare Midgley, 'Introduction', in Clare Midgley (ed.), *Gender and imperialism* (Manchester: Manchester University Press, 1998), p. 7; Gouda, 'Nyonyas', p. 318.

32 On gender and poor whites elsewhere in the British Empire see, for example, Elizabeth Buettner, 'Problematic spaces, problematic races: defining "Europeans" in late colonial India', *Women's History Review*, 9:2 (2000), pp. 277–98.

33 Kay Daniels, *Convict women* (St Leonards, NSW: Allen & Unwin, 1998), p. x.

34 Padma Anagol, 'Indian Christian women and indigenous feminism, c. 1850-c.1920', in Midgley, *Gender*, pp. 79–80.

35 Damousi, *Depraved*, p. 44.

36 AOT CSO 19/8, pp. 258–9.

37 See in particular: Alan Atkinson, 'The first plans for governing New South Wales, 1786–87', *Australian Historical Studies*, 24:94 (1990), pp. 22–40; Alan Atkinson, *The Europeans in Australia* (Melbourne: Oxford University Press, 1997); and Aveling (now Quartly), 'Imagining'.

38 See: Atkinson, *Europeans*; Paula-Jane Byrne, 'A colonial female economy', *Social History*, 24:3 (1999), pp. 287–93; Daniels, *So much hard work*; Patricia Grimshaw, 'Women and the family in Australian history', in Elizabeth Windschuttle (ed.), *Women, class and history: feminist perspectives on Australia, 1788–1978* (Melbourne: Fontana/Collins, 1980), pp. 37–52; Monica Perrott, *'A tolerable good success': economic opportunities for women in New South Wales, 1788–1830* (Sydney: Hale & Ironmonger, 1983); Aveling (now Quartly), 'Bending'; Aveling (now Quartly), 'Imagining'.
39 Alan Atkinson, 'The freeborn Englishman transported: convict rights as a measure of eighteenth-century Empire', *Past & Present*, 144 (1994), pp. 88–115.

CHAPTER ONE

Visions of order

Gender, sexual morality and the state
in early Van Diemen's Land

If there was an imperial blueprint for early Van Diemen's Land, it was quickly discarded. For the first decade and more, the infant colony was virtually ignored, a neglect which reflected London's preoccupation with war against France. The decision to establish the southern settlements had anyway been formed against the backdrop of this conflict, and was initially designed to do little more than secure British claims to the Bass Strait.[1] For David Collins (1803–10), the first Governor at Hobart, the southern of the two new settlements, the silence from London was an acute disappointment: why, he asked repeatedly in his despatches, had his settlement gone for so long 'so totally unnoticed'?[2] He was to die, in 1810, without an answer. Things were little better for William Paterson (1804–8), Governor at Port Dalrymple, the second settlement in the north. No communications, instructions, convict ships or supplies came direct from Britain until the later 1810s. Instead, everything travelled through the governors-in-chief at Port Jackson (Sydney) who, with more than enough on their hands, paid an at best wavering and partial attention to matters Van Demonian. Britain largely forgot the new settlements until questions of economic retrenchment, imperial expansion and domestic repression made themselves felt in the post-Napoleonic world. It was in this context that London finally intervened, sending Commissioner John Bigge to New South Wales and Van Diemen's Land in 1819–20. His report would lay the basis for a fundamental re-organisation of the convict system and of the wider colonial order, including the separation of Van Diemen's Land from New South Wales in 1825. Prior to Bigge, however, the impetus for colonial design came primarily from within.

Long conceived of as tyrannical and despotic, the early Australian state has enjoyed a rehabilitation of image in recent historical works. An older emphasis upon coercion and brute force, the gallows and the lash has been substantially modified by recognition of change over time, the ideological variation and sophistication informing methods of rule and the extent to which notions of liberty and consent also always mattered.[3] A number of historians have, in particular, been concerned to highlight the 'Enlightenment' and revolutionary credentials of Australia's founding moments. Here Alan Atkinson's work has been of particular importance as he was concerned to explore the significance of the fact that settlement took place in the 1780s, at the 'climax of the European Enlightenment' and thus in 'a decade of extraordinary creativity'.[4]

If there were aspects of the new in the first plans for governing Botany Bay, these were, nevertheless, interwoven with older themes, as Atkinson makes clear. Drawing up his plans for Botany Bay in the 1780s, Lord Sydney had been concerned to ensure convict rights both because as an 'old-fashioned Whig' he was informed by a 'fundamental suspicion of the executive' and because the American Revolution had enhanced his belief in the 'liberty of the subject'. Rather than an unaccountable despotism or Antipodean Gulag, Sydney sought to achieve a balance between authority and consent. Convicts, he ordered, were to have rights in land: their civic independence was to be grounded in their socio-economic liberty as small freeholders, and this was to provide a crucial check upon the power of the executive.[5]

The vision upon which the colony had originally been founded had therefore looked primarily to the seventeenth and eighteenth centuries for its inspiration, drawing variously upon Lockean political discourse, in which manly independence and civic virtue were derived from land proprietorship, and Enlightenment moral philosophy, which stressed the inter-relationships between environment and reform. Far from unique to Botany Bay, this ideological cluster gave shape to many of Britain's other eighteenth- and early nineteenth-century colonies.[6] While some versions of this imperial agrarian model emphasised the 'improving' role to be played by large landowners and men of capital, it was the sturdy, yeoman farmer who stood steadfastly at the heart of the early Antipodean vision. While this partly reflected concerns for liberty, the yeoman ideal was also central because it addressed contemporary understandings of crime in a variety of ways.

Criminality was reputedly the product of an undisciplined self, a disordered appetite and a passion for over-indulgence in all matters of the senses from excessive eating and drinking to indiscriminate sexual encounters. In an agrarian-based settler society the beguiling seductions of modern luxuries were, however, supposedly absent. 'New situations make new minds', William Godwin mused on the subject of transportation in the 1790s. 'The worst criminals, when turned adrift in a body, and reduced to feel the churlish fang of necessity, conduct themselves upon reasonable principles, and often proceed with a sagacity and public spirit that might put the proudest monarchs to blush.'[7] Property, it was argued, also fostered civic virtue because it laid the basis for a new order founded in independence and moral individuality. French naturalist François Péron noted on a visit to New South Wales in 1802, expressing just this kind of view, that convicts had abandoned their 'anti-social manners' because they were 'obliged to interest themselves in the maintenance of order and justice for the purpose of preserving the property which they have acquired'.[8] Exile was designed to provide a stimulus to the much-heralded virtues of industry and labour. Through such means, Collins commented, convicts might in time become so 'purified in the furnace of punishment and adversity as to become the ornaments of that society of which they had formerly been the bane'.[9]

In the penal settlements, the land was idealised, therefore, as the medium and reward for civic virtue and moral progress. By living on the land, the convict was morally sanitised; by living through the land he acquired moral agency, caught up, as he was, in a wider imperial project of settlement, 'improvement' and 'civilisation'. It was partly this kind of belief in the cleansing powers of land that had encouraged Governor King, in his despatches home, to promote the idea of extending the settlements to Van Diemen's Land. King's belief that a new colony was needed to relieve Port Jackson was considered wise policy back in London. Botanist Joseph Banks promoted the new settlement in terms that suggested he regarded convicts as crops in need of rotation.[10] The land at Port Jackson, he argued, was temporarily exhausted and needed to be laid fallow for a period before more convicts were transplanted. 'If you continually send thieves to one place, it must in time become super-saturated', Banks observed. 'Sydney, I think, is now completely saturated. We must let it rest and purify for a few years and it will be again in condition to receive.'[11]

Profoundly gendered notions of social order, liberty and authority were, of course, implicit in the yeoman ideal. This was the case not least because transportation and re-settlement were designed to foster a particular kind of manhood. From the supposedly disordered, dependent, licentious convict body was to step an independent, self-disciplined and thus morally virtuous colonial masculinity. The idealised social model around which Botany Bay was designed also imagined explicit places for men and women. If transportation was intended, on the one hand, to 'convert the most hardened villains, the most daring robbers, into honest and peaceable citizens' and 'industrious agriculturists', then it was hoped it would 'operate the

[19]

like revolution in the vilest prostitutes', by transforming them into 'faithful wives and excellent mothers'.[12] From the outset, Marian Quartly notes, 'the men who . . . thought of a British colony in New South Wales assumed a society shaped by gender'.[13] This was reflected not only in the persistent attempts to order colonial society into small settler households in which men were 'husbands and workers' and women were 'wives and mothers' but also, in turn, in the ways in which the interface between state and society was idealised. A 'patriarchal political and gender order' was 'intended'; New South Wales was to be 'ruled publicly by the head of state and privately by heads of families'.[14]

A belief in the link between labour, land and reformation, therefore, had informed policy from the start. Phillip, the first governor of New South Wales, had been instructed to issue every convict man with thirty acres of land when the First Fleet arrived in 1788.[15] In 1812, the Select Committee on Transportation noted approvingly that time-expired convicts were still being granted land, tools and stock and access to the government store for a period and so 'an opportunity of establishing themselves in society'.[16] Until 1820 all land grants were authorised at Port Jackson; enabling Lachlan Macquarie, Governor-in-Chief throughout the 1810s, to exercise a particular influence over the shape of the new settlements.[17] The son of a west coast Scottish tenant farmer, Macquarie was committed to the development of a smallholding society, and he believed in the possibilities of redemption through labour. Arguing that a convict's civil disabilities should be temporary only, he disavowed the idea put by some free settlers and officers that convict origins should lay the basis for a permanently hierarchical and exclusivist society. Macquarie was still promoting the small farmer ideal in Van Diemen's Land as late as 1821, recommending to Governor Sorell (1817–24) that 'the Tract of land lately discovered near George Town and which I have called Cimitière Valley shall be settled and small farms of thirty acres given to industrious Ticket of Leave men to be cultivated'.[18] These ideas helped to create a society dominated by smallholding, largely subsistence, farming. By 1819 around three-quarters of landowners in Van Diemen's Land had holdings of less than 100 acres.[19]

The multiple interconnections and solidarities to which a small, self-sufficient agrarian settler community ideally gave rise were designed to strengthen the ideological and material structures of colonial authority. The interdependence of each social part was to be realised in the body of the governor who stood, literally, at the head of everything. From Collins and Paterson to Davey (1813–17) and Sorell, the early governors were formally responsible for every aspect of life and death from land grants and stock to town planning, labour, discipline and relations with indigenous peoples. Although Arthur (1824–36) would set a more formal authoritarian tone, the extent of the intervention in the minutiae of daily life to which the first governors *aspired* remained unparalleled. Collins 'aimed for total control', his biographer notes, with the result that:

> few aspects of life in the settlement escaped his attention. He determined the hours at which the convicts rose and when they went to sleep, the hours they laboured and the hours they rested. The regulation of bakers, the placement of privies and the preservation of native swans were the subjects of just a few of his printed edicts which, from time to time, also offered useful advice on the dangers of bathing in the heat of the day, the most satisfactory method of growing hemp and the anti-scorbutic properties of kangaroo meat.[20]

All this was designed to sustain a government based upon an intensely individualised paternalism. In this sense, events in Van Diemen's Land again mirrored those of the elder settlement at Port Jackson where Phillip in particular had pursued a paternalistic patriarchy drawing upon the model family for inspiration.[21] There is much to suggest that Collins, who had served under Phillip in those early days at Port Jackson, sought a similar system of order in Van Diemen's Land. He repeatedly fashioned himself as a father figure and promoted a highly personal form of rule based substantially upon individual discretion. His insistence on personally attending all corporal punishments that he had ordered reflected his belief that convicts were errant children to be chastised and corrected whenever need arose. Likewise, he purported to believe that those who, in his opinion, expressed genuine contrition and regret had 'learnt their lesson' and did not need further punishment.[22]

This familial model of authority was replicated in the wider socio-economic and cultural power structures of early colonial society. Just as the governor fashioned himself as the 'father' of his 'infant' colony, so each smallholder was ideally to be the father of his household. Such a model was designed to simultaneously concentrate and diffuse authority: distributing power through heads of households only to focus it once again in the governor. Colonial society was to be simultaneously one family and a multitude of families. On arrival at the Derwent, and despite the relative absence of women, Collins took almost immediate steps to organise the convicts into 'households'. Despite the urgent public demands on labour in the early weeks and months of settlement, Collins ordered that Sundays and religious and civil holidays like Good Friday and the King's Birthday be devoted to the private needs of convicts on the condition that they worked at constructing their huts.[23] Convicts who were married received particular privileges: they were allotted additional time and resources to build shelters for themselves and their families.[24] Collins here was working *with* the people as much as *over* them: there can be little doubt that many convicts were eager to acquire the 'comfortable residences' to which their governor's orders alluded.[25]

It was through repeated overlaps of this kind between the interests of state and subject that the household model of authority drew much of its long-term strength. However, if consent and cooperation were to the forefront here, more coercive and authoritarian instincts were never far behind. The huts simultaneously created private spaces *and* arenas for the intervention of public power. Once constructed, the convicts were allocated into groups and one convict in each case instructed to act as 'family' head. Through such means, even the first rudimentary households became sites for the orderly distribution and control of the population. The names of all inhabitants were publicly displayed on boards attached outside each hut. 'The People, being now distributed into Huts', Collins noted in April 1804, they 'are not upon any account to change their habitations without orders'. The camp had been domesticated. The close inter-penetration of public and private authority such spatial ordering assumed was extended through the use which Collins then made of domestic authority figures as channels through which his own authority might travel. The huts, he ordered, were 'to be kept clean both within and without', noting that he would 'hold the person whose name stands the first in each hut as responsible for the cleanliness, good order and appearance of each member thereof, whenever called upon for that purpose'.[26]

A symbolic rendering of this idealised notion of the early colonial community as a 'family' can be seen in the attempts to direct Collins's funeral in 1810. The *Derwent Star* 'deplored' the death of a man who had been 'truly a father and a friend' to 'all the respectable and honest inhabitants of this Colony'. Collins was the caring father of the 'infant' colony: 'graceful and commanding' in person, 'affable' 'kind', 'instructive and amusing' in manners and conversation. Characterised by 'conspicuous humanity', he had been 'ever more ready to pardon than punish' and had always had their 'real interests at heart'.[27] 'All descriptions of persons will most readily come forward on this melancholy occasion ... to pay the last tribute of respect to the memory of their late beloved Governor', Edward Lord asserted. The funeral was designed to reflect the social and gendered hierarchies of the colonial order. Led off by a detachment of marines, the cortege was followed by the military and civil officers, officers' wives, the 'domestics of the

Lieutenant Governor in mourning', then by the wives of the military, convict superintendents, several hundred settlers, followed by their wives and children, and last and most definitely least, by 'a numerous attendance of male and female prisoners'.[28]

Beneath the surface, however, things were not all that they seemed and Collins's funeral provides one sign of this. The image of the governor as a benign patriarch anxiously fussing over his infant settlement would be beguiling was it not for the fact that these expressions of grief-stricken loyalty jar. Their unsettling nature partly derives from the fact that they emanated from Edward Lord, the settlement's senior military officer and a man who had hardly been Collins's friend in life but who had, in fact, spent much of his time since their arrival at the Derwent attempting to bully Collins into keeping Lord's own, very exclusive, 'interests at heart'. This was a man who knew the value of public spectacle as a conduit and affirmation of personal power. Lord's attempts to direct the funeral and his extravagant expenditure upon the ceremony, choosing, among other things, to bedeck everyone in new suits of black, spoke as much to his attempts to monopolise Collins's mantle as any sense of genuine loss. In the event, he was unsuccessful for, although assuming temporary command, he was swiftly replaced by Captain John Murray, sent from Port Jackson until a proper successor could be appointed by London. Lord's purpose had nevertheless been served: he departed for Britain on leave, having convinced Macquarie that he had been Collins's 'particular friend', a largely manufactured loyalty which would bring its rewards in ample acres of colonial land, among other indulgences.[29] On leave in Britain, he resigned from the army and gave himself over fully to the pursuit of wealth. Returning to Van Diemen's Land as a merchant and settler, Lord was rapidly to become, with a little help from his 'friends', one of the richest men in the colony.

Not all those who followed Collins's cortege were there for the 'wrong' reasons. Some were clearly grief-stricken. Convict James Grove was one: applying the engraving skills that had got him transported for forgery, he inscribed a silver plaque to adorn the coffin lid. But Grove's grief, while deeply felt, was naturally enough also shaped by his personal dealings with Collins. Like a few select others, Grove had basked in the full filial warmth of Collins's paternalism. Befriended by the Governor, probably partly for his literate and educated company, Grove had enjoyed Collins's patronage from the outset. When the convicts had been set to labour in the first stages of settlement, Grove had been exempted to pursue his own entrepreneurial ambitions. He was also, through his wife, one of the earliest recipients of land. And, despite his life sentence and the serious nature of his crime, which included the implication of treason during wartime, at Collins's recommendation Grove enjoyed an extraordinarily swift pardon.[30]

Collins, however, had not been a father whose subjects enjoyed equal favours, and the partiality of his rule spoke to his wider weaknesses and failings as a governor. Unlike his successors Collins did not pursue his own interests, but he did systematically advance those of his friends. Signs of the impending trouble had emerged on the voyage. Writing to his brother from Rio de Janeiro, Deputy Surveyor-General Harris complained both of Collins's perceived penury to his officers – he had refused to extend more than five pounds of credit to any of them while in Rio, thereby making it difficult for them to stock up cheaply on those objects which would be in demand upon their arrival at the Derwent – and of his failure to spend time with them. Collins, he wrote, 'has behaved extremely odd & strange to all his Officers Civil & Military – We are six altogether Civil & Military on board the *Ocean* and we have never been invited on board the *Calcutta* since we left England tho a week in harbour at Teneriffe [*sic*] & a fortnight here'.[31] Affronted by this, and the extent to which their Governor over-rode fraternities of class to socialise with convicts like Grove, Collins's officers became an increasingly disgruntled and difficult bunch. At least some of them regarded his actions as a licence to do their own thing and became consumed in endless efforts at self-enrichment through practices such as embezzlement, smuggling and corruption.[32] The 'actions' of the officer class, one convict remembered of Collins's time, 'were so dirty in those days that it was a business for any poor man to keep any accounts of the villainy that was going on'.[33] This was partly because the officers worked so hard to cover their tracks. On hearing of Collins's death a group of them took immediate steps to burn the settlement's official documents.[34]

There were also signs of open dissension at the funeral. Although 'the Reverend Mr Knopwood . . . gave the poor inhabitants to understand that they should lament the loss of our good and well beloved Governor in a sermon he preached . . . there was', convict Robert Bayles noted, 'little attention fixed to what he said'.[35] Bayles's obituary wandered far off the official script: 'thus died a servile creature to his superiors . . . and a great Tyrant to his inferiors', he commented in his diary.[36] The 'General Orders' regarding the funeral had anticipated such trouble. The fact that 'melancholy' and 'lamentation' were considered matters for government command is telling: 'the Commanding Officer trusts he need not order any one', Lord began, before proceeding to do precisely that. Lord also felt it necessary to warn the convicts that they were 'expected' to 'shew their respect . . . by sober and peaceable behaviour'. The death of their Governor, Lord dictated, was a 'loss' that 'must and will be universally felt and deplored'.[37] The *Derwent Star* also anticipated a divided response, attempting to silence anyone who might be so 'despicable' and 'devoid of humanity' as to 'rake up the ashes' by casting 'reflections' on Collins's memory. The Governor, the obituary noted, was now 'equally insensible to the blandishments of flattery and the shaft of censure', a remark which implies much about the ways in which ingratiation and denigration had variously dominated relationships between state and subject under Collins.[38]

Collins's personal relations and conduct caused problems in other ways, too, for he was also a hypocrite in matters of the heart. Selecting a sexual companion for himself in the shape of Hannah Power, wife of convict Matthew Power, was one thing; turning a blind eye to his own affairs while ruthlessly punishing the parallel actions of others was quite another. In 1804, he wrote to the Colonial Office to object that Mary Whitehead had received a paid passage to the colony by falsely claiming to be the wife of convict Andrew Whitehead. Mary had, in fact, been Whitehead's de facto wife prior to his conviction, but this cut little ice with Collins. Her 'shameful imposition on Government' was made even more outrageous in Collins's eyes by the circumstances of its discovery. Although Mary had seemed 'respectable' during the voyage, when she had travelled in a separate cabin with the wives of a select number of wealthier convicts and had been considered morally fit enough to act as a witness at one of the first baptism ceremonies, Collins reported that she 'threw off the Mask' on the final leg of the journey to Hobart, when she 'Desert[ed] the Man whose Wife she had pretended to be [and] went openly to live with another Person'.[39]

Mary had, in fact, re-aligned herself with Leonard Fosbrook, one of Collins's officers and an obviously more judicious choice of partner than a convict. It is difficult to separate either her motives or Fosbrook's behaviour from those of Hannah Power and Collins. The key difference, however, was one of power, as Whitehead discovered when Collins exiled her to Port Jackson 'to be disposed of by the Governor in Chief'. 'This', Collins noted with moral disdain, 'was the second Circumstance of the kind which occurred among these People', but in that instance the Parties wishing to be married, I directed the Clergyman to perform the Ceremony'.[40] The same clean-up operation could not extend to Whitehead because, it transpired, she already had a husband in Britain. It was, in fact, should we choose to count the affair between Hannah Power and Collins, at least the third such 'Circumstance of the kind'. Although Hannah was also in no position to marry her paramour she nevertheless got to stay. This was not the last time that Collins blatantly disregarded moral equality. When, for example, he sentenced Private Woolley to 200 lashes for drinking with a convict, a breach of the regulation that forbade social intercourse between bond and free, the Reverend Knopwood noted caustically that Collins had that very same day breakfasted with Hannah and Matthew Power; 'she always lives at the Colonel's table', he commented.[41]

Collins's affair with Hannah Power caused long-term ructions. Although the cause was partly moral, the problems were also deeply rooted in a range of social conflicts. The insults caused by overlooked fraternity were key. Not only did Collins fail to invite his officers to his table but he added insult to injury by dining instead with the Groves and the Powers, convict couples who, by all known and respected rules, ought to have been of thoroughly marginal status. These kinds of insults, whether deliberate or not, were clearly deeply felt. Writing home to his mother in England in October 1805, Harris bemoaned the fact that he and his new wife were still living in a 'miserable Hovel a Ground floor of 2 Rooms about the size of a Nutshell'. There was, Harris noted:

> very little probability of getting into a better for Governor Collins has not paid the least attention to the wants of his Officers in this respect – Only one Officer has yet had a House built him – all the rest have either been obliged to build for themselves or else to hire houses or live in Marques [sic] tho God knows he has had time enough for it since he has built *elegant houses for Convicts*, where the Wife was a *favourite*.[42]

Recently married, Harris was repeatedly anxious thereafter in his letters about the absence of a respectable 'society' in whose circles his wife might safely move. The 'miserable' nature of their abode undercut Harris's ability to establish a proper family home and thus to construct a secure sense of himself as a respectably domesticated man. In addition, and as a direct result of the Governor's failure to look after his officers, Harris was required to spend the exorbitant sum of fifty pounds a year in rent. Combined with the fact that 'everything [here] is most abominably dear', this put considerable strain on his already limited resources, threatening Harris's attempts to acquire the 'means of getting on'. Social advancement, as Harris's repeated discussion of the theme in his letters home reveals, was as dear to him as his new wife, because it alone promised to provide the foundations for the 'respectable' family life to which he aspired.[43]

Collins had, in fact, extended a broad range of privileges to convict Matthew Power, including land, preferential work allocation and an early pardon. Largely as a result, Power was able to become a successful trader, and so a competitor to Lord and his ilk. Matthew and Hannah, who never separated despite her relationship with Collins, both gained from the affair. By 1809 they had accumulated enough capital to finance their return to England.[44] There was much to justify Edward Lord's allegation, voiced deliberately in front of Collins, that Matthew Power was the Governor's pimp. Enraged by the situation, Lord refused to salute Collins when he passed him in the street, citing as his justification the fact that the Governor had Hannah Power 'hanging publicly' on his arm. Collins had Lord arrested for disrespectful conduct, an injudicious decision that underscored his fragility and growing isolation. The magistrates resigned and Collins's officers broke publicly from him, creating a 'major rift in power structure'.[45] Matters were only resolved when Collins climbed down, releasing Lord and allowing him to leave the colony for a time to enable a cooling off. Collins, notably, never crossed Lord again.

Collins's private behaviour also became problematic because of the ways in which it interacted with a series of deeply rooted public conflicts. Here, the conditions created by scarcity were key. Remembering the experience of famine in early New South Wales, Collins had endeavoured to make sure that the new settlement at the Derwent was relatively well provisioned, organising, prior to departure from London, for supplies sufficient to sustain it for up to two years. Shipboard losses, as well as rotten rations and poor quality tools, eroded such hopes.[46] Distance from London combined with official neglect and erratic supplies from Port Jackson further confounded them. Restricted rations, hunger and even famine were the results. Scarcity thus became a key force destroying the fabric of the state. Provisioning of the inhabitants was explicit in the colony's design. An assumption of mutuality between governor and governed was part of the contract between state and subject in Van Diemen's Land: protection and paternalism were to be exchanged for duty, loyalty and respect. By making their way along the quickly worn paths between their rudimentary homes and the Commissariat Store where rations, tools and seeds, as well as life's other vital necessities, were issued, the colony's inhabitants were supposed to receive regular lessons in loyalty. By helping to punish the disloyal, the Store also acquired a punitive function. When, for example, a group of settlers crossed Collins in 1808, a number of them were ordered, with their families, to be permanently removed from the Store.[47] Through these kinds of processes of exclusion and inclusion, the Store was designed as a vital means of discipline. But if scarcity reigned, this rebounded: when the state failed to fulfil its duty of care, many of its subjects were tempted to wander off path. Executive authority, therefore, tended to wax and wane with the harvests.

As governors, Collins and Paterson both took their paternal responsibilities seriously and the burden pressed hard. Collins reported that his limited ability to provide, despite repeated pleas for help, 'made my heart sick'.[48] He returned repeatedly and voluminously in his despatches to endlessly mundane details about food, stock and crops. Among these multiple missives were letters pleading for blankets to keep 'the People' warm in winter, returns of children vaccinated, and details about the special measures he had adopted to prepare a kangaroo and vegetable soup to be fed to those with scurvy.[49] This kind of attention to detail reflected Collins's desire to extend the arm of state care to his people, especially the weakest, and when it came to pressing their needs Collins knew few bounds. He was, he explained, only 'interested in the welfare of the little colony which I have established here' and was determined to do his best to 'give it permanence and vigour'.[50] Just as the poorly provisioned situation ate away at the sinews of his state, so too it stretched relations between Collins and the centres of power at Port Jackson and London to their limit. Things got so bad at times that irritation crept into the Governor's tone. He need not, he considered, even 'trouble' Castlereagh 'with a formal return of the remains of Provisions in His Majesty's Stores' for 'they are literally next to none'. This, Collins reported, was 'truly painful to me'.[51] In a private letter to his son written shortly before his death, Collins was more outspoken still. 'Leaving me to depend upon Port Jackson', he raged, 'has been nearly as bad as strangling a babe in its infancy'.[52]

Collins was fully aware of the extent to which a poor harvest, bad weather or sick cattle could undercut the broader legitimacy of his power and dissipate his authority. Writing to London in 1806, he commented:

> The most painful part of these Disappointments and Delays, and the necessity that has existed for victualling the People upon more than merely a reduced ration, is the Impediment thrown on the Public Labour, and the Temptation that is furnished to the evil disposed to rob and plunder whatever they can lay their hands on; of which description, there are many in this Settlement, too many, who are ever lying in wait to exercise their Industry, particularly in Seasons of distress.[53]

'In October last', he recalled on another occasion, 'I had not an ounce of any article of bread to issue to upwards of a thousand people, and I began to tremble for the consequences.'[54] Paterson faced similar problems at Port Dalrymple, 'a Species of Discontent' manifesting itself in response to the paucity of rations there.[55] Alert to these dangers from the outset, both governors had moved immediately upon their arrival to separate the Store from their settlements, locating them on islands in their respective harbours. With the immediate business of setting up camp completed, Collins set the convicts to build a secure stone building for the Store, followed by a powder magazine.[56] Paterson took similar steps. This mix of concerns about provisions and gun-powder says much about the lineages of their states.

Despite their attempts to protect it, the Store quickly became the centre of a deeply corrosive force, a hub linking stock-thieving gangs and convict bushrangers with corrupt officers and profiteering traders. In the absence of reliable state supplies, colonists – convicts and free – quickly looked to their own resources to make ends meet. While some farmed or fished, others headed for the bush, armed with guns and dogs. The supplies of kangaroo and game with which they returned were a vital means of staving off the collective hunger. From the beginning, these off-stage provisioning activities relied on close and enormously lucrative working relationships between officers and convicts. As early as August 1804, Deputy Surveyor G.P. Harris was able to report that his two dogs 'catch me one or two [kangaroos] from 30 to 60lbs weight 5 or 6 times a week'; 'to get the latter', he claimed, 'is only a little exercise for my Gamekeeper & Dogs'.[57] The partnership between Edward Lord and A.W.H. Humphrey, the settle-ment's mineralogist, also did well, with their convict men capable of delivering over a thousand pounds (weight) of kangaroo per week. During the same period, the Reverend Knopwood made over a hundred pounds (cash) in one two-month period via the kangaroo brought back from the bush by his convict servants.[58] These were substantial bonuses for men whose official salaries hovered between one and two hundred pounds a year. The rewards might, moreover, be invested in a more secure future: Harris, for one, diverted at least some of the kangaroo meat his men brought in as wages-in-kind to get convicts to work privately for him outside government hours building that much desired home on his farm.[59]

Although these activities began legally enough, they gradually spiralled out of control. Anticipating this, Paterson wrote to King in 1805 of his concerns about the 'spirit of buying and selling Dogs' and 'hunting Kangaroos' that so pervaded his settlement. 'If a stop is not soon put to it', he observed, 'it will in the end be the cause of much idleness, and consequently the neglect of Cultivation'.[60] Governor King shrugged these concerns off, recommending, with an eye to economy, that Paterson should extend the hunting and issue kangaroo in part exchange for the meat component of the government ration.[61] The dangers were, nevertheless, increasingly obvious to those on the ground. At both settlements, some had fast tracked the process of supplying the Store through organised stock theft – raiding government herds and settler farms alike. Others developed a mutually beneficial arrangement with convict bushrangers whose continued existence beyond the boundaries of official settlement and freedom from penal constraints was possible largely because they funnelled meat into the Store. Most were in league with individual officers and settlers. As a result, whenever bushrangers were brought in, the allegations and rumours their testimonies fuelled were breathtaking in their expanse, implicating almost all those in positions of order and authority. In the north, things were, if anything, worse. 'The Inhabitants', Paterson warned again in 1807, were fast becoming 'a set of Wood-rangers' as a result of the almost total dependence on kangaroo. 'Labour stood still', with the result that that inculcation of 'industrious habits' so crucial to 'an infant Settlement' had become a difficult and protracted process.[62] By the end of the first decade, several officers at Port Dalrymple, including both the Deputy Commissary Officer and the Deputy Surveyor, the latter armed with invaluable topographical knowledge, had given up even the pretence of legality, changing sides to become bushrangers in their own right.[63]

Theft and disorder, therefore, went to the very heart of the state both because these methods were increasingly crucial to the supply lines and because they had become a major means of income for so many of the officers. A state designed to channel authority through the body of the governor was being slowly but surely undermined. Power was dissipating and some of it, following the supply lines, was running into the woods. When convict bushranger Michael Howe later proclaimed himself 'the Lieutenant-Governor of the woods', he was therefore displaying more than mere bravado.[64] The bushrangers had long represented an alternative pole of authority, and the activities of these men were all the more destabilising when they gave voice to alternative belief systems. Declaring that he was 'fully determined to be like Turpin to rob from the rich and give to the Poor', Howe constructed himself as a paternalistic anti-authority willing and able to care for the weak where the governors had failed.[65]

Like a number of other bushrangers who adopted gentlemanly mantles for themselves, Howe also pursued a self-image that was chivalric, morally ordered and manly.[66] Visiting the home of T.A. Lascelles in 1816, Howe was reputedly keen to ensure that his gang maintained a morally ordered gendered decorum. He allegedly ordered his second-in-command to prevent 'those noisy fellows' (Lascelles's convict servants who had been drinking and dancing with the Howe gang for some hours by this stage) from indulging in more drink, instructing him to 'gag them if they used any improper or indecent language to disturb the females and children'. Evoking a vision of a world carefully structured by moral economy, he urged the convicts to observe both its rules and those of manly self-discipline. 'I find', Howe reportedly commented, that:

> you are the servants of a good and human master . . . but now you have taken the bushrangers as a cloak for you and eat and drink more like beasts than human beings . . . your kind master can have but little faith in such servants as you appear to be after what he has seen of you this afternoon, [nor] . . . can any of you look up to him for indulgence. I certainly used the freedom of treating you all that would partake of the good cheer placed before us by your bountiful master, but not with a view that any present should eat or drink to excess.[67]

Lascelles, Howe asserted, was 'a gentleman by birth' and thus a far cry from those masters whose 'cruelty' had forced 'unfortunate men like myself' into the bush. He and his gang 'would willingly throw down our arms at the feet of Mr Lascelles, if we could be again admitted into society', Howe informed the servants. Governor Davey was a much lesser man by comparison to Lascelles, because he was 'almost always either drunk or crankie'.[68] His weaknesses made him an injudicious governor and a failure as an authority-figure: the bushrangers would come in, Howe, claimed, but only if a deal was brokered through gentlemen like Lascelles with the more moral Governor-in-Chief at Port Jackson. Davey's individual failings of temper and appetite therefore spoke both to his personal weaknesses as a man and to the wider collective failings of his state. To restore order it was necessary, in Howe's view, to go over the Governor's head.

Just as the material pressures upon the early state led to the partial disintegration of the governor's paternalistic authority, so the off-stage provisioning and trading activities also began to rework the relationships between colonial households and the state. Rather than acting as microcosms of moral order, as mirrors to the state, a number of households re-orientated themselves with the result that their families formed hubs of disorder. As historian Peter Macfie notes, a series of 'stock-theft clans', based upon ties of family, kinship and inter-marriage stood at the forefront of the 'system of plunder'.[69] 'A large portion of the Community', possibly 'half or more of the people', Sorell later commented, lived in 'direct defiance of the Law' by 'preying systematically upon the honest and the industrious'.[70] While fathers and sons ran with the gangs, wives and daughters frequently operated the butchering and retailing side of the operation. These were genuinely family-run businesses: thus the women within households like that of Richard Morgan, a convict settler who headed one such clan, owned their own livestock.[71]

The thin veneer that separated the stock thieves and bushrangers from some of the officers was equally expressed through household associations and personal interconnections. Although Knopwood's links appear to have been purely platonic, he nevertheless spent substantial amounts of time dining and drinking in the home of Denis McCarty, smuggler and stock thief. The links between other individuals were more intimate still. Maria Sergeant, de facto wife of Matthew Bowden, assistant colonial surgeon, was, for example, connected with sheep-stealing operations through her assigned convict servants.[72] Fanny Anchor, wife of convict Daniel Anchor, was involved in an affair with Leonard Fosbrook. As Commissary Officer, Fosbrook had charge of the Store, and would eventually be court-martialled for his repeated corruption. One wonders whether it was a mere coincidence that Daniel Anchor was Hobart Town's butcher, or if the relationship between Fanny and Fosbrook testified to a wider nexus of stock theft and illicit butchering between these three. Daniel certainly accumulated a host of appearances before the magistrates, charged, among other things, with stealing from the Store and illegally killing sheep.[73] Family and household connections also facilitated the interests of those officers whose minds were firmly fixed on self-enrichment. Unable to trade in their own right while they retained their commissions, a number of these men used convict wives – legal and de facto – as business fronts. The most successful of these partnerships was the arrangement between Edward and Maria Lord; the latter's astute business acumen and moneymaking abilities served her officer husband well.[74] Rather than sources of order and authority, families were, in a host of different ways, fast becoming both catalysts to, and emblems of, a world turned upside down.

* * *

If the bushrangers and their networks represented one alternative source of authority within early colonial society, an increasingly wealthy corps of traders and merchants, many of them military and civil officers, formed another. The two groups were, as we have seen, closely intertwined anyway. Power was once again shifting along illegitimate and destabilising trajectories. The extent of this problem became fully evident when William Bligh, who had just been deposed as Governor-in-Chief, sailed into the Derwent in 1809, ostensibly on his way home to London from Port Jackson. Bligh had been overthrown by a rebellion on the mainland, which, although to some extent popularly supported, had been led by some of the richest officers of the New South Wales Corps anxious to protect their wealth and privilege.[75] If Bligh's presence at the Derwent helped to ensure that the rebellion's reverberations were felt in Van Diemen's Land, equally important were the criss-crossing connections between officer traders which, although centred on Port Jackson, spread outwards from there to include men like Edward Lord and Captain Anthony Fenn Kemp. Kemp, who had been part of Paterson's original party at Port Dalrymple and who was destined to become an increasingly important player in the Van Demonian economy, had played a prominent part in the rebellious proceedings at Port Jackson. Men like these had much to lose should Bligh be restored.[76]

Recognising weakness when he saw it, Bligh attempted to exploit the divisions between Collins, the officer entrepreneurs and the small settlers. The developing confrontation, drawn out over the nine months that Bligh stayed, vainly awaiting reinforcements from Britain, tested Collins's authority to the limit and revealed the extent to which men like Lord were firmly ensconced behind his throne. Throughout the affair, Collins played a double game, courting Bligh yet simultaneously, and largely at the bidding of those officers who supported the rebel party, taking steps to undermine him. Bligh, however, did nothing to ease his situation. From the moment the deposed Governor stepped off the boat, he began to build popular alliances. Although 'salutations and Marks of Respect' were extended to him on arrival, and the Governor's house was given over to him, Bligh nevertheless 'appeared dissatisfied' because he had not 'been addressed by the Settlers'. His motives quickly became apparent; 'I could observe', Collins reported, that 'upon every Occasion he was endeavouring to impress upon the Minds of the Settlers and Convicts the Idea that he was the Governor-in-Chief, and still possessed of the power and authority of that Office'.[77] Collins was less guarded in a letter to his brother. Bligh, he told George, was 'possessed of every bad quality that can enter into the composition of the worst of tyrants' and 'has been skulking here . . . endeavouring to do me all the mischief in his power by exciting my settlers, and declaring he would ruin me'.[78]

At Port Jackson, cartoons and gossip lampooning Bligh as an unmanly coward hiding under the bed while his daughter confronted the mutinous soldiers on her own had accompanied his overthrow.[79] Others had attempted to undercut his manly character through accusations of sexual immorality. Writing to London to justify the rebellion, acting Governor-in-Chief Foveaux claimed that Bligh had squandered public resources and convict labour in 'erecting and ornamenting a residence for one of the several prostitutes whom (not withstanding his constant professions of religion and morality) he was in the habit of maintaining'.[80] In Hobart, the deposed Governor-in-Chief tried to turn the tables, deploying discourses of familial duty and gendered morality in an attempt to rebuild his base. Collins's household was an obvious target. The Governor, Bligh reported, was 'inattentive' to 'particulars of etiquette' and 'decorum'.[81] Although his affair with Hannah Power had ended, Collins was now cohabitating with Margaret Eddington, adolescent daughter of a Norfolk Island settler. By the time Bligh arrived she was pregnant. Writing to London, Bligh claimed that he had been forced to retreat from Government House back to HMS *Porpoise*, moored in the Derwent, by his concerns for moral propriety. Collins, he explained, not only walked 'with his kept Woman (a poor, low creature) arm-in-arm about the Town' but also brought her into the presence of Bligh's daughter. In 'a moral and civil point of view', this, Bligh asserted, was 'as great an insult as could be offered'. Similar blows were aimed at Edward Lord: condemning his wife Maria as 'a Convict Woman of infamous character', Bligh argued that her pardon, because it had been awarded by Foveaux, now ruling in Bligh's place, was illegal.[82]

Bligh focused his claims upon the immoral, unrespectable and disordered character of the households of those who opposed him. In a society in which household supposedly mirrored state, to depict the households of those in power as disordered was to call the legitimacy of government into doubt. By disputing the private 'character' of figures such as Collins and Lord it was possible to challenge their right to public authority. Such a challenge partly rested on its undoubtedly gossip-fostering qualities, of course, drawing upon and spreading sensational stories that everyone already 'knew' to be true. But there was more to it than this. Most gossip, as anthropologist James C. Scott reminds us:

> is a discourse about social rules that have been violated. A person's reputation can be damaged by stories about his tight-fistedness, his insulting words, his cheating, or his clothing only if the public among whom such tales circulate have shared standards of generosity, polite speech, honesty, and appropriate dress. Without an accepted normative standard from which degrees of deviation may be estimated, the notion of gossip would make no sense whatever.[83]

Bligh's appeal was deeply rooted in an amalgam of 'normative standards' about household, family, authority and state. These standards not only structured Bligh's own world view, they also underpinned that of the small settlers whom he was most keen to rally to his cause.

Power, for Bligh, as for many of those who supported him, was a profoundly familial matter. The appeal was to an ideal of authority in which the King attended to his subject in just the way a father cared for his child: the nation was a metaphoric family. Bligh's authority

Anon, 'The arrest of Governor Bligh' (1808)

was thus simultaneously an expression of filial duty to his monarch and an embodiment of the fatherhood of the King. Although deeply hierarchical in structure, this familial ideal simultaneously naturalised and yet promised to check power. This was so because the family was also believed to engender reciprocal bonds of love, duty and affection: a nation state modelled on the family was, therefore, one in which there were guarantees against tyranny or the misuse of power.[84] Chief among these was the duty of paternal care and affection, which good fatherhood supposedly fostered. Humanity was thus literally embodied in the paternity of the King, or, by extension, the governor as his representative. 'I have', George Suttor wrote to Bligh, expressing exactly this type of sentiment, 'endeavoured to preserve my Allegiance to the best of Kings by a faithful and loyal attachment *to the person* of your Excellency'.[85] Bligh's anger at the rebels was likewise partly rooted in his belief that they had, through their mistreatment of him, engaged in a *personal* affront to the King. Visited on one occasion by two of the rebel officers, he recorded his relief that 'the portraits of our beloved Majesties' that hung in 'my Drawing Room' 'were veiled ... on so extraordinary a Visit'. This, he observed, was 'a fortunate circumstance' because it meant that 'His Majesty saw nothing of the transaction'.[86]

[35]

This model of patriarchal authority was, historian Catherine Gallagher explains, based upon 'an identity theory of family and society': the private and the public were imagined as unitary rather than contiguous or separate spheres.[87] Power was perceived, therefore, as rightly personal, intimate and immediate. But this, in turn, relied extremely heavily upon the character and conduct of the individual who embodied that power. The system worked only in so far as the head of the household (or nation) was a moral, caring father. This, Collins, if Bligh's denunciations were to be believed, was clearly not. Bligh's actions, by contrast, not least in leaving Government House in order to ensure propriety for his daughter, positioned him as a moral man and a caring father. The exchanges between Bligh and the small settlers at the Derwent were repeatedly imbued with the language of fatherhood and family. In a series of proclamations, Bligh offered the people his paternal protection and professed his 'readiness to hear and redress any Complaints they would lay before him'.[88] Even his decision to remain in the settlements rather than depart for London should, he suggested, be read as a testament of his determination to defend the interests of those 'good' but 'honest' settlers who were suffering as a direct result of the Rebellion. The 'Free Man, but poor', the emancipist and the 'unhappy Prisoner' were, he told London, 'all now look[ing] with anxious hearts to [their] hour of relief by their Gracious Sovereign'. 'I have not been able', he reported, 'to render them any personal service, except remaining in the Territory'.[89]

Bligh also drew a contrast between the impoverished honesty of the small settlers and the blatant self-interest, maladministration, profiteering, engrossing and monopolising that he believed to characterise the rebels in New South Wales and Van Diemen's Land.[90] Seeking to exploit such divides, the deposed Governor-in-Chief placed placards around Hobart's parade ground, the symbolic centre of power, calling on anyone who 'felt themselves agreeved [sic] to come to Bligh for redress'.[91] In addition to these public proclamations Bligh also paid personal visits to as many settlers as possible. 'These poor people', he reported, 'say they suffered and are still suffering the greatest hardships'. 'I have visited many of them and', he assured London, 'their situations ... do not contradict their assertions'. To settler ears this 'fatherly' intervention was welcome. A number of the settlers consequently ignored Collins's orders forbidding communications with Bligh and sought instead to make common cause with the deposed Governor-in-Chief by issuing a joint address in which they took the time to compliment Bligh on his 'Parental Kindness'. 'May your Amiable Daughter', they concluded, 'find that consolation in her present Afflictions which must evidently result from Parental Kindness and filial duty'. The petitioners equally hoped that this paternal care would extend to them and that their duty and loyalty would guarantee 'consolation' from the 'Afflictions' that then beset them.[92]

The settlers' attachment to familial notions of duty and authority found sustenance and confirmation in the material realities of their lives. Those who signed the address farmed their lands and ran their households through systems of paternal authority, family loyalty and labour. Interlinked through marriage, a broader sense of family and kin also informed their sense of community. Bligh's paternalism thus appealed both to the political sensibilities and to the lived experiences of these men. 'Legitimacy of power and principle' was, Alan Atkinson notes, partly rooted for these settlers 'in the familiar order' of their 'own household[s]'. To 'be a good subject and a painstaking father' were their interlinked ambitions.[93] Bligh was their natural hero. Sent from London with orders to clean up New South Wales, he had attempted to restructure colonial power and property relations in ways that favoured the small settlers, adopting measures to restrict market monopolisation and speculation, helping smallholders to pay off their debts, and giving them a larger share of convict labour.[94] Although the rebellion was more complex than a straightforward conflict between rich and poor, powerful and weak, Bligh had, nevertheless, gained the support of a substantial swathe of small settlers.[95] His vision, he told London, was of a future in which 'the industrious man will see his increasing Family a blessing to him; he will feel the produce of his labours realized in the comforts of life; and a general confidence will take place to give tranquillity to all Classes of His Majesty's Subjects'.[96] His actions and pronouncements encouraged the small settlers at the Derwent to believe that Bligh would look out for their interests, and that by securing the foundations of their families, he would reaffirm their status as independent heads of household and so their position within the wider hierarchies of imperial power. By 1808, many of these settlers had good reason to fear both for their prosperity and for their liberty. Bligh's appearance brought a series of longer-term socio-economic and political conflicts between the settlers and the Van Demonian state to the surface, and, by provoking a crisis, it forced that state's repressive tendencies into the open thereby heightening settler fears for their freedom.

When James Belbin, unofficial leader of the small settlers, went to Bligh's boat in search of an audience with the deposed Governor-in-Chief, Collins had the elderly widower arrested, imprisoned without trial and severely flogged. Belbin felt that his rights to political expression and an impartial judgement under the 'rule of law' had thus been threatened. He had, he noted, been 'deprived of all Communication with his friends (surrounded by all the Systems of Terror)' and 'sentenced to an unjust, Cruel and illegal punishment'.[97] The Address to Bligh, prepared by 'the loyal settlers and inhabitants of Norfolk Island', had, he noted, also been 'forcibly taken from me'.[98] Having 'kicked' and 'thrown' him down in the mud', Edward Lord had moreover informed Belbin that he 'would hang me for a mutineer'. In court, while Knopwood 'behaved as a gentleman, acting with candour and impartially', Lord was 'turbulent and prejudiced' and 'upbraided' Belbin with having 'once being [sic] a Convict'.[99]

Belbin's response to this treatment, recorded in his diary and in his later petitions for redress, reflects much about the way in which his concerns for his liberty and character were interwoven with his sense of family and household. His role as father informed his sense of self and, combined with his affection for his children, it drove his economic endeavours. Despite being caught in a life-threatening crisis, Belbin continued to pay keen attention to material matters. His account of his treatment was repeatedly interspersed with economic news: the cargoes of visiting ships, the price of food and an array of other details about ongoing trade and entrepreneurial activity. These activities were at the forefront of Belbin's mind because of the vital role they played in sustaining his household.

The impact of his arrest upon his children was also a central concern: 'was forcibly dragged from my children and my dwelling' by Edward Lord, he wrote in his diary. He reiterated this fatherly outrage in his petitions of protest to London. He had, he complained, twice been 'unjustly and illegally ... torn from Amidst of his family (Five Motherless Children)'.[100] As it turned out, Belbin had good reason to fear for his family: while he was in prison, his children were locked out of the house, his daughter Elizabeth 'seduced', and his son James badly attacked. The final insult came in the form of a request for 'my daughter Kitty', to 'live at Government House to nurse' the Governor's illegitimate infant. This Belbin inevitably refused, with the result, he claimed, 'of prolonging my punishment'. 'Sergeant Davis told me that the Governor meant to release me that day', Belbin wrote, 'only that I denied him my daughter'.[101]

The effect of Belbin's arrest and the others that followed was to further de-legitimise Collins. His retribution against the settlers only served to confirm those who believed the Governor depended upon 'aggression and tyranny'.[102] Underpinning such interpretations was the belief that the state was compromised by the corruption and self-interest of many of its officers. Belbin's arrest and imprisonment without trial, combined with the extreme severity of the flogging (500 lashes) he received, helped to crystallise a view of the state as partial.

Bayles, for example, was convinced that the officers he mockingly dubbed 'the chandlers' (the shopkeepers) were the real force behind Belbin's treatment.[103] So powerful were they, and so 'beloved' by Collins, he argued, that at least one of those punished for loyalty to Bligh had had the 'shadow of a trial but prejudged by these Chandlers'. Certainly, the evidence suggests that Lord, in particular, had propelled Collins to take action to crush Belbin and had tried to ensure that the Governor, despite concerns for Belbin's age and health, saw it through to the final lash.[104] 'There is no justice shewn to the Inhabitants of these Colonies', Bayles asserted, 'all the established Magistrates are . . . Clerks or Shopkeepers [and] If there should be an officer a Magistrate and he a just man . . . where he do not keep shop or farm the other Magistrates will [get] him out of the way before they will sit if they have any dirty work to carry on'.[105] These views were interwoven with concerns about the dishonourable overlaps between public duty and private interest. The officers, Bayles claimed, were men who 'neglect their duty to look after their own private concerns'.[106] Both the settlement's failure to thrive and the tendencies towards tyranny were deemed products of this systematic advance of private interest at public expense.

Belbin's condition also spoke to a more collective settler drama and revealed the state's failure to fully consolidate and secure itself. The tensions and conflicts between the free community and the state were profoundly worrying signs because the former had been conceived of as a crucial stabilising force, a backbone of order and settlement upon which the governors might depend. Unlike the settlement at Port Jackson, which had initially been settled only with convicts, the presence of free settlers in Van Diemen's Land had been part of the original design plan. Many of the earliest reports had dwelt upon the island's rich potential as a site of free colonisation, and efforts had been made from the outset to facilitate the arrival, survival and expansion of a settler community.[107] A handful of settlers had arrived with Lieutenant Bowen's advance party from Port Jackson in September 1803 and others had travelled with Collins.[108] Overall their numbers were, however, tiny and to offset this, King planned to provide the new settlements with major infusions of free colonists from Norfolk Island.[109] Between November 1807 and October 1808, over 550 of these men, women and children arrived at the Derwent. Others went to Port Dalrymple.[110]

Most of these men and women had originally been transported as convicts to New South Wales, but by the early 1800s, many had been working small properties on Norfolk Island for several generations and were solidly established smallholders. Their replanting in Van

Diemen's Land was envisioned as part of an endeavour to settle the natural *and* social landscape of the southern settlements. 'None but good Characters will be sent', King promised, envisaging that their established 'habits of Industry' would 'benefit [the] Settlement' both by providing a source of agricultural produce and by the example they might set the convicts.[111] Collins, too, was relatively optimistic at the outset, expressing his opinion that at least some of these settlers would 'manifest a disposition for Industry [and] in Process of Time . . . as they acquire Property in the Country . . . will become interested in its Welfare, and prove a valuable Addition to its internal Defence'.[112]

The plan misfired from the start, however. Forced to leave Norfolk Island because of an official decision to abandon that establishment, the settlers had understandably only done so upon receipt of repeated official promises that they would be fully reimbursed for their losses.[113] Government, however, failed to follow through. As a result, Collins and Paterson not only lacked the means to provide for the Norfolk Islanders but also the paper work necessary to calculate and settle their claims.[114] A vast expansion in the size of their communities was, moreover, the last thing that either of them needed in the midst of the famine years. Expecting the land, rations, stock and labour they had been promised to re-establish their farms and households, the settlers instead discovered that the state faced an uphill struggle just to keep them alive. Their stake in the system began to look less secure, and Collins and Paterson rapidly faced murmurings of discontent. Several 'ignorant and low Characters', Collins reported, 'have not hesitated to express their Dissatisfaction with myself, because it has not been in my Power to fulfil the Promise of Government to the extent of their Claims'.[115]

Although confident that he had 'nothing to apprehend' from such complaints because he could depend on the loyalty of his military detachment, the fact that Collins had had to turn to thoughts of force was in itself a sign of his weakness. At other points, moreover, Collins clearly felt much less secure. In January 1808, he expressed his hope that abundant supplies would shortly be sent or, he noted, 'we shall not be able to fulfil the Promises of Government to these Settlers'. Expressing anxiety about his small military force, he explained that if more Norfolk Islanders were to arrive he would need 'a reinforcement' of troops.[116] A scheme that had begun with the project of creating a carefully balanced mutuality of interests between state and subject had quickly deteriorated into a less sophisticated, and correspondingly more fragile, resort to the threat of force.

Collins and Paterson were caught between a rock and a hard place. Although they might have openly acknowledged that they were unable to deliver the settlers' requirements, this strategy would have made men whose claims to ultimate personal authority were paramount to state order appear weak. Both Governors instead pursued a tight-lipped and seemingly unsympathetic approach, dismissing the settlers' demands as irritating and unjustified. 'I found', Collins complained, blithely feigning ignorance of what could possibly have given them such notions, that the Norfolk Islanders were 'prepossessed with an Idea that all their Wants could be supplied at this Settlement'.[117] Paterson was equally unsympathetic: 'what trouble I have had with the Settlers', he informed King, 'they really have ideas that everything they do is to oblige me, and if I was to give them all the stores in the Settlement, and cultivate their Ground into the bargain they would not be satisfied'.[118]

Although this strategy maintained the facade of total control, it nevertheless focused discontent upon the Governor and helped to foster the impression that those in power elsewhere would be more caring and responsive. James Belbin, therefore, headed for London when he was released, the trip reflecting his belief that Collins alone was to blame for failing to honour the promises that had been made to the Norfolk Islanders. Appealing over the Governor's head, Belbin was convinced that a righteous and paternalistic metropolitan authority would restore the 'rule of law' and so his rights as an Englishman. In London, as it turned out, he also gained his reward for his loyalty to Bligh in the form of a recommendation for a land grant. Belbin deserved this privilege, Bligh asserted, because he was a 'firm and loyal subject' and had 'the Character of an industrious Man'.[119] The fact that Belbin returned to Van Diemen's Land with land meant that he, and no doubt others among the Norfolk Islanders, was never disabused of the idea that their problems stemmed from the failings of the local rather than imperial state. This was certainly the conclusion to which Bayles held fast. 'There are men set over us', he claimed, who are 'a mockery to the Laws of God and Man' and 'are more fit to be in Bedlam than to hold an office under our gracious Sovereign'.[120]

Collins undoubtedly deserved some of the blame: he had certainly exacerbated his inability to deliver to the community at large by making sure that there was always something in hand to bestow upon a select few. This unequal treatment helped to render his private life a matter of public disapprobation and dissent, and it meant that when colonists approached him for help his apparent indifference was interpreted less as a sign of the state's broader difficulties and more as an indication of the Governor's own personal failings. Instead of being a caring father to his people, ever willing to listen and respond to their needs, Bayles claimed that under Collins 'there was no time or place appointed for any one to speak to him [with the result that] if you wanted any business with him, you must catch him in the street'.[121] Keen to acquire a small plot to farm, Bayles waited nervously upon the parade ground after muster had ended one day, urged on by 'wellwishers' whose low opinions of Collins apparently conformed to his own. 'Go now', they told him, or 'he will soon be off, go now you fool, he will soon be housed and you will not see him today anymore'. Having begun his approach, he saw Collins:

> take out his snuff box ... and begin to shovel it up his nostrils by fistfuls. I then stoped [sic] at a respectable distance, thinking His Honor would call me and ask me if I wanted him, as I have known all gentlemen do, but no he let me stand there and took no notice of me but ... ran off towards his house and I after him, but as he was going up the steps of his house, I said, I would beg leave to speak to His Honor, he turned round and looked on me with all the disdain imaginable and said what do you want Sir, I told him I would thank him to allow me a Farm, if his Honor pleased, who are you Sir [Collins asked] I am a servant to Mr Folly, settler from Norfolk Island [Bayles replied] ... I cannot let you go [Collins told him] ... till more Prisoners come out into the Country and [he] asked me when my time was out, O I must inquire into that [Collins said] and [he] stopped the door in my face.[122]

No one, Bayles recorded, was to tell him until afterwards that 'if you wanted any favor of [Collins] you must take great notice of how he took his snuff for if you see him put it up his nostrils by handfulls [sic], it was ... best ... to leave him for that day'.[123] In a few short lines, Bayles had conjured up an image of a governor who was distant and tyrannical, prone to fits of temper and unpredictable passions, and whose addiction to snuff and failure to observe the rules of decorum structuring relations between those at different points of a supposedly paternalistic social hierarchy were signs of his failed qualifications to manly virtue. He was, in addition, a man who was apparently willing to override the word of the law by refusing to liberate convicts if this went against the settlement's labour needs. The account reveals much about how at least some colonists saw Collins.

Even worse, this conduct was not confined to the Governor but was seemingly of a piece with the wider failings of an officer class which was, in Bayles's view, composed of 'self-created Gentlemen' who had made large fortunes in a 'depraved and scandalous manner' and who regarded 'wealth and power' as 'a sanction for every species of villainy'. As on the mainland, so in Van Diemen's Land, competing assertions of manly character and honour helped to feed the crisis.[124] Thus Bayles sought to exploit the fact that many of those who held power in the colony were of decidedly marginal background, their claims to gentlemanly status fragile and based largely on their extremely recent colonial elevation.

The economic dominance created by the officers' abuse of power threatened, moreover, to distort the market by creating monopolies. Their attempts to manipulate state power to advance their own interests, therefore, threatened tyranny not only because it undermined the neutrality of government and the rule of law but also because, by eroding the property of others, it threatened to destroy what the small settlers regarded as the cornerstone of their liberty. In questioning the gentlemanliness of such men, and condemning their techniques of corruption and tyranny, Bayles imagined the colony as a site for a different type of manhood. The progress of these 'base infamous Wretches' had, he alleged, been made at the expense of those 'free men of honest character', whose energy and industry made them ideal colonists, capable of transforming waste lands into 'fine scopes of . . . cultivation'.[125] A properly ordered, moral government ought to have acted in *their* interests.

This conception of the colonial state owed much, however, to past dreams and little to present realities. It derived both from the Norfolk Islanders' own experiences and from the first visions of Botany Bay as an egalitarian society based upon liberty-loving, small-holding agriculturists. By the early 1800s, growing civic and socio-economic inequalities, driven partly by an increasingly ruthless and competitive quest for colonial wealth, were bringing systematic pressure to bear upon these older structures and ideals. Those settlers who continued to cling to the original model of an independent and moral yeoman-based paternal authority were increasingly being squeezed by the forces of disorder. Disappointed by Collins's limited ability to extend paternal care, they also felt surrounded on all sides by corruption and immorality, in the form of stock-thieving clans *and* the illicit and self-serving relationships of many of the officers. Their situation heightened Bligh's appeal as a governor who appeared willing to put the colonial house in order, and it gave the familial model of authority an increasingly oppositional edge.

For all these reasons, the settlers around Belbin condemned the colonial state in systematically gendered terms, their critiques infused with moral disquiet at what they perceived as the sexual and gender disorder of the officer class. While some of this condemnation stemmed from the ways in which these officers abused their public positions in order to pursue their private interests, it also derived from the belief that the officers' perceived failure to control their passions – by disinterested and disciplined government – was profoundly un-manly. Bayles's view of Murray's command is instructive. Arriving from Port Jackson to assume temporary control after Collins's death, Murray was a man who, in Bayles's view, had 'long been launched into the vortex of dissipation'; his ambition was only to outdo those around him in their 'ostentatious and licentious practices'. Murray, he reported, 'brought a kept miss with him', a woman 'whose taste was congenial to his own for every fashionable folly' and who was driven by a taste for luxury and 'the most profuse extravagance'. 'Our Commandant', Bayles claimed:

> is now seen in his true Character, he is continually in a state of inebriated stupidity and allowing all manner of vice to be carried on, Cockfighting, Horse racing, roasting sheep and bullocks whole on the Parade and allowing the soldiers to commit all sorts of insults and outrage on the inhabitants, breaking down their Garden fences, and beating people with the Palings.[126]

From sexual indiscretions to fashionable follies, Murray had been undone, and with him any pretence of colonial order. In these kinds of interpretations, the immoral sexual relationships pursued by so many of the officers were constructed as both cause and effect of their uncontrollable and unmanly tastes and desires. These stood in sharp contrast to the idealised frugality, order and discipline of the settler household, and the extravagant habits of those in authority were consequently deemed to threaten the 'utter ruin' of the colony.[127] Men incapable of governing themselves could not be expected to govern a colony, not least because their uncontrollable tastes for fast and luxurious living apparently drew them into the very webs of disorder and corruption which threatened to undermine the settler household.[128]

A wider vision of British imperial order and historical progress was equally at stake. When Edward Lord had a convict woman flogged, Belbin emphasised the archaically brutal notions about femininity that the act, for him, revealed. 'Can this be a land of Christians or one of savages only', he asked, 'where such an exhibition is permitted?'[129] These kinds of incidents were emblematic for men like Belbin of a breakdown in the 'rule of law' and of the very notion of progress itself. Belbin notably developed these themes by situating himself within wider debates about the relationships between Britishness, gender, humanitarianism and authority within the empire and by drawing upon the contemporary controversies surrounding the trial of Thomas Picton in particular.

The ex-Governor of Trinidad, Picton had stood trial in London for torture in 1806. His alleged victim, a Creole called Louisa Calderon, had been just ten or eleven years old when Picton had had her imprisoned and tortured in order to force her to reveal evidence in a larceny trial. Calderon was depicted in court as the subject of immense cruelty *and* the victim of seduction. It was reported that she had, despite her 'tender age', 'been induced to live' with one Pedro Ruiz, 'in a state of concubinage'.[130] Trinidad had been a Spanish colony until occupied by Britain in 1797 and its population remained largely Spanish in origin. British audiences could therefore read practices such as child concubinage as evidence of their already established beliefs about Spanish otherness. Picton's implicit failure to rescue Calderon from Ruiz threw both his manliness and his British character into question. Calderon was presented as a fitting feminine object of manly pity: she was, newspaper reports claimed, of 'very genteel appearance' and 'dressed in white', and 'her person was slender and graceful'.[131] These ideas of gender were, in turn, linked with images of un-British despotism that were more fully drawn out during the trial. Picton defended himself on the grounds that his treatment of Calderon was consistent with the Spanish law and precedent under which Trinidad was still partially governed. In response, the prosecution linked authority within the British Empire to the promotion of freedom-loving, humanitarian and 'modern' principles such as chivalry, manly sensibility and the rule of law. It had, the prosecution claimed, been Picton's 'duty' to:

> impress upon the minds of the people of that colony the great advantages they would derive from the benign influence of British jurisprudence; and that, in consequence of being received within the pale of this Government, torture would be for ever banished from the island. It is therefore not sufficient for him to establish this sort of apology . . . This governor ought to have been aware that torture is not known in England; and that it never will be, never can be, tolerated in this country.[132]

The prosecution interpreted both Picton's original actions and the tenor of his defence as evidence of his otherness. Thus the prosecuting attorney argued that Picton, was 'a British Governor; he had an English heart, and ought to have been governed by the laws of British humanity, and should not have thus inflicted the cruel torture upon that most unhappy female'.[133] Picton was therefore a 'disgrace' to 'the British name'; 'the first man to stretch authority' and 'order torture to be established' in a British colony.[134]

Thousands of miles and many months away, James Belbin drew comfort from the reports of the trial, which were eventually brought to Van Diemen's Land through the London newspapers, and he took time, in the midst of the crisis which enveloped him, to copy the details of the case into his diary.[135] Picton's trial, he believed, presented 'a necessary example to other British Governors that the meanest British subject if Oppressed would one day have an opportunity of meeting his Oppressors face to face in a country where equal Justice was administered to the Rich and Poor'.[136] The parallels between Collins and Picton appeared striking. Here were two colonial governors who seemingly combined an acceptance of unmanly seduction and immorality with a passion for torture, tyranny and despotism. The decision to make Picton face trial in the British courts therefore gave grist to Belbin's mill, re-affirming his belief that the imperial state would support his vision of the empire as a place of manly liberty and morality, humanitarianism and progress.[137]

This vision was more widely shared among the colonists. Bayles, for one, advanced a similar theme. 'We are very apt', he noted, recounting the Belbin affair in his memoirs:

> to condemn the Day of Algiers and a number of other Nations as contemptable [sic] savages but Oh Englishmen! when you come to hear all the Tyranny of English Officers when invested with a small share of authority over their fellow creatures and them committing by far worse crime than it is in the Power of the low order of People to commit, give them but power and the life of a poor man is no more in their hands than a Fly for they will be lashing them by Candelight there not being day light enough for their savage practices.[138]

What could be expected of such men other than the sexually immoral practices which routinely accompanied the conduct of the 'savage' and the 'barbarian'? According to Bayles, the officers kept 'an open Bagnio' or harem in the centre of Hobart. These kinds of accusations of sexual otherness were part and parcel of his attempt to represent the officer class as alien and un-British. The presence of 'harems' – routinely associated with visions of 'Oriental' despotism and tyranny – in Van Diemen's Land was a sure sign that things were rotten in this supposedly British colony.

*   *   *

By the time that Bligh arrived the settlers' grievances had festered into an open sore. Settler families who had not resorted to stock theft or smuggling were struggling to keep their heads above water. An officer–merchant cabal, whose lifeblood was that very same system of illegality, was slowly tightening its economic grip, indulging in economies of scale and price fixing in order to dominate and control the market.[139] The officers, Bayles claimed, not only failed to allow the settler 'to have a fair chance of the market' but were also 'known to concert to their own use anything they might have in their charge belonging to Government'.[140] Bligh reported that Edward Lord, in alliance with the Naval Officer, 'keeps a shop', and together they 'engross the advantages of Trade to the great injury of the Settle-ment'.[141] Settler anger was the righteous rage of once successful farmers and contented heads of household, men who had left flourishing properties on Norfolk Island on the word of a supposedly nurturing and paternalistic state. Angered by past events, many of the settlers were equally nervous about the future. Deep unease about the widespread corruption, plunder and profiteering beset them. Bligh's sentiment that Hobart was 'a Sydney in miniature', a place where 'all the indulgencies [sic] were put into the hands of a few to accumulate Wealth, and the Poor the Sufferers', was bound to appeal to them.[142]

James Belbin and his compatriots were farming on quicksand. In the years to come, many would slide into debt and lose their properties. When wholesale reform finally came, it did not generally benefit them. The shift to large-scale, more heavily capitalised farming, which Commissioner Bigge recommended, simply cleaned up, consolidated and confirmed the patterns of wealth accumulation begun by bushranging, stock theft and corruption. In defeat, Bayles for one, nevertheless drew comfort from stories about Collins's death: Governor Macquarie, he claimed:

having heard of his Honor Lieutenant Governor Collins's behaviour to his Excellency Governor Blythe [sic] and to the free inhabitants of Hobart Town and of his keeping common prostitutes in his House in derogation of God's honor and the corruption of good morality, sent him a very severe letter on that Head ... it was said that when [Collins] read this letter, it dropd out of his Hand and he fell on the floor and expired in a short time after.[143]

There is no evidence to support such an account, but the glee with which Bayles recorded it years later suggests that the tale had an energy and longevity all of its own. Bligh's moralising commentary on Collins's household had apparently borne fruit. 'The Great Tyrant' was gone.[144] Virtue, at last, had *seemingly* had its day.

Notes

1 On the motives for the new settlements see: *HRA* I, 4, pp. 247–9; *HRA* I, 3, pp. 436–8, 490, 697–9, 737; *HRA* I, 4, pp. 8–23 & 643–6; *HRA* I, 5, pp. 22–4, 209; *HRA* I, 6, p. 203; *HRA* III, 1, p. 603.
2 *HRA* III, 1, p. 362.
3 For interpretations which stress the authoritarian nature of the early Australian state see: R. W. Connell and T. H. Irving, *Class structure in Australian history* (Melbourne: Longman Cheshire, 1980); Alastair Davidson, *The invisible state: the formation of the Australian state, 1788-1901* (Cambridge: Cambridge University Press, 1991); Robert Hughes, *The fatal shore: a history of the transportation of convicts to Australia, 1787-1868* (London: Pan, 1988); Michael Roe, *The quest for authority in eastern Australia, 1787-1852* (Carlton, Victoria:

Melbourne University Press, 1965). A series of revisionary works challenge these views – see, for example: Alan Atkinson, *The Europeans in Australia* (Melbourne: Oxford University Press, 1997), Vol. 1; Marian Aveling (now Quartly), 'Imagining New South Wales as a gendered society, 1783–1821', *Australian Historical Studies*, 25:98 (1992), pp. 1–12; J.B. Hirst, *Convict society and its enemies: a history of early New South Wales* (Sydney: George Allen & Unwin, 1983); David Neal, *The rule of law in a penal colony. law and power in Early New South Wales* (Cambridge: Cambridge University Press, 1991); W. Nichol, 'Ideology and the convict system in New South Wales, 1788–1820', *Historical Studies*, 22:86 (1986), pp. 1–20. The emphasis upon physical coercion has also diminished as historians interested in economic matters have become aware, through comparative historical works on slavery in particular, that terror alone has a limited ability to extract productive labour from unfree workers. See, for example: S. Nicholas (ed.), *Convict workers. reinterpreting Australia's past* (Cambridge: Cambridge University Press, 1988) and, for an important critique, Raymond Evans and William Thorpe, 'Power, punishment and penal labour: *Convict Workers* and Moreton Bay', *Australian Historical Studies*, 25:98 (1992), pp. 90–111.

4   Atkinson, *Europeans*, Vol. 1, p. x. See also John Gascoigne, *The Enlightenment and the origins of European Australia* (Cambridge: Cambridge University Press, 2002).

5   See: Alan Atkinson, 'The first plans for governing New South Wales, 1786–87', *Australian Historical Studies*, 24:94 (1990), pp. 22–40; Atkinson, *Europeans*, Vol.1, pp. 53–4.

6   Christopher Bayly, *Imperial meridian: the British Empire and the world* (London: Longman, 1989), especially pp. 156–60.

7   Godwin cited in Gascoigne, *Enlightenment*, p. 146.

8   Péron cited in Gascoigne, *Enlightenment*, p. 146.

9   David Collins, *An account of the English colony in New South Wales* (London: T. Cadell & W. Davies, 1798), Vol. 1, cover page.

10 On Banks's significance in formulating colonial policy, particularly as regards Australia and the Pacific, in the era prior to the formation of the Colonial Office, see John Gascoigne, 'Joseph Banks and the expansion of empire', in Margarette Lincoln (ed.), *Science and exploration in the Pacific: European voyages to the southern oceans in the eighteenth century* (Woodbridge: Boydell Press in association with the National Maritime Museum, 1998), pp. 39–54.

11 Banks cited in John Currey, *David Collins, a colonial life* (Melbourne: Melbourne University Press, 2000), p. 176. Elaine Hadley notes that the idea that certain types of emigrants (criminals, juveniles, paupers) could be re-planted on colonial lands, where they might act as 'potential fertiliser' if 'sound principles of husbandry' were applied, drew upon a 'nostalgia-tinged agricultural philosophy and agrarian rhetoric'. See Elaine Hadley, 'Natives in a strange land: the philanthropic discourse of juvenile emigration in mid-nineteenth-century England', *Victorian Studies*, 33:3 (1990), pp. 411–40.

12 *Brewster's Encyclopedia* cited in 'Notes on Transportation and Secondary Punishment', *BPP* XXXVIII (582), 1839, pp. 1–2.

13 Marian Aveling (now Quartly), 'Bending the bars: convict women and the state', in Kay Saunders and Raymond Evans (eds), *Gender relations in Australia: domination and negotiation* (Sydney: Harcourt Brace Jovanovich, 1994), p. 145.

14 Aveling (now Quartly), 'Imagining', p. 5.

15 *Ibid.*, p. 2.

16 'Report of the Select Committee on transportation', *BPP* II (341), 1812, p. 13. Bayly suggests that the yeoman-inspired imperial vision was particularly Scottish in intellectual origin, and this perhaps accounts partly for its continued pursuit, under Macquarie's command, in early VDL. See Bayly, *Imperial meridian* pp. 134–6, 151–2.

17 Sharon Morgan, *Land settlement in early Tasmania: creating an antipodean England* (Melbourne: Cambridge University Press, 1992), p. 10.

18 *HRA* III, 4, p. 19.
19 Irene Schaffer (ed.), *Land musters, stock returns and lists: Van Diemen's Land, 1803–1822* (Hobart: St David's Park Publishing, 1991), pp. 130–52.
20 Currey, *Collins*, p. 235.
21 Aveling (now Quartly), 'Imagining', pp. 5–6.
22 Currey, *Collins*, pp. 208, 214, 236–7, 239; *HRA* III, 1, p. 335.
23 *HRA* III, 1, p. 266.
24 For details see Mary Nicholls (ed.), *The diary of the Reverend Robert Knopwood, 1803–1838* (Hobart: Tasmanian Historical Research Association, 1977), p. 66. The same policy had been pursued during their brief period at Port Phillip. *Ibid.*, p. 28.
25 *HRA* III, 1, p. 271.
26 *Ibid.*, p. 267.
27 *Derwent Star*, 3 April 1810.
28 *Ibid.*
29 *HRA* III, 1, pp. 451–2.
30 For Grove's account see: Benjamin Bensley (ed.), *Lost and found; or light in the prison: a narrative with original letters, of a convict, condemned for forgery* (London: W. Wells Gardner, 1859).
31 Harris, 17 July 1803, in Barbara Hamilton-Arnold (ed.), *Letters of G.P. Harris, 1803–1812* (Sorrento, Victoria: Arden Press, 1994), pp. 24–5.
32 A similar pattern had established itself in early New South Wales. In 1797, Governor Hunter had complained to London of the 'rage for speculation and traffic' among the officers, arguing that if they could not be made to place their public duty first they should be removed from office. See *HRA* I, 2, p. 22.
33 Robert Bayles, Diary, AOT NS 395/1, p. 105.
34 Marjorie Tipping, *Convicts unbound: the story of the Calcutta convicts and their settlement in Australia* (Victoria: Viking O'Neil, 1988), pp. 137, 144.
35 Bayles, Diary, p. 118.
36 *Ibid.*, p. 118.
37 *Derwent Star*, 3 April 1810.
38 *Ibid.*
39 *HRA* III, 1, p. 262.
40 *Ibid.*
41 Nicholls, *Diary*, p. 65.
42 Hamilton-Arnold, *Letters*, pp. 64, 72. Emphasis in original.
43 *Ibid.*, especially pp. 72–3.
44 Tipping, *Convicts*, pp. 301–2.
45 See Currey, *Collins*, pp. 241–5 for an account of these conflicts.
46 *HRA* III, 1, pp. 232–3.
47 Free settler William Paterson who also 'apply'd to (Bligh) and stated my grievances . . . Conceiving him as the Representative of My Soverign [sic]', suffered the same fate; *HRA* III, 4, p. 841.
48 *HRA* III, I, p. 328.
49 *Ibid.*, pp. 257, 286, 346.
50 *Ibid.*, p. 340.
51 *Ibid.*, pp. 369–70.
52 Collins cited in Currey, *Collins*, p. 295.
53 *HRA* III, 1, p. 362.
54 Collins cited in Currey, *Collins*, p. 295.
55 *HRA* III, 1, p. 676.
56 *Ibid.*, pp. 220, 224, 231, 247.
57 Hamilton-Arnold, *Letters*, pp. 64–5.
58 Tipping, *Convicts*, p. 119.
59 *HRA* III, 1, p. 17.
60 *Ibid.*, p. 645.
61 *Ibid.*, p. 648.

62 *Ibid.*, p. 668.
63 *HRA* III, 2, p. xvi; *HRA* I, 8, p. 264; and 'Report of the Commissioner of Inquiry into the state of the colony of New South Wales', *BPP* XX (448), 1822, p. 108.
64 For a contemporary account of Howe, originally published in 1818, see: Thomas Wells, *Michael Howe: the last and worst of the bushrangers of Van Diemen's Land. Narrative of the chief atrocities committed by this great murderer and associates during a period of six years in Van Diemen's Land, with an introduction by George Mackaness* (Sydney: D.S. Ford, 1945).
65 *HRA* III, 2, p. 163.
66 On the bushrangers see: Hamish Maxwell-Stewart, 'I could not blame the rangers: Tasmanian bushranging, convicts and convict management', *Tasmanian Historical Research Association*, 42:3 (1995), pp. 109–26.
67 Reminiscences of Alexander Laing, District Constable, Pittwater, Tasmania, 1819–38, NS 1116/1, pp. 5–6.
68 *Ibid.*
69 Peter MacFie, *Stock thieves and golfers: a history of Kangaroo Bay and Rosny Farm, Tasmania, 1803–1998* (Rosny Park, Tasmania: Clarence City Council, 2002), especially pp. 5, 15–16. In 1817, for example, Sorell noted that Thomas Crahan was 'one of the worst and most notorious plunderers in the Colony' and that, 'with his Sons', he had 'carried on for years, in combination with a Bush-ranger and robber named Watts, a system of Sheep-stealing to the extent of Hundreds in a year'; *HRA* III, 2, p. 282.
70 *HRA* III, 2, pp. 194, 282.
71 MacFie, *Stock thieves*, especially pp. 5, 15–16.
72 *Ibid.*, p. 15.
73 The relationship between Fanny and Fosbrook was long-term, however, and they returned to London together in 1813; see: Tipping, *Convicts*, pp. 131, 140, 159.
74 On Edward and Maria Lord see: Kay Daniels, *Convict women* (St Leonards, NSW: Allen & Unwin, 1998), pp. 1–28.
75 On the rebellion against Bligh see: Atkinson, *Europeans*, Vol. 1, pp. 264–91; Michael Duffy, *Man of honour: John Macarthur – duellist, rebel, founding father* (Sydney: Pan Macmillan Australia, 2003); and H.V. Evatt, *Rum rebellion: a study of the overthrow of Governor Bligh* (Sydney: Angus & Robertson, 1938).
76 On Kemp see: Nicholas Shakespeare, *In Tasmania* (London: The Harvill Press, 2004).
77 *HRA* III, 1, p. 426.
78 Collins cited in Currey, *Collins*, p. 295.
79 Geoffrey Chapman Ingleton, *True patriots all or news from early Australia as told in a collection of broadsides* (Sydney: Angus & Robertson, 1952), p. 48. According to Ingleton, the image of Bligh cowering under the bed was the subject of several contemporary drawings and was also among the transparencies shown during the bonfires that celebrated Bligh's arrest. Ingleton, *True patriots*, fn. 35, p. 262.
80 *HRA* I, 6, p. 663.
81 *HRA* I, 7, p. 126.
82 *Ibid.*, pp. 128–9.
83 James C. Scott, *Domination and the arts of resistance: hidden transcripts* (New Haven, CT: Yale University Press, 1990), pp. 142–3.
84 On these theories see: Carole Pateman, *The sexual contract* (Oxford: Polity, 1988); Gordon Schochet, *The authoritarian family and political attitudes in seventeenth-century England* (London: Transaction Books, 1975).
85 *HRA* I, 7, p. 131. Emphasis added. Suttor ended up in Sydney gaol for his loyalty to Bligh.
86 *Ibid.*, p. 120.
87 Catherine Gallagher, *The industrial reformation of English fiction. Social discourse and narrative form, 1832–1867* (Chicago: University of Chicago Press, 1980), p. 117.

88 *HRA* III, 1, p. 426. Settler William Paterson approached Bligh for example to complain that he had been unfairly dismissed as Superintendent of Convicts; *HRA* III, 4, pp. 840–4.

89 *HRA* I, 7, pp. 115–16. Five settlers were imprisoned at Sydney for their continued loyalty and support and others sent him letters and Addresses before he left New South Wales; *HRA* I, 6, pp. 116, 125.

90 *HRA* I, 7, pp. 123, 129.

91 Currey, *Collins*, p. 283.

92 *HRA* I, 7, pp. 120–1, 130, 159–60. For the order banning communications with Bligh see *HRA* I, 7, pp. 165.

93 Atkinson, *Europeans*, Vol. 1, p. 315. One wonders how far any clear-cut division between the 'respectable' and the 'unrespectable' actually existed, however. Belbin shared a house in Hobart with Daniel Anchor for a period and Bayles seems to have been imprisoned for bushranging; see Tipping, *Convicts*, p. 250; *HRA* III, 4, p. 620.

94 Aveling (now Quartly), 'Imagining', p. 9. For examples of these orders see: *HRA* I, 6, p. 204. In practice, however, Bligh's actions, particularly over property, also lost him support among this class, hence the rebellion's partially popular base, particularly in Sydney; Atkinson, *Europeans*, Vol. 1, pp. 273–91.

95 On settler support for Bligh see Duffy, *Man of honour*, especially pp. 249, 252–7 and 276.

96 *HRA* I, 7, p. 164.

97 *Ibid.*, pp. 686–7.

98 James Belbin, Pocketbook, University of Tasmania Library, RS 90/1, 25 April 1809.

99 *Ibid.*, 26 April 1809.

100 *HRA* I, 7, pp. 686–7.

101 Belbin, Pocketbook, 7 November 1809.

102 Bayles, Diary, p. 107.

103 Bayles claimed Collins had settler Richard Pitt punished for taking vegetables to Bligh and another settler flogged for 'speaking in favour of the Governor in Chief and against his so much beloved chandlers'; Bayles, Diary, p. 107. Bligh reported that Pitt and McCloud were imprisoned for provisioning his ship; *HRA* I, 7, p. 161.

104 Tipping, *Convicts*, pp. 140–2.

105 Bayles, Diary, pp. 122–3.

106 *Ibid.*, p. 110.

107 See, for example, *HRA* III, 1, pp. 610–11, 613–23.

108 For details of these early settlers see: *HRA* I, 4, p. 153, Tipping, *Convicts*, p. 330.

109 On the relocation of the Norfolk Islanders see: *HRA* I, 4, pp. 304–6, 643; *HRA* I, 5, pp. 5, 25 and 539; *HRA* I, 6, pp. 70–5, 156.

110 *HRA* III, 1, p. 420.

111 *Ibid.*, p. 245.

112 *Ibid.*, 1, p. 404.

113 The Norfolk Islanders were promised that they would be victualled from the Store for 12 months after their arrival, that buildings would be erected for them at government expense and that they would be supplied with implements from the stores. The first two of these conditions were largely unmet; *HRA* III, 2, p. 758. Macquarie made efforts to resolve the situation when he visited in 1811. The settlers had petitioned him for assistance; *HRA* III, 1, p. 440.

114 See, for example, *HRA* III, 1, pp. 394–5, 399–401, 407–8.

115 *Ibid.*, p. 404.

116 *Ibid.*, p. 395.

117 *Ibid.*, p. 399.

118 *Ibid.*, p. 651.

119 *HRA* I, 7, pp. 685–6.

120 Bayles, Diary, p. 125.

121 *Ibid.*, p. 111.
122 *Ibid.*, pp. 111–12.
123 *Ibid.*, pp. 110–12.
124 On notions of gentlemanly honour in New South Wales, see Duffy, *Man of honour*.
125 Bayles, Diary, pp. 110, 123, 126–7.
126 *Ibid.*, pp. 129–30, 133–4.
127 *Ibid.*, p. 130.
128 There can be little doubt of Murray's corruption. See *HRA* I, 9, pp. 39–41.
129 Belbin cited in Atkinson, *Europeans*, Vol. 1, p. 314.
130 *The Times*, 25 February 1806.
131 The trial of Thomas Picton, 24 February 1806, in *The Newgate Calendar*, www.exclassics.com/newgate/ng477.htm (accessed 6 May 2004), p. 2.
132 *The Times*, 25 February 1806.
133 *Ibid.*
134 Trial of Picton, p. 4.
135 Belbin cites *The News*, 2 March 1806 as his source; Belbin, Pocketbook, 2 July 1809.
136 *Ibid.*
137 By 1808, Trinidad was, moreover, petitioning for the British Constitution to be extended to the colony; *The Times*, 27 August 1808. Picton was convicted in 1804 but won an appeal in 1806. For an account of the first trial see *The Times*, 4 May 1804. The argument for a re-trial again revolved around 'reputation' and character. Picton's defence claimed Calderon was an 'infamous character' who lived 'in open prostitution', while he was 'a person of respectability and character in his Majesty's service'; Trial of Picton, pp. 4–5.
138 Bayles, Diary, pp. 124–5.
139 For a discussion see Hamish Maxwell-Stewart, 'The bushrangers and the convict system of Van Diemen's Land, 1803–1846' (PhD dissertation, University of Edinburgh, 1990), pp. 165–7.
140 Bayles, Diary, p. 110.
141 *HRA* I, 7, p. 129.
142 *Ibid.*, p. 129.
143 Bayles, Diary, pp. 117–18.
144 *Ibid.*, p. 118.

CHAPTER TWO

Regulating society, purifying the state
Gender, respectability and
colonial authority

'Perpetual petty squabbles and quarrels', settler Louisa Meredith noted of Van Diemen's Land in the early 1850s, are 'especially rife in this little fraction of a world'. A 'frightful amount of *snobbishness*', she bemoaned, 'prevails here'.[1] Not even 'in the most moral circles of moral England', she went on, is 'a departure from the paths of propriety or virtue more determinedly or universally visited by the punishment of exclusion from society than in this "Penal Colony"'. 'Nowhere', Meredith concluded, 'are all particulars and incidents of persons' past lives more minutely and rigidly canvassed, than in the "higher circles" of this little community; and nowhere are the decent and becoming observances of social and domestic life more strictly maintained'.[2] Meredith was far from alone in her grumble: Hobart, George Thomas Lloyd commented, was a city dominated by 'classes, cliques and bitter jealousies'. 'Everybody', he proceeded to remark, 'knows everybody's birth, parentage, and education, either from facts, or from the inventions of their own fertile imagination'.[3] Even in Sydney, Lady Jane Franklin likewise observed that there was 'nothing ... like the squabbling rancour' that existed in Van Diemen's Land.[4]

Access to Government House was particularly jealously guarded. Despite her complaints about the 'squabbling rancour' that beset Van Diemen's Land, during her period as the Governor's wife in the late 1830s and early 1840s, Jane Franklin, in fact, repeatedly endeavoured to investigate and exclude those she considered unsuitable for admission to colonial 'society'. Her determination to oversee and censor the guest lists for official functions at Government House was one sign of this. Although her actions inevitably caused offence, Franklin refused to back down. Visited on one occasion by a Mr Thornton – demanding to know why 'he had not been deemed fit by his conduct to be invited to the ball' – Franklin noted that he was 'a miserable looking creature' who bore signs 'of sottishness'; 'the latter', she remarked, 'is his habitual condition'. There was simply no way, in Franklin's view, that, given Thornton's lack of 'sobriety' and 'deportment', he 'could have been admitted into decent society'. 'I was as cold as I could well be to him', she noted in her diary, with the result that 'his visit was shorter than I had expected'. On his departure, she concluded, 'I gave orders that he should never be admitted to the house again'.[5] Franklin was, moreover, willing to be even more proactive in her efforts at moral regulation than this. On the arrival of one young lady in the colony, a Miss Gregg, Franklin 'begged' that 'enquiries . . . be made about her'. Upon discovering that Gregg had left the West Indies under a cloud and had recently married 'in a great hurry', Franklin concluded that 'she was unfit to be visited'.[6]

Sir William and Lady Denison, the Franklins' successors at Government House, were inclined to be more forgiving. In Lady Denison's view, accusations about the past were best avoided. 'Whatever the history was', she commented in the case of one woman, 'it was long ago, and I believe it is well known that she has been living most respectably for many years'. Sir William appears likewise to have thought it 'better not [to] rake up old stories' or to 'know more than is forced upon us of the private feuds or jealousies of people about one another'.[7] Many of their contemporaries nevertheless appear to have disagreed with them with the result that the Denisons were repeatedly pushed into taking actions similar to Franklin's. Their attempt, shortly after their arrival in Van Diemen's Land, to organise 'a small dance' ended in near disaster when they narrowly escaped a 'dreadful fracas' caused by a dispute over seating. There had, Lady Denison explained, 'been considerable difficulty . . . in arranging the matters of precedence; for among the guests were two Legislative Councillors and their wives, and which of these two was to be first?' In an attempt to seek a solution, it was decided that

> the wife of the greatest man should be the greatest woman, and that Mr ____ who was both the oldest councillor and the oldest man, should have the precedence. All was done accordingly; Mrs ____ was advanced to the post of honour, and we were all charmed with her; for she seemed a nice, respectable, motherly old lady and pleased us all very much.[8]

The next morning, however, the Denisons discovered that they had committed a major faux pas. 'A____ burst into the room', Lady Denison recorded, and exclaimed that 'we were within an ace of having half the people who came to dine here last night walk out of the room', because, he explained, 'Mrs ____ is the most infamous character that can be!'[9] Just a month after this incident, Denison was inundated by complaints from individuals demanding to know why they had not been invited to a ball at Government House. The main purpose of these complaints, Denison reported, was 'to enquire whether His Excellency has heard anything prejudicial to their character, or whether it is considered that their situation disqualifies them from receiving the honour of an invitation; and stating that, in duty to themselves and their connections, they cannot allow such an insult to be passed unenquired [sic] into'. So serious were these matters considered to be that some of those who felt offended went so far as to write to the government in London to complain 'of the indignity caused to them'.[10] 'The being or not being, admitted here is', Lady Denison was forced to concede, 'in this place considered as the great criterion of a person's social position'.[11]

Although these tendencies became more accentuated with time, a determination to deploy discourses of gendered respectability and moral propriety in an attempt to delineate and police the boundaries of colonial 'society' had, as we saw in chapter one, been evident in Van Diemen's Land from the outset. There 'is no society' here, Deputy Surveyor-General G.P. Harris had complained in a letter to his mother as early as 1805. 'I cannot visit *with* my wife most of my brother Officers because', he explained, 'they have female Companions', by which he meant they were cohabiting, many of them with female convicts. The social results were dismal: 'we seldom therefore visit except to Captn. Sladdens (Marines) who is married', he noted. Beyond this, the only other source of company which Harris deemed acceptable was his wife's own family. These were 'the only females', Harris asserted, with whom his wife could properly 'associate'.[12]

The boundaries that Harris attempted to construct around his household speak to the ways in which his sense of self was bound up with a specific set of domestic circumstances and with his ability to re-enact the same standards of wifely propriety and family morality he had known at home. Unlike those of his fellow officers who had succumbed to the temptations of cohabitation, Harris's marriage shortly after their arrival at the Derwent had enabled him to leave what he perceived as the 'exile' of the 'ocean' and yet to avoid the 'rock' of colonial sexual immorality by entering the security of the home, a place he notably christened his 'Harbour of happiness'.[13] His concern with the moral conditions of the broader colonial community also spoke to the ways in which family values facilitated the construction of a more collective, class-based colonial identity for these kinds of men. For it was not just the unmarried that Harris sought to place outside the family home but equally those who were married but of lower class. Captain Sladden was far from being the only other husband in the settlement; rather he was the only other

[55]

married 'brother officer'. Even in these very early years there were families to be found among the convicts and poorer free settlers but none, it would seem, that Harris considered fitting for his wife, in particular, to visit.

With the onset of considerable free emigration in the late 1810s and early 1820s, these tendencies become increasingly pronounced. This was partly because many of these new settlers were heavily family oriented; having left Britain as a result of financial pressures, they were determined to secure, through empire, the material means for the independent maintenance of their households. Indeed, Van Diemen's Land was explicitly marketed to prospective emigrants in just this way from the mid- to late 1810s onwards.[14] A commitment to family and to domesticity was, as a consequence, deeply embedded within the settler world view from the outset, and the requirements of colonial life, with its emphasis upon household production and family labour, only served to heighten this.[15] The fact that large numbers of religious settlers came to Van Diemen's Land from the late 1810s onwards – inspired, as they were, to live a 'God-fearing life of self-sufficiency on a small farm' – further consolidated and extended these emphases upon family and morality.[16]

The determination of these new settlers to observe high standards of domestic and familial propriety was, as with G.P. Harris before them, also heavily bound up with their sense of self and status. Many of the new arrivals were concerned, in particular, to avoid too close an association with ex-convicts or their offspring. The attitude of one recently arrived emigrant speaks volumes. Writing a letter to her sister in 1821, Janet Ranken noted:

> Mr Lord a man worth half a million money is married to a convict woman. . . . Mrs Lord sent her daughter Miss Lord and her sister Mrs Simpson to call upon me when I came here but I have never returned the call yet nor shall I although wile Governor McWharie [sic] and his lady were here paying there last visit Mrs Lord was Mrs McWharies most intimate friend and I have been advised to visit her but they say 'evil communication corrupts good manners' so I shall rather be without the kindnesses that Mrs Lord has in her power to show me rather than visit her.[17]

Ranken's strategy in the face of the 'abominable' practices which supposedly beset colonial 'society' was therefore to be ruthlessly exclusive about the company she kept. Despite her wealth and power, Maria Lord was therefore openly snubbed, and Ranken instead sought the company of 'respectable' emigrants like Major Bell and his wife, and the colonial surgeon and his wife. Colonist Octavia Dawson, writing a few years later, adopted a similar strategy to deal with her fears about the social origins and moral status of Van Diemen's Land's other inhabitants. Despite her evident loneliness, she chose to be 'on visiting terms' with just two couples, both of whom had come free to the colony and were of respectable and solidly middle-class means.[18]

The intense anxieties about social place that these practices reveal were partly a product of the dislocation and resulting sense of disorientation caused by emigration and empire. 'Colonists', Penny Russell notes of nineteenth-century Melbourne:

> were acutely conscious that in this new society, a social order and its associated relationships had not to be challenged or protected, but created: and created of individuals who all had a sense of their place in an older order but who were now compelled to relate to each other in new ways ... Strangers ... were strangers indeed, thousands of miles from acquaintances who could reveal the truth about their antecedents, and a minimum of six months away from a response by mail to any request for information sent 'Home'. ... The colonies were ... a place of severance from family or past life ... In the context of such real or imagined hazards, the stranger ... represented a significant problem, and the question 'Who are you really?' could be a profoundly worrying one.[19]

These anxieties about origins and status were inevitably particularly pronounced in a penal colony. As Janet Ranken's determination to exclude Maria Lord from her company reveals, it was often extremely difficult for ex-convicts to escape their past. By the mid- to late 1810s, Maria and Edward Lord were not only among the wealthiest inhabitants of Van Diemen's Land but Maria, as Kay Daniels notes, was also increasingly attentive to matters of domestic propriety, anxiously overseeing her family's conduct and her children's education.[20] Free colonists like Ranken nevertheless still sought to spurn her. Others endured similar discrimination. Despite being a major colonial landowner and having been sent to England for his education, the fact that colonist Richard Dry was the son of a convict continued to count against him in certain circles.[21] 'Plebein [sic] blood', colonial socialite Annie Baxter Dawbin noted in part reference to Dry's company, 'is beneath my notice'. Dawbin also expressed a more generalised and 'thorough contempt' for 'the community at large'; 'they have no blood to be vain of', she sneered.[22]

If these attitudes partly spoke to a sustained prejudice against convict origins, they were also intertwined with the development of a more generalised colonial class-consciousness. The emergence of a more deeply polarised social structure was accompanied in these years in both New South Wales and Van Diemen's Land by the development and elaboration of what some historians have referred to as an ideology of 'moral ascendancy'.[23] This was far from unique to the Australian colonies. Domestic propriety and moral respectability, historian Kirsten McKenzie notes, were central to the construction and consolidation of notions of difference and claims to authority within a range of British colonial communities in this period. An emphasis on gender and sexual morality, she stresses, was one of a number of ways 'in which ... colonisers neutralised potential divisions amongst themselves, emphasised their distinction from the colonised, and reassured themselves of their separate identity and right to rule'.[24] As elsewhere in the empire, so in Van Diemen's Land questions of gender and sexual morality became increasingly crucial social and cultural dividing lines. Against this backdrop, a number of major colonial players notably made efforts to eschew some of their more illicit past practices and to sanitise their reputations. It was, for example, during these years that Edward Lord endeavoured to publicly distance himself from his ex-convict wife Maria – blithely ignoring his own history of serial adultery while pursuing her through the courts on a charge of having engaged in 'criminal conversation' with another man. Others chose this moment to marry women – many of them ex-convicts – with whom they had previously happily co-habited.[25]

Colonists who looked back on the colony's history and development from the more secure perspective of the mid- to late nineteenth century were often likewise keen to emphasise the idea that this period had marked a key cultural and moral turning point. Central to these claims was the notion that a crucial shift had occurred in the domestic order of the colony with the arrival of free emigrants of reputedly higher social and moral status. This shift was supposedly reflected in the changing physical vista which colonial settlement presented. Hobart, they emphasised, lost its 'exceedingly primitive appearance' in these years as previously 'slovenly' houses 'of wood' were replaced with 'new buildings ... either of brick or stone', and huts 'of all orders of low architecture', few of which were deemed 'worthy' of 'the designation of dwelling houses', disappeared.[26]

These changes in the substance and layout of the colonial home were, in turn, interpreted as the product of a systematic moralisation of domestic order and of the ostensibly related development of a virtuous and heroic settler masculinity. The early settlers, the Reverend John West asserted, had lacked the requisite moral virtue to properly pursue colonial progress and civilisation. They 'neither possessed nor desired' large areas of land; rather, he claimed:

> They drew their rations from the Royal stores, and bartered away their homesteads for a few bottles of spirit; and it was no idle boast, that a keg of rum was worth more than a common farm. Their hopeless and

dissipated state is remarked in every document of the times: their frail dwellings soon exhibited all the signs of decay and their ground was exhausted by continual cropping. ... The transactions of those early days are scarcely colonial: charged with debauch and outrage, they denote a time of social disorganisation – the dark ages found in the history of every country.[27]

It was, West concluded, only with the arrival of a new breed of settler that the colony's potential had begun to be realised. It was to these new emigrants that Van Diemen's Land was deemed to belong. Men of energy, 'character' and 'principle', their 'influence soon began to be felt in an improved state of things' with the result that their arrival, from the early 1820s onwards, 'imparted a new tone to the social character of the young colony'.[28]

So convinced was colonist David Burn of this that he insisted on dating the colony's 'birth', 'its *virtual* nativity', to 1820 on the grounds that it was at this point that free emigration had 'utterly annihilated the convict ascendancy; imparting to the infant settlement' the 'highly moral and intelligent tone for which ... it at present stands conspicuous'.[29] In Burn's eyes, all that had gone before was irrelevant; early settlement had taken the form of a morally dissolute stillbirth. The architects of colonial 'progress and prosperity' were those 'resolute' free colonists whose influx from 1820 onwards had 'subdued and overawed the licentious' and who had 'gradually extract[ed] harmony' from the 'discordant'.[30] Idealised notions of gender difference and domestic order, therefore, took the form of an ideological punctuation mark, serving to radically separate the convict, and hence morally dubious, origins of early settlement from the ostensibly higher moral endeavour that drove colonial 'progress' thereafter. This process of differentiation, by denigrating the efforts of the early (mostly ex-convict) settlers in particular, enhanced the wider claims to moral ascendancy on the part of the newly emerging colonial middle and ruling classes.

Although settlers would later remember these processes of change as natural and inevitable, their narratives and histories seamlessly associating the moral transformation of Van Diemen's Land with the moment of their arrival, the refashioning of the colony in these years was an inevitably more complicated and, at times, conflict-ridden matter. This was partly because, despite their attempts to distance themselves from the past, the new arrivals often had more in common with those who were already in the colony than some cared to admit. A similar concern with family and with domestic morality had, as we saw in chapter one, been an integral part of the world view of many of the ex-convict small settlers who had been transported to the settlement in its first twenty years. The pressure to conform in the decades thereafter also came as much from above as below: while informal practices such as settler gossip, moral surveillance and social exclusion would play an important role, so too would a substantially enhanced state regulation and intervention. Thus, while settler pressure would lead, on the one hand, to the purification of the state and to the re-ordering of governorial authority, so these processes would, in turn, stimulate growing pressures on colonists themselves. The result was a major, and largely simultaneous, reworking of the colonial private and public spheres.

*　*　*

One of the first signs that a major shift was under way came in the late 1810s and early 1820s with a series of divisive and increasingly public rows over the personal habits and moral conduct of Governor William Sorell. Sorell had arrived in the settlement in 1817 with a woman he treated as his wife, lived in adultery with her at Government House, had several children with her, and saw no problem in introducing her into 'society'. Indeed, Sorell appears to have considered a colonial life a solution to their problems: in Britain he had emphasised the need for secrecy and discretion; in Van Diemen's Land he felt able to conduct the relationship in public.[31] The controversies over Sorell's conduct were, in some ways, simply a re-run of the kinds of arguments that had once enveloped Collins; they were inspired by the same kinds of jealousies and divisions and by a determination on the part of some powerful colonists to manipulate, and even usurp, state authority. In a number of other ways, they were, however, a product of the shifting socio-economic and cultural landscape. The questions raised by Sorell's private life would, consequently, also intersect with a range of new questions and, in particular, with the growing determination of an expanding colonial elite to consolidate its position and to delineate and regulate its boundaries.

The deserted Mrs Sorell, left languishing in Britain, was among the first to act. Writing to Lord Bathurst in mid-1818, she sought financial recompense for herself and seven children, claiming that Sorell had abandoned them when he had taken up a position at the Cape over a decade before. With at best limited assistance from Sorell over the years, the family had struggled to survive. Their goods had been seized for unpaid rent, Mrs Sorell had been crippled in a fire, and eventually they had ended up in the workhouse. When in 1817 Sorell was ordered by a London court to pay £3,000 damages to the husband of the woman with whom he was living Mrs Sorell was encouraged to act. 'I will not tire your Lordship', she commented, 'by a painful recital of the many miseries and hardships I have most undeservedly suffered from the Cruel neglect of him whose duty it undoubtedly is to afford Comfort and Consolation'. Instead she simply 'threw' herself upon Bathurst's 'goodness', asking that he direct some of Sorell's salary to his 'helpless wife' and children. In response, Bathurst ordered that a hundred pounds a year be advanced to the family direct from the Governor's salary. He had taken this action, Bathurst informed Sorell, on the basis of his 'full Expectation' that 'your own feelings will prompt you to make such a provision' and because Mrs Sorell's claim was 'as much inconsistent with your Public as with your Private character to refuse'. This was his 'one great error of conduct' in life, Sorell admitted in response, and it was one, through the damage done to his 'prospects', for which he believed he had already partially atoned. Seeking to reassure Bathurst that he was nevertheless fit for the job, Sorell claimed the continued 'esteem' of 'many distinguished persons', including, importantly, the 'confidence' of Governor-General Macquarie.[32]

If Sorell had thought to separate his private life from his public prospects by heading for Van Diemen's Land, he could not have been more wrong. As Bathurst's comments reveal, a governor's authority was considered to depend upon his whole character, and not merely his public conduct. Neither was this simply a matter of individual moral codes for, as the colonial gossip mills were about to reveal, Sorell's private conduct directly undermined the state's claims to respectability and authority. Thomas Davey and Anthony Fenn Kemp were among the first colonists to exploit the public–private dissonance created by Sorell's lifestyle. Aggrieved by his own recent dismissal, ex-Governor Davey sought to repair his reputation by attacking Sorell. 'I feel inexpressibly proud', Davey informed Bathurst, that 'during the time myself and family were representatives at Van Diemen's Land, Religion, Virtue, Morality and Example was the order of every Succeeding day; but now, my Lord, I with sorrow perceive a disregard of all moral restraint and even timid attention to principle'.[33] While Davey's allegations about the current immorality were designed to cast doubt upon London's decision to replace him, and so to help restore his reputation, they were also partly related to his land claims. Although he had petitioned for 5,000 acres of land in 1814, this had still not been granted; something that Davey believed was due to the 'vile reports . . . dark and invidious insinuations' that had 'gone abroad' about him. These insinuations had come largely from Macquarie, who had written repeatedly to London to accuse Davey of 'dissipation and profligacy', alleging that 'he spends almost his entire time in drinking, and every other Species of low depravity in Company with the basest and meanest of people'.[34]

The relationship between Macquarie and Davey had been strained from the outset. Even before Davey had assumed office in 1813, Macquarie was complaining of the 'extraordinary degree of frivolity and low buffoonery in his manners'.[35] While Macquarie believed that Davey's personal habits debased his family, a fact which was 'gross and offensive' in itself, he also considered them inimical to good government. In Macquarie's view, Davey's inability to keep 'sight of that Manly and dignified deportment' which his rank and office required made him 'totally incapable of executing the Public Duties of his Station'. Davey was not only 'dissipated and profligate in his private life' he also misused his office. 'He is extremely venal and corrupt in his public Capacity', Macquarie alleged, accusing Davey, among other things, of turning a blind eye to the clandestine trade and smuggling at the Derwent and of financial dishonesty. In his place, Macquarie sought a new type of governor: one with the 'activity, zeal and intelligence' that he believed the office required.[36] Influenced by these allegations, Bathurst sacked Davey on grounds of 'licentious conduct'.[37] Understandably keen to undo the damage to his reputation – and well aware of the capital value of character – Davey responded by repeatedly stressing his credentials as a family man and by emphasising that he had conducted himself 'in all parts of the World, without the Smallest reproach or blemish' during forty-five years of government service.[38] His attack on Sorell – which notably coincided with his renewed requests for colonial land, labour and livestock – was almost certainly partly designed to throw his own claims to respectability into even sharper relief.

It was, however, Anthony Fenn Kemp who would do Sorell most damage. The conflict with Kemp began the moment that Sorell arrived and it primarily revolved around Kemp's concerns to prevent the new Governor from obstructing his interests. By 1817, Kemp was in business with George Gatehouse, ex-convict trader and farmer. Sorell, apparently inadvertently, managed to offend Gatehouse almost immediately by striking his name from a list of people invited to a function to welcome the new Governor. Although Sorell had not taken any of the actual decisions about the guest list, he had nevertheless approved when told that 'care would be taken to avoid any mixture of persons beyond an admissible line' by excluding 'characters' of a 'questionable nature'. Offended by their lack of invitation, Kemp and Gatehouse were also understandably fearful that it signalled the onset of an official policy of discrimination against ex-convicts. Partly as a consequence, they interpreted Sorell's refusal to appoint Gatehouse to the coveted position of Hobart auctioneer and his refusal to allocate more convict workers to their firm as evidence of just such a policy and they framed their protest to Macquarie in these terms. Defending his decisions, Sorell noted that the men had, in fact, been refused additional labour not through any 'injustice or hostile feeling' but because of a generalised 'scarcity of Men'. Ironically, his decision about the auctioneer position had arisen, it turned out, not from any negative opinion of Gatehouse – 'a quiet and well conducted Citizen' – but because of Sorell's objections to Kemp. The latter, Sorell asserted, was 'the most seditious, mischievous' man in 'this whole Settlement' and, given that the 'interests' of Kemp and Gatehouse were so 'blended', the Governor considered that 'the nomination of Mr Gatehouse as Auctioneer' would be 'highly pernicious to the order of this Settlement'.[39]

Viewing Sorell as a threat, Kemp endeavoured to put the new Governor in his place. He resorted initially to allegations of financial impropriety. Although entirely unsubstantiated, the fact that Kemp was a magistrate lent his accusations an air of official authority. Were it not for this, Sorell noted, he would have been willing to overlook the fact that Kemp was 'in the daily habit of disseminating the grossest falsehoods and calumnies against my public Acts and conduct'. Kemp's determination to 'compromise' Sorell's 'authority' inevitably forced matters to a 'crisis'. Intent on mobilising public opinion, Kemp 'talked of convening the Settlers'. The action carried with it the strong scent of rebellion for it was just such a public assembly that had sparked the mutiny against Bligh, an event in which Kemp, of course, had played his part. Kemp deliberately played upon this association, raising the spectre of 1808 by combining a declaration about 'convoking the Settlers' with a direct allusion to the events surrounding 'Admiral Bligh's removal'.[40] Pushed to his limits, Sorell dismissed Kemp from the Bench and recommended that civil and criminal actions against him be considered. Sensing the danger, Macquarie ratified these decisions and expressed his public support by ordering that Kemp's dismissal be published as a Government Order.[41]

Beaten on this occasion, Kemp simply changed tack. The next conflict blew up over Kemp's refusal to obey a Police Order for every householder to complete a Muster return. Although Kemp had complied with this perfectly routine request in previous years, he now sought to use it to undermine Sorell.[42] The muster was an important expression of state authority because it was a moment when all heads of households appeared in person before the governor. Sorell's secretary wrote to Kemp that the Governor:

> would conceive himself to be very ill maintaining the rank of the Chief authority in this Settlement, if, upon *a great public occasion, upon which his duty requires him to sit in person* to receive generally the Reports and Returns of the population … he were to admit the

right of exemption in any class or Body ... to make them otherwise than in person.[43]

Kemp's obstinacy, however, appears to have won him something of a following, and crisis once again threatened Sorell. Among Kemp's supporters was Edward Abbott, Chairman of the Bench and, as Deputy Judge Advocate, Van Diemen's Land's chief law officer. When Kemp was ordered to appear before the magistrates, Abbott refused to hear the case and instead used his appearance on the Bench to side publicly with Kemp.[44] Kemp was 'a person of respectability and Fortune', Abbott argued, and ought not to have been summoned for a breach of police regulations. Sorell was incandescent. 'Can it be intended', he asked:

> that any Man's Fortune or Condition entitles him to resist the Laws, or be exempt from obeying them? ... If such considerations were allowed to influence the Bench of Magistrates every seditious and turbulent Demagogue, who has money, would at once feel himself above their Jurisdiction, and would of course set them at defiance.[45]

In Sorell's eyes, moreover, there was more at stake here than a simple defence of the 'rule of law'. In cases of 'contempt or breach of Law and Regulation there is', he argued, 'double reason for enforcing obedience and punishing contumacy, when the example of the Recusant may, from his property or Station, be likely to encourage others'.[46] Here was the seed of an idea – to be pursued more fully under Arthur – that a new colonial elite had to be fashioned, capable of consistent moral leadership and thus of more fully commanding authority.

Kemp's refusal to attend Sorell in person had, from the outset, rightly been perceived as a direct challenge: the Governor, Kemp was informed, 'will not wave [sic] to you any particle of what belongs to his official situation'.[47] Abbott's defiance deepened this challenge. A key 'principle' was at stake, Sorell argued, for:

> if it be once conceded that Magistrates ... are warranted in exercising any latitude or discretion with respect to carrying into effect the Colonial Laws and Regulations emanating from the Supreme authority ... the whole may become subject to doubt and question. ... Thus would the Magistrates ... be in fact possessed of a controlling power over the Lt Governor.[48]

Fortunately for Sorell, the situation was quickly contained. Within days, Abbott had been made to see sense, publicly declaring – at Sorell's insistence – that he had been wrong; he also recalled the Bench and proceeded with Kemp's trial. The latter was prison bound, albeit briefly.[49]

Kemp, however, was far from done, for he had been waging a simultaneous campaign against Sorell's 'immorality'. His 'tongue', Sorell complained, 'spares none in its slander'.[50] By late 1818, these attacks upon Sorell's private life had become the centre point of Kemp's strategy, provoking several letters to Bathurst. He wrote, Kemp claimed, not from 'personal pique' but out of his sense of 'duty' to his family and he repeatedly drew attention to his status as a married man and the father of six children. Sorell's governorship, Kemp alleged, was 'attended with . . . serious injury to the Morals of the rising Generation of this Infant Colony'. Not only was the Governor an adulterer, but the affair was being conducted openly 'in *Government House!*' It would have been one thing, Kemp asserted, had Sorell kept 'Mrs Kent privately', but 'he consistently attends her abroad' and even 'publicly paraded' her 'in an equipage bought at Government Expense'. These acts were too 'insulting to Public Decency' to 'be forgiven'.[51] 'It is', Kemp concluded, 'not the private indulgence of which I complain, but the public Insult', for even 'if Vice itself can be excused, there is yet a certain display of it, a certain outrage to decency and violation of public decorum, which for the benefit of Society should never be forgiven'. Rejecting the claims of the Governor's 'friends' that his 'private Character has nothing to do with his *Public One*' as 'demoralised' and 'absurd', Kemp stressed 'the disadvantages an Infant Colony receives from the example of the Highest Authority living in a state of Adultery'.[52] Following so closely on the complaints from Mrs Sorell and Davey, Bathurst had little choice but to order Commissioner Bigge to launch an official enquiry, a process that would lead eventually to Sorell's dismissal.

While Kemp may have genuinely feared for the moral injury that Sorell's adultery was doing to the settlement, his contemporaries were doubtful. Many held Kemp in low regard; Robert Bayles, for one, colourfully denounced him as a man who 'studied law behind a [shop] counter by the yard and gallon', claiming that 'money' was the only 'god he worshipped'.[53] Others considered him 'weak, vindictive and malignant'.[54] Some were specifically hostile to his campaign against the Governor. Those who agitated against Sorell, colonist Charles Rowcroft asserted, were 'the vermin of the social body', individuals who 'daub with their filthy tongues all persons and institutions' and 'who too fond of the sound of their own voices to forebear their ceaseless talk' will 'exhaust old scandal and imagine new'.[55] Even Bigge, who, as a visitor, was a more neutral judge, was dubious: 'with the Knowledge that I have of the conduct of Mr Kemp, and his bitter animosity towards Lieutenant Governor Sorell, I may venture', he noted, 'to question the sincerity of his Parental Solicitude'.[56] These doubts rested partly on Bigge's discovery that Kemp had continued to visit Sorell 'some time after' he 'had been acquainted with the circumstances of his Domestic Life and the real character of the Lady who was living with him'. Attempting to explain this discrepancy, Kemp revealed the extent to which his material interests dominated. He had, he conceded, been 'loath to offend a Person who had it in his power to obstruct my mercantile views'.[57]

Kemp's letters to Bathurst reveal similar inconsistencies and they were, in addition, riddled with misrepresentations, exaggerations and even outright fabrication. Two further clues tend to confirm the central role of rhetoric and self-interest in Kemp's campaign. The first was his own hypocrisy, the second his later fairly breathtaking U-turn. Kemp had a decidedly mixed past; he was, his biographer suggests, 'roistering' and 'corrupt' from an early age.[58] A gambler, he had been imprisoned for debt among other things, and he had also at one stage enjoyed his own de facto relationship – with ex-convict woman Judith Simpson, whom he later abandoned, along with their infant child. Indeed, the need to escape his own past figured high among his reasons for being in the Australian settlements at all.[59] In his hypocrisy, Kemp was far from alone; other self-appointed guardians of colonial public morals had equally shaky records. Indeed, insecurity of character and reputation often partly motivated these kinds of outbursts. Although the empire appeared to offer a fresh start, the potential for character re-invention also tended to make colonial reputations insecure, rendering colonies fertile sites for gossip and accusation.[60]

In 1824 Kemp also did an abrupt about-turn. As chairman of a meeting of 'the Landholders, Merchants and Free Inhabitants of Van Diemen's Land' called in the Governor's support, it was Kemp who was nominated to write to the King seeking Sorell's continuance in office. 'At an early period of His Honor's Administration', Kemp commented, in a breathless display of understatement:

> a difference arose between him and me, chiefly from want of explanation, and too much warmth on both sides; and, considering myself aggrieved, I represented him to Earl Bathurst; but, after witnessing for nearly seven Years his unremitting Attention to the duties of his Station, and his high Talent for Public Business, I sunk all remembrance of private Feeling, and cheerfully joined my Fellow Colonists in forwarding a Public Measure, from a deep conviction that our Personal Rights and the General Security of Property will hardly find a more able and upright Protector than Lieutenant Governor Sorell.[61]

Both Kemp's reversal of attitude and the moralising terms in which he waged his campaigns were embedded within the wider shifting dynamics of the colony's socio-cultural order in these years. Although

Sorell's early actions had appeared to bode ill for men like Kemp, his period in office had in fact laid the foundations of a major transition in the Van Demonian economy. An earlier ban on commercial trade with the colony was lifted, the free emigration of 'men of capital' began to take off and the boundaries of settlement expanded. Although these processes would only be fully consolidated after Bigge and under Arthur, Sorell played a key role in getting things started. He moved to suppress disorder by crushing the bushrangers and by establishing sites of confinement and secondary discipline. He rationalised the convict system to facilitate a greater efficiency in the distribution of labour and enhanced discipline. He deployed labour and public resources to infra-structural works such as new roads and bridges, encouraged commercial developments and agricultural pursuits, and promoted the whaling industry and the development of trade in products like merino wool, hops and wheat. Finally, anticipating the take-off in demand for land that would coincide with increased free emigration, he sent out parties to explore and survey Van Diemen's Land systematically. In a variety of different ways, then, Sorell had revealed that he was fully committed to using the state as a lever for colonial social and economic development.[62] For all these reasons, merchants like Kemp were increasingly aware that their interests lay with the Governor rather than against him.

The process of creating a greater colonial order nevertheless initially fostered conflict as well as cooperation. Men like Kemp were too used to having things their own way and to subverting, if not actually breaking, the law when it suited them.[63] Kemp, after all, was a representative of that wider class of 'self-created Gentlemen', many of whom, as we saw in chapter one, had made their 'fortunes' in a 'depraved and scandalous manner' and against whom Belbin and others had attempted to take a stand a decade before.[64] Many of the larger merchants and landowners continued to benefit from the existing status quo, enjoying what one competitor angrily denounced as a 'systematic mode of extortion'.[65] Kemp and Gatehouse, in particular, were among a select group of individuals who, by acting as profiteering middlemen between the smallholders and the state, had reaped substantial profits by manipulating the contract system through which government endeavoured to supply the Store.[66] Sorell's reforms threatened this. The opening of the colony to free settlement and commercial development demanded the end of the old system, and in 1823 a free market in the key staples of wheat and meat was introduced.[67] Determined to retain his market share, Kemp again attacked Sorell. In February 1823, a month after the contract system had been abolished, he again accused the Governor, this time of profiteering by illegally using convict labour on government land illicitly to supply the Store with wheat.[68] Although Bigge later exonerated Sorell of these charges, wider doubts about the Governor's morality, kept alive by Kemp's gossip about Sorell's private life, undoubtedly helped to give them a degree of credibility.

Despite the opposition, Sorell was clearly determined to stifle the 'roguery' of the past. Indeed, he had been instructed explicitly by Macquarie to do so and to keep an eye on a range of 'designing characters' in an effort to 'restore' Van Diemen's Land to 'Peace, tranquillity and respectability'.[69] Consequently, within weeks of his arrival in the settlement, a spate of investigations and arrests into stock theft had begun, one sign of Sorell's determination to 'sift this train of infamy to the bottom'.[70] Commissary General Broughton, sent by Macquarie in 1816 to take command of the Store specifically to help suppress the corruption, was impressed by Sorell's 'firmness' of 'character', believing that it would 'tend to check the few turbulent persons in this Place, whose sole study has been to oppress the poorer orders of People'.[71] 'I find', Broughton continued, that he is:

> [a] keen discerning Man, and, without the assistance of any one, has formed a pretty perfect knowledge of the characters of the disaffected, to whom I do not hesitate to say he will be a terror. ... And I am as fully persuaded he will encourage the honest and industrious by a fair and impartial distribution of favors, in proportion to their exertions.[72]

Crimes, Broughton claimed, 'were committed with the greatest impunity' but how could it be otherwise, he asked, when the 'very heads, with but few exceptions, set the very worst examples'. 'Not even Villainy is kept a secret', he reported, 'for there are some who boast of their iniquity and glory in their misdeeds'. Among the activities that Broughton investigated was the 'diabolical scheme' of 'Financiering' run 'by Gentlemen here'. Although he was uncertain about Governor Davey's actual involvement in the corruption, Broughton considered him incapable of overseeing any real change, accusing him of 'mismanagement' and of allowing 'many improprieties to pass by with impunity'.[73] To effect fundamental reform in Van Diemen's Land, Broughton and Sorell both realised that it would be necessary to confront some of the settlement's wealthiest and most powerful vested interests.

For a variety of reasons, men like Kemp simultaneously resented and were attracted by these attempts to suppress the corruption and other illicit activities and to place colonial capitalism on a more secure, regulated and legal basis. To some extent, they recognised that they had exploited the existing system to its limits and, in light of this, some now sought to secure their fortunes and consolidate their positions. Consequently, at the same time as they were making endless trouble for the likes of Sorell, some of these same merchants and landowners were also looking increasingly to the state for protection and assistance. Disputes over property ownership, which became almost endemic in these years, illustrate the paradox. Although none of the early governors in Van Diemen's Land had been empowered to allocate land without permission from Sydney, all of them had done so, resorting, among other things, to verbal contracts, temporary titles and limited tenures. As a result, property claims were often confusing and tenuous, and historic problems with surveying meant that boundaries were also often indistinct.

From the mid-1810s onwards, the state began to mediate these kinds of disputes, establishing questions of succession and inheritance, ordering financial settlements and, in some cases, revoking title. One of the first signs of this new spirit of interventionism was an Order issued by Macquarie in 1816 which decreed that 'all Grants or Leases of Lands or tenements' made in Van Diemen's Land, either in the past or the future, 'by incompetent authority' would 'be deemed null and void'.[74] Kemp and Gatehouse were among a host of individuals who suffered as a consequence. In 1818 Macquarie ordered that a Hobart allotment over which they claimed ownership was to be restored to settler George Guest, whom Macquarie considered to have prior claim on the grounds that it had not been 'alienated by any sufficient authority' to anyone else. Guest, moreover, was ordered to pay only part compensation for the house that Kemp and Gatehouse had built on this plot.[75]

Although Kemp and Gatehouse had clearly lost out in this particular case, other incidents taught men like them that considerable benefits were to be gained from the enhancement of state power and that the old system of corruption had its costs as well as its benefits. In 1816, along with a number of other colonists, they complained that Patrick Hogan, the then Commissariat Officer, had fraudulently obtained money from them and now refused to pay his debts.[76] Hogan, who would eventually be court-martialled for his activities, was involved in a wide range of illegal pursuits, including the forging of bills designed to look like government notes. Although Macquarie initially told the complainants that he had no powers to take action, several months later Broughton reported that enough evidence had now been gathered to bring charges. By this stage, the action had extended to involve a substantial number of the settlement's leading merchants and entrepreneurs to whom several thousand pounds were owed, almost

£800 of it to Kemp and Gatehouse alone. With over £20,000 of public property at stake, the state too had its own good reason to act.[77]

This case was symptomatic of a deeper problem, testifying, as it did, to the relative insecurity of property in the settlement and to the inability of many creditors to enforce payment. Allegations of fraudulent activities against some of the settlement's key officers, a feature that was the legacy of almost two decades in which official appointments had been used as a base for colonial entrepreneurship, exacerbated these problems. The collusion, if not active corruption, of many of the officers, created the potential for these cases to spill over into the public domain where they became a conduit for wider debates and conflicts about the morality and legitimacy of authority. Thus, for example, when merchant Rowland Loane brought actions against George Weston Gunning and A.W.H. Humphrey, accusing them of refusing to pay for livestock that he had delivered to them, the case quickly became a magnet for broader grievances. Besieged by Edward Lord, Gunning, Humphrey and others and faced with their tactics of illegal arrest and imprisonment, Loane gained the public support of a group of smaller settlers who issued an Address in his favour both because they regarded his battle as a lever against the 'systematic Extortion so regularly practised in this Settlement' and because of their concerns that if 'fraudulent Sales of property . . . be allowed', they would 'become the Order of the Day'.[78]

These kinds of conflicts could run deep, far beyond the relatively wealthy and increasingly order-oriented layers of the major merchants and landowners, outwards into the wider community and right down to its labouring base. In 1818, in yet another episode in this drawn-out saga, a large crowd gathered to watch the arrest and removal under force of Humphrey from Government House, through Hobart's streets, to the jail. The scene appears to have been a deliberately designed piece of retributive theatre. The two law officers involved used the excuse of a civil summons issued by Loane against Humphrey to arrest the latter as he left Government House and, repeatedly refusing to accept his bail, told him they would 'not be satisfied with any thing but [his] Body'. A crowd had waited outside the Court much of the morning, expecting to see Humphrey there, and 'ready to cheer and huzza' his arrest.[79] Both the actions of the law officers and the appreciative crowd testifies to the extent to which a range of conflicts had attached themselves to the confrontation between Loane and Humphrey and, while these encompassed the grievances of some merchants and farmers, they also emanated, more dangerously still, from the fact that Humphrey was a magistrate and, as Superintendent of Police, the key figure in Sorell's reformed system for distributing and disciplining convict labour.[80] As a central lynchpin of colonial order and authority, Humphrey's implication in dirty dealings and biased court proceedings was potentially explosive. As these kinds of incidents revealed, the interests of the state, the major merchants and landowners, in stifling colonial corruption and the spirals of disorder that it created, were increasingly beginning to overlap.

It is against this much broader backdrop that Kemp's reversal of opinion towards Sorell must be situated. At a superficial level, his decision to switch sides and blithely to front the campaign to retain Sorell was probably partly the product of the somewhat disturbing news of the Governor's imminent replacement by Lieutenant-Colonel George Arthur. Having used accusations of immorality in an attempt to crush and manipulate Sorell, Kemp *et al.* now found themselves somewhat outdone: the morally austere, resolutely independent and discipline-oriented Arthur was, almost certainly, not quite the outcome they had sought. Arthur's alleged penchant for authoritarianism was, also, a worrying sign that he might be less willing than Sorell to protect 'our Personal Rights'.[81] At another level, support for Sorell was also undoubtedly based on his considerable achievements. The petition requesting he be allowed to stay on as governor dwelt upon the transformations which had occurred in the settlement during his seven years in office and, in particular, its enhanced security, 'flourishing appearance' and greater prosperity. These achievements, the petitioners claimed, were largely the result of the 'utmost solicitude' that Sorell had 'constantly and unceasingly exhibited ... to ameliorate our condition and give prosperity to our exertions'.[82] Again, Arthur's reputation undoubtedly preceded him: he had already been the subject of sustained controversy and of a pamphlet war over the actions he had taken, as Superintendent of Honduras, against the slave-owners there.[83] Unlike Sorell, whose public reputation as an efficient and intelligent administrator was now firmly established in the settlement, it was less certain whether a new governor, and especially one with such a record, could be trusted to act so systematically in the interests of the propertied. Where Arthur was unknown, Sorell was 'tried and proven'.[84] 'No successor', the petition claimed, 'even with the greatest talents and the best disposition towards us, can be possibly expected to bestow all that general and Individual attention to our wants and wishes, without the lapse of much time and much probable increased inconvenience'.[85] Those who now backed Sorell based their support on their growing recognition that the reformation and restructuring of the legal and social foundations of the settlement's economy were vital to its future stability and expansion.

Despite his achievements, Sorell's private life nevertheless inhibited his ability to command, making it difficult for him to clean up the wider disorder that beset his state. Although he was determined to suppress the corruption and disorder, the impact of his measures was limited necessarily by the example he himself set. In some areas of the settlement, the intra-state conflicts that the lack of discipline and rectitude among the officers created were so rife that government had become virtually impossible. In Launceston and George Town, for example, conflict and dispute between the officers had become so commonplace that the state barely functioned. Sorell's adultery tended to exacerbate these problems. Thus, after a sustained investigation, Bigge was forced to conclude that Sorell's misconduct was contagious. His enquiries revealed not only an alarming rate of indiscipline among the state's officials but also a web of connections between this indiscipline and the wider colonial disorder. Bigge discovered, for example, that Captain Barclay – one of just three justices of the peace in the north – had, through his cohabitation with a convict woman, encouraged other convicts to subvert discipline. Barclay had not only exempted his lover, Mary Smallshaw, from attendance at church but also from the weekly muster, a key moment at which the state exercised its authority over convicts. Moreover, according to Reverend Youl, chaplain at Launceston, this favour had not been confined to Smallshaw alone but extended to 'others in the same situation'.[86] The 'notoriety' of this, Bigge concluded, had 'produced its natural effects upon the minds of other prisoners' who in turn 'justified their own absence from church by the interested connivance of their superiors in the breach of that regulation'.[87] Bigge concluded that it was partly as a result of this type of conduct that so many of the settlement's magistrates failed to 'command the personal respect of the inhabitants'.[88]

While in the north, Bigge also investigated the case of convict Alice Blackstone, who, in 1818, had been made to march thirty-five miles wearing a five and a half pound iron collar around her neck while carrying her newborn infant.[89] The incident not only flew in the face of contemporary theories of punishment but also contravened early nineteenth-century notions of femininity. To make matters worse, it had originated from a now notorious debacle between Alice, her convict husband Richard Blackstone, and W.E. Leith, Inspector of Public Works at George Town.[90] Leith had sent Blackstone into the woods to work as a sawyer, where he sometimes stayed for weeks at a time, and the Inspector had used the opportunity this absence created to conduct a public affair with Alice. 'The foulness of Mr Leith's intercourse with my wife', Richard Blackstone reported, 'spread abroad, owing to their publickly pleasuring and boating together'.[91] Leith had not only abused the convict labour system and legitimised adultery by his acts but he had also deployed state power for his own ends. When Alice eventually left Richard for Leith, her husband's attempt to reclaim his wife and to gain access to their infant child resulted in Leith setting the police on him and later on his being arrested at gunpoint, imprisoned and shackled in irons.[92]

In Bigge's eyes, the misconduct of men like Leith and Barclay was simply unacceptable, and it came at a price which the Commissioner considered too high for a penal state, charged with the control of a multitude of convicts in the absence of a substantial armed force, to pay. The frequency of these kinds of incidents undercut Sorell's attempts to introduce a reformed system of convict discipline based upon 'perpetual reference and control'.[93] While Sorell's firmness of *public* character and his willingness to confront entrenched interest groups were not in doubt, his *private* indiscretions weakened him, undermining his authority by enabling his opponents to question and criticise his power. Kemp's refusal to attend the muster was just one indication of the ways in which Sorell's private life might be used against him. Kemp had been able to dress up his insubordination as moral righteousness – his principled refusal to appear, either socially or on official occasions like the muster, before an adulterer. Sorell's private life equally inhibited his ability to take action against disorderly officers. When, for example, he dismissed Assistant Surgeon Younge for drunkenness and insubordination, it backfired on him. Younge, urged on, as it transpired, by Kemp and Loane, published a scurrilous letter in the settlement's newspaper accusing the Governor of a range of sins.[94] Bigge's remit from London was to create a blueprint for colonial economic development, the expansion of free emigration and the systematic enhancement of the terror of transportation. If colonial society were to undergo such a wholesale transformation, it would require a fully cleansed state machine and a governor without a chink in his moral armour.

* * *

Sorell's departure and Arthur's arrival marked a key turning point in the relationship between the state and the regulation of colonial gender relations and sexual morality. The new order demanded a new breed of governor. Where Collins womanised, Davey drank and Sorell committed adultery, Arthur practised what he preached, turning his energies to the construction and elaboration of an efficient, expansive and purified state machine. Arthur, as the Reverend John West writing in the early 1850s made clear, was very much the man of a particular moral moment. 'The domestic circumstances of Arthur', West commented, 'were more favourable to his authority as a censor; and happily for our ultimate welfare, he resolved to discourage violations of social decorum'.[95] 'Concubinage', Kemp had informed Bigge, was widespread; 'many settlers', including some 'who have land and stock and are respectable', were allegedly living in this state.[96] 'With proper example and encouragement', Kemp suggested, some might be inclined to marry.[97] Under Arthur, this encouragement was systematised. From the early 1820s, those who lived outside marriage, and who were either unwilling or unable to legitimise their relationships, or who offended in other ways, found themselves increasingly excluded from state office and official favour. 'They were placed under a ban', West recorded, 'the favours of the government were denied them' and those who were officers 'were dismissed'.[98] The tide had, in fact, begun to turn before Arthur. Bigge's visit had not only led to Sorell's dismissal but also to the removal from positions of power and authority of several others who had strayed morally.[99]

Arthur's appointment marked the beginning of a fundamentally reworked relationship between state and society. From the moment he arrived, the new Governor looked to the free settlers as agents of discipline and morality. 'It is to your exertions', and still more to your example', he addressed the delegation of gentlemen who greeted him on his arrival, 'that I mainly confide . . . for any effectual reformation in the moral character of a very large class in this community'. Their role as moral exemplars was linked to their self-interest: their moral leadership was 'a measure most essential to the security of your personal property and domestic peace'.[100] This link was forged above all by convict assignment, a coerced labour system designed to supply free settlers with convict workers. 'Bentham's notion that gaolers should possess a personal interest in the reform of convicts is beautifully realised in Van Diemen's Land', Arthur claimed, for:

> [the settler's] prosperity depends not only upon the control and discipline, but also upon the selection of his servant. If a convict . . . in any way sets a bad example to his fellow(s) it is in the master's interest, if he appears irreclaimable, to get rid of him as soon as possible, and the result is that according to the character of his offence . . . he is sent to a road party, a chain gang or perhaps a penal settlement. There is thus maintained throughout the colony a continual circulation of convicts, a distribution of each in his proper place; in short a natural and unceasing process of classification.

'The mainspring' of the system, Arthur asserted, 'is not the authority of the government, but the silent yet most efficient principle of self-interest'.[101] This principle was so powerful, colonist James Ross concurred, that it was able to transform settlers of even indifferent character into moral masters. 'There is no settler . . . in the colony', Ross contended, who 'does not spend more than one-half of every day of his life in watching, advising and actually reforming his convict servants. If he did not do so, he would soon find that they were his masters and not his servants'.[102]

The reformed convict labour system, therefore, depended on a much closer inter-relationship between state and settler, making it necessary not only to achieve greater control over convicts but also to create mechanisms for the enhanced regulation of the free. This was achieved through the extension and withdrawal of a range of state privileges on the basis of moral conduct and by the broader construction of a colonial 'society' whose boundaries were governed by strict codes of gendered morality and domestic respectability. While the latter was partly the autonomous product of the shifting cultural prescriptions and social composition of the free community itself, the state, particularly under Arthur, also played a key role. Indeed, the relationship between state and 'society' was, in this sense, reciprocal and dynamic. As the anxieties caused to colonists by their access, or otherwise, to Government House suggest, invitations from, and association with, the governor were one key means of identifying the 'respectable' and thus of securing character in the unknown and relatively anonymous world of the empire. Arthur was acutely aware of this and he sought to exploit it as one means of ordering and regulating the community. A fairly systematic discrimination against those who had been convicts formed one aspect of this system of informal regulation. The 'time expired or emancipated convict has still been a Felon', Arthur commented, 'and in my judgement, if it is desirable to distinguish between Virtue and Vice, he is thereby precluded from being the private friend or companion of a Public Officer in a Penal Colony'. It was by these principles, he noted, that he endeavoured to 'regulate my own conduct'.[103]

Government House acted as a filter for colonial 'society' more generally. By paying careful attention to the reputation and character of those he 'received at' his 'table', Arthur was confident that he had done much to establish 'a clearly defined line in this Colony between characters of real respectability and others'.[104] These practices were important even at a relatively informal level. The position of a new emigrant on arrival in the colony, as well as his chances of success, was partly secured by the Governor's initial response to him. Towards 'respectable persons', and especially those carrying letters of introduction from the Colonial Office, he had, Arthur explained, always endeavoured to extend the hand of friendship – 'a little special assistance or advice in the selection or location of land', 'the accommodation of a horse from my stable to inspect the Country' and 'a few dinners', which, he explained, 'helps to stamp a character as respectable on his first arrival and is ... useful to him as an introduction in his newly adopted country'.[105] Recognising the material benefits of such practices, one colonist was also gratefully aware of their broader purposes. The 'letters of introduction' he had taken time to arrange for before departing Britain had proved crucial upon his arrival, James Ross noted, and consequently he would urge no man to travel to the settlements without them, for:

> so many doubtful characters come to the colony from time to time, who, without any fair pretensions, contrive to work themselves into the confidence of the credulous or unsuspicious, that a doubt is sometimes apt to be thrown even on deserving strangers who have been so forgetful as to neglect this necessary duty to themselves in leaving home.[106]

Although Sorell had likewise been conscious of the importance of these informal practices of inclusion and exclusion, the disordered nature of his own household undoubtedly undermined their effectiveness. If Janet Ranken was determined to avoid the company of the ex-convict Maria Lord, she was also clearly perturbed by Sorell's domestic arrangements. 'Governor Mr Sorell is married', she noted in her correspondence, 'but he left his own wife in England and brought another man's wife with him in her stead'.[107] Sorell's inability to create a coherent site for the delineation and regulation of 'respectable' society formed one part of Kemp's complaints against him. 'All the married men of Respectability feel severely the example of Lieutenant Colonel Sorell and it leads to great schisms', Kemp asserted.[108] Kemp was especially exercised by the inability of his own wife, and those of men like him, to visit Government House while Sorell remained in residence.[109] Ex-Governor Davey's allegations were strikingly similar: 'during my administration', he claimed in a letter to Bathurst, 'the Government House on the birthdays of our most Gracious Queen was throng'd with the most respectable females, married and unmarried of both Settlements. But now, my Lord, alas! not a female appears at Government House. Thus unhappily circumstanced, Society sinks into oblivion'.[110] By rendering some sites of colonial power moral 'no-go areas' Sorell's behaviour had tended to undercut the nascent socio-cultural unity of the colonial elite. Arthur's properly ordered domestic relationships and high standards of manly propriety created no such problems.

These informal mechanisms were backed up by a swathe of much more formal government measures. State attempts at the moral surveillance and regulation of settlers began, in fact, even before they departed from Britain. Indeed, selection criteria had been applied to settlers for years. As early as 1812, the Select Committee on Transportation had expressed its approval that 'greater precautions' were being taken in 'the selection of these persons', involving both an assessment of their property and the submission of 'satisfactory testimonials and recommendations from persons of known respectability'.[111] Most prospective emigrants applied to the Colonial Office for permission to settle. The ability to supply letters of recommendation or to have patrons capable of testifying to character was crucial, resulting in an advance letter of introduction being sent to the governor and a recommendation for land. Letters from the Colonial Office transmitting these recommendations combined comments about the occupational history of the emigrant with remarks about the size of his capital and the quality of his character.

Two types of emigrant were especially preferred: those with an agricultural past, in the belief that they would make better colonial farmers, and retired military and naval officers, because they supposedly brought a class of individuals with invaluable experience of authority and discipline to the colony. In 1828, Arthur responded to the extremely favourable character references provided for John Boutcher and Abraham Skinner by Sir Thomas Acland MP with delight. Both men, Acland testified, were 'the sons of very respectable Yeomen Tenants . . . and have or will have a fair Capital', and Boutcher, in particular, already had an established reputation as 'a steady active farmer'.[112] 'Acland has recommended two young men of the class the most desirable in a new Colony', Arthur enthused, 'pray be so good as to desire him to send a dozen more of his Country friends', 'it is impossible we could have a more acceptable importation'.[113] 'Respectable Yeomen', he commented, would provide a 'Class of Settlers, which of all others is decidedly the most suited to improve the moral character of the people, and to infuse a proper feeling and some industry into the Colony'.[114]

Arthur, an army man, considered ex-military officers equally indispensable to colonial authority, and he regularly relied upon them to supplement state authority not only as masters but also as district police magistrates, justices of the peace, convict superintendents and the like.[115] Recommending one prospective settler, Captain Morrow of the 40th Regiment, to the favourable attention of the Colonial Office on the grounds that he was 'an Officer and a Gentleman', Arthur concluded, 'I should be highly gratified to receive a thousand such Settlers into the Colony'.[116] In an attempt to promote this kind of settlement, the government in London instituted a range of measures designed as a 'temptation ... to induce them to proceed' to the Australian settlements. These provided ex-officers with more favourable rates of quit-rent in return for their commitment to settle for a period of at least seven years and to invest capital in their land equal to at least half its value, privileges that were later extended to retired officers from the Royal Navy and the Marines.[117] These arrangements were designed to 'hold out to Officers of the Army, such inducements to become Settlers in the Australian Colonies as would secure to the public the Services of a valuable and intelligent class of persons'. 'There is', Arthur commented in approval, 'no measure more likely to be advantageous to the Colony, more especially if they are married men, provided it is well guarded and strong recommendations of character insisted upon as absolutely indispensable'.[118]

Past service to the nation alone was, however, insufficient: officers wishing to emigrate were also required to provide 'satisfactory testimonials of conduct of an unquestionable character'.[119] One of the keys to the establishment of such respectability, as Arthur's comment reveals, appears to have been marriage; thus at least one emigrant 'married before he left England' in the belief that 'he might have more the appearance of making a permanent lodgement in the Colony'.[120] State preference for married settlers was, moreover, at times a matter for explicit direction. In 1812, when Macquarie informed acting-Governor Geils (1812–13) that permission had been given by the Admiralty for marines who belonged to the detachment soon to depart from Hobart town and who wished to stay on in Van Diemen's Land to be given land and other assistance to enable them to become settlers, he stressed that this indulgence was only to be extended to 'such of the Marines as are *Married, have Families*, and are *Men of good Character*'. So important was this qualification that Macquarie returned to it a paragraph later, concerned lest Geils be forgetful or misled: 'this option', he reiterated, is 'confined to the *Married Men*; those who are not so not being permitted ... to remain in the Colony as Settlers'.[121]

Character and capital together governed both the numbers of acres to be issued to a prospective settler and the extent of their 'introduction' to the governor. While some prospective emigrants were simply furnished with a standard pro forma, those who provided more impressive character recommendations, particularly from powerful patrons, or who had sizeable capital received preferential treatment. The Colonial Office provided them with more detailed and enthusiastic introductions and encouraged the governor to go beyond the usual bounds by providing not only his personal assistance but also the possibility of extra land and sometimes an official appointment. Arthur not only responded to each and every Colonial Office introduction, but he also followed them up, writing to London about the progress of settlers and reporting, in particular, when they failed to meet standards. In 1826, for example, he notified the Colonial Office that Lieutenant Blair, ex-Royal Navy, had, despite his avowed 'respectability', proved less than 'worthy of indulgence' because he was 'exceedingly addicted to drinking'. 'I fear', Arthur later noted, 'that he is not a gentleman likely to make a valuable addition to our emigrant population'.[122]

Character continued to govern the distribution of land even after an emigrant had arrived. In 1828, a Land Board was established to survey those lands already distributed, report upon their 'improvement' and to make recommendations for additional grants.[123] One of its purposes was to provide information about settlers who had avoided the Colonial Office's moral net. The Board was, therefore, instructed by Arthur to enquire into the physical progress of those applicants who had originally brought out orders from the Secretary of State but to report additionally upon the *moral* character of all others. Native-born youths, Arthur further ordered, would only be granted land once the Board had made enquiries as to their 'age, character and connexions', and landowners who intended to be absent from their estates had to provide detailed accounts of the 'respectability' of their 'overseer or agent'. The ability to provide testimonials from 'credible persons of Known respectability' in the colony who 'have had an opportunity of being acquainted with' each applicant's 'character, means and intentions' was considered vital in all these cases.[124]

Even settlers of apparently established reputation had to submit to investigation. In 1828 Arthur responded to the Colonial Office's recommendation that William Allardyce be granted additional land. Allardyce, son of a Scottish clergyman, had received 800 acres upon his arrival in the colony in 1822. Now wishing to extend his holdings, he had had a number of influential men, including two magistrates, three clergymen and the MP for Aberdeen, intercede with Viscount Goderich, Secretary of State for the Colonies, on his behalf. These powerful and favourable testimonials were, however, insufficient. Although responding positively, Goderich reminded Allardyce's patrons that it was 'unusual' to distribute additional grants to settlers already in the colony without 'previous reference to the Governor', and he stipulated to Arthur that the additional grant was only to be made 'provided encouragement could be afforded with propriety'. Arthur consequently caused 'immediate enquiry to be made through the Police of the District' in which Allardyce lived 'as to his improvements, pursuits etc'. Only when this confirmed Allardyce's 'reputation of being a very respectable, industrious young Man, residing on, and improving his Farm' did Arthur confirm the additional grant.[125]

The question of 'character' was never set in stone. Rather, Arthur used the system creatively and as a constant regulator, punishing those who stepped out of line, while holding out the potential of a future reward for rehabilitation. Grants therefore might eventually be awarded, even when previously refused, if a settler could convince the governor that his lesson had been learned. Thus, despite his profoundly negative opinion of David Blair's drinking habits, Arthur continued to reserve his land grant for him long after he had left Van Diemen's Land, and he promised London to take his case into consideration once again *on the condition* that Blair return and take up residence. He was likewise willing to recommend that a ban on additional land grants to settler William Young be lifted. Young had suffered under this prohibition for two years as punishment for his attempt to acquire extra acres by fraudulently applying for land in the names of his infant sons. By 1829, Arthur was ready to forgive this indiscretion. 'Mr Young', he reported to London, has 'proved himself an industrious settler'. He was, no doubt, partly influenced by the views of the Land Commissioners who had reported that Young was 'an industrious steady Man, with a large young Family, who has built a neat Pisa House, enclosed a large Garden and Orchard, and has cleared and fenced a considerable quantity for the time he has been here'. Ordering that the ban be lifted Bathurst noted that Young had 'retrieved by his subsequent conduct the misrepresentation which he . . . practised on a former occasion' and had therefore 'made sufficient atonement for the impropriety'.[126]

Arthur's conviction that ex-officers and yeoman farmers were ideal settlers was partly grounded in his belief that men of more moderate capital made the best masters. 'The most wealthy settlers, or those with large Establishment', he commented, 'are not the most likely Masters to succeed in reforming their Servants, but such as having but few as are daily over them, and with them, and are witnesses to every part of their conduct'. Wealthy, often absentee, masters were much less reliable agents of reformation than settlers who 'were so humble as to associate with their men'.[127] When the large landowning class was allowed to dominate, James Ross, one of Arthur's most loyal colonial supporters, argued that the 'grand and economical engine of maintaining and reforming the prisoner is clipped of its machinery'.[128] This was a view that Bigge also shared, expressing his fears of a system in which convicts, particularly those employed as shepherds, were spread out across the land and were too distant to allow for regular surveillance. The 'principal object' of his regulations was, Bigge explained, 'to induce persons of respectability to engage personally in the rearing of sheep and cattle ... and to provide as much control as possible' for convicts 'through the presence of their masters or a free overseer'.[129]

This emphasis upon resident masters as moral guides for convict workers also partly informed Arthur's unwillingness to grant land to women. Where his predecessors had emphasised the alleged inability of women to work the land properly, Arthur's stressed their unsuitability as employers of convict labour. 'It is to be regretted', he commented, that 'Ladies should ever attempt the management of a Farm with servants whom they cannot control', a factor which he took into account when considering female petitions for land.[130] The contribution of 'ladies' to convict reformation focused on their role within the household where as moral mistresses it was believed that they were able to exact an appropriate authority over, and influence upon, their assigned *female* convict servants. Settler males were recognised by the state as the proper heads of household and the most efficient means of disciplining convict workers. Land policy under Arthur was, therefore, profoundly influenced by his desire to create a particular type of masculine authority: middling-class men, resident upon their land, personally active in its improvement, and willing and able to intervene in the lives of their convict workers.

If land was one crucial means of regulating and rewarding character, labour was another. The assignment system was a key mechanism for the discipline and control of settlers. Governors enjoyed wide-sweeping powers in the assignment of convict labour, including the largely undefined and therefore almost discretionary authority to 'modify' individual assignments and to establish regulations 'in such manner as justice and good policy may require'.[131] A central aspect of this process was the 'most essential' nature of the need to 'get a large insight into the characters of the Free Settlers' in order to assess 'how far they are, or are not, proper persons to be entrusted with Convicts'.[132] Arthur's arrival marked the onset of increased surveillance in this respect. He had, he reported in 1826, already been 'rather more strict in investigating the manner of life of those who have applied for Crown Servants' than Sorell. 'All possible care', he declared, 'should be taken to avoid placing [convicts] in circumstances of great temptation, or in open immorality'.[133]

As a result, Arthur's subordinates were charged with the responsibility of matching convicts to moral employers. In 1827, John Lakeland, Principal Superintendent of Convicts, reported to Arthur that he had 'refused ... a very considerable proportion' of applications for convict servants on the grounds that they had 'been made by exceptionable characters'.[134] On Lakeland's death the following year, Arthur insisted on replacing him with James Gordon, whose suitability for the job was largely based upon his veteran status in the colony and his experience as a magistrate, factors which meant that he possessed 'an intimate acquaintance with the Characters of the settlers'.[135] Arthur was partly driven in these measures by his decidedly mixed opinion of the free population. Although he differentiated between the 'better' and 'lower' classes of settlers, claiming that those who had originally been transported were chiefly one-time 'pickpockets' and 'vagrants' who were 'dissolute to a proverb' and 'drunkards beyond redemption', he was also dubious about those who had come free.[136] They were, he commented, 'generally very needy and not quite so respectable as they have been represented at home'.[137]

In Arthur's view, little could be expected of the older settlers as employers of convict labour. The 'lower' class, he claimed sweepingly after just three months in the colony, was characterised by 'a universal propensity to excessive drinking' with the result that its members 'corrupt rather than reclaim the Servants who are assigned to them'. He had, he reported, taken steps to deal with this problem by removing the convicts assigned to this class of individuals whenever possible. Even the 'better' class of settlers created problems, however, because, in Arthur's opinion, they too tended to encourage the 'dissipated propensities' of their servants, both out of the general 'dread' which they entertained of convicts, and 'from the desire to prevail with them to work on any terms'.[138] Settlers, he noted, 'want the Prisoners as Servants, and pamper or neglect them at the very time these Prisoners should be kept at hard labour for their Offences'.[139] The tension between profit and punishment was, of course, constant and integral to assignment and this was one reason why the surveillance and regulation of employers was considered so vital.

Although aware that his determination to investigate settler character was provocative, Arthur nevertheless, persevered.[140] Government, he asserted, had the backing of 'every Settler whose opinion and support are worth consideration'. Complaints were natural, he alleged, tarring his opponents with the brush of immorality, because his measures were bound to interfere with the 'former Habits' and 'private interest' of 'a certain Class of the Community'.[141] 'Just laws and regulations', he argued, once again morally marginalising those who opposed him, 'are only felt as severe by those who offend them'. The state's right to enquire into settler character was, moreover, the price which free emigrants had to pay for the privileges of land and labour and for the fact that they had chosen to live in what was, first and foremost, a penal colony. 'In exacting many of the most wholesome

[82]

restrictions on the Prisoners', he argued, 'it is frequently necessary to trench upon that unrestricted liberty which is claimed by the free Population'. 'The whole Island', Arthur claimed, 'must be considered in the light of a Gaol'. The 'Free Inhabitants', developing a theme which he would apply with equal resolve to conflicts over the freedom of the press and settler political representation, should therefore 'be looked upon as Visitors' in the colony and as such 'liable to submit to the Rules established for [its] general peace and order'.[142] These attitudes unsurprisingly generated manifold grievances and a body of colonial opposition to Arthur's rule.

Despite the propensity of state surveillance to give 'offence', Arthur argued for a 'still greater discrimination and scrutiny into the claims of Settlers'. Employers, he asserted:

> should be impressed generally with the idea that such servants are assigned to them with the confident hope of their being reformed in their Service under the influence of their example and patient manage-ment; and it should be fully understood that, if the Servant should be removed by a Magistrate ... for any fault of the Master, the latter is not to expect any renewal of the indulgence.[143]

So important did Arthur consider the process of assignment and its related task of accumulating knowledge about the character of prospec-tive employers that, during his first few years, he assumed personal command of the system and invested considerable time and energy in its establishment and development. The process of acquiring detailed information on convicts and settlers 'cost me much continued applica-tion for three Years', he informed London in 1828:

> I am in my own office generally two hours in the summer, and one hour in the winter before my breakfast hour (which is eight o'clock) every morning, and am seldom occupied less than ten, most generally, twelve hours every day, and constantly until a late hour at night, and I may add that I have thus persevered for upwards of four years. The Private Secretary and two Clerks are of course equally hard worked![144]

This intense effort was crucial to the smooth running of the convict system. There 'is no part of the Administration of a Penal Colony, more anxious in its nature, or more important in its results, than a right direction of Convicts labour', Arthur commented. 'One of the most anxious duties in this Colony', he noted, 'is the assignment of Prisoners to prevent their falling into improper hands'. It was con-sequently 'of paramount importance to bestow the greatest attention in directing and enquiring into the nature of their employment'.[145] It is, he reiterated, 'extremely desirable ... that either through the Police or Principal Superintendent ... the most conclusive information should always be obtained of the character of the applicant and all circumstances connected with the family'.[146] The system, Chief Police Magistrate John Price later conceded, was necessarily 'very inquisitorial'.[147]

By the end of the 1820s, with the foundations of the assignment system securely in place, a highly efficient bureaucratic infrastructure, centred upon officers like the Principal Superintendent of Convicts, the Muster Master, chief district constables, police magistrates and the Colonial Secretary, was more fully in play, and Arthur's individual burden declined to an extent. In 1830, one of the most powerful, and invasive, mechanisms for the regulation of free settlers was created in the form of the Assignment Board. Composed of the Chief Police Magistrate, the Principal Superintendent of Convicts and a military officer, the Board's remit was not merely to distribute convict labour but to review all cases where settlers were accused of contravening regulations or of committing other offences.[148] Employers whose character was called into question in any way, including on the word of their convict workers, were thoroughly investigated and, at times, forced to go to great lengths to clear their names, including, in every case, submitting to a thorough investigation by the District Police Magistrate.[149] Blanket prohibitions were also placed upon specific groups of employers. Publicans and innkeepers, individuals who had breached state regulations and ex-convicts were, for example, banned from receiving assigned servants.[150] Although many of these prohibitions applied equally to male as female convicts, regulations for the assignment of women were particularly tight. Single men were, for example, among a longer list of groups prohibited from receiving women servants.[151] 'Every effort', Arthur insisted, ' is made to prevent a female being assigned to any service, except such as there is every expectation that she will be taken care of'.[152]

Combined, these measures ensured that the colonial state had both the will and the means to direct investigations into the characters and lifestyles of settlers, regulating not only how they behaved but also whom they lived with.[153] Numerous individuals had their convict workers removed as a result. The charges ranged from drunkenness and suspicion of immoral conduct to permitting convicts to eat Christmas dinner with the family or to partake in harvest celebrations through to more general breaches of regulations, including the failure to submit the regularly required returns and reports on convict servants.[154] Even settlers with otherwise apparently impeccable character references could fall foul of this system. In February 1829, just a year after Arthur had recommended an additional land grant on the basis of a favourable report, William Allardyce was fined for 'allowing an assigned servant of a neighbouring settler to tipple in his house' and for having drunk spirits with 'this man, his own three assigned servants, two other convicts and several other persons free by servitude'. In addition to the sentence of the court, the undoubtedly more punitive measure of an order for the removal of all convict workers assigned to his service was issued. Allardyce, the Colonial Secretary commented, was particularly deserving of punishment because he had 'so much abused the confidence which the government reposed in him'.[155] A month later, government nevertheless relented: as Allardyce had 'expressed contrition for the offence', the order for the withdrawal of all his servants was revoked, Arthur expressing his 'hope' that Allardyce would 'be more circumspect in his conduct in future'.[156]

This kind of chastising power over the free was remarkable and it rested, above all, upon the fear that if a settler crossed the state's moral line, the vital labour force of convicts would be removed. The power of this penalty should not be underestimated for the effects could be disastrous. Sarah Bromley was left without any servants whatsoever as a result of several accusations of immorality against her. As a result, she had, she noted, 'no servants to work on the farm, to attend the house or to attend me during my illness'. Writing again several months later, her situation had become even more desperate: she suffered from 'severe rheumatism', had three young children to support on her own, and now her harvest, the family's main income, was about to go to waste. Despite the immediacy of this latter concern, it was another month before, as a merely interim measure, some of Bromley's workers were temporarily restored.[157] The withdrawal of her servants, Mary McAuley likewise testified, had also very swiftly and 'seriously' affected 'my interests'. In a society so heavily dependent on convict labour, these colonists were almost certainly not alone in fearing 'ruinous consequences' as a result of this kind of state sanction.[158]

The withdrawal of convict servants also had profound implications for one's reputation, and hence one's place, within colonial 'society'. 'I am', Robert Bell complained upon the removal of his female convict servant, 'the sufferer of this both in regard to losing my female servant' and because it 'cannot do any good to my character having a servant taken away in such a manner'.[159] James Fenton was equally aware of the potential damage to his reputation which the refusal to assign a female convict servant to his household entailed, understanding only too well that such a decision must rest upon 'some gross misrepresentation ... respecting either my character or situation'.[160] Defending Arthur's system, James Ross explained that the effects of such 'strict' and 'summary' sanctions were both planned and welcome. The 'public disgrace' involved in having one's servants removed served as a powerful and constant incentive to good conduct among the settler population, he contended, and when this penalty was imposed, the desire to have it lifted served, in turn, to produce an 'amendment in' the settler's 'life and habits'.[161]

Combined, the pressures to conform created a finely honed device for state supervision and intervention. The minute knowledge of individual households that the state was able to accumulate, often with the compliance of a particular settler, was astonishing. Richard Troy for one, desperate to overcome the ban on his acquiring female convict servants for the sake of the health of his 'exhausted' wife, willingly invited the state, in the form of local Police Magistrate George Weston Gunning, to inspect his home. Troy, Gunning noted, had, as earlier reports suggested, once been a heavy drinker, but was now of 'such a worn out constitution' that he had had to stop. Since he had been refused as 'a very improper person to have a servant', other improvements to the household had also been made. A strict regime now operated in the home, Gunning informed Arthur. Troy was 'severe upon his servants' and 'will not allow them to do wrong', and there was much to support Troy's pleas that his establishment was now subject to an 'orderly regulation' and that he had reconstructed himself as a moral and disciplined household patriarch. There were, Troy desperately sought to reassure Arthur, 'few farmers in Van Diemen's Land' who had 'paid as much attention to the bringing up and education of their children as I'. Upon receipt of this detailed account of Troy's apparent reform, Arthur relented, assigning a female servant to the household. Through an ongoing process of official supervision, scrutiny, surveillance and sanction, Troy had been taught the appropriate moral script: the power of the state to enforce this meant that Troy, like others who suffered similarly, almost certainly paid more than mere lip-service to it.[162]

* * *

Visiting Van Diemen's Land on a tour of inspection in 1828, Archdeacon Scott commended Arthur on the many changes which he believed had taken place since his previous visit in 1824, noting the decrease of drunkenness, the increased rate of marriages and baptisms, the decline of illegitimacy and the diminution of crimes such as burglary, highway robbery and murder. 'I cannot attribute this change', he wrote to Arthur, 'but to the system of Police and Vigilance in every Department established by Your Excellency, the example you have set yourself, and the inflexible adherence to the Duties of Religion and Morality'.[163] In matters of respectability, the colony had apparently come a long way. A key part of this was undoubtedly state endeavour. Government House under Arthur, historian W.D. Forsyth argued many years ago, was 'a conning-tower from which the autocrat saw through a thousand eyes and heard from hundreds of listening posts'.[164]

But, for all that Arthur's success rested upon a transformation of the colonial state, the heightened emphasis upon moral respectability was just as crucially rooted in the shifting composition and culture of the settler population, many of whom, because of their profound attachment to family and to ideals of domesticity, shared Arthur's emphasis upon the importance of moral regulation and respectability. If some undoubtedly resented the peculiar degree of state intervention in the private sphere which life in Van Diemen's Land entailed, dubbing Arthur a tyrant and his system inquisitorial, many were therefore also willing, for material as well as cultural reasons, to be actively complicit with it. The emphasis upon personal and family morality was, in turn, partly bound up with the ideologies and practices of class rule, and this was further stimulated, as we will see in chapter four, by the ways in which the reformed assignment system was underpinned by a particular version of domestic ideology.

Notes

1 Louisa Meredith, *My home in Tasmania during a residence of nine years* (London: John Murray, 1852), Vol. 1, pp. 29, 32. Emphasis in original.
2 *Ibid.*, p. 36.
3 George Thomas Lloyd, *Thirty-three years in Tasmania and Victoria* (London: Houston & Wright, 1862), p. 283.
4 Journal of Lady Jane Franklin, NLA MS 248/86, p. 157.
5 Franklin, Journal, MS 248/87, pp. 34–5.
6 *Ibid.*, pp. 186–8.
7 *Ibid.*, p. 36.
8 William Denison, *Varieties of vice-regal life* (London: Longmans, Green & Co., 1870), Vol. 1, pp. 35–6.
9 *Ibid.*, pp. 35–6.
10 *Ibid.*, pp. 43–4.
11 *Ibid.*, p. 58.
12 Harris, Hobart, 12 October 1805, in Barbara Hamilton-Arnold (ed.), *Letters of G.P. Harris, 1803–1812* (Sorrento, Victoria: Arden Press, 1994), p. 73.
13 *Ibid.*, p. 72.
14 See, for example, Anon, *The farmers, or, tales for the times: addressed to the yeomanry of England* (London: C. & J. Rivington, 1823).
15 For a more detailed discussion of these themes see: Kirsty Reid, 'Family matters: masculinity, domesticity and power in early nineteenth-century Britain and Australia', unpublished paper presented to the 'British World' conference, Melbourne, July 2004; available from the author.
16 Shayne Breen, 'Land and power in the district of Deloraine, 1825–75', *Tasmanian Historical Research Association*, 37:1 (1990), p. 26.

17 Janet Ranken, Hobart, December 1821, in Patricia Clarke and Dale Spender (eds),
    Lifelines: Australian women's letters and diaries, 1788–1840 (Sydney: Allen &
    Unwin, 1992), p. 151.
18 Octavia Dawson, Van Diemen's Land, 11 August 1829, in *ibid.*, pp. 154–6.
19 Penny Russell, *'A wish of distinction': colonial gentility and femininity*
    (Melbourne: Melbourne University Press, 1994), pp. 6, 10–11.
20 Kay Daniels, *Convict women* (St Leonards, NSW: Allen & Unwin, 1998), pp.
    24–7. On the relationship between Maria and Edward Lord more generally see
    pp. 1–28.
21 Despite this kind of prejudice, Dry would later become an elected member of the
    colony's Legislative Council and the first Premier of Tasmania. See: A. D. Baker,
    The life and times of Sir Richard Dry (Hobart: Oldham, Beddome & Meredith,
    1951).
22 Lucy Frost, *A face in the glass: the journal and life of Annie Baxter Dawbin*
    (Port Melbourne: Heinemann, 1992), p. 12. Russell suggests that Dawbin's snobbery
    was partly motivated by her own insecurity of circumstance. Her first husband
    had committed suicide and her second was bankrupt; Russell, *'Wish of distinction'*,
    p. 56.
23 See, in particular: R.W. Connell and T.H. Irving, *Class structure in Australian
    history: documents, narrative and argument* (Melbourne: Longman Cheshire,
    1980), pp. 62–3; and W. Nichol, 'Ideology and the convict system in New South
    Wales, 1788–1820', *Historical Studies*, 22:86 (1986), pp. 1–20.
24 Kirsten McKenzie, 'Women's talk and the colonial state: the Wylde Scandal,
    1831–1833', *Gender & History*, 11:1 (1999), p. 42. See also: Kirsten McKenzie,
    Scandal in the colonies: Sydney and Cape Town, 1820–1850 (Carlton, Victoria:
    Melbourne University Press, 2004).
25 Daniels, *Convict women*, pp. 17–22. Captain Andrew Barclay, J.P. and convict
    Mary Smallshaw were, for example, married in November 1821, just months after
    Commissioner Bigge had criticised their de facto relationship. According to Currey,
    Lord fathered a string of illegitimate children; John Currey, *David Collins, a
    colonial life* (Melbourne: Melbourne University Press, 2000), p. 256.
26 Henry Widowson, *The present state of Van Diemen's Land* (London: S. Robinson,
    1829), p. 22; Lloyd, *Thirty-three years*, p. 8. Throughout the nineteenth century,
    Anne McClintock notes, notions of social and racial difference drew repeatedly
    upon an 'iconography of domestic degeneracy' or 'barbarism', particularly, she
    argues, in situations 'where skin color as a marker of power was imprecise and
    inadequate'; Anne McClintock, *Imperial leather: race, gender and sexuality in
    the colonial contest* (New York: Routledge, 1995), p. 53.
27 John West, *The history of Tasmania* (Launceston: Henry Dowling, 1852), Vol. 1,
    p. 38.
28 James Fenton, *History of Tasmania* (Hobart: Melanie Publications, 1978),
    pp. 51–2.
29 David Burn, *A picture of Van Diemen's Land* (Hobart: Cat & Fiddle Press, 1973),
    pp. 6, 14. Emphasis in original.
30 *Ibid.*, pp. 5–6.
31 *HRA* III, 2, pp. 782–3.
32 *HRA* III, 2, pp. 337–9, 376–7, 782–3. *HRA* III, 4, p. 684.
33 *HRA* III, 2, pp. 633–4.
34 *HRA* I, 8, pp. 458–9.
35 *HRA* III, 2, p. xiii.
36 *HRA* I, 8, pp. 458–61.
37 *HRA* III, 2, p. xx. For Macquarie's many complaints against Davey see: *HRA* I,
    8, p. 458; *HRA* I, 9, p. 113; *HRA* III, 2, pp. 176–9. For Davey's counter-charges
    see: *HRA* III, 2, pp. 193, 636–7, 644–5.
38 *HRA* III, 2, p. 651.
39 *Ibid.*, pp. 328–30.
40 *Ibid.*, p. 332.

41 *Ibid.*, p. 350.
42 *Ibid.*, p. 666.
43 *Ibid.*, p. 667. Emphasis added.
44 *Ibid.*, p. 668.
45 *Ibid.*, pp. 670–1.
46 *Ibid.*
47 *Ibid.*, p. 666.
48 *Ibid.*, p. 670.
49 *HRA* III, 3, p. 215.
50 *HRA* III, 2, p. 331.
51 *Ibid.*, pp. 684, 686. Emphasis in original.
52 *Ibid.*, pp. 684, 687. Emphasis in original.
53 Robert Bayles, Diary, AOT NS 395/1, p. 116.
54 *HRA* III, 4, pp. 820, 847.
55 *Ibid.*, p. 472.
56 *Ibid.*, p. 683.
57 *HRA* III, 3, p. 228.
58 Nicholas Shakespeare, *In Tasmania* (London: Harvill Press, 2004), especially pp. 17, 40–3.
59 *Ibid.*, pp. 17, 40–3.
60 For a discussion see: Russell, *'Wish of distinction'*; McKenzie, *Scandal*.
61 *HRA* III, 4, p. 547.
62 *Ibid.*, pp. 641–57.
63 *HRA* III, 3, p. xi.
64 Bayles, Diary, p. 123.
65 *HRA* III, 4, p. 724.
66 *HRA* III, 4, pp. 640–1.
67 *Ibid.*, p. 353.
68 *Ibid.*, pp. 685–7.
69 *HRA* III, 2, pp. 240, 611.
70 *Ibid.*, pp. 194–5.
71 *Ibid.*, pp. 150–61.
72 *Ibid.*, pp. 613–14.
73 *Ibid.*, pp. 591–6.
74 *Ibid.*, p. 191.
75 On Gatehouse's property claims see: *HRA* III, 2, pp. 335–7, 352, 360–2, 307–9, 372, 676–80.
76 *Ibid.*, pp. 598–9.
77 *Ibid.*, pp. 611–12. On the Hogan case see also: *HRA* I, 9, p. 550; *HRA* III, 2, pp. 623–8; and *HRA* III, 4, pp. 693–5.
78 *HRA* III, 4, p. 784. On the conflict between Loane, Lord and others see: *HRA* III, 4, pp. 721–809.
79 *Ibid.*, pp. 833–4.
80 On Humphrey's powers see: *HRA* III, 3, pp. 271–2.
81 *HRA* III, 4, p. 548.
82 *HRA* III, 4, pp. 548–51.
83 On Arthur see: *A.G.L. Shaw, Sir George Arthur, Bart., 1784–1854: superintendent of British Honduras, lieutenant-governor of Van Diemen's Land and of Upper Canada, governor of the Bombay presidency* (Carlton, Victoria: Melbourne University Press, 1980).
84 *HRA* III, 4, pp. 548–50.
85 *Ibid.*
86 *HRA* III, 3, p. 443.
87 'Report of the Commissioner of Inquiry into the state of the colony of New South Wales', *BPP* XX (448), 1822, p. 111.
88 *Ibid.*, p. 111.
89 *HRA* III, 3, p. 408.

90 *Ibid.*, pp. 852–68.
91 *Ibid.*, p. 858.
92 *Ibid.*, p. 859.
93 *Ibid.*, p. xii.
94 *HRA* III, 4, pp. 813–22.
95 West, *History*, Vol. I, p. 98.
96 *HRA* III, 3, p. 219.
97 *Ibid.*, p. 221.
98 West, *History*, Vol. I, p. 98.
99 Leith, for example, was dismissed for his 'gross immorality'. *BPP* XX (448), 1822, p. 46. In 1831, to take one example, Arthur preferred a situation in which the colony was 'effectively ... without a Supreme Court' for a period, rather than have Alexander Macduff Baxter sworn in as Puisne Judge. Baxter, who had arrived from Sydney where he had previously served as Attorney General, offended Arthur on a number of counts: he was insolvent, he drank and he had 'a scandalous domestic life'; *HRA* III, 7, fn. 245, p. 762.
100 Arthur cited in Mary Nicholls (ed.), *The diary of the Reverend Robert Knopwood, 1803–1838* (Hobart: Tasmanian Historical Research Association, 1977), pp. 422–3.
101 *HRA* III, 7, p. xxi.
102 James Ross, *An essay on prison discipline, in which is detailed the system pursued in Van Diemen's Land* (Hobart: James Ross, 1833), pp. 42, 90.
103 *HRA* III, 5, p. 444.
104 *HRA* III, 5, p. 669.
105 *HRA* III, 7, p. 624.
106 James Ross, T*he settler in Van Diemen's Land* (Melbourne: Marsh Walsh Publishing, 1975), pp. 20–1.
107 Ranken in Clarke & Spender (eds), *Lifelines*, p. 151.
108 *HRA* III, 3, pp. 220–1.
109 *Ibid.*, pp. 220–1.
110 *HRA* III, 2, p. 634.
111 'Report of the Select Committee on Transportation', *BPP* II (341), 1812, p. 9. Steps to tighten up the selection procedures had been introduced from the early 1800s. See, for example: *HRA* I, 1, fn. 72, p. 732; *HRA* I, 3, p. 434; *HRA* I, 4, p. 35.
112 *HRA* III, 7, p. 394.
113 *HRA* III, 7, pp. 681–2.
114 *HRA* III, 5, p. 436.
115 Examples include Lieutenant Henry Boden Torlesse and Captain Patrick Wood. Torlesse served in the Royal Navy for 21 years before emigrating to VDL in 1828 with a recommendation for land from the Colonial Office. He was one of the first emigrants to VDL to benefit under the Admiralty Order of 11 August 1827. This extended many of the privileges already enjoyed by military officers to those from the navy. Torlesse settled in Hamilton, was appointed a justice of the peace in the district on his arrival and later as Assistant Police Magistrate. He also served as Deputy Chairman of the Court of Quarter Sessions; *HRA* III, 7, pp. 321, 774. Wood had served in East India, Mauritius and America before emigrating in 1822. He settled at the Clyde River where he had nearly 8,000 acres of land by 1828 and was appointed a magistrate for the district; *HRA* III, 7, pp. 322, 675, 774.
116 *HRA* III, 5, p. 142.
117 *HRA* III, 6, pp. 117–18, 150–1, 376; *HRA* I, 13, p. 596; *HRA* III, 7, fn. 64, p. 709; *HRA* III, 7, p. 702. In the 1820s, Sorell and Arthur both proposed similar measures to attract ex-East India Company officers to retire to Van Diemen's Land, arguing that 'their character, capital and services' would bring innumerable benefits to the colony; *HRA* III, 4, p. 575; *HRA* III, 8, p. 375.
118 *HRA* III, 5, p. 683.
119 *HRA* III, 7, fn. 64, p. 709.
120 *HRA* III, 7, p. 624.

121 *HRA* III, 1, pp. 466–7. Emphasis in original.
122 *HRA* III, 5, p. 35, *HRA* III, 8, p. 453. For a similar case: *HRA* III, 5, p. 390.
123 On the Land Board see: Anne McKay (ed.), *Journals of the land commissioners for Van Diemen's Land 1826–28* (Hobart: Tasmanian Historical Research Association, 1962).
124 *HRA* III, 7, pp. 328–9.
125 *HRA* III, 6, pp. 148–50, *HRA* III, 7, p. 91.
126 McKay, *Journals*, p. 17; *HRA* III, 8, pp. 365, 714, 888–9. For Arthur's earlier opinions of Young see: *HRA* III, 5, p. 211–13.
127 *HRA* III, 5, p. 680.
128 Ross, *Settler*, p. 109.
129 *BPP* XX (448), 1822, p. 161.
130 *Ibid.*, p. 47.
131 Anne McKay, 'The assignment system of convict labour in Van Diemen's Land, 1824–42' (MA thesis, University of Tasmania, 1958), p. 112.
132 *HRA* III, 7, p. 654.
133 *HRA* III, 5, p. 52.
134 *HRA* III, 7, p. 302.
135 *Ibid.*, p. 673.
136 *HRA* III, 6, pp. 421–2.
137 *Ibid.*, p. 421.
138 *HRA* III, 4, p. 161.
139 *HRA* III, 5, p. 153.
140 The use of these powers was one source of the colonial opposition to Arthur. See McKay, 'Assignment', p. 129.
141 *HRA* III, 5, pp. 443–4.
142 *Ibid.*, p. 683.
143 *Ibid.*, pp. 679–80.
144 *HRA* III, 7, pp. 643–5, 654–8.
145 *HRA* III, 5, p. 279 ; *HRA* III, 6, pp. 364–5.
146 AOT CSO 1/172/4450.
147 AOT CSO 22/50, p. 191.
148 W.D. Forsyth, *Governor Arthur's convict system: Van Diemen's Land 1824–36* (Sydney: Sydney University Press, 1970), p. 51.
149 For examples: AOT CSO 1/164/3933; 1/562/12462; 1/456/10165 and 5/43/910.
150 McKay, 'Assignment', pp. 85–95.
151 AOT CSO 1/577/13104.
152 George Arthur, 'Select Committee on Transportation', *BPP* XIX (518), 1837, p. 312.
153 For examples see: AOT CSO 84, pp. 15, 17, 36, 49, 77, 83, 99, 107, 197, 233, 238, 278 & 492.
154 For examples see: AOT CSO 88, pp. 15, 22, 26, 31, 40, 45, 57, 60–2, 66–7, 73.
155 AOT CSO 84, p. 278.
156 *Ibid.*, p. 308.
157 AOT CSO 1/562/12462.
158 AOT CSO 1/244/5920.
159 AOT CSO 1/840/17791.
160 AOT CSO 1/497/10907.
161 Ross, *Essay*, p. 69.
162 AOT CSO 1/164/3933.
163 *HRA* III, 7, p. 143.
164 Forsyth, *Arthur's convict system*, p. 55.

CHAPTER THREE

Production and reproduction

Colonial order, convict labour and the
convict private sphere, *c*.1803–17

From the moment that the First Fleet landed in 1788, Governor Phillip took steps to encourage family formation and to direct convicts into marriage and parenthood. Noting 'the illegal intercourse between the sexes as an offence which encouraged a general profligacy of manners' and was thus 'in several ways injurious to society', Phillip's speech to the convicts on their disembarkation 'strongly recommended marriage, and promised every kind of countenance and assistance to those who, by entering into that state, should manifest their willingness to conform to the laws of morality and religion'.[1] David Collins, who was then Judge-Advocate of New South Wales, alleged that some of the first marriages at Botany Bay, a batch of thirty celebrated in February 1788, were motivated, as a result, by the idea that 'the married people would meet with various little comforts and privileges that were denied to those in a single state'.[2] Although somewhat cynical about these marriages and their prospects for long-term success, Collins recorded that Phillip nevertheless persevered with a permissive approach to family formation. 'None who applied' to marry 'were ever rejected', he noted, 'except when it was clearly understood that either of the parties had a wife or husband living at the time of their leaving England'.[3]

Although Phillip clearly shared Lord Sydney's belief that household and family formation were integral to convict reform, his approach was also guided by pragmatism. Keen to restrict the privileges of an independent household and family circle to those who 'deserved' it, he also held out the prospect as an incentive to those he considered of particular value. Here, convict William Bryant provides an interesting, if unsuccessful, example. A fisherman from Cornwall, Bryant's ability to help feed the early settlement was highly valued. 'Every encouragement' was held out to him, not only to put as much of his energy as possible into fishing, but also to resist trading the catch on the side. Bryant had been among the first of the convicts to marry; convict Mary Braund, also from Cornwall, had become his wife in February 1788. The two had had a baby on the voyage and a second child was born in February 1789. Phillip ordered that a 'hut' be built for Bryant and his family, and efforts were made to ensure that the Bryant household 'wanted for nothing'. Despite these relative privileges, Bryant was soon punished for selling fish, and in March 1791 he, his wife, the children and seven male convicts made a permanent (and famous) escape by boat.[4]

If Bryant bucked Phillip's system, James Ruse provided a much better early example of how things were supposed to work. Ruse was the only one among a group of newly time-expired convicts who, in late 1789, took up the offer to become a settler. The others were determined to go home. A farmer by upbringing, Ruse was judged 'industrious' and keen to return to his formerly 'honest habits and pursuits'. Phillip saw him, therefore, as an ideal role model: 'the governor', Collins commented, wished 'to hold him up as a deserving character'. Keen, in addition, to prove that it was possible to farm successfully in New South Wales, Phillip issued Ruse with land, tools, seed and some livestock from the Store.[5] It was perhaps for both these reasons that Phillip chose to call the land that he gave Ruse 'Experiment Farm'. Convicts were ordered to clear an acre for Ruse and to build him a hut. In September 1790, Ruse, although he already had a wife and children in Britain, married convict Elizabeth Parry or Perry, who had arrived just three months before. Over the next decade, they had several children together. Ruse's first harvest, in March 1791, was rewarded by full title to his land, and continued successes over the next few years saw him granted additional acreage.[6]

Phillip also encouraged Ruse by extending privileges to him through his family. In 1792, Elizabeth was granted an early absolute pardon, a reward, Collins recorded, for:

> the good conduct of the wife, and the industry of the husband, who had for some time supported himself, his wife and child and two convicts, independent of the public store ... [these] were the reasons ... which restored her to her rights and privileges as a free woman ... [and which resulted in Phillip] extending to her the hand of forgiveness.[7]

Over the following four decades, Ruse and his wife acquired several hundred more acres. Combined, Ruse's independence, economic success, family and domesticity were clearly integral to his sense of self. On his death in 1837, his headstone, carved by himself, recorded his success as the man who had 'sowd the forst grain' in the colony, and he claimed also to have been raised in domestic respectability;

my mother 'reread me tenderley ... with me she took much paines', Ruse noted.[8] These kinds of professions of domestic loyalty and emphases upon the respectability of family origins were more common; often providing standard openings to male convict accounts of their lives, suggesting that Ruse was far from alone among convicts in valuing such matters.[9] Through these kinds of overlapping interests, state policy and convict desire had the potential at times to merge.

Despite growing reservations about the alleged laxities of transportation, London continued throughout several decades after 1788 to encourage the governors to promote marriage as a means of moralising the settlements. Phillip's promotion of 'matrimonial connexion', combined with the steps he had taken to 'protect' those among the women convicts he deemed virtuous, had been immediately sanctioned by the government in London, who responded that such a 'measure', by 'tend[ing] to the improvement of ... morals' was considered 'indispensably necessary for securing the general peace and happiness of the convicts'.[10] Just as Phillip before them, so too almost all the other early governors continued to be attentive to family life, and to direct convict women, in particular, into colonial homemaking. Marriage, Governor Hunter reported, 'was a thing we encouraged upon all occasions'.[11]

A central aspect of the state's rationale in pursuing these kinds of policies was to reform convicts by domesticating them. So much value was attached to this project that official encouragement of household and family formation began even before the very survival of the settlements had been secured. Writing to London to inform Lord Sydney of the First Fleet's arrival, Phillip included a request for more women in this, his very first, despatch from Australia. 'The very small proportion of females', he noted, 'makes the sending out of an additional number absolutely necessary'.[12] In the midst of the famine years in Van Diemen's Land, Collins issued similar requests, expressing his gratitude whenever women were sent from Port Jackson. 'The Women you destine for this Settlement', he told Governor King in late 1804, 'will be welcome'.[13] Writing early the next year to thank King for thirty women who had just arrived, Collins expressed his hope that more would soon come from England.[14] Given that women performed less of the vital labour required to keep the early settlements alive, these demands, made when survival was still an at best distant prospect, almost certainly reflected the importance attached by the state to the policy of convict reformation through domestication.

A similar policy of promoting family formation extended to the new settlements in Van Diemen's Land. As preparations for the departure of HMS *Calcutta* were being finalised, nineteen male convicts received permission for their wives and children to 'accompany them into exile'. This, Lord Hobart noted, was designed as a reward for 'some favourable circumstances' in their 'characters'.[15] To these already constituted family groups, Collins extended other rewards and privileges including land, stock, seed and tools. Men with wives and families were also given additional time off labour to build homes and shelters for themselves. Almost all of these families, no doubt partly as a result of this early indulgence, would do well in the colony.[16] These kinds of policies continued to be pursued long after Collins's death. In 1813, on the arrival of the male convict ship *Indefatigable*, Macquarie ordered Davey to look out for the interests of several men who had been 'strongly recommended' by 'Persons of respectability in England'. They included William Jemott, a convict who had, probably as a result of these same interventions, been allowed to bring his wife and children with him. In view of his previous 'respectability' and his status as a family man, Macquarie ordered that he be 'permitted to go on his own hands immediately' and that he be issued with 'some land to cultivate, say 30 acres'. To give the family time to find their feet, they were also permitted to receive victuals from the Store.[17]

The importance of the household as a basic unit in society was reflected in land grant policy more generally. Where single time-expired convicts received thirty acres, married convicts were given a further twenty acres, with a further ten acres for each child born at the time of the grant.[18] Land policies also reflected the extent to which those in power regarded the adult male as the 'natural' head of household. They sought to establish and sustain a system of household patriarchy that mirrored the patriarchal structures and authority of the state. Thus, as the settlement became more established, land, a key source of colonial wealth, became an overwhelmingly male preserve. Although some early grants had been made to free women, normally the wives of convicts, their rights were largely temporary. Once emancipated, their husbands were able to legally acquire property again and thus to fully resume their position as head of household. At this stage, most of these acres slipped, almost imperceptibly, from female to male hands. The case of Ann Peters is illustrative. In 1805, Collins issued Peters with forty acres and ordered that her convict husband Thomas be assigned to her to help work the farm. By 1807, however, and despite the fact that he was still under sentence, Thomas Peters was classified as a settler and all of the family land, crops and stock was listed in his name.[19] While Bruce Kercher is undoubtedly right that the fact that property rights were vested in wives during the term of a husband's sentence, and that convict men could be assigned to, and thus subjected to discipline by, their wives requires historians to 'rethink the notion of patriarchy' in the penal colonies, these kinds of examples tend to suggest that this kind of colonial transformation of masculine domination was both temporary and fragile.[20]

In the years after Collins's death, land became an increasingly male preserve. When Macquarie discovered in 1813 that Davey had issued land to Mrs Jemott he immediately intervened. 'I cannot on any account authorize Mrs Jemott to receive Lands in her own right', he noted, 'it being against the rules I have laid down'.[21] Husbands meanwhile, even while under sentence, could receive land. Acknowledging that a convict might not legally hold a grant of land, Macquarie ordered Davey to circumvent this regulation by giving men like Jemott the right to cultivate a smallholding 'till they are emancipated'.[22] Macquarie appears to have been opposed to the idea of women as landowners more generally.[23] He always refused applications from single women, he explained to Bigge, believing 'such persons' to be 'incapable of cultivating Land'. Sorell pursued a similar policy into the early 1820s, arguing that he could 'not give Land to Ladies' without explicit authorisation from the Secretary of State for the Colonies.[24] The effects of these kinds of gendered policies are clear. In the first two decades of settlement 96 per cent of grantees were men.[25] Heads of household were to be father figures: family power structures were to mirror the power structures of the state.

State support for the household as a model of a good society also fostered an enduring commitment to order and fashion the built environment in particular ways. During his 1811 tour of Van Diemen's Land, Macquarie issued instructions for the re-design of Hobart and George Town and for the erection of a string of village-style communities across the settled districts. His villages, or 'townships', were devised around an idealised model of small-scale proprietorship and family settlement. In 'Elizabeth-town', a settlement notably named after his wife, Macquarie subdivided the land 'into regular allotments' and ordered the government in Hobart to 'afford every facility and encouragement' to 'sober, honest, industrious Tradesmen to go to reside and settle there'. A school was to be established both for the children of these tradesmen and for the families of the surrounding farms in the district of New Norfolk. In Macquarie's view, the fact that there were good facilities for river transport to the township and beyond would enable the surrounding settlers to market and sell their produce with ease, and this, combined with the area's fertile lands, would, he hoped, stimulate the further expansion of rural settlement in this district. By providing their surrounding regions with facilities such as skilled tradesmen, markets, churches and schools, settlements such as Elizabeth-town were designed to serve a dual role as economic stimuli and centres of manly morality and ordered domesticity within frontier society.[26] Macquarie's plans for the settlement at Cimitière Valley were, as we saw in chapter one, influenced by a similar emphasis upon the settling of 'industrious', reformed and family-oriented men across the colonial landscape.[27]

Domesticated models of order continued to have their advocates throughout the period of early settlement and beyond. In 1820, A.W.H. Humphrey defended the domestic and privatised distribution of convicts then prevailing in Van Diemen's Land, under which the majority of convicts lived in independent households. These arrangements were driven partly by pragmatic considerations. In the absence of adequate funding and sufficient public institutions to accommodate and confine convicts, the state had necessarily to rely upon private provision. As the numbers transported to Van Diemen's Land increased in the later 1810s, convicts were compulsorily billeted upon existing households where they were allowed to lodge until they acquired the time and resources to build homes for themselves.[28] However, Humphrey regarded this system as a matter of principle too. Encouraging convicts to live in households was more 'natural', he claimed, and therefore contributed 'more to their moral improvement than confining them all indiscriminately in barracks'. The latter, Humphrey contended, should only be used for 'disorderly' characters requiring greater discipline and punishment.[29]

Humphrey's confidence in the existing system was partly founded upon the fact that these households, while locating convicts within the more 'natural' space of the domestic sphere, were, nevertheless, in practice only semi-private. 'The Constables', Humphrey informed Bigge, were 'empowered' to use spot checks 'to visit houses where Convicts reside during the night'.[30] Convict homes provided the state with useful regulatory sites in other ways too: ledgers listing the residences of all convicts, including ticket-of-leave holders, were compiled and maintained by the Hobart police from 1816 onwards. These were designed to show and fix 'the place of abode' of every convict in the town. Information gleaned through regular musters and the pass system supplemented and updated this.[31] Convicts were required to spend their evenings in these registered abodes: those found on the streets after the eight o'clock bell risked being apprehended and imprisoned.[32] Private households, through these and other means, provided ideal mechanisms for distribution, surveillance and control, enabling Humphrey to develop a 'sufficient personal knowledge' of each and every convict resident in and around Hobart by keeping them all under his 'own eye'.[33] One result of all this was that the

[97]

separation of public from private spheres was never that meaningful or secure for some sections of colonial society. As any reading of the surviving police and lower court records will reveal, the Van Demonian police force continued to survey convict and other colonial working-class homes and to walk into them with astonishing ease for decades thereafter.[34]

Partly as a result of the official promotion of family life, household formation was a prominent characteristic of life in early Van Diemen's Land. Between 1804 and 1819, 594 adults tied the knot at the Derwent, decidedly impressive figures given both the extremely low numbers of women, particularly single women, and the fact that Hobart's adult population averaged around just 450 between February 1804 and January 1810 – even as late as November 1817 it was only a little over 2,000.[35] In 1818, six out of ten free adult females resident in Hobart, the majority of them ex-convicts, were listed as married.[36] Relationships and families equally flourished in the north. On a visit to Port Dalrymple in 1819 – a town with a population of around just 700 – the Reverend John Youl married forty-one couples and baptised fifty-six children.[37] Extra-marital arrangements further increased the number of early households. There was, Reverend Knopwood commented, 'a great deal' of concubinage in and around Hobart. In 1819–20 all the convict women resident in Launceston, with the exception of two who were married, were cohabiting with male prisoners. Matters were much the same at George Town, where almost all of the women were reportedly living with male convicts.[38]

The state's ability to sponsor marriage and family life was, however, undoubtedly hampered by the initially tiny numbers of women. 'It is to be regretted that a certain proportion of females do not accompany the convicts', a Home Office official noted in early 1803, as preparations for the colonisation of Van Diemen's Land were being finalised. 'This', he commented, was 'a grand blot in the first establishment at Port Jackson'. 'Pray do not forget the Women', he urged, 'to begin with a Colony of Men . . . will do for nothing in nature'.[39] The decision to place a number of wives on the boats was probably partly an offshoot of these concerns. Despite this, there were to be relatively few women and, more importantly for legitimate family formation, few single women in particular, throughout the first years. The starting point was decidedly unpropitious: women accounted for just 6.6 per cent of the adults who settled at the Derwent in February 1804 and the vast majority of them were already married.[40] These figures were even worse than in very early New South Wales and they were also slow to shift.[41] As late as 1824, women averaged only just over 19 per cent of the adult European population of Van Diemen's Land.[42]

[98]

With the arrival of several large parties of settlers from Norfolk Island from 1807 onwards this balance nevertheless gradually began to alter. The two to three hundred children who accompanied these first groups of immigrants marked, in particular, a major increase in the number of colonial families. With time, the numbers of women also inevitably grew.[43] By the 1810s, some of the first native-born female children were old enough to be considered potential spouses. Many married young and in doing so they seem to have established a pattern for ensuing generations. Married by fourteen and fifteen years old, some of the Norfolk Islander daughters were already grandmothers by the mid-1820s. 'Though we by no means approve the system of young persons being married and becoming parents at so early an age . . . it is impossible', the *Hobart Town Gazette* nevertheless concluded, in a decidedly celebratory tone, 'not to be amazed at the probable result of so rapid a series of progression in the numbers of the people, fastened and augmented as it must be by the advantages of this prospering Colony'.[44] In the early days, some men also made their own arrangements to secure a female partner: like Edward Lord, a few of the officers travelled to the mainland and brought convict wives and partners back with them. Others, including a number of convict men, looked to Aboriginal communities, establishing a variety of relationships there that ranged from the more consensual to the fully coercive.[45]

Crucially, however, the demographic imbalance meant that the various importations of convict women, although intermittent, unpredictable and limited in their size until the 1820s when female convict ships finally began to arrive regularly and directly from Britain, were absolutely vital to colonial family formation. These facts gave female convicts extra importance as potential wives and mothers and undoubtedly invested them with a degree of bargaining power and some room for manoeuvre in their relationships both with individual men and with the state. Through marriage and cohabitation, many of the convict women transported in these early years moved swiftly, and in some cases practically directly, from the boat to the family. Typical of this group were women such as: Ann Horan who married free settler Richard Wilson within days of her arrival at Launceston; Mary Ford who married John Coffee just six weeks after disembarking; and Eleanor Toomey who was married to William Copperweight within a month.[46] Their experiences reflected the generally brisk nature of the trade in convict brides throughout the first couple of decades. Of the female convicts who arrived in Van Diemen's Land between 1820 and 1822 and who married within that period, 19 per cent did so within three months of their arrival.[47]

Such were the opportunities to marry and cohabitate that it was, to the dismay of growing numbers of employers, often remarkably difficult to find and then keep a female servant. In 1819 the Reverend Youl reported that although there were numerous female convicts in Launceston still, his wife could not find one to 'do a day's work'. Almost all of them, as at George Town, were instead living with male convicts.[48] Anthony Fenn Kemp complained that convict women in the southern settlement, even those assigned as servants on their arrival, were 'very soon after ... inveigled away from their masters'. 'Such is their scarcity', he noted, that 'they are useful only for a month'.[49] Convict Ann Bass provides a perfect example: arriving in August 1817, she had, within a month, twice been punished for riotous and disorderly conduct in her service. The cause of the disorder was her desire to 'quit her service'; the source of her desire was one John Gwynn. Gwynn, who had been a convict but was now free, was fined five pounds for these attempts to persuade her to leave her place. Despite this and her employer's opposition Bass prevailed, marrying Gwynn just three months later.[50]

Many convict women in these years would not only marry but would, in an economic sense at least, marry relatively well. Given the shortages of women, the acquisition of property was often as much a prerequisite for, as a product of, family formation for many men. There can be little doubt that a degree of wealth enhanced a man's prospects in these very early years in what was, after all, a deeply competitive marriage market. William Richardson was in many ways typical: arriving as a convict in 1804, he had accumulated a flock of sheep by 1819, and in 1822 he bought fifty acres of land on which he built a house, stockyards, a barn and some pigsties. It was only then that he finally married: in 1823 convict Elizabeth Winrow, who had arrived just months before, became his wife.[51] Many of the men transported on the *Calcutta* would, like Richardson, have to wait until the late 1810s and 1820s to marry, if at all, and it is noticeable that among those who successfully formed colonial families, many, if not most, had property to their name. The wealthiest among them were, in turn, and despite their often advancing years, those most likely to be able to marry a second, and sometimes even a third time, when widowhood struck. If marriage and family formation were key routes to property accumulation, property was likewise also a vital means through which to open the door to marriage. The prospects for those men who acquired neither property nor family were often much more bleak.[52]

These facts also meant that many women in the early period were convicts in name only, seeing out their sentences in colonial family homes. The experience of these women differed quite substantially from that of their male counterparts, many of whom had to delay hopes of marriage or other intimate or familial relationships.[53] This, combined with the gendered nature of state policy and the early colonial labour regime, meant that convict men were much more likely than women to experience their sentence in these years as a form of servitude. While large numbers of men were directed to work for government or private employers in these early years, the majority of convict women, by contrast, left assigned service relatively quickly, exchanging it for marriage, family and household and thus an existence that was relatively independent of the state. State policy tended, deliberately or otherwise, to facilitate this pattern. It was general knowledge, Knopwood explained, that when a female convict married she was 'exempted or nearly so from Government labour or assigned service'.[54]

The pursuit of family life was, however, always much more than a response to official policy. It was equally grounded in the settlement's socio-economic structures, and, as a part of the everyday cultural heritage of the people, it also played a key role in promoting personal security and a sense of well-being. Powerful ideological sinews aside, the small settler familial ideal flourished because it made perfect material and emotional sense. The small landholding and farming character of the early settlements placed a continuing premium on the household as a site of economic activity and upon the family as labour. As in the other nineteenth-century Australian colonies, the labour of women was crucial to the survival of small farms. Rural households were sites of intense labour; isolation and frugality required that many operate as largely self-sufficient units. The production of numerous everyday items took place in the home: food was grown, pickled, brewed, cured, preserved and cooked, and items such as cloth, clothes, candles, soap and footwear were prepared. Home life in rural Van Diemen's Land, settler Louisa Meredith reported, revolved around a series of 'ever-recurring' tasks.[55]

Women also contributed to household income through their labour in the towns. Ex-convict Maria Lord, wife of Edward, was responsible until the early 1820s for the management of the family business, and her entrepreneurial skills contributed substantially to their great wealth and power.[56] Other women likewise played important economic roles in urban families. Convict Mary Martin, sent by Macquarie from Sydney in 1815 with orders that she be employed as a schoolmistress, provides one example.[57] On her arrival, she married ex-convict Thomas Fitzgerald who was then running the town's only school from his Hobart house. Together they did so well that they were able to move to bigger and better premises within a few years. By the early 1820s,

[101]

almost all of Hobart's children had passed through their school: the fees paid by parents combined with salaries and subsidies from government provided a lucrative income source with which to sustain their household and growing family. When Thomas died in 1824 Mary, despite being left pregnant and with three young children, was soon able to open a new and more upwardly mobile institution in the form of Hobart's first 'Academy for Young Ladies'.[58]

The reproductive capacities of women were as important as their productive endeavours. The importance of the family as a source of labour was reflected in the emphasis placed upon female fertility in these years. Catherine O'Neill earned a special mention in the *Hobart Town Gazette* when she gave birth to triplets in 1819, despite the fact that the babies quickly died. 'It is singular', the *Gazette* reported, that 'this good woman has been delivered of four sons within the space of eight months'.[59] Some women had very large families indeed: Maria Nicholls, one of those Norfolk Island girls who married in her teens, bore seventeen children with ex-convict husband William Mansfield.[60] Even while young, children made an invaluable contribution to family survival: their particular significance in rural families is probably reflected in the fact that those who settled in the towns had fewer children than their farming counterparts. 'The more numerous the farmer's family', colonist David Burn commented, 'the better'.[61]

The greater material success experienced by men with wives and children reinforced the central importance of the family form, and this found reflection in the contours of the land system. Whereas only 40 per cent of initial grants in the early period were made to married men, almost two-thirds of those who received additional grants were married and over half had children.[62] Whether it was the case that extra land grants were made as a reward for matrimony, or that access to family resources ensured the development necessary for extra acreage, or even that convict women disproportionately preferred men who already had some material success under their belts, the lessons in family morality and economy were clear. The family, both as concept and as lived reality, was central to the exercise of power and to the accumulation of property.

Finally, many convicts had powerful personal and emotional motives for seeking out household and family life. Reprieved from death, but sentenced to transportation for life, James Grove was all but shattered by the prospect of his impending exile. 'Tis impossible', he wrote to friends in 1802 as he waited in Warwick Gaol to be taken to the convict ship *Calcutta*, that 'I can find words properly to convey my feelings. Sometimes on the pinnacle of hope – at others in the mire

of unbelieving darkness. Am well in body – bewildered in mind'.[63]
Sitting in his cell, some four decades later, waiting to be sentenced
to transportation and feeling a 'vile', 'miserable object in truth',
John Ward had similarly disarranged thoughts. 'All my feelings and
passions now rushed upon me at once', he noted, 'all was confusion'.[64]
Transportation, not least because it occasioned a forced separation
from friends and family, threatened a sundering of the self. 'How
difficult it is for a man to exist', the twentieth-century exile Alexander
Solzhenitsyn commented, 'divorced from his own place, his familiar
territory. Everything is wrong and awkward'.[65] 'My wife', 'my wife',
James Grove cried out, 'here hangs the weight, the heaviest weight
that . . . rivets me more closely to the world than the possession of
all its wealth would do'.[66]

* * *

Attitudes to convict labour in the early period were shaped profoundly
by the official emphasis upon household and family formation. While
men were regularly assigned to labour, either for the state or private
employers, the women were deemed largely unavailable for such
work because it was assumed they were occupied in household tasks
and the care of children. 'It was', Governor Hunter reported from Port
Jackson in the 1790s, 'so common to see' the women 'with a young
child in their arms that they had not time to work'.[67] Governor King
was likewise unconcerned by the 'little assistance' derived by the
government from female convict labour, because he too assumed that
most of the women were otherwise fruitfully engaged in domestic
pursuits.[68] Practical considerations such as the demands of mothering
were reinforced, in turn, by a set of gendered cultural prescriptions:
Phillip's penchant for 'humanitarian authoritarianism' encouraged him,
as Atkinson shows, to bring female convicts under the paternal care
and 'protection' of his state.[69] Added to this was the growing belief
that women who performed heavy physical labour, particularly in the
fields, would be de-feminised and demoralised.

In very early New South Wales, as a result, a sexual division of
labour had quickly emerged. As Marian Quartly notes, Phillip was
'always reluctant to set women to labour in the public sphere, in the
backbreaking work of growing food and building shelter for the whole
community.[70] 'Women were, as a result, kept to a relatively restricted
set of tasks: including needlework and mending, lighter agricultural
work such as husking corn and weeding, and making pegs with which
to fasten the roofs to buildings.[71] Even women without partners or
children were often kept busy with domestic labour. 'Those who are
not fortunate enough to be selected for wives', George Thompson

[103]

commented in a visit to New South Wales in 1792, 'are made hut-keepers'. These women, he explained, were responsible for the care of groups of between fourteen and eighteen men who shared huts at settlements like Toongabbie and Parramatta. The men, Thompson reported, worked all day 'under the heat of the sun' and the eye of their 'merciless' overseers, 'felling trees, digging up stumps, rooting up shrubs and grass, turning up the ground with spades and hoes, and carrying the timber to convenient places'.[72] The women, meanwhile, were responsible for cleaning, cooking and provisioning the huts. Female labour was thus by no means unimportant for it made an important contribution to the efficient reproduction of the men's labour-power. The alternative, after all, was to reduce the working day in order to give the men time to cook and care for themselves.[73] At a time when labour was scarce and the prospects for survival fragile, this was not a particularly viable strategy.

The destruction of so many of the early settlement records in the immediate aftermath of Collins's death in 1810 undoubtedly hampers any understanding of labour patterns in very early Van Diemen's Land. However, it seems likely that the same kinds of assumptions shaped official attitudes there, not only because of Collins's first-hand experience, and approval, of Phillip's regime but also because government strategy in the southern settlements continued to be shaped partly by the governor-generals at Sydney until the two colonies were officially separated in 1825. The surviving documents are also suggestive. They tell us, for example, that every one of the convicts who arrived with Lieutenant Bowen's advance party in September 1803 was expected to work: while the men were employed caring for stock and erecting buildings, the three convict women were assigned to grass-cutting, a task designed to prepare land for farming and to provide fodder and materials for roofing.[74] During their brief stay at Port Phillip, en route to the Derwent, Collins had also overseen a gendered division of labour. Although an exception was made for James Grove, whose previous 'respectability', marital status and friendship with the Governor set him apart, almost all the other convict men were occupied in intensely physical labour.[75] While the women stayed mostly in and around the camp, and confined themselves to what James Tuckey, First Lieutenant on the *Calcutta*, referred to vaguely as a series of more 'lively' pastimes and employments, the men were kept busy unloading the ships, cutting down trees, shifting timber, erecting huts and clearing paths. Impressed by their progress, Tuckey was nevertheless also much struck by their plight. 'When', he commented:

> I viewed so many of my fellowmen, sunk . . . and by their crimes degraded to a level with the basest of mankind; when I saw them *naked*, wading

to their shoulders in water to unlade the boats, while a burning sun struck its meridian rays upon their uncovered heads, or yoked to and sweating under a timber carriage, the wheels of which were sunk up to the axle in sand, I only considered their hapless lot, and the remembrance of their vices was for a moment absorbed in the greatness of their punishment.[76]

As at Port Jackson in its first years, male convict labour in very early Van Diemen's Land was almost entirely divided between agriculture and construction. With autumn coming, Collins was understandably concerned to set up camp, clear land and get 'the Grain in the Ground' as quickly as possible.[77] Woodcutting, land clearing, planting wheat, oats, rye and potatoes, stonemasonry, lime-burning, brick and tile manufacture, hut building and wharf construction consumed the men's days.[78] At least until the working day was cut as a consequence of the reduced rations and illness, the men were kept to long hours of labour. 'The Prisoners', Paterson reported at the end of their first month at Port Dalrymple, 'have worked from daylight till dark every day since we arrived'.[79] In an effort to increase productivity, many of the male convicts were organised into gangs, and supervisors were appointed from among the settlers.[80] Of the organisation and intensity of the women's work we know little, but it seems to have revolved around a range of domestic-support tasks. In early 1805 all thirty-five female convicts at the Derwent were employed in laundry work, much of it probably for the male convict workforce, soldiers and civil officers.[81] The women may also have been responsible for food preparation. The 'copper' that Collins ordered be 'erected for cooking' and the 'public oven' established at Port Dalrymple certainly suggests an initially collective approach to eating.[82]

Collins's chief concern throughout the first years was undoubtedly with the productivity of his male labour force. He faced three main problems: physical incapacity, labour shortage and worker bargaining. Repeated requests for extra labour to be sent were combined with complaints about the quality of his existing workforce. 'I never could imagine', he complained to London:

> that among those who were intended to form a New Settlement, there would be found a collection of old, worn out, useless Men, or children equally as useless. Such a description of People, your Lordship will readily conceive must be a Burthen to a Young Settlement, and . . . the Provisions which they consume would be more usefully employed, had they been allotted to Artificers or stout and Labouring Men. Of these I am sorry to observe, I have but very few.[83]

Interestingly, none of these complaints concerned convict women, suggesting that Collins did not consider them a particular 'burden' –

as he had at points during his term of office in early New South Wales.[84] Indeed, along with healthy labourers and 'artificers', Collins was repeatedly grateful whenever women were sent.[85] Perhaps the fact that the numbers of women at the Derwent were so tiny, even by comparison with New South Wales in its first years, undercut any fears that Collins might have had about the size of his 'dependent' populations and their demands on his meagre supplies and already overstretched labour force.

Collins's constant anxiety about matters of health and nutrition reflects the initial premium upon physical force. In a settlement 'where so much is to be done by manual labour', he noted shortly after arrival, 'the health of the people is to be preserved with the utmost care'.[86] Despite his best efforts, sickness, disability and hunger impeded labour power, undermining state attempts to sustain efficiency in the public works and making it difficult to provide the settlers with servants.[87] The situation was further complicated by the unequal toll which the long hours of hard labour, insufficient rations and poor living conditions had upon the men: 'the halest men', Samuel Bates, Deputy Judge Advocate at the Derwent from 1805 until 1814, later remembered, 'appeared to me to be the most affected'.[88] Certainly they appear to have been particularly badly hit by sickness and death: of nine convicts lost to scurvy between August and November 1804, 'several' were 'useful Men', including a number of sawyers and carpenters, whom Collins reported he 'could ill spare'.[89] The gendered labour regime may then have benefited female convicts in some ways, perhaps leading, as at Port Jackson in the first few years, to a situation in which the women led 'more comfortable' lives.[90] Gendered sensibilities also meant that the women were less likely to be subjected to certain punishments. Certainly the furore created by the flogging of one convict woman in 1808 suggests that the infliction of physical discipline on women was exceptional. George Harris complained that at no point in the settlement's first five years had he ever 'seen a precedent for the public punishment of a Woman' in such a manner.[91] Given the potential of punishments such as flogging and hard labour in chains to occasion injury and illness, these facts no doubt also contributed to the relative corporeal well-being of the women.

If the men did badly in some ways, they nevertheless benefited in others. In particular, those with continued strength and/or skill were able to use the enhanced bargaining power produced by relative scarcity to their advantage. Several groups were thus able to force Collins, despite his opposition, to concede task work arrangements. 'I am well aware', he noted in May 1804, that:

far more labour is obtained from the Prisoners by Task than Day work, yet I cannot but prefer the latter on the principle that the less time these people have to themselves, the less Opportunity they can have of concerting Mischief. I have it is true, in Order to prepare a Quantity of Ground for Wheat, allowed the Gang employed at the Farm to be tasked, and it has answered my purpose; but it is a practice which I shall not continue.[92]

This optimism was ill grounded: by July 1804, the sawyers and carpenters too were working by the task rather than the hour.[93] These kinds of arrangements gave some male convicts time each day to work for themselves. Hiring their services out to the officers and settlers, they were, despite government efforts to organise employer combinations and fix labour rates, able to command high wages. The fact that these state attempts to set wages included no reference to any female task whatsoever suggests that these benefits were almost entirely enjoyed by the men.[94] Neither do these advantages appear to have been fleeting in nature. As late as the mid-1820s, colonists were complaining of the exceptionally high wages commanded by some ex-convict workers and of the fact that the skilled in particular were too frequently able to earn enough 'in two to three days' work a week 'to keep them in a state of intoxication during the rest of the week'.[95]

Although almost all the available convict labour was initially deployed for public benefit, the interests of the private sector were never far from government's mind. Both Paterson and Collins were instructed to consider the convicts, and 'all' that they produced, as a part of the 'Public Stock'.[96] Along with the seeds, livestock and tools in the Store, the state was authorised to distribute convict labour to settler and officer hands, and both Paterson and Collins endeavoured to do this whenever possible.[97] In practice, however, their ability to do so was seriously hampered by the shortages of labour and supplies. The interests of the settlers had, initially at least, to be set to one side and their needs would only really begin to be properly satisfied during the early-to-mid 1810s when the numbers of convicts transported began to increase. A spate of orders from the government in Sydney at this time directing that this labour be channelled towards settlers further facilitated the process. The arrival of the *Indefatigable* in 1812, with 199 convict men, marked something of a turning point both because it was the first transport to come direct to Hobart (instead of via New South Wales) and also because Macquarie ordered that all the men, with the exception of any skilled mechanics, should be 'given to the Settlers'.[98]

A series of similar instructions over the next few years began to underpin a fairly major transition of male convict labour away from public works and towards the private sector.[99] While this was to some extent a product of growing settler demand, it was also one part of a broader effort to reduce state spending. Facing pressure from London to cut costs, Macquarie ordered the governors at Hobart to reduce the numbers provisioned by the Store. The remit, he instructed Davey, was to 'strike off as many Persons as you can from the Victualling Books'.[100] Redirection of labour away from public works was linked with a determination to make employers pay for their workers' support. 'The more Convicts' he could 'get the Settlers to take *off the Store* the better' Macquarie advised Sorell.[101] Other forms of state support for settlers also began to be more regulated and limits were placed upon the time a new settler might receive public assistance. From 1813 onwards, no new settler was to be 'Victualled ... beyond *Eighteen Months*' and additional care was to be taken that 'no person' receive state support 'who is not strictly and justly entitled to that indulgence'.[102]

The determination to reduce state spending not only affected labour policy, it also stimulated a much broader and fairly systematic restructuring of relations between public and private spheres. The concern with government retrenchment consequently would become one of three major factors fostering a re-working of the colonial gender and familial order in these years. The others, as we will see, included a growing concern with labour discipline and class subordination and a heightening determination on the part of the state to achieve a greater control over colonial morality and to impose an increasingly prescriptive model of family and personal relations. One of the most important signs that fundamental change was under way came in the first two decades of the 1800s when systematic attempts began to be made to reduce the practice of provisioning from the Store. It had become common practice in New South Wales and Van Diemen's Land to pay salaries in kind to a range of government employees including superintendents, overseers and constables by keeping them, their wives and families on the Store. Given the high price of many basic commodities, this was almost certainly an invaluable income supplement for many households. Significantly, large numbers of women were also maintained by the Store – regardless of their partners' status or employ – and the high numbers of young children on the books suggests that mothers were disproportionately likely to receive this kind of support.[103] Official promotion of the family in these early decades, therefore, appears to have extended to a number of pro-maternal welfare measures.

A series of government orders, implemented during the 1800s, had, however, all but abolished these family provisioning practices on the mainland by the time of Macquarie's appointment as Governor-in-Chief in 1810.[104] These had, nevertheless, still to be effectively applied in Van Diemen's Land. Visiting in 1811, Macquarie was astonished to discover that all the wives and children of the 73rd Regiment were still supported by the Store. Ordering that half these families be 'struck off the Victualling Books' immediately, he then limited the numbers to be provisioned to twelve women per Company.[105] The numbers provisioned by the Store fell precipitously thereafter as the application of policy in Van Diemen's Land came into line with the rest of the settlements. By late 1816, the number of convict women supported by government had consequently dropped to negligible levels. While the majority of convict men remained in receipt of public rations (a fact that probably reflected their continued concentration in public work, despite the beginnings of a shift towards the private sector) the maintenance of female convicts had been thoroughly privatised. Thus, just nine of the ninety-five convict women then at the Derwent were on the Store, compared to 311 of the 391 convict men.[106]

These attempts to reduce state spending inevitably led to a broader restructuring of relations between public and private spheres, facilitating, in particular, a growing emphasis upon the responsibilities of parents, and particularly husbands and fathers, for family sustenance. Although these emphases upon household independence and male breadwinning would not become systematic parts of official policy until the 1820s and 1830s when, as we will see in chapter four, they informed new regulations governing both convict marriage and convict family reunion, these ideas were nevertheless increasingly important influences upon family policy from the first two decades of the 1800s. Thus, when Lord Bathurst gave permission for ten women, the wives of convicts in New South Wales, to travel to the colony in 1812, he emphasised that the ability of these couples to support themselves independently of the Store was to be a central part of the 'experiment'.[107]

A growing determination to make female as well as male convicts work towards the cost of their maintenance was also fostered by the shift away from state support. The convict experience of state support had been initially strikingly differentiated by gender. For male convicts, the Store had served as an important disciplinary mechanism from the outset. While Phillip had partly relied upon various eighteenth-century precedents to enforce servitude, it was not until the 1824 Transportation Act that forced labour actually became a fully legal part of the sentence of transportation. On-the-spot disciplinary sanctions were therefore as important to the early governors as any abstract legal powers. Reflecting this, the Store quickly became a tool for the extraction of labour. Within days of their arrival in 1788, Phillip was threatening convicts with the withdrawal of their rations: 'he assured them', the settlement's surgeon George Worgan noted, 'that those who would not Work, should not Eat ... *That* they should perform, or *Starve*'.[108] Store support was therefore decidedly double-edged for many convicts. The ration kept hunger at bay, but it came with a requirement to labour and so a loss of independence.

The relationship between convict women and the Store had, however, been fashioned rather differently. This was partly, as we have seen, because the government assumed many convict women were engaged in domestic labour and child-rearing within their own households and it thus tended to provision them without seeing any need to account directly for the work they performed. Until the first two decades of the 1800s, however, a similar generosity also extended to those female convicts who were neither married nor assigned to private employers.[109] These women were by no means inconsequential in number but accounted for around one in four of the female convicts under sentence on the mainland in the first decade of the 1800s.[110] This willingness to support female convicts regardless of their marital or family status also reflected the state's initial desire to 'protect' women. The female convicts, Collins noted in 1792, were 'on account of their sex ... not harassed with hard labour'. Despite this, he noted, they 'shared of such little comforts as were to be procured in the settlement'. Even as the food began to run out and male rations were cut, Phillip, in what Collins described as a spirit of 'conspicuous ... humanity', 'directed that no alteration should be made in the ration to be issued to the women'.[111]

The state's ability to extract productive labour from women had also been hampered by practical constraints. The government had an initially limited ability to provide suitably 'feminine' and yet economical forms of female public employment. The erosion of unconditional government maintenance for women consequently occasioned various efforts from the late 1790s onwards to provide more female convicts with public sector work, much of it in textile manufacture at Parramatta. By the early 1800s a majority of the convict women in the mainland settlements who were neither married nor assigned to private service were employed making cloth.[112] Others were variously found employment as hospital nurses and midwives, in the Orphan Institution, in spinning and picking oakum, at lighter forms of agriculture, in the government dairy and as sail-makers.[113] Through these kinds of means it had, according to King, become possible to ensure that the female convicts 'maintained by the Crown' were no longer 'altogether useless'.[114] One sign of the shift in attitudes was the production, from the early 1800s, of regular statements of the labour performed by government-maintained convicts. Indicative of the growing insistence that everyone, regardless of gender, age or health, be made to contribute towards their upkeep, was the fact that these employment returns now included women as well as men.[115]

These years also witnessed the beginning of a broad assault upon convict freedoms. This was part and parcel of an attempt to establish an enhanced discipline over convict labour and to increase class subordination. A series of new regulations introduced in the mainland settlements therefore sought to limit the ability of convicts, male and female, to be 'on their own hands'. These included the organisation of regular musters and the introduction of vagrancy and pass legislation and of regulations fixing the hours of work, setting wages and requiring settlers to provide up-to-date lists of all servants in their employ.[116] At the heart of these labour policies was a growing concern that the independent working and living conditions maintained by many convicts were inimical to discipline. Significantly, the attempts to reshape colonial labour relations were combined with the onset of a more restrictive official approach to convict personal relationships, marriage and family formation. A number of influential commentators began to argue, in particular, that real change would only be forth-coming when attempts to reform the convict labour system were conjoined with efforts to check the ability of convicts to establish and maintain their own households. The result was the development of measures designed to place household formation and other personal relationships under greater state regulation. These would extend, most notably, to measures to restrict the mobility of female convicts.

Convicts, the wealthy and influential settler John Macarthur alleged, only became more 'confirmed in their habits of idleness' during their time in New South Wales. 'Permitted to dispose of their time as they think proper themselves', many of these men allegedly supported themselves through a mixture of government maintenance and 'plunder' rather than labour.[117] The reformed system advocated by Macarthur promised, by contrast, to combine state economy with moral order by placing convicts under the eye of 'industrious and vigilant master[s]'.[118] Writing to London in the mid-1810s, Nicholas Bayly, who, like Macarthur, was a one-time officer in the New South Wales Corps, suggested similarly that convict men be assigned more systematically to labour upon private farms. 'Nothing', he wrote of the men:

> has so good an effect upon them, or is more likely to produce a reform in their immoral and Vicious habits, or to make them good Servants and hereafter useful Members of Society, as the Prospect of obtaining

their Emancipation after they have spent a certain number of years in Industry and Morality.[119]

To assist in this production of moral and industrious workers Bayly argued that the women must be 'confined to a Penitentiary Home' where they could be 'entirely separated from the Men'.[120] The women would benefit from this discipline, he declared: kept separate from the broader community, they would be denied the opportunities they currently enjoyed of forming relationships with colonial men from the moment that they disembarked. Confined to institutions and kept to labour, they would instead have time to 'reflect on their past Conduct' and might turn away from the 'state of Debauchery'.[121] By such means, female convicts might be transformed into exemplars of femininity and proper agents of moral order, while the men would be encouraged to become dutiful and obedient workers.

It was not so much that men like Macarthur and Bayly objected to convict families and households per se but that they wished to see those relationships formed on terms and conditions more conducive to their own interests as large employers of labour. Politically conservative, they tended to favour a hierarchical paternalism in which the family, or more specifically the master's family, operated as a site of authority, labour discipline and moral fashioning. This view of the family had been a mainstay of British systems of discipline and socialisation for centuries.[122] It revolved around the idea that young men and women would leave their own families to enter the households of others, as servants or apprentices, and that their masters and mistresses would, by taking on an extended parental role, impart occupational knowledge, an understanding of social place and an appreciation of the virtues of discipline to them. The early colonial system had, however, produced a different family structure, one in which the household tended towards being a self-sufficient unit and in which men and women laboured largely for themselves. Larger colonial employers and landowners, therefore, had good economic reasons to pursue a different productive and reproductive order. For the older system not only helped to sustain smallholders who, by drawing on the unpaid labour of their families continued to compete with the larger agricultural concerns, it also provided convicts and other workers with a variety of options for survival, thus facilitating a substantial independence of labour.

On an official visit and survey of the settlements in Van Diemen's Land in 1810, the colonial explorer and soon-to-be Surveyor-General John Oxley, set out a detailed model for a parallel system there. The employment of male convicts in public works was, he argued, not only economically wasteful, it had also failed to reform. Convicts should neither be 'suffered to go on their own hands' nor be maintained by government but should instead be 'distributed to settlers'. Great savings could be made by cutting the numbers maintained by the Crown and, by dividing the men up among settlers spread across the colony, a rudimentary system of separation and classification might be introduced. Through a system of regular employer returns and reports, Oxley believed that government could come to 'know with greater certainty' the 'conduct and general character of the men'. By such means, some at least of the 'dangerous and at present useless characters' allegedly to be found among the male convicts might be reclaimed. Meanwhile, those who failed to reform could be worked 'in gangs on the roads, and wherever else hard labour is required' before being confined 'at night'.[123]

Oxley's plans for the female convicts involved a similar emphasis upon segregation as the models that were beginning to be devised on the mainland. The women, Oxley complained, moved too easily beyond the eye of government: seven out of ten of them, he asserted, were 'taken off the stores within a week' of their arrival, a practice which for Oxley signified widespread 'immorality', presumably because he believed it to facilitate practices such as prostitution and cohabitation. Under Oxley's reforms, measures would be taken to 'employ them beneficially' until the women were either 'legally married' or their term of transportation had expired.[124] The 'greater part of the women convicts', Oxley claimed, were 'unable from ignorance' to work even if they 'possessed the inclination'. These failings were ostensibly a reflection of the fact that they had from 'their youth been brought up in every scum of wickedness'. 'Reclaiming ... such characters' and 'bringing' them 'into habits of industry' would therefore be no easy task. A 'public factory' (Female House of Correction) was to be the solution: providing the means of keeping the women apart from the community and subjecting them to much greater discipline while also cutting costs by making them more economically 'useful' to the government. If his House of Correction was not to be quite 'a nunnery' – for Oxley imagined that some of the women might be free to go out for part of each day if they worked efficiently – the idea that 'such wretches' as the female convicts might 'be let loose on society without any restraint' nevertheless clearly filled him with horror. If the women were institutionally confined, he believed that they 'would be kept out of harm's way', prevented from doing mischief' and given an opportunity for 'individual amendment'.[125]

The repeated emphasis in these plans upon separating the men from the women was grounded in the idea that the under-regulated nature of personal, familial and household relationships underpinned

[113]

much of the current disorder. Free to live in their own households, and to maintain themselves through a variety of different means, convict workers were allegedly able to work when and for whom they desired. Under the present system, one commentator asserted, the convicts were therefore able to 'abandon themselves entirely to habits of idleness and debauchery'. This 'evil', he argued, was rooted in 'the custom' of allowing convicts to be 'at large' without 'any special controul [sic] or obligation'. Convicts not only failed, as a consequence, to acquire 'habits of industry', the men and women also enjoyed 'unrestrained association' with one another.[126] The epitome of the existing disorder, Macarthur concluded, was the way in which convict men laboured not for the benefit of moral masters like himself but for 'convict prostitute women', by which he meant variously their wives and de facto wives as well as other, more fleeting, sexual partners.[127] Under existing conditions, Bayly likewise asserted, male convict workers were too often tempted into crime and disorder by their ready access to the women. They committed robberies, he asserted, both to pay for their own lodgings and to house and sustain their female partners, and presumably also, although Bayly did not refer to it, to pay for sex.[128]

One illustration of the kinds of practices that these men were complaining about can be seen in George Town, in northern Van Diemen's Land in these years. There, relationships between men and women were clearly integral not only to what their superiors perceived as crime and disorder but also to a striking degree of independence. Although the male convicts in George Town were largely assigned to the public works, some of these men were making money on the side. They were able to do so through the active collaboration of their common-law female convict partners. The women, Bigge discovered, were regularly travelling to the nearby town of Launceston where they not only sold the furniture and other items that had been made by the men in preference to their government work but also allegedly trafficked in stolen property. To make matters worse, some of the male convicts, granted extra free time in order that they might build huts for themselves and their partners, had apparently endeavoured to extend this privilege by building themselves houses and then 'wantonly' setting fire to them.[129] The fact that these men and women lived in their own households – and that the women in particular enjoyed considerable mobility and freedom from the requirement to work – was therefore helping to foster a semi-independent convict sphere and, by creating alternative sources of income, undermining the ability to discipline labour. The key to changing this kind of situation, one Colonial Office official advised, was to reform the

[114]

hitherto 'improper *mode of disposing*' of the convicts, '*especially the females*, after their arrival in the Colony' and thus to force the men and the women to 'apply themselves to pursuits of an industrious reputable nature'.[130]

The growing emphasis upon the need to exercise greater control over the convict women dovetailed with government's increasing determination to regulate colonial morality and to suppress cohabitation and prostitution. With these kinds of aims in mind, Bligh introduced a series of measures in an attempt to regulate the labour of convict women and to restrict their freedom to move. These began with their disembarkation: the female convicts, he ordered, were to be taken directly from their ships to a 'very comfortable place to retire' where 'their persons' were to be 'guarded by superintendents'. The aim was to ensure 'that no person could be allowed to mix with them'. Women who remained unassigned to private service were 'ordered to the Factory' at Parramatta where they were to be placed under the control of 'proper persons' until suitable employment was found for them.[131] Bligh insisted, in addition, that all those making applications for female convict servants had to be subjected to a character inquiry. The only way to ensure that convict women genuinely became servants – as opposed to prostitutes or the common-law partners of men – he claimed, 'rested' in the state's ability to acquire knowledge about the 'moral character of those who received them'.[132] Macquarie's emphasis upon married couples as suitable employers of female convict labour reveals a similar agenda.

Macquarie built upon these measures during the course of the 1810s by ordering that all female convicts be carefully mustered before they were disembarked from their ship. On the basis of this muster data, they were then either to be 'assigned to such Married persons as require them for Servants' or 'sent to work at the Government Factory'.[133] Like Bligh, his aim was to 'prevent' the 'Intercourse' of the female convicts 'with the People of the Town, until such time as they should either be Married or Assigned as domestic Servants to Married persons'.[134] For similar reasons, the government also took steps to fix female convicts more securely in place. In 1810, for example, Macquarie introduced the idea of an indenture. From now on, he declared, any settler who wanted a female convict servant would have to sign a bond promising to retain them in their service for three years and to provide them with 'humane and proper treatment'.[135] These measures were also extended to Van Diemen's Land. When forty female convicts arrived at the Derwent in 1810, Davey was consequently instructed by London to adhere strictly to Macquarie's 'measures' for their 'disposal'. The government in London, Davey was advised, agreed with Macquarie that female convicts 'when landed' should always:

> be as much as possible kept separate until they can be properly distributed among the Settlers, and that their Services shall not be allotted to any Person, who does not enter into a Written Agreement to receive them for at least three years, and who does not become bound under a Penalty to treat them well during their Period of Servitude.[136]

On the mainland, these shifts in policy certainly seem to have had some effect. During 'Bligh's time', Thomas Robson, Commissary Clerk from 1806 until 1810, remembered, 'prostitution' (by which he meant cohabitation) was suppressed, because the Governor 'would not suffer a woman to be taken off the stores by any man, without being married, unless it was as servant to an officer'.[137] Convict women, John Palmer likewise recalled, were more generally distributed as 'servants' during this period than 'for the purposes of prostitution'.[138] Symbolic of the growing constraint suffered by female convicts was the fate of those women whom government deemed to be neither suitably employed nor married. These women, Macquarie ordered, should be sent to the House of Correction at Parramatta. Thus, the thirty-two women who arrived on the ship *Canada* in 1810 and who 'remained undisposed of' as servants on their arrival were very shortly afterwards 'employed in the Government Cloth Manufactory'.[139] Although a lack of 'suitable buildings' initially undermined the effectiveness of these regulations, because it meant that many of the women, supposedly confined to this Factory, were, in fact, still free to move around during part of each day and at night, Macquarie determined to make his system more fully effective by rebuilding and enlarging the institution and enclosing all the women behind 'a high Stone wall'.[140]

All this suggests a somewhat different reading of the rationale behind the establishment of the Female Houses of Correction than that previously provided by historians. Existing accounts tend to explain the decision to build these institutions as a sign of government's recognition that the women required refuge and protection from a supposedly profoundly misogynistic colonial culture.[141] While Macquarie may indeed have considered his actions to be chivalric and paternalistic, his intent appears to have been to segregate the women in order to prevent them from forming relationships as and when they chose and to preclude them from seeking out illicit and independent means of support. For similar reasons, Bligh and Macquarie were equally concerned to effect a greater state control over female convict labour. Assigned service was, almost certainly correctly, considered a route into cohabitation, prostitution and other forms of semi-independence for some convict women. 'Cohabitation', William Hutchinson, the Principal Superintendent of Convicts at Sydney told Bigge, was 'the frequent consequence' of assignment.[142] 'Female convict servants', Bigge concluded, were continually being 'seduced from the houses of their masters' and finding 'asylums in the houses of single men, under the pretence of service'.[143]

While the newer measures undoubtedly provided some convict women with a degree of protection from unwanted sexual advances and abuse, enabling them to find accommodation and employment in the homes of 'suitable' employers, they also marked a substantial diminution in female freedoms and the beginnings of a marked shift towards a substantially enhanced servitude. The government had begun to undermine the ability of convicts, and of convict women in particular, to move freely and so to select either sexual partners or places of employment for themselves. These attempts to regulate the convict private sphere more tightly and to intervene in the processes of household and family formation were linked with a broader determination to reduce convict freedoms by enforcing greater labour discipline. One of the central long-term remits of these reforms was thus to achieve the enhanced exploitation of convict labour, female as well as male. Much of what these early governors had begun, Commissioner Bigge was about to seek ways to complete and extend.

Notes

1 Arthur Phillip, *The voyage of Governor Phillip to Botany Bay with an account of the establishment of the colonies of Port Jackson and Norfolk Island* (London: John Stockdale, 1789), pp. 66–7. On the ways in which ideas about gender shaped Phillip's plans, see: Marian Aveling (now Quartly), 'Imagining New South Wales as a gendered society, 1783–1821', *Australian Historical Studies*, 25:98 (1992), pp. 1–12; and Alan Atkinson, *The Europeans in Australia* (Melbourne: Oxford University Press, 1997), Vol.1, pp. 65–6, 129–30.
2 David Collins, *An account of the English colony in New South Wales: with remarks on the dispositions, customs, manners & c of the native inhabitants of that country. To which are added some particulars of New Zealand; compiled, by permission, from the Mss. of Lieutenant-Governor King, by David Collins Esquire, late Judge Advocate and Secretary of the colony. Illustrated by engravings* (London: T. Cadell & W. Davies, 1798), Vol. 1, p. 18.
3 *Ibid.*
4 *Ibid.*, pp. 54–5. Bryant, the children and several of the male convicts died on the voyage, but Mary made it home and became a popular cause. Attempts to re-transport her and the four surviving men consequently failed. See: C.H. Currey, *The transportation, escape and pardon of Mary Bryant* (Sydney: Halstead Press, 1963). For biographies of Braund and Bryant see Mollie Gillen, *The founders of Australia: a biographical dictionary of the First Fleet* (Sydney: Library of Australian History, 1989), pp. 46–7, 57.
5 Collins, *Account*, Vol. 1, p. 92.
6 *Ibid.*, pp. 158–9. For Watkin Tench's descriptions of the farm's progress and an account by Ruse himself, see: Watkin Tench, *A complete account of the settlement at Port Jackson* (Melbourne: Text Publishing Company, 1996), pp. 157–8, 223.

7   Collins, *Account*, Vol. 1, p. 225.
8   Gillen, *Founders*, pp. 318–19.
9   For examples see: Ian Duffield (ed.), *Jack Bushman, passages in the life of a lifer* – http://iccs.arts.utas.edu.au/narratives/bushman1.html (accessed 12 April 2006); Martin Cash, *The bushranger of Van Diemen's Land in 1843–4: a personal narrative of his exploits in the bush and his experiences at Port Arthur and Norfolk Island* (Hobart: J. Walch & Sons, 1870); Diary of John Ward, convict, 1841–42, NLA MS 3275.
10 *HRA* I, 1, p. 120.
11 John Hunter, 'Select Committee on Transportation', *BPP* II (341), 1812, p. 20.
12 *HRA* I, 1, p. 23.
13 *HRA* III, 1, p. 293.
14 *Ibid.*, p. 315.
15 *HRA* I, 4, p. 10.
16 See chapter one for a discussion. John Fawkner and Thomas Peters, for example, both became substantial landowners and colonial businessmen partly as a result of these early indulgences. For their biographies see Marjorie Tipping, *Convicts unbound: the story of the Calcutta convicts and their settlement in Australia* (Victoria: Viking O'Neil, 1988), pp. 272, 299.
17 *HRA* III, 2, p. 25.
18 For details of these policies in NSW see: *BPP* II (341), 1812, p. 21.
19 For a biography of the Peters family see: Tipping, *Convicts*, p. 299. For the original grant in Ann's name, see: *HRA* III, 1, p. 568. Tipping describes this as a 'mistake' in the Return but it seems more likely that it reflected the ever-present assumption that property belonged to the male head of household. The very design of the Returns – with separate columns for each proprietor, his wife and children reflects this. See, for example: *HRA* III, 1, pp. 500–1.
20 Bruce Kercher, 'Perish or prosper: the law and convict transportation in the British Empire, 1700–1850', *Law & History Review*, 21:3 (2003), www.historycooperative.org/journals/lhr/21.3/forum_kercher.html, para. 150 (accessed 13 April 2006).
21 *HRA* III, 2, p.35.
22 *Ibid.*
23 On Macquarie's attitude to this question see: *HRA* I, 12, p .348, *HRA* III, 6, fn. 24, p. 883, *HRA* III, 6, pp. 158 & 531. Arthur stuck to a roughly similar course, agreeing that women had the right to land in principle, but often denying them in practice. See for example: *HRA* III, 7, pp. 47–8
24 See: *HRA* III, 7, fn. 45, p. 704.
25 Sharon Morgan, *Land settlement in early Tasmania: creating an antipodean England* (Melbourne: Cambridge University Press, 1992), p. 25.
26 *HRA* III, 2, p. 16; Lachlan Macquarie, *Journal to and from Van Diemen's Land to Sydney in New South Wales*, www.lib.mq.edu/all/journeys/1811/1811.html, p. 13 (accessed 12 December 2005).
27 As Aveling (now Quartly) notes, Macquarie's zeal for planned settlement and rational architecture derived from his belief that 'ordered lives' depended, above all, upon a 'cultivated landscape', a commitment which reflected his commitment to Enlightenment ideals; Aveling (now Quartly), 'Imagining', p. 9.
28 Samuel Bates, 'Select Committee on the state and description of gaols and other places of confinement, and into the best method for providing for the reformation as well as the safe custody and punishment of offenders', *BPP* VII (579), 1819, p. 132.
29 'Report of the Commissioner of Inquiry into the state of the colony of New South Wales', *BPP* XX (448), 1822, p. 49.
30 *HRA* III, 3, p. 276.
31 For examples see: *HRA* III, 3, pp. 542–3.
32 *BPP* XX (448), 1822, p. 43.

33 *HRA* III, 3, p. 277.
34 In 1840, for example, various inhabitants of George Town protested against these kinds of practices, complaining that the constabulary were entering the homes of some free mechanics at will; Police Office George Town, 14 May 1840, POL 211/2.
35 'Return of baptisms, marriages and deaths within the district of Hobart Town, 1804–1819', *HRA* III, 3, p. 510. For population figures see: *HRA* III, 1, pp. 227, 258, 298, 318, 341 & 722–3; *HRA* I, 5, pp. 614–15. *HRA* I, 7, pp. 284–5. See also: Irene Schaffer (ed.), *Land musters, stock returns and lists: Van Diemen's Land, 1803–1822* (Hobart: St David's Park Publishing, 1991), pp. 46–7, 49–50.
36 Schaffer, *Musters*, pp. 119–24.
37 *Hobart Town Gazette*, 6 February 1819; *HRA* III, 2, p. 527. Until Youl took up his appointment in 1819, the northern settlement had been without a chaplain, and a civil ceremony, performed by a justice of the peace, had had to suffice; *HRA* III, 3, fn. 189, p. 957.
38 *HRA* III, 3, pp. 365, 384, 410.
39 John Currey (ed.), *Records of the Port Phillip expedition* (Melbourne: The Colony Press, 1990), Vol. 1, p. 42.
40 *HRA* III, 1, p. 227. By comparison, women accounted for 28.2 per cent of the adults on the First Fleet in 1788; *HRA* I, 1, fn. 52, p. 727.
41 Women had averaged an unspectacular 20 per cent of the adult European population at Port Jackson during its first decade. In the first decade in Van Diemen's Land, their numbers hovered around 16 per cent at the Derwent and just 14 per cent at Port Dalrymple; *HRA* I, 1, pp. 203, 298–9, 342–3, 399, 436–7, 468, 501–2, 597–8, fn. 52, p. 727; *HRA* III, 1, pp. 258, 298, 318, 341; *HRA* I, 5, pp. 614–15; Schaffer, *Musters*, pp. 46–7, 49–50.
42 *Statistical returns of Van Diemen's Land or Tasmania from the date of its first occupation by the British nation in 1804 to the end of the year 1823* (Hobart: James Barnard, 1856), pp. 7, 9–11, *Statistical returns of Van Diemen's Land from 1824 to 1839* (Hobart: William Gore Elliston, 1839), Return 17.
43 At least initially, however, the arrival of the Norfolk Islanders did little to alter gender ratios among the adult population. Men outnumbered women among the Norfolk Island settlers by just over two to one and there were just nineteen single adult females among the arrivals; *HRA* III, 3, p. 582.
44 *Hobart Town Gazette*, 9 December 1826.
45 For examples: *HRA* III, 1, p. 359; Tipping, *Convicts*, pp. 261, 317. On Aboriginal-European relations more generally, including relations between men and women see: Marie Fels, 'Culture contact in the county of Buckinghamshire, Van Diemen's Land, 1803–11', *Tasmanian Historical Research Association*, 29:2 (1982), pp. 47–79; J. Kociumbas, '"Mary Ann", Joseph Fleming and "Gentleman Dick"?: aboriginal-convict relationships in colonial history', *Journal of Australian Colonial History*, 3:1 (2001), pp. 28–54; Maria Moneypenny, 'Going out and coming in: cooperation and collaboration between the Aborigines and Europeans in early Tasmania', *Tasmanian Historical Studies*, 5:1 (1995–6), pp. 64–75; Lyndall Ryan, *The Aboriginal Tasmanians* (St Lucia: University of Queensland Press, 1981); Rebe Taylor, *Unearthed: the Aboriginal Tasmanians of Kangaroo Island* (Adelaide: Wakefield Press, 2002).
46 Phillip Tardif, *Notorious strumpets and dangerous girls: convict women in Van Diemen's Land 1803–1829* (Sydney: Angus & Robertson, 1990), pp. 349–50, 354–5, 417.
47 *Ibid.*, pp. 345–67.
48 *HRA* III, 3, p. 442.
49 *Ibid.*, p. 249.
50 *Hobart Town Gazette*, 27 September 1817. For details of Bass see: Tardif, *Notorious strumpets*, p. 270. For a biography of Gwynn see: Tipping, *Convicts*, p. 279.
51 Tipping, *Convicts*, p. 305; Tardif, *Notorious strumpets*, pp. 666–7.
52 Tipping, *Convicts*, pp. 249–326.

53 It was the late 1810s and 1820s before many of the men transported on the *Calcutta* married; *ibid.*, pp. 249–326.
54 *HRA* III, 3, pp. 285, 365.
55 Louisa Meredith, *My home in Tasmania* (London: Murray, 1852), Vol. 2, p. 22. See also: Frances Cotton, 'Home life in Van Diemen's Land', *Tasmanian Historical Research Association*, 21:4 (1974), pp. 178–80; Sharon Morgan, 'George and Mary Meredith: the role of the colonial wife', *Tasmanian Historical Research Association*, 36:3 (1989), pp. 125–9; and Morgan, *Land settlement*, especially pp. 27–30. On the Australian colonies more generally see: Katrina Alford, 'The drover's wife and her friends: women in rural society and primary production in Australia, 1850–1900', *Australian National University Working Papers in Economic History*, 75 (Canberra: Australian National University, 1986); Patricia Grimshaw, Chris McConville & Ellen McEwen (eds), *Families in colonial Australia* (Sydney: George Allen & Unwin, 1985), pp. 173–97.
56 On Maria Lord see Kay Daniels, *Convict women* (St Leonards, NSW: Allen & Unwin, 1998), pp. 1–28.
57 Tardif, *Notorious strumpets*, p. 88; *HRA* III, 2, p. 117.
58 Mary remarried in 1829. Her second husband was William Nicholls, also a relatively well-to-do ex-*Calcutta* convict; Tipping, *Convicts*, pp. 151–3, 273–4.
59 *Hobart Town Gazette*, 9 January 1819.
60 Tipping, *Convicts*, pp. 154, 293–4.
61 *Ibid.*, p. 173; David Burn, *A picture of Van Diemen's Land* (Hobart: Cat & Fiddle Press, 1973), p. 182.
62 Morgan, *Land settlement*, pp. 6–7, 27–9.
63 Benjamin Bensley (ed.), *Lost and found; or light in the prison: a narrative with original letters, of a convict, condemned for forgery* (London: W. Wells Gardner, 1859), pp. 38, 100.
64 Diary of John Ward, pp. 1–2.
65 Alexander Solzhenitsyn, *The gulag archipelago* (London: Collins & Harvill, 1978).
66 Bensley, *Lost and found*, p. 100.
67 Hunter, *BPP* II (341), 1812, p. 20. For similar comments see: Collins, *Account*, p. 84.
68 *HRA* 1, 4, p. 483.
69 Atkinson, *Europeans*, Vol.1, pp. 129–44.
70 Aveling (now Quartly), 'Imagining', pp. 6–7.
71 For other accounts of women's work in these early years see: Collins, *Account*, Vol. 1, pp. 29, 125, 132; George Dyer, *Slavery and famine: punishments for sedition or an account of the miseries and starvation at Botany Bay by George Thompson who sailed in the Royal Admiral, May 1792, with some preliminary remarks by George Dyer* (Sydney: D.S. Ford, 1947), pp. 35–7; Tench, *Account*, pp. 124, 159; and *BPP* II (341), 1812, pp. 20, 32, 34.
72 Dyer, *Slavery*, pp. 36–7.
73 As Miriam Dixson observes, women frequently play central, if undervalued, economic roles in society because 'they produce, and often sustain, the direct producers'; Miriam Dixson, *The real Matilda: women and identity in Australia 1788 to 1975* (Ringwood, Victoria: Penguin, 1976), p. 122.
74 *HRA* III, 1, p. 200.
75 For James Grove's experiences see: Bensley, *Lost and found*.
76 James Tuckey, *A voyage to establish a colony at Port Philip on Bass's Strait on the south coast of New South Wales, in His Majesty's Ship Calcutta, in the years 1802-3–4* (London: Longman, Hurst, Rees & Orme, 1805), p. 59.
77 *HRA* III, 1, p. 224.
78 *Ibid.*, pp. 220, 265, 287, 608, 627, 645.
79 *HRA* III, 1, p. 607. On hours of labour see: *HRA* III, 1, pp. 219, 265.
80 One of these was a punishment gang for convict men set to hard labour in irons. For details of the gangs and their supervisors see: *HRA* III, 1, pp. 219–20, 226, 232, 241, 248, 265, 608–9.

81 *Ibid.*, p. 319.
82 *Ibid.*, pp. 220, 652.
83 *Ibid.*, pp. 230–1. On the need for extra labour see: *HRA* III, 1, pp. 230, 254, 641.
84 Collins, *Account*, Vol. 1, pp. 118–19.
85 He complained only once and then the issue was not incapacity but morality. On the arrival of Elizabeth Leonard alias Kelleyhorn, Collins noted, 'I well remember (her) to have been long a Nuisance at Sydney'. He considered her 'a Veteran in Infamy'; *HRA* III, 1, p. 315.
86 *Ibid.*, pp. 265–6.
87 *Ibid.*, pp. 310, 327, 403.
88 Samuel Bates, *BPP* VII (579), 1819, p. 130.
89 On death and its impact see: *HRA* III, 1, pp. 264, 286, 288 & 290. According to Aveling (now Quartly), mortality rates during the famine years in New South Wales may likewise have been higher among the men; Aveling (now Quartly), 'Imagining', pp. 6–7.
90 Dyer, *Slavery*, p. 36.
91 Harris to Collins, 7 December 1808, in Barbara Hamilton-Arnold (ed.), *Letters of G.P. Harris, 1803–1812* (Sorrento, Victoria: Arden Press, 1994), p. 109.
92 *HRA* III, 1, p. 241.
93 *Ibid.*, p. 274.
94 *Ibid.*, pp. 269–71.
95 *Hobart Town Gazette*, 2 and 9 December 1826. For a detailed breakdown of wages by area and trade in the 1830s see: 'Statistics for 1838', CSO 5/178. Demand for female labour meant that women too enjoyed relatively high wages. For a discussion see: Kirsty Reid, 'Work, sexuality and resistance: the convict women of Van Diemen's Land, 1820–39' (PhD thesis, University of Edinburgh, 1995), especially chapter 5.
96 See, for example: *HRA* III, 1, p. 591.
97 See for example: *ibid.*, p. 239, 240, 242, 248, 591.
98 *HRA* III, 2, p. 6.
99 For similar orders see: *HRA* III, 2, pp. 14, 27, 395, 398.
100 *Ibid.*, p. 33. For similar instructions see: *ibid.*, pp. 5, 16 & 18–19.
101 *Ibid.*, p. 314. Emphasis in original. See also: *ibid.*, p. 33. For similar measures on the mainland see: *HRA* I, 1, pp. 422 & 495; *HRA* 1, 3, pp. 255, 399, 576.
102 *HRA* III, 2, p. 16.
103 Of the free population, for example, just 12.2 per cent of men compared with 48.5 per cent of women were on the Store at the December 1799 muster. If women were more likely to receive support than men, women with children stood an even better chance. There were 0.8 children to every adult woman victualled compared to 0.2 children to every adult female not victualled; *HRA* I, 2, p. 468.
104 See for example: *HRA* I, 3, p. 467; *HRA* I, 4, p. 483.
105 *HRA* I, 7, p. 601.
106 *HRA* III, 2, pp. 599–600.
107 *HRA* I, 7, pp. 539–40.
108 George Worgan, *Journal of a First Fleet surgeon* (Sydney: Library Council of New South Wales/Library of Australian History, 1978), pp. 19, 27. Emphasis in original.
109 In the very early days this may, however, have been different: Worgan notes that Phillip was addressing both male and female convicts when he issued the instruction that they must work or starve. Worgan, *Journal*, p. 27.
110 *HRA* I, 2, p. 617; *HRA* I, 4, pp. 93, 318, 506 & 618; *HRA* I, 5, pp. 45, 185, 314, 502, 604, 613, 618, 664, 782; and *HRA* I, 6, p. 181.
111 Collins, *Account*, Vol. 1, pp. 84, 204. In early Van Diemen's Land, women likewise appear to have received a stable share of available supplies, remaining on a two-thirds' allowance despite the fact that they were burning fewer calories at work. See, for example: *HRA* III, 1, p. 227.

112 Two-thirds of these women were so employed in 1804, 1805 and 1806. Their numbers continued to increase thereafter; by mid-1807, three-quarters were employed in this way. For returns see: *HRA* I, 2, p. 617; *HRA* I, 4, pp. 93, 318, 506, 618; *HRA* I, 5, pp. 45, 185, 314, 502, 604, 613, 618, 664, 782; and *HRA* I, 6, p. 181. Men also worked in the manufactory but, with the exception of a few able men employed as weavers, the majority were 'invalids or cripples'. The labour was divided by gender: women did the sorting, picking, washing, carding and spinning, and the able men did the weaving; *HRA* I, 3, p. 439; *HRA* I, 4, p. 493. Some convicts, male and female, were also employed at a 'flax manufactory' also based at Parramatta; *HRA* I, 3, pp. 125, 156.

113 *HRA* I, 2, p. 617, *HRA* I, 4, pp. 93, 318, 506, 618, *HRA* I, 5, pp. 45, 185, 314, 502, 604, 618, 664, 782, *HRA* I, 6, p. 181. Some of these women appear to have received a wage in addition to government rations. In 1802, Ann Sandilon, employed as cook at the Orphan School, received £8 8s for a year's work, while Ann Gaunterry, housemaid at the same institution, received £6 6s. Three teachers, Mary Peat, Mary Cosgrove and Elizabeth Edwards, were given £1 11s 6d 'in consequence of (their) good behaviour'; *HRA* I, 4, pp. 96–7, 102–3.

114 *HRA* I, 4, p. 483.

115 The first of these quarterly returns dates from March 1803. See: *HRA* I, 4, p. 93.

116 There were numerous such regulations and orders – their repetition suggests that the government faced difficulty in enforcing them. See, for example: *HRA* I, 2, pp. 201, 215, 359–61; and *HRA* I, 3, pp. 48, 254, 470–3, 466–7, 621.

117 *HRA* I, 2, pp. 90–3.

118 *Ibid.*, p. 92.

119 *HRA* I, 9, p. 198.

120 *Ibid.*, fn. 44, pp. 856–7; *HRA* I, 9, pp. 197–200.

121 *Ibid.*, p. 200.

122 On the Macarthur family see: Alan Atkinson, *Camden* (Melbourne: Oxford University Press, 1988).

123 John Oxley, 'Remarks on the country and settlements formed in Van Diemen's Land', *HRA* III, 1, pp. 578–9; John Oxley, 'Remarks on the settlement of Port Dalrymple', *HRA* III, 1, p. 767.

124 Oxley, 'Remarks on the settlement of Port Dalrymple', *HRA* III, 1, pp. 766-7.

125 *Ibid.*

126 *HRA* I, 7, pp. 204–10.

127 *HRA* I, 2, pp. 90–3.

128 *HRA* I, 9, p. 199.

129 *BPP* XX (448), 1822, pp. 46–7.

130 *HRA* I, 7, pp. 204–5. Emphasis in original.

131 Bligh, *BPP* II (341), 1812, p. 32.

132 *Ibid.*, p. 32.

133 *HRA* I, 9, p. 503.

134 *Ibid.*, p. 504.

135 *Ibid.*, p. 113.

136 *HRA* I, 7, pp. 524–5.

137 Robson, *BPP* II (341), 1812, p. 52.

138 Palmer, *ibid.*, p. 61.

139 Macquarie, *ibid.*, p. 113.

140 *HRA* I, 7, p. 614.

141 For a history of the House of Correction at Parramatta, see Annette Salt, *These outcast women: the Parramatta Female Factory, 1821–1848* (Sydney: Hale & Ironmonger, 1984).

142 *BPP* XX (448), 1822, p. 68.

143 *Ibid.*, p. 106.

CHAPTER FOUR

Sex and slavery

Convict servitude and the reworking of the private sphere, c.1817–42

The decision to send Commissioner John Bigge to the Australian settlements in 1819–20 was informed by an imperial government programme of retrenchment, repression and reform. In the wake of the Napoleonic Wars, and with huge public debt, cost cutting acquired an influential bearing upon policy both in Britain and throughout the empire. Reform of the convict assignment system not only promised to stimulate colonial economic development but also to reduce state spending by systematically redeploying convict labour to the private sector. The wars and the period immediately after them were also characterised by a turn to repression, which included an expansion of the state's regulatory and policing powers, the planning of new penitentiaries and houses of correction, enhanced curbs upon political liberties and freedom of speech, and coercive labour legislation.[1]

Coincident with these shifts, a range of reforms began to curb the so-called 'Bloody Code'. The continuing decline in rates of execution inevitably further heightened the state's reliance upon transportation as one of *the* most significant forms of secondary punishment. This was extended by a post-war 'crime wave', a companion to the social dislocation caused by military demobilisation and economic depression.[2] The exponential growth in the numbers transported speaks for itself. While just over 15,000 convicts had arrived in the Australian settlements between 1788 and 1815, 11,885 men and 1,381 women were transported between 1816 and 1820 alone. Their numbers remained high thereafter. An average of 3,737 convicts arrived in the two colonies every year between 1816 and 1840, an almost seven-fold increase on average annual arrivals in the early period.[3] Against this backdrop it was crucial that the dread of transportation be consolidated and enhanced. As he departed from London, the government ominously instructed Bigge to avoid 'any compassion or desire to lessen the convicts' sufferings'.[4]

During his stay in the settlements, Bigge became convinced of the need for a fundamental shift of policy, one that linked colonial socio-economic development with a systematic enhancement of the terror of transportation. His proposals rested on two key pillars: the encouragement and facilitation of wealthier free emigration and the transformation of convicts into an unfree labour force. Bigge considered that transportation's aims of punishment, deterrence and reformation would only be achieved if convicts were systematically channelled into the hands of large rural employers. These reforms would bring the vision of order and authority in the Australian colonies much more firmly into line with thinking elsewhere in the empire. The 'dominant tone' of the 'new imperial age' (c.1780–1830), historian Christopher Bayly explains, was 'agrarianist and aristocratic'; 'disposable property in land and agrarian improvement' were considered 'virtues' because supposedly they would 'reveal a natural hierarchy' based upon social and racial difference.[5]

The link between land, labour and moral reformation, which had informed state practice throughout the first period of settlement, was to be pursued, therefore, in a fundamentally different way. The agrarian vision was to be redrawn, the earlier emphasis upon the convict as yeoman replaced by a greater focus upon the gentleman farmer. Although paternalism was to remain crucial to colonial authority, its forms and functions were to shift. Convicts, Bigge recommended, were to be assigned as far as possible to 'the large estates of the most respectable settlers, where the advantages to be derived from good character will be appreciated, and those of example in the master, and good conduct in the servant, will be reciprocally felt'.[6] The civilising project of convict discipline and reformation was to be achieved through the simultaneous economic exploitation and moral superintendence of bonded convict workforces by free men of capital.

The new system depended, of course, on the existence of a sufficient supply of free settlers of adequate social and moral status. Happily for Bigge, the emigration of these kinds of individuals had begun in earnest in the mid-1810s, and he recommended that the imperial state facilitate the future expansion of their numbers by making land and labour available to those who arrived with £500 of capital or more. Although relatively few of the great landowners around whom Bigge planned his system would settle in Van Diemen's Land, Arthur was, as we saw in chapter two, anyway always more persuaded of the disciplinary and supervisory potential of middle-class settlers, and many such men and women arrived in this period. Free emigration, Arthur later declared, had resulted in an 'infusion of healthy blood into the constitution of the colony', which by 'sprinkling . . . religious and moral characters ... over the face of the country at large' had ended a situation where the 'materials for coercion had been wanting'.[7]

In Arthur's view, the settler home was ideally suited to the application of Benthamite thought because of the ways in which it brought settler self-interest to bear upon an environment with a peculiarly 'natural' capacity to socialise and transform. The master would exercise great vigilance and discipline because, Arthur contended, he knew that should he ever 'relax the discipline of his establishment the convict would presume upon his forbearance, or weakness. His household would then become a scene of disorder revolting to his feelings, and destructing of his property'.[8] Each member of the family into which a convict was assigned therefore had a direct self-interest in 'watching his behaviour'.[9] The convict was, as a result, to all effects and purpose, a 'slave'; 'at the mercy of his master', he or she was also rightly 'exposed to the caprice of all the family to whose service he may happen to be assigned'.[10] Made 'alive to the degradation of compulsory servitude', the convict would be woken to a requisite sense of shame; 'reflection', Arthur confidently asserted, 'follows'.[11]

Interpretations of the settler home as a miniature 'panopticon' or prison house drew fulsomely upon understandings of the domestic sphere as a 'natural' site. Assignment, Governor John Franklin (1837–43) observed, provided a form of discipline in which 'the convict is the least removed from the natural condition'. It was to be considered therefore 'the least artificial of all punishments'.[12] These kinds of views were partly founded in the belief that the home was 'natural' in the sense that it was the timeless and trans-historical foundation of 'civilised' society. Contemporaries, historian John Tosh explains of the nineteenth century, believed that it was 'ordained by nature' and that 'its function and structure predated civil society and were the precondition for its reproduction'.[13] The home was also a site in which hierarchies of power and authority, and the exercise of discipline, had long tended to be naturalised and thereby rendered opaque. Yet, as Anne McClintock notes, domesticity 'denotes both a *space* (a geographic and architectural alignment) and a *social relation to power*'. 'The verb to domesticate', she comments, is etymologically 'akin to dominate, which derives from *dominus*, lord of the *domum*, the home' and, until the late twentieth century, it 'carried as one of its meanings the action "to civilise"'.[14]

Power-ridden meanings repeatedly informed understandings of the reformed convict assignment system. Thus convicts were, in addition to being perceived as 'slaves', also imagined as animals in need of taming. The role of the settler, Arthur asserted, was to take his convict servant and to break him in as if he were a horse. Deemed 'primitive', 'savage' and at best semi-civilised, the convict was also considered child-like. 'Delinquents', Bentham had advised:

> especially of the more criminal descriptions, may be considered as a
> particular class of human beings, that, to keep them out of harm's way,
> require for a continued length of time that sort of sharp looking after,
> that sort of particular close inspection, which all human beings, without
> exception, stand in need of, up to a certain age. . . . They may be
> considered as a sort of grown up children, in whose instance the mental
> weakness attached to non-age continues . . . beyond the ordinary length
> of time.[15]

The reworked system of assignment depended upon notions of 'civilisa-tion' through domestication and upon a conceptualisation of settler families as crucibles of moral re-fashioning. 'The habits of a people', one colonial clergyman asserted, 'are formed by the circumstances in which they are placed'. Assignment worked, he explained, because convicts were:

> introduced into the settlers' houses and establishments, as permanent
> domestic servants, or labourers, where, they entered into a new associa-
> tion, many became completely reformed, and rose to respectability, and
> independence; and all were in a great degree restrained from vice and
> influenced towards good.[16]

'The mind' of the convict, another commentator agreed, was 'chameleon-like' and 'so constituted as to take [on] the hues of surrounding objects'.[17] In the domesticating atmosphere of the colonial home, each convict would therefore 'take on' moral character while simultaneously learning the value of labour. Not surprisingly, given the contemporary emphasis upon the home as the proper site of a moral and ordered femininity, commentators considered that this system had particular resonance for convict women. 'There is no means more conducive to the reformation' of female convicts 'than a proper system of assignment', Josiah Spode, Principal Superintendent of Convicts, explained: 'The prisoner has the example of virtuous women and [has] habits of cleanliness and industry enforced which are not now. The prisoner . . . mingles with the children and forms an attachment which she does not like to break and which very much softens her disposition.'[18]

Similar ideas were nevertheless extended to the men: assignment, Franklin declared, had the power to transform even a London pick-pocket, that symbol *par excellence* of urban and metropolitan deviance in this period, into a useful and industrious farm servant. 'The heart and understanding of the convict may be acted on', Franklin explained. Through assigned service, the convict acquired 'a new affection' for work and through 'intercourse with his master ... a field for the cultivation of those sentiments which determine the character of a man; gratitude, benevolence, conscientiousness'.[19]

As these comments reveal, a belief in the reformative power of the home was, in turn, interwoven tightly with notions of class and with the commitment to the production of a particular type of social order, one that was hierarchical yet bound by 'familial' ties of mutual affection and care. Assignment, Franklin counselled, promised to 'rouse the sympathies of the convicts' and to 'create between him and society affinities of a higher and better order'.[20] The convict system was thus to be conducive to the creation of an organic and putatively 'natural' society, which, mirroring the family, was to be bound together by ties of benevolence, duty and obligation.

In Van Diemen's Land, Sorell had already embarked upon a major overhaul of the system prior to Commissioner Bigge's arrival. Alphabetical convict conduct registers formed the centrepiece of this new approach. Designed to create a 'system of perpetual reference and general control', these registers brought together all the information on an individual in one place and were kept rigorously up to date by the chief police magistrates.[21] Reference to the register would, from 1817 onwards, inform all decisions about an individual convict's progress: whether he or she ought to be subjected to additional punishment and discipline or might marry, be granted a ticket of leave, pardon or other indulgence. New regulations also instructed all male convicts to appear at a weekly Sunday muster, before compulsorily attending church. Additionally, the establishment of a pass system required convicts to prove to the police that they had 'not deviated from [their] time or destination'. By establishing 'a perfect unity of management throughout the Island respecting Convicts', Sorell declared he had created 'a perfect check upon their loco-motion'.[22]

Sorell's reforms included a series of measures to streamline the distribution of convict labour. All convicts who arrived after 1817 were subjected to an interview and a muster. A 'list or muster roll of the convicts' was prepared, Bigge explained, 'describing the number, name, time and place of trial ... sentence, age, native place, trade, description of person and character' of each convict. A detailed physical description of each convict was then compiled and kept by the police magistrate 'as a future guide to the identity of their persons'.[23] While this process was crucial to the construction of the new convict registers – confirming and extending the state's knowledge of each individual – it also facilitated the placing of convicts in work. On the basis of the occupational data collected, government either reserved a convict for public work or made him or her available for assignment. As settler demand for convict labour rose and distribution became correspondingly more competitive and elaborate, the muster's inter-rogation and information-gathering functions became increasingly vital to the efficient operation of assignment.

Efforts were also made to impose greater control over convict working conditions. New regulations introduced between mid-1817 and early 1822 attempted to fix wages for assigned servants, set their hours of labour, keep them in service, discipline them when they were guilty of misconduct and generally prevent them from being 'upon their own hands'.[24] These measures – which notably were extended to the women as well as the men – were designed to undermine the ability of convict workers to change their service at will, work and live independently, move around freely, and bargain over terms and conditions. The high wages commanded by colonial labour were a particular source of anxiety and Sorell sought to curb them by setting official convict wage-rates and by punishing those who attempted to bargain beyond these. Ticket-of-leave holders were, for example, to be penalised by demotion to full convict status whenever they were found to have made 'an exorbitant demand' for wages.[25]

The fact that these orders were re-issued regularly implies, however, that government enjoyed at best partial success. The evidence gathered by Bigge tends further to confirm this.[26] Despite prohibitions placed upon the practice, settlers who were unable to afford to pay their convict servants the set wages continued to permit them to seek work elsewhere from 3 p.m. each day.[27] Many smaller settlers also evaded the regulations that stipulated that they must keep an assigned servant for a minimum of one year by employing them during periods when their 'labour needs' were most 'pressing', such as harvest, but then allowing them at other times to 'go' illicitly 'on their own hands'.[28] Artisans and skilled tradesmen were, in addition, regularly permitted by their masters to work freely at their trades in return for paying these employers a share of their income and rations.[29] Similar freedoms even extended to convicts employed in public works, most of whom were free to do as they pleased from 3 p.m. on weekdays and mid-morning on Saturday.[30] This was necessary, Major Bell, the Inspector of Public Works at Hobart, explained, in order for these men to earn the five shillings a week required to pay for lodgings. Limited state accommodation meant that only a minority could be kept confined. While the 'industrious' worked during this free time, many other convicts allegedly were to be seen 'lounging about the Streets, gambling and robbing'.[31]

Continued shortages of labour were one key factor bedevilling almost all of the government's efforts to curb and control convict workers in these years. 'Many employers', Anthony Fenn Kemp informed Bigge, simply did not consider it 'practicable', 'from the Few Labourers we have', to adhere to the regulated rates for convict labour.[32] The 'great number' of convicts who were to be seen 'idling about and ... unemployed' in the streets was, ex-Chief Constable Wade explained, a sign of the fact that high wages enabled many to 'earn enough in two days for the rest of the week'.[33] Matters were much the same in some rural districts where, according to magistrate James Gordon, convicts commanded wages at double the official government rate of ten to ten pounds seven shillings per man per annum.[34] The relatively limited means of state coercion also undermined efforts to discipline convict labour and enforce regulations. The 'difficulty that is experienced by the Settlers in compelling and enforcing the Labour from Convict Servants', combined with 'their distance from Magistrates' and the costs of a trip to the courts, meant, Wade explained, that the 'Settlers are obliged to incur greater expense to encourage and induce their servants to Work'.[35] Chronic insufficiencies in the state's ability to incarcerate and punish offenders further complicated matters. The 'only means of lodging' the 'bad characters' employed in the public works at Hobart, for example, was a two-room hut and a small watch-house. Convicts in Van Diemen's Land were, as a result of all these factors, allegedly 'much more daring' in these years than their counterparts in New South Wales.[36]

Arthur tackled these problems by systematically restructuring and expanding the police and judiciary and by splitting the colony into a number of distinct police districts.[37] The formal separation of Van Diemen's Land from New South Wales also helped by placing the governor's authority on a more fully independent and secure footing. Of similar significance was the establishment of Courts of Quarter Sessions and, in 1824, a Supreme Court making the imposition of discipline a simpler and swifter prospect. The creation of a body of new criminal offences, many of them dealing exclusively with convict labour, and the institution of summary jurisdiction over convict servants were further crucial markers of the state's developing power. Arthur's police and surveillance systems were such, in addition, that it was increasingly difficult, although never impossible, for settlers to overlook the offences of their servants. Convict offences that previously had 'passed by undetected or disregarded ... now undergo full enquiry and consequent punishment', Arthur declared at the close of 1827.[38] As a result, assigned servants, Franklin later reflected, had gradually been made subject to punishment for a range of 'offences so minute as not to be known as such in England'.[39]

The period from the early 1820s onwards also witnessed a massive expansion in the punitive resources of the state. Perhaps most crucially of all, given the ramshackle and markedly insufficient resources that the state had previously been forced to rely upon, new institutions for the accommodation and punishment of convicts opened, including a string of gaols and watch-houses, convict barracks, houses of correction for both men and women, and several penal stations at remote sites like Macquarie Harbour, Maria Island and Port Arthur. These institutional developments were essential because they provided the state with a wide range of places of incarceration and punishment. The extreme discipline, deprivation and isolation of sites of secondary exile like Macquarie Harbour enabled new levels of terror to be struck into the male convict population.[40] Chain and iron gangs, and the threat of hard labour, had a similar effect. The construction of gaols, prisons and barracks across the settled districts also made possible a much wider range of sanctions including solitary confinement, the imposition of bread and water diets, and periods of hard labour on the treadmill, thus creating a much greater flexibility of response.

This shift underpinned the introduction of a much more rigorous system of separation and classification, enabling Arthur, from the late 1820s onwards, to place male convicts into one of seven newly defined and hierarchically ordered classes.[41] The ability to classify and grade had, Arthur explained, allowed the state to place each convict in a position 'commensurate' with his 'conduct'. The 'scale', he explained in 1832, had gradually been made 'as complete as possible' so that it now descended:

> on the one hand from the least severe species of punishment, in the service of the settlers, by regular steps, through the usual public service, road-gangs, chain-gangs, the penal settlements of Port Arthur and Macquarie Harbour (a last alteration, next to capital punishment), and ascending on the other, by encouragement to reform, through the links of probationary service in the field-police, and other descriptions of duty in the public service, distinguished by some mark of conferring different degrees of liberty by conditional, and lastly by absolute pardons.[42]

The ever-present prospect of moving up this scale, as well as the perennial fear of being sent down, created a vital resource, which, historian Hamish Maxwell-Stewart notes, enabled the state to draw in an increasingly sophisticated fashion upon both 'coercion and incentive-based management strategies'.[43] The 'facilities' for discipline conferred by this scheme had, Arthur asserted, helped to 'render' the whole colony 'one of the best and most economical prisons ... that could be devised'.[44]

Of equal significance was the way in which these new institutions facilitated a major restructuring of the colonial public sphere and an assault upon the labour conditions, freedom and independence of convicts. As we saw in chapter three, until the early 1820s, most convicts made their own housing and domestic arrangements, and consequently they were relatively free to live and work as they chose, particularly in their own time. The opening of convict institutions like the Hobart barracks in the early 1820s marked the beginning of the end for these kinds of freedoms and there can be no doubt that this was a key part of the government agenda. 'Every Prisoner in the Island who is not in the Service of the Settlers', should, Arthur urged, 'be securely lodged in some Public Barrack at night, and at all times kept under the strictest Superintendence'. The alternative, he reminded London, was to continue to allow those employed in the public works or not in assigned service, 'so many hours in the day to work for themselves as a means of procuring Lodgings at night'. During this time, he warned, these men were 'entirely upon their own hands' and thus able to revel 'in every species of debauchery and vice'.[45]

Wholesale reform of the system therefore depended upon the state's ability to redirect convicts systematically from their own lodgings or homes either into settler households or government accommodation.[46] This assault upon the foundations of the convict private sphere was an implicit part of the Bigge plan. The right of convicts to earn wages and to hold and accumulate property could only be abolished if the state assumed full responsibility for their maintenance and support. Likewise, any possibility of enhancing the rate of exploitation and intensifying punishment by increasing servitude depended upon the state's ability to suppress and penalise convict labour bargaining. The expansion of facilities for confinement made it more difficult for convicts to search legitimately for alternative work or to be 'on their own hands'. Convicts found out of barracks or related institutions or away from the property of their assigned employers were now more likely to be regarded with suspicion and thus as legitimate targets for police action. Once confined, convicts also had a more limited capacity to enjoy their own patterns of culture and leisure. Much of the non-work time of those confined to institutions was instead increasingly consumed by state-directed religious and educational pursuits.

The new spatial ordering enabled the state to suppress attempts by convicts to work independently or in their own time and thus to enforce a greatly enhanced servitude. On the back of these shifts Arthur moved to abolish convict wages and to institute in their place a fixed basic ration of food and clothing.[47] The payment of wages, Bigge had observed, was 'inconsistent with that state of servitude' which convict workers were 'bound to endure'.[48] The right of convicts to acquire or access their property while they remained under sentence was also removed.[49] A savings bank was established and orders issued for all money to be taken from convicts upon their arrival and deposited there. A key purpose of such measures, the government in London reminded Arthur, was to prevent convicts from having any means to acquire 'indulgencies' [sic] during their period of assigned service.[50] Another sign of the scale of the transition in these years was that the very concept of convict time shifted. New regulations imposed in the 1820s dictated that convicts were no longer to be permitted to end their official work at 3 p.m. but were instead directed to 'devote their whole time and their best services from morn to night' either to their assigned employer or in the public works.[51]

Significantly, given the emphasis that historians conventionally have placed on the role of gender in shaping the convict system, most of these measures were applied with equal force to the women as the men. By comparison with the period of early settlement, when the government had emphasised their marital and reproductive potential, female convicts were increasingly reconceived as a source of unfree colonial labour. As with the men, this shift towards a substantially enhanced servitude was accompanied by government efforts to close down the spaces for female convict independence both from the state and from assigned service. Like the men, shortages of labour had previously enabled the women to access a range of alternatives to assignment and to bargain over their terms and conditions. Throughout the first decades, moreover, marriage and cohabitation had offered female convicts important additional escape routes from servitude. It was, Sorell complained, nearly impossible 'to keep assigned female Servants in their places' given 'the offers they generally receive of Marriage or more advantageous employment'.[52]

These opportunities to circumvent assignment were also grounded in the fact that men so vastly outnumbered women. Writing in 1818 to thank Macquarie for the sixty female convicts he had recently sent to Van Diemen's Land, Sorell asked for 'forty or fifty more' to be sent as soon as possible. Additional numbers, he explained, were crucial if the state was to have any chance of keeping convict women in their place.[53] While colonial demographics would become more balanced in the decades thereafter as the numbers of women arriving in the colony began to rise, the ongoing imbalance between the numbers of males and females almost certainly continued to endow women with a degree of bargaining power both at work and in the marriage market. 'It may appear . . . a strange remedy', Arthur was still commenting as late as 1838, but 'if a great many more' women were transported 'their situation would be altogether very greatly improved'. 'There are too few females in the colony', he explained, with the result that convict women in assigned service continued to be 'liable to great temptations'.[54] Although historians have tended to consider the marked imbalance between the numbers of colonial males and females as profoundly disadvantageous to women – on the grounds that it fostered a masculine-dominated culture – it seems likely that female convicts nevertheless also benefited from this situation in a number of ways.

From around the late 1810s, two key changes began to enable the colonial state to impose assigned service upon the majority of convict women for the first time. First, state policy underwent a fundamental transformation. The government issued a number of instructions dealing specifically with female convicts as *labour*, and these speak to the beginnings of a crucial shift away from marriage and towards assignment. As late as 1817, Sorell had continued to approach the distribution of convict women with an eye to their marriage as much as their labour. Upon sending a party of seventeen female convicts to northern Van Diemen's Land in September that year, he instructed the Commandant there 'to assign a portion of them' to the 'public officers and respectable Settlers' but also to allow others to marry 'the overseers or most decent prisoners' if they so desired.[55] From early 1818 onwards, however, the government began systematically to assign newly arrived female convicts and to place corresponding limits on their initial freedom to marry.[56] In 1820, for example, all the applications from convict men to marry the women who had arrived recently at George Town from the ship *Janus* were turned down and these women were instead assigned.[57] Like convict men, moreover, new regulations were also introduced in these years to fix convict women much more securely in their place of service. Settlers were, for example, warned that any failure to notify the authorities immediately should a female convict leave her assigned service would result in the employer being 'excluded from the indulgence of receiving Government Servants' in future.[58]

These shifts in policy were both occasioned and facilitated by the second key change of these years: the beginnings of a sustained take-off in colonial demand for female convict labour. This was a product of the expansion of free settlement and the consequent growth in the market for household servants. The decision to transfer sixty women from Sydney in February 1818 and another thirty in the September was one sign of the state's growing confidence that female convicts sent to Van Diemen's Land would be found employment. Macquarie commented to Sorell that there would be 'no difficulty in disposing' of these women as servants 'amongst the Settlers'.[59] Indeed, despite their gradually expanding numbers, the government in Hobart even began to complain of the overly limited supply of female labour. Asking for more convict women to be sent in March 1820, Sorell explained that the 'want' of female servants was 'pressing'.[60] And, despite the extra supplies sent that June on the *Princess Charlotte*, 'demand for female Convict Servants' continued to 'exceed the Number' available, with the result that all forty-one of these women were assigned to service immediately 'except such as were sick and incapable'.[61] This marked the beginning of a long-term trend. From the late 1810s until the female convict assignment system was abandoned in the early 1840s, convict women were overwhelmingly assigned to private service immediately upon their disembarkation in the colony. Throughout this same period, moreover, women in assignment formed a consistent majority of all female convicts under sentence in Van Diemen's Land.[62]

The emergence of a much more coherent and universally applied system of female convict servitude was accompanied by a correspondingly marked escalation in the state's determination to discipline and coerce convict women. As the proportion of women under sentence who were married or otherwise living 'on their own hands' began to fall, and the proportion assigned to compulsory service started to climb, so too the percentages of women who were incarcerated and undergoing punishment in the colony began to rise notably. In 1822, just under 10 per cent of convict women under sentence were confined to a gaol or other similar institution. Within a decade this figure had more than doubled, reaching 21 per cent in 1832, almost 30 per cent in 1835, and just over 35 per cent by 1842.[63]

This shift was, in turn, a product of the state's growing ability to punish convict women. Despite repeated requests from Sorell for funds to build a female house of correction in Hobart, Macquarie had continued to recommend instead that he send those women who required punishment either to the house of correction at Parramatta or to the penal settlement at Newcastle, to the north of Sydney.[64] As late as 1819–20 there were, as a consequence, next to no facilities in Van Diemen's Land itself for the disciplining of female convicts. At Launceston, Bigge discovered that while the women might be sent to the stocks, there was 'no fit place of confinement' for them.[65] In Hobart, although it was possible to confine women to the town's gaol, this building was badly built, overcrowded and physically insecure, with the result that conversations and trafficking were possible with passers-by in the street and the women were barely separated from the men.[66] 'The want of a proper place of punishment', Bigge was forced to conclude, had resulted in a situation in which the female convicts in Van Diemen's Land 'were not in a state of very effectual control'.[67]

From the 1820s onwards, a number of important steps were taken to redress this situation. These included the establishment of a major female house of correction at Cascades, on Hobart's outskirts, in 1829 and the opening of a house of correction at Launceston, in the north of Van Diemen's Land, in the early 1830s. Although, as in New South Wales, these institutions would perform a range of functions – including acting as depots for women who were unassigned, as lying-in hospitals for pregnant female convicts, and as places of care for the sick and elderly – their founding rationale and primary purpose was labour discipline. Pressing the case for a local house of correction, Sorell had emphasised the 'want' of 'a place of restraint or labour for Female Convicts' and had informed Bigge that until such an institution was built there would be 'no alternative . . . but to allow the Mass of the Females . . . to go at once at large'. Just as importantly, there was also no way of stopping those women who were already in assigned service from 'quitting their places', something, Sorell reported, that was at that point 'nearly impossible to prevent'.[68] The various places of confinement that were built by Sorell's successors undoubtedly helped to fill this gap. For, as the regular house of correction returns reveal, the majority of women confined to these institutions were, throughout the 1830s and 1840s, undergoing punishment for offences committed in their assigned service.[69] As with the men, the shift towards servitude therefore had been underpinned both by a major spatial re-ordering of the female convict population – away from their own households and towards either settler households or the houses of correction – and by a marked extension in the disciplinary power and punitive resources of the state.

Despite the growing parallels between the experiences of convict men and convict women, a number of distinctions nevertheless continued to prevail. While some of these disadvantaged the women, others were almost certainly to their benefit. In particular, it seems likely, as a number of historians have suggested, that the domestic or household nature of female assigned service often resulted in a more restricting and confining experience for convict women than men.[70] This was certainly true during the working day when, as the repeated bickering, rows and even open explosions of anger that occurred between convict women and their mistresses, in particular, reveal, female convicts were often forced to work under an extremely close supervisory eye.[71] Attempts were also made to impose greater supervision upon convict women during their time off work and many of them were locked inside their employer's houses at night. The men, by comparison – even when they worked as domestic servants in and around the house – were mostly accommodated in separate buildings or huts on their master's property and consequently they enjoyed greater facilities for independent relaxation and socialisation. Not surprisingly, given this, the women frequently sought to escape the house for the huts.[72]

While the closer confinement suffered by some female servants was partly a product of the primarily household nature of their work, it was also an offshoot of gender ideology and a sign of the state's greater determination to regulate femininity. Convict women, colonist Henry Widowson remarked in the late 1820s, can only 'be assigned to such persons as are married'. In addition, he reported, 'the settler previous to their going to him, is obliged to sign a bond, enjoining that the women shall sleep every night in his house; thus manifesting on the part of government a praiseworthy attention to the moral welfare of these fallen creatures'.[73] Settlers who failed to observe these kinds of rules were regarded as inadequate and demoralised masters. Gender ideologies also shaped the treatment of male convict servants who were frequently kept locked out of the house at night because of settler fears about the sexual and moral 'threat' that they supposedly posed not only to the women servants but also to the female members of the family.[74] Thus, although the domesticating and paternalistic discourses that linked the settler household to convict reform were applied to men as well as women, these were nevertheless inflected somewhat differently.

Discourses of femininity also tended to benefit convict women in some ways, not least by placing major prohibitions upon the state's ability to coerce and punish them.[75] Conditions in the female houses of correction were undoubtedly frequently poor – the buildings were damp and cold and the food inferior and inadequate. Despite this, convict women were never subjected to anything like the extreme physical deprivation and suffering endured by those men who had been sentenced to be flogged or to undergo punishment in the chain gangs or at the penal stations.[76] With the exception of just two women, moreover, execution was also applied solely and exclusively to men.[77] These differences were the product of a series of profoundly gendered contemporary notions about the greater weakness and susceptibility of female bodies and minds. Penal reformers feared, in addition, that degrading, physical punishments might simply further 'harden' women offenders, make them more masculine and thus achieve the opposite of 'reform'.[78] As one colonial observer noted, 'you may put a Man upon the Chain Gang, and make him work so as to draw forth the Sweat of his Brow; but you cannot punish a Female in that Way. This was the real practical Difficulty we always met with in my Time with regard to the Female Convicts'.[79] As a result of these concerns, a range of punishments that had previously been used primarily to discipline convict women – including the stocks, iron collars and head shaving – were also increasingly being phased out by the late 1820s and 1830s. For similar reasons, Arthur, in particular, refused to entertain the idea that convict women be sent to penal stations.[80]

This limited range of sanctions had a two-fold impact upon the women. First, unlike the men, who, as we have seen, were sorted into an increasingly complex hierarchy of classes – a ladder of promotion and demotion – the majority of the women were organised into just three groups in this period: those who held a ticket of leave; those in assigned service; and those confined to a house of correction. Second, and as a direct consequence of this weaker management structure, the colonial state and colonial employers were more likely to be thwarted in their attempts to control convict women. In the absence of sufficient negative sanctions ('stick'), it seems likely that some employers resorted more frequently to positive sanctions ('carrot'), giving in to female convict worker demands for indulgences like extra rations and free time where they might perhaps otherwise have attempted to stand firm.[81] This was certainly the conclusion that various colonial authorities reached. 'With respect to the discipline of the female convicts, it is', Josiah Spode concluded, 'I confess, much more difficult to bring it to a system of coercion than towards the males'.[82]

Within a decade of Bigge, the terrain upon which convict labour relations were fashioned had decisively shifted. According to Arthur, at the time of his arrival in 1824 the convicts had been 'kept quiet by a system of extreme indulgence'. By the early 1830s, this had been replaced with a 'systematic scheme of coercion'.[83] The cumulative effect of reform – for women as well as men – was a significant escalation in the scale and intensity of convict servitude and constraint. 'To the mass of prisoners', Arthur concluded, 'transportation is perfect slavery, and a most severe punishment'.[84] Although ongoing resistance on the part of many convict workers, combined with the fact that settlers were keen to encourage their servants to work, meant that many employers continued, despite the new regulations, to concede incentives such as free time and extra rations to their assigned servants, Arthur undoubtedly had a point.[85]

*   *   *

Reform of the convict system in the 1820s and 1830s extended to a wholesale retreat on the part of the colonial state from its older, effectively permissive approach to convict marriage and family formation. The established approach – introduced by Phillip in 1788

[137]

and designed to promote marriage wherever and whenever possible – had persisted until at least the end of the 1810s. Visiting the settlements in 1819–20, Bigge noted that the government was still extending indulgences to all convicts 'who entered into the marriage state' and that convicts continued to be 'at all times allowed to marry'.[86] All this was about to change, however. Over the period that followed, many of the established incentives to marry were withdrawn: in particular, the practice of awarding convicts tickets of leave upon marriage was abandoned.

The success of an application to marry also became increasingly dependent upon a couple's ability to meet a growing number of conditions. These included evidence of good conduct, reformed character and the capacity to maintain a family independent of state support. Most convicts were, in addition, no longer permitted to marry immediately upon their arrival but were required to serve at least part of their sentence in order even to become eligible for consideration. At the same time, petitions to marry were subjected to increasingly formalised administrative procedures and to growing state scrutiny, and partly as a result, they were more likely to fail. A series of associated reforms heightened the state's control of convict family relations more generally, helping to determine such matters as their access to their children and the prospects of family reunion. Cumulatively, these changes meant that convict access to marriage, family and private life would become progressively more delayed, restricted and tenuous.

The impact on convict women, who had previously been largely concentrated in and around their own households, was particularly striking. The proportion of women convicts under sentence who were married fell precipitously from the early 1820s onwards, from an average of 44.8 per cent in 1822 and 1823 to just 7.4 per cent throughout the decade from 1832 to 1842.[87] As we saw in chapter three, large numbers of women transported in the first two decades had married and effectively left the convict system within months, and in some cases weeks, of their arrival. From the early 1820s, few women would escape so easily. The majority of those who arrived between 1824 and 1842 would spend at least three to four years in assigned service. Four out of ten remained assigned for between five and six years and over a quarter were still assigned some six to seven years after their arrival.[88] A profound restructuring of female convict experience had occurred.

While the decline of early marriage partly reflected growing colonial demand for female convict labour, it was also the product of conscious state policy. Throughout his term in office, Arthur endeavoured to prevent convict women from marrying 'as soon as they arrived in the colony'. Instead, he explained, all women were made 'subject to the punishment of being placed in assigned service at least for two or three years'.[89] A series of rules governing tickets of leave and pardons helped to achieve this. In 1829, these were supplemented by a new regulation dictating that a woman convict could only petition for permission to marry once she had completed a minimum of twelve months in assigned service without committing an offence.[90] The quick marriages and minimal female assignment of the first period had been replaced by longer periods of servitude and delayed family formation. From this point onwards, it was simply no longer the case, in Van Diemen's Land at least, that 'female convicts under sentence ... could marry without difficulty'.[91]

The experiences of male convicts were similarly transformed. Once again, this was a combined product of the shifting convict labour regime and of government policies specifically targeting marriage and family formation. The majority of convicts – and particularly those who were married and who had children – previously had been allowed at least some free time to work for wages. The abolition of these rights in the 1820s directly undermined the material foundations of the convict household. Only convicts holding tickets of leave now had the legal right to work for wages, but tickets of leave were now no longer automatically issued upon marriage. This situation was made worse by the introduction of a number of associated reforms. In particular, married convict men increasingly were unlikely to be given permission to live with their families. Only in exceptional circumstances (and then under very strict conditions), Arthur reported in the early 1830s, did he ever now allow men to reside anywhere other than the government barracks or their place of assigned service.[92] The related practice of assigning men to their wives also went into sharp, and decisive, decline.[93] The ability of convict men under sentence to maintain their wives and families had thus been undermined systematically. Yet, at the same time, government policy sought increasingly to reify a male breadwinner family form. From the 1820s onwards, convict men were required to provide written testimonials of their ability to support a wife as part of their petition to marry. The success or failure of any application increasingly turned upon this factor. Combined, these changes meant that convict men generally had to wait even longer than women – often until the very last years of their sentence at least when they had regained a degree of freedom and with it the ability to earn an income – before they were even in a position to begin to consider marriage.

Government, of course, had not turned its back on the idea that convicts were more likely to be reformed if married and nor would it ever. But, although Bigge shared the contemporary belief that the family was a potentially powerful redemptive site – tending to agree that marriage provided 'a corrective to vicious propensities' – he nevertheless expressed some serious anxieties about the way the current system worked.[94] In particular, the promotion of marriage did not appear to have resulted in either genuine or widespread convict reform. Instead, the use of incentives seemed to have encouraged convicts to marry for the wrong reasons. 'Great difficulty', Bigge concluded, 'is found in distinguishing between the real and pretended motives for applications of convicts to be married ... and no doubt is entertained, that the marriage obligation is contracted for the purpose of making an alteration in the civil condition of the parties'.[95] Too many convicts, in other words, were apparently marrying simply in order to be free.[96] Indeed, some convicts did not even bother to go that far: in Van Diemen's Land, Knopwood informed Bigge, men were in the habit of falsely claiming an intention to marry solely in order to receive a ticket-of-leave.[97] Faced with this kind of evidence, officials feared that the existing system was rewarding duplicity and fostering a largely instrumentalist and thus surface commitment to the family form.

The state's pursuit of pro-family policies likewise appeared to be at odds with transportation's ability to punish and deter. Inspired by their hopes of marrying and making a fresh start in the colonies, women, in particular, appeared, in Bigge's view, to have decidedly limited reasons to fear a sentence of transportation. 'The moral effects of separation from their native country are less sensibly felt by the female convicts'; 'their minds', Bigge concluded, 'are more elevated by the prospects before them, than depressed by the recollection of those they have just quitted'.[98] Marriage and family also seemed to confer inappropriate freedoms upon convicts by cutting sentences prematurely short. Knowing that they would almost certainly be immediately assigned to their husbands upon their arrival and thus effectively set free, Bigge believed that some women were even deliberately committing crimes in order to be transported. Men who married colonial women or whose wives and families travelled out to Australia to join them could anticipate similar freedoms. 'Your presence here will free me from bondage', convict Thomas McCulloch wrote from Sydney to his wife in Scotland in 1821, 'as any man's wife that comes out here ... can take her husband from Government employment or being a servant'.[99] This kind of 'abrupt' alteration in civil status was, in Bigge's view, inconsistent 'with a just notion of punishment'.[100] The family, it seemed, had, in a variety of different ways, become an overly easy and rapid route to colonial freedom.

By extending and prolonging the separation of convicts from their families and friends and delaying the processes of household formation more generally the state also hoped to increase the sense of loss and disorientation created by transportation. One way of achieving this was to make greater efforts to segregate newly arrived convicts from family and friends already in the settlements. Bigge was clearly appalled by the latter's apparent current ease of access to the former. Whenever a convict ship arrived in the harbour, boats immediately sailed out to greet it and when the convicts were disembarked large crowds gathered to welcome them. Despite attempts to police the disembarkation process, Bigge reported that convicts were still able to communicate freely with the 'people in the streets', to exchange property and make 'hasty . . . bargains' with them, and to experience the 'noisy and joyous recognition of their friends'.[101] There were mutual benefits in such moments: while newly arrived convicts were understandably keen to recognise a familiar face in the crowd and to seek advice which would help them in their new lives, the prospect of news from home and the chance that a relative, friend or neighbour from the past might be among the new arrivals was also of significance to those who had already been in the settlements some time.

Bigge was particularly perturbed by the ways in which some convicts, male and female, used the time immediately after their arrival to their advantage. 'The interval that elapses between the arrival of a convict ship . . . and the debarkation of the convicts is one that affords the fullest exercise of their ingenuity in the arts of imposition and concealment, and also in devising the means of their future indulgence', he reported.[102] Communication between ship and shore was central to this because informal information-gathering exercises, mirroring but undermining the state's mechanisms of muster and interview, helped convicts to work out how to position themselves to best effect.[103] By such means, mechanics keen to avoid government work were advised to deny they had a trade, while others, hoping to stay in Sydney, were told to claim that they were skilled.[104] Women were allegedly encouraged to mislead Convict Department clerks about their marital status, some in the hope that this would clear the path to future colonial unions.[105] Others used this time to invest any capital or sell property that they had brought with them, and many relied upon the advice of friends and family already resident in the colony to maximise their profits. Finally, convicts also used these contacts to ensure that they would be assigned to particular people and places and to secure 'advantageous situations in the service of their friends'.[106]

This manipulation of the labour market and the convict system not only clashed with the convict worker's coerced status, it also undermined transportation's psychological effects. Preventing newly arrived convicts from communicating with the colony's inhabitants would, Bigge asserted, help to increase the 'salutary apprehension and uncertainty' many felt on arrival 'respecting their future fate' and would 'open their minds', in particular, to 'one of the worst characters of their condition, the hardships they have to endure in the service of an unknown master'.[107] Determined to suppress these forms of convict communication, Bigge urged extra vigilance to prevent boats from 'hovering round the convict ships' while they remained in harbour and argued for sentries to be posted on deck and for convicts to be disembarked only under guard.[108] Convicts were also no longer to be allowed to make their own accommodation arrangements upon their arrival. As things currently stood, Bigge reported, the 'first resort' of many convicts upon their disembarkation was 'naturally' to the homes of 'their relations, or to their former associates in crime'. 'The effect of restraint is thus lost', he commented, 'at the moment when it ought to be most sensibly felt'.[109] In future, he instructed, convicts who were not assigned immediately to private service were to be systematically confined. Noting that this had begun to happen in Sydney as a result of the opening of the Hyde Park Barracks in 1819, Bigge ordered that immediate steps be taken to construct similar facilities in Van Diemen's Land.[110]

The attention that female convict ships attracted was particularly intense and so required even tighter supervision. 'All the precautions that I have already recommended in preventing access to the ships . . . are doubly necessary in the case of a female convict ship', Bigge remarked.[111] He was consequently impressed to discover that Sorell had already made the disembarkation of female convicts a matter of his own personal overview and command, and he recommended the extension of this practice throughout the settlements. In the years thereafter, the Van Demonian state would become so determined to prevent contact between the colonists and newly transported female convicts, in particular, that it began to disembark the women only under cover of night. By the late 1820s, four o'clock in the morning had become a preferred time.[112] These early morning landings appear to have been informed both by a desire to 'protect' and shelter the women and by a determination to prevent them from using the moment of their disembarkation to make contact with friends, family or prospective male partners. It was this latter aim that almost certainly informed the recommendation that the women be forced to disembark in the drab regulation dresses provided by the Naval Board. There was, Bigge argued, nothing 'more unsuitable' than 'the appearance' that the women had previously been allowed 'to make on their arrival'.

They should, in future, he insisted, be prevented from using 'their property and dress' in any way which might help to afford them 'the means of present indulgence'. They were thus to be removed from the boats and taken to their 'places of servitude in the naval dresses' and 'in no others'.[113]

A range of additional measures was implemented to separate convicts from their families and to prevent them from moving straight from the boat into their own colonial homes. From this point onwards, when members of the same family were transported they were much more likely to be kept apart. Eleanor Owen and her husband, transported to Van Diemen's Land in 1825, were among the first to suffer under these new conventions. Assigned upon their arrival to different places of service, it was only some six years later, and as her husband's sentence drew to an end, that Eleanor gained permission to live with him once again.[114]

An increasingly intransigent approach was also taken when family members, transported to the different colonies, petitioned either to be transferred from New South Wales to Van Diemen's Land or vice versa. In Colonial Secretary Burnett's view, these petitions ought to be refused: it was, he explained, often the Secretary of State's deliberate intention that families should be divided in this way 'as a punishment'.[115] To send 'married prisoner couples' to the same colony was self-evidently impolitic, one colonial newspaper agreed, because it directly undermined efforts 'to make transportation a punishment'.[116] By keeping couples apart, it was also possible to crush the idea that transportation was simply an alternative form of emigration. Thus, although Arthur believed that it was always in principle 'desirable' for a husband to 'be with his wife', he nevertheless considered the separation of convict couples to be part of the debt that they owed 'to public justice'. It was, he explained, no part of government's design to allow 'these people to become comfortable settlers'.[117]

Part of government's broader purpose was to prevent convicts from evading assignment and thus effectively cutting their sentences short. One of the primary aims here was to shore up transportation's ability to deter. Thus, Arthur's decision to prevent convict women from marrying 'as soon as they arrived in the colony' was, he explained, informed by his belief that such a policy would only encourage 'the promotion of crime' in Britain.[118] Governor Franklin was of like mind: no convict woman, he asserted, should ever be allowed to marry 'until she has first passed through a period of suffering and privation'. 'It is obvious', he explained, that the 'contrary course ... would be destructive of all deterring example to her own sex at home, and an absolute encouragement to the commission of crime'.[119] Much the

[143]

same reasoning underpinned the decision effectively to abandon the practice of assigning convict men to their wives. This form of assignment had been largely phased out by the early 1830s on the grounds, as Sir Francis Forbes, Chief Justice of New South Wales, explained, that it had tended 'to do away with the punishment' imposed by a sentence of transportation.[120] It was, as a result, much less possible for men to appeal, as Thomas McCulloch had once done, for their wives to travel to the colonies to free them from bondage and it also became more difficult for convict men to secure their liberty from service by marrying free colonial women.

The determination to make all convicts undergo a period of servitude upon their arrival in the colony also had a profound impact upon state attitudes towards parenthood. While the childbearing capacities of female convicts had been much remarked upon and celebrated throughout the first period of settlement, convict women under sentence who had children were increasingly viewed as problematic. Employers were rarely willing to take mothers as servants and, although state-run orphan schools had existed in New South Wales since the late 1790s, Van Diemen's Land lacked such facilities.[121] In their absence it was virtually impossible to adopt a comprehensive policy towards convict women by making them all equally available for assignment. Thus, when convict Honor Baldwin arrived in 1827, Arthur conceded that he had no choice but to 'stretch . . . our present regulations'. 'It will', the Principal Superintendent of Convicts informed him, 'be almost impossible for me to get her into service from her having brought three children with her'. The problem was more easily resolved in Baldwin's case than most by the fact that her husband James had travelled out to join her in the colony. A seaman by trade, he had worked his passage on the same boat that had transported his wife. In the event, Arthur chose not only to assign Honor to her husband – a position in which she saw out her entire life sentence – but he also took steps to ensure that James had the means to support his wife and family by appointing him the 'keeper' of a 'small gaol in the interior'.[122]

These kinds of individual solutions were, however, by their very nature ad hoc and piecemeal and, by requiring government to 'stretch' the rules, they tended actively to undermine attempts to construct a more comprehensive and uniform system of convict discipline. Determined to overcome this, government approved a plan to build two orphan institutions – one for boys, the other for girls – on the outskirts of Hobart. From the moment that these opened in the late 1820s, the children of convicts were much more likely to be institutionalised.[123] Although the schools were designed to perform a range of functions, one of their key tasks was to facilitate the assignment of convict mothers. Thus, in July 1828, fourteen of the eighteen children who arrived with the convict women on the *Mermaid* were placed in the orphan schools and their mothers made available for service.[124] By sending the infants of convict women who became pregnant while in assigned service to the orphan schools once they had been weaned, it was, Arthur noted, also now possible to subject these mothers to punishment for their illegitimate pregnancies before making them once again 'disposable to' the settlers as servants. These measures, Arthur noted, had the additional benefit of preventing both the convict woman *and* her child becoming a financial 'burden upon the Colonial Government'.[125]

The creation of state-run child-care facilities increased the government's ability to put convict discipline first. Exceptions to the rules no longer had to be made where convicts had children to care for and families to maintain: punishment could, as a result, be more uniformly applied. This new situation also shaped the state's approach towards convict fatherhood. Ann Banks's petition to have her convict husband, William, returned to the family home in Hobart from a period of colonial punishment was, as a result, denied despite the fact that she had two young children, one a mere fortnight old, and that she was, in William's absence, living in 'a state of absolute destitution'. 'When the wives of convicts under punishment are unable to support themselves', Arthur advised the Colonial Secretary, the men were not to be returned to their families but their children instead admitted to the orphan schools. This was to be considered the governing principle in all such cases: no indulgence, Arthur emphasised, should 'ever' be 'granted to the prejudice of convict discipline'.[126]

In an effort to retain a modicum of control over their personal lives convicts, not surprisingly, attempted to resist and evade these kinds of measures. Thus, despite government instructions, issued in the late 1820s, that employers return all convict servants to the house of correction immediately their pregnancies were discovered, there to undergo punishment once the baby had been weaned, some men and women continued to try to circumvent these regulations by making their own private arrangements for the birth and subsequent care of their child. A number of female convicts consequently were able to avoid both imprisonment and separation from their infants because their lovers – almost certainly at times with the active collusion of the woman's employer – paid for accommodation and nursing during the labour and for independent child-care arrangements after the birth.[127] Other men did their best to marry a woman when she became pregnant and some even cited the imminent birth of the child as additional grounds for the state to grant their petition. Ex-convict Thomas Hagan considered Mary Sawyer's pregnancy sufficient grounds to hope that government would overturn its previous decision – taken some six months earlier – to refuse their application to marry. In '*the expectation*' that his first memorial would be '*complied with*', he explained to Arthur, '*a connection*' had '*been formed which is likely to end with an increase in number*'. Pointing both to his 'industry as a bricklayer' and to the good influence of his future wife's 'sober habits', he argued that the marriage would not only enable him to support Mary and their child but that it would also make him 'happy'. Unimpressed, Arthur refused to budge.[128]

The case of William Skelley and Jessie Thompson provides a particularly poignant example of these kinds of convict struggles to retain some control over personal and family matters. In November 1834, Skelley (an ex-convict) simply removed convict Jessie Thompson from her assigned service in order to care for her during the birth of their child, and it was only when the baby was a month old that she eventually returned. When she did so, her master Thomas Fenton complained, 'she was ornamented with every description of flowing white ribbon' and seemed determined to do no work. While this lack of industry almost certainly reflected the fact that Thompson was busy caring for her baby, it seems likely that she was also attempting to exact revenge upon her master because he had, several months before, not only refused to support her petition to marry but also withdrawn his permission for Skelley to visit her. With the added complication of a new baby, it is possible that Thompson believed Fenton might now be forced to acquiesce: her master was certainly convinced that her behaviour was deliberately designed 'to wear me out'.[129]

A week after returning to her service, however, their baby became ill and died. Skelley, who lived nearby, returned immediately and, despite the fact that Fenton had banned him from his property, he demanded to see his baby's body. He then accused Fenton of murdering the infant, declared that 'it should not be buried until a doctor had seen it' and promised to 'see into the rights of it [even] if it cost him £100' and even to 'write to the Governor'. Although these attempts to force an inquest failed, Fenton was unable, despite his best efforts, to prevent Skelley from accompanying Jessie either to the funeral or to the subsequent wake. Neither ultimately was he able to stand in the way of their marriage – later that same year – a union that would lead, in 1838, to the birth of their second child, this time in their own home.[130] The predicament faced by Skelley and Thompson not only reminds us of the personal toll which the shift to greater servitude

took upon convicts' intimate and family lives but also of the willingness of convict and ex-convict men to provide and care for their partners
and children. These kinds of images and accounts – although often
surviving in only fleeting and fragmentary form in the archives –
provide an important counterbalance to the still far too well established
idea that convict men were, by virtue of their class and criminality,
almost universally anti-familial and misogynistic brutes.[131]

The reorientation of official attitudes and policies towards marriage
and the family had thus enabled the state substantially to enhance
its authority over convicts. Preventing them from cutting their period
of servitude short was, however, only the start of the process. Marriage
was also reconceived as 'an indulgence' and a 'favour', with the result,
colonist John Barnes explained, that permission to marry was only
ever granted to 'a deserving convict', one 'who has been some time
in the colony, and whose conduct has been generally correct'.[132] Making
hopes of marriage, parenthood and family reunion increasingly dependent upon sustained good conduct in service substantially extended
the state's ability to discipline convict workers. Recognising these
kinds of imperatives, convict couples repeatedly sought to emphasise
their credentials as reformed individuals and good colonial workers.
George Bagshaw and Mary Sullivan were typical. Petitioning Arthur
for permission to 'be united in the Bond of Matrimony', they asked
him to take into consideration 'their length of servitude' and stressed
that 'their conduct' in their service had been 'generally steady,
industrious and sober'.[133] The new rules dictated that all petitions for
permission to marry and for related indulgences had to be forwarded
to the Colonial Secretary via the convict's employer. One's master or
mistress was also expected to provide a written testimonial of support
– without this a petition was highly unlikely to succeed. This gave
masters and mistresses enhanced powers over convict workers,
tightening their disciplinary hold by rendering convict servants who
wished to marry or be reunited with a spouse heavily dependent upon
the goodwill of the employer.

The link between the new approach to convict families and colonial
labour discipline was particularly clearly delineated in the regulations
guiding female applications to marry: from 1829 onwards, a convict
woman could only petition for permission to marry once she had
served twelve months in the *same* service without 'any fault being
recorded against her'.[134] Welcoming this measure, the colonial press
highlighted its powerful disciplinary potential. 'This is a very judicious
regulation', the *Colonist* asserted; it has the power 'to induce all female
prisoners, who have any regard for their own welfare, to conduct
themselves properly, while in their respective service'. It must, the

paper urged, be uniformly and systematically applied.[135] Employers used the regulation carefully and deliberately to reward the good conduct of their servants and to punish those who failed. 'I am known to be . . . most anxious to promote marriage', the Reverend W.H. Browne noted, 'as is evident from the number of persons married from my service'. He was, however, unwilling to sanction the marriage of his assigned convict servant Bridget Kelly to Valentine Soper, a ticket-of-leave man. The 'indulgence' of marriage should never 'be given without some reasonable period of good conduct', Browne asserted, and, believing that Kelly's conduct in his service had not been good enough to deserve it, he refused to recommend her petition.[136]

The new rules placed convict women desirous of marriage under intense pressure and onerous constraint. 'Very few' women were able 'to accomplish' the 'twelve months good behaviour' in their service which the regulation required of them, settler Peter Murdock asserted.[137] Josiah Spode, Superintendent of Convicts, likewise reported that it was an 'utter impossibility' for female convict servants to continue for 'long periods . . . without exhibiting such conduct and committing such offences as would necessarily preclude their Mistresses recommending them' for indulgence. As domestic servants, he explained, they had to endure an almost 'constant' and 'vigilant controul' and this, combined with the fact that many of the women resented 'working under compulsion', created a state of 'constant warfare' between their employers and themselves.[138] For a woman to stay in the same service and be industrious and obedient for a full twelve months was thus no mean task. This was the case not only during the year that the woman was required to wait before she submitted her application but also for the weeks and sometimes months that it then took the state to process and reply to it. Even when permission had been granted, many couples remained in a state of anxious limbo for a time because colonial clergymen were often slow to read the banns. All it took for the prospects of a marriage to fail was one small step out of line during any of these waiting periods. It was this which caused Jane Turnley's wedding to be called off at the last minute: her hard-won permission to marry was suspended when, as a result of a single act of misconduct in her service, she was ordered to wait until her mistress was once again willing to furnish 'a favourable report of her behaviour'.[139]

Access to marriage and family life was also considered a powerful weapon in the disciplining of convict men. This was particularly the case for men serving longer sentences. In colonist John Barnes's view, the knowledge that they were only ever likely to gain permission either to gain a ticket of leave, to marry or to 'get a wife from home' if they conducted themselves well in their service made men sentenced to fourteen years and to life more 'malleable'. A seven-year convict, by comparison, often had less to lose by being 'troublesome' because, Barnes explained, he 'knew that there was a certain period at which his punishment would cease and he would become a free man'.[140] As with female convicts, the success of a man's petition to marry depended on his being able to furnish a clean conduct record and a good character reference from his employer. Although many men applied to marry after their period of assignment had ended, they were still required to furnish their employer's written testimonial as part of their application. In an attempt to strengthen their case, some men also provided references from other local authority figures, including chaplains, magistrates and the police. The desire to be married not only increased the pressure to conform at work but also tended to make convicts and ex-convicts careful of their conduct more generally and deepened their dependence upon local power and patronage networks.

Permission to marry could, as with the women, also be suspended or removed from a man even once it had been granted if he committed any kind of offence. Even the suspicion of misconduct was, in some circumstances, sufficient. Permission for convicts Charles Wicks and Ellen McKay to be married, for example, was suspended – despite the fact that the banns had already been called twice – when it was discovered that Wicks recently had been charged with sheep-stealing. The fact that he had been acquitted by the Supreme Court was not enough to dissuade the authorities from preventing the wedding: the hint of a dishonest character was all that it took for the district police magistrate to recommend that their permission to marry be revoked.[141]

Male convicts who wished to marry or be reunited with family members at an earlier stage of their sentence were particularly heavily dependent upon their employers. Unlike convict women who generally were released from their assigned service upon their marriage if their new husband either was holding a ticket of leave or was free, convict men who were still in the assignment stage of their sentence remained in service regardless of the civil status of their wife and were consequently only able to proceed with their plans for marriage if they gained their master's written undertaking to support both their prospective spouse and any offspring for the duration of their sentence. The alternative was for a man to wait until he was in a position to apply for a ticket of leave, but this entailed at least four years for a man sentenced to seven years' transportation, six years for a man sentenced to fourteen years and eight years for men sentenced to life.[142]

Once again, the regulations guiding convict marriage arrangements had obvious labour disciplining functions. To inspire a master to undertake to support a man's wife and children a male convict servant had to render himself invaluable and be able to prove, over a sustained period of time, his capacity for loyalty and industry. As the New South Wales settler James Mudie explained, it was only when a master had a male convict servant that he was 'anxious to keep and whom he believes to be well behaved' that he was willing to grant him this kind of permission to marry.[143] Mudie, for one, also provided these men with the materials and time off work to build private huts for their brides upon his estate and with additional rations for the new family.[144] These kinds of official and unofficial provisions, the sense of gratitude as well as the physical attachment to a new home that they inspired, almost certainly helped to stabilise colonial labour relations by tying some male workers, both during and after their sentence, to particular masters and estates.

Exactly the same reformatory and disciplinary imperatives drove the convict family reunion scheme. Permission to petition government to have a spouse and children brought to the colony from Britain and Ireland at the state's expense increasingly depended upon evidence of good conduct. From Sorell's period onwards, petitions were only transmitted to London after enquiries by the colonial police had confirmed the convict's character.[145] In the state's eyes, family reunion provided both an excellent incentive and a useful reward for reformed conduct. Repeatedly extolling the scheme's disciplinary benefits, Sorell explained that 'the presence of their wives and children so much contributes to the commencement or the confirmation of habits of reform and industry [that] even the acceptance of the petition and the expectation thereby created that its prayer would be successful, has in some instances caused an immediate change of conduct'.[146]

During Arthur's period, the reunion scheme became an increasingly sophisticated disciplinary mechanism. Regulations introduced in 1826 prevented convicts from applying for family reunion immediately on their arrival in the colony by instituting a minimum twelve-month waiting period during which time an applicant's conduct might be assessed. Prior to this point, as Arthur explained, 'no attention' had been 'paid to the period of a Prisoner's residence' because it had 'always been considered desirable that their Families should join them as early as possible'.[147] From the mid to late 1820s onwards, petitioners were also increasingly required to include evidence of their ability to maintain a family independent of state support; something which the colonial government, under pressure to keep spending within limits, was increasingly anxious to police.[148] This requirement was

[150]

substantially stepped up when, in 1829, regulations made it mandatory for all applicants to provide the written guarantee of their employer to 'receive and maintain' the convict's 'wife and family' until 'the husband shall be eligible for a ticket of leave'.[149] Ticket-of-leave holders – similarly required to provide evidence of their ability to support their families – were often obliged to enter into similar arrangements.

These measures brought the reunion scheme into line with the regulations governing convict marriage and once again tended to make convicts heavily dependent upon the combined goodwill of employers and the state. Success under the scheme often demanded high levels of self-regulation and constraint. Even the slightest slip could stand in the way of family reunion. Petitioning for his wife and seven children, aged between four and fifteen years, to be brought to the colony, convict Richard Hurst noted that reunion with them was 'the only consolation' he could possibly look forward to or 'receive'. 'This convict', Josiah Spode noted with disdain on Hurst's petition, 'prays that his wife and family be sent out as the only consolation he can receive; but, as I perceive he was not only disorderly, but *drunk* on the 30 June last I presume, he finds some consolation in Public Houses – refused'.[150] The pressure upon convicts who were desperate to see their families again must have been immense at times. Convict Thomas Flanagan's desperation to bring his wife and eight children from Ireland in the late 1840s and early 1850s, for example, is palpable. His fears for them were undoubtedly amplified by news of the Famine and his knowledge that they were living 'in great distress'. 'He is', his master William Archer reported, attempting to intervene with government on his servant's behalf, 'a hardworking, sober, well conducted man' but 'at more than fifty years of age, is denying himself comforts, to enable him to send a further sum for their relief'.[151]

Time was an additional pressure in these kinds of cases: convicts were only eligible to apply for family reunion under this scheme while they remained under sentence. Those who waited until they were free to petition for reunion had, as ex-convict John Barry would discover to his cost, waited too long. He had, he noted in his petition, left a wife and four children in Ireland in 'a manner unprovided for and unprotected' when he had been transported some twelve years before. Now free by servitude, Barry had 'a very anxious desire to have the society of his dear wife and family restored to him once more after such a long and painful absence'. He was, he reported, renting a small farm in the district of New Norfolk and was able to support his wife and family but not to pay for their passages to the colony. Despite a string of testimonials in his favour, confirming his character as reformed and respectable, Arthur noted that Barry was not eligible under the reunion scheme because he was no longer a prisoner.[152]

Unlike applications for marriage, then, which normally were submitted either towards the end of a man's sentence or after it had finished, the desire for reunion had the greatest disciplinary effect upon convict workers in the earlier stages of their sentence – those who were assigned or holding tickets of leave. Given the pressures, convicts who applied under the scheme were, not surprisingly, those who had unusually clean conduct records and favourable character references and who had in addition, in many cases, achieved a remarkably stable record of colonial employment.[153] Many, indeed, had been in the continuous service of one master since their arrival in Van Diemen's Land, and their ability to apply for permission to have their wives and children brought out from home was founded in their willingness, and the agreement of that master, to stay on in the same service for the foreseeable future. Like the regulations guiding marriage, then, the reunion scheme was designed in such a way as to bind convict workers much more tightly to their masters.

The desire for family reunion had a powerful effect upon convict women, too. The threat of separation from their children was used to discipline convict mothers confined to the female houses of correction. Those whose conduct was judged to have been good were more likely to be allowed to stay on as nurses in the children's wards after their babies had been weaned but before they had been removed to the orphan schools. Permission to remain with their children for this extended period was regarded as a reward: convict mothers considered 'it a punishment to be taken from their children and sent into assigned service', Mrs Slea, matron of the nursery ward at Cascades, reported.[154] The separation of mother and child was also undoubtedly deployed as an incentive to good conduct more generally. Those in power certainly linked the two. When a convict woman approached her in tears and informed her that she was 'breaking' her 'heart' as a result of the removal of her two children to the orphan school, Lady Denison advised her that 'if she conducted herself well . . . she would be allowed to see them'.[155] In Slea's view, the 'hope of being permitted to see their children' served as an incentive to discipline in service: it was, she claimed, often the 'only inducement' that these women had to 'conduct themselves well in assignment'.[156]

A woman's ability to visit her child in the orphan school while she remained under sentence depended upon her master or mistress giving her a pass and the necessary free time. Once again, the intimate and family concerns of convicts had become embroiled with their discipline and control at work. Keen to remain in contact with their children, some women endeavoured to bargain over their access to free time. When these attempts failed, direct conflict sometimes resulted. Thus, Ann McGregor's refusal to give convict servant Eleanor Murphy leave to 'go to the Orphan School' on the grounds that 'it was not (then) convenient' sparked a confrontation in which Murphy allegedly became 'very insolent' and ultimately refused to work.[157] Mary Lambert's belief that her mistress was being similarly unreasonable led to a total breakdown in relations. Having denied her permission to talk to a visitor who had come with news of her children confined in the orphan school, Lambert stormed through the house demanding that her mistress 'turn her in'. She would not work for her any longer, Lambert declared, because 'her place would not suit her if she could not see proper who came to give her an account of her children'. After continuing, over several more days, to demand that her assignment be terminated and that she be returned to government, Lambert finally took matters into her own hands and absconded.[158]

For most convict mothers, hopes of being reunited with their children in the long term depended not only upon conduct in the workplace but also upon their ability to marry and re-establish a family home in the colony. In order to reclaim their children from the state, convict mothers had to produce a certificate of good conduct and of their ability to support them.[159] This had a dual effect. First, like the regulations governing marriage, it heightened a woman's dependence upon a positive character reference from her employer. Freedom – whether through marriage, a ticket of leave, or a pardon – was key to any long-term hope of family reunion. While a woman remained in assignment and under sentence she stood next to no chance of successfully reclaiming her children. Second, the need to prove one's ability to support a child almost certainly encouraged women to seek out, and formalise, relationships with men. Lower female wages made it harder for a single woman to convince government that she had the ability to maintain a family. Dominant-class models of gender and family reinforced this by equating feminine respectability and morality with dependence. Convict women who married were therefore in a better position to apply to have their children taken out of the orphan school than those who did not.

Much the same principles governed attempts by convict women to have their children brought to the colony from Britain and Ireland. Although convict women were eligible under the family reunion scheme, relatively few applied: most of those who did had waited until they were married. Jane Street was in many ways typical: transported in 1827, it was late 1831 before she was in a position to petition for her two children to be brought to the colony. Significantly, her application was submitted within months of her marriage to John Brown. Although Street stressed that she too was able and willing to contribute to family income, it was Brown alone, a free man and a shoemaker by trade, who was in a position to sign the official guarantee that the children would 'not in any way become chargeable to the Government after their arrival'.[160] If the requirements of the family reunion scheme pushed men towards a breadwinning role, they tended to propel women into marriage.

*   *   *

Historians have long tended to situate women outside the boundaries of the convict system, arguing that the formal logic and lived experiences of exile were both fundamentally differentiated by gender. It was Anne Summers who took this argument furthest when she claimed that two entirely separate systems in fact existed. The women, she argued, were sent for primarily sexual and reproductive purposes and their experiences were consequently radically different to those of the men. Their punishment, she famously asserted, 'comprised transportation plus enforced whoredom'.[161] As we saw in chapter three, marriage and family formation had, indeed, been a key government concern throughout the early years of settlement, with the result that the convict system was profoundly marked by gender. The system as it developed post-Bigge was, by contrast, characterised by a series of striking parallels between the treatment and experiences of men and women. Although ideas about gender remained influential and continued to exercise a powerful influence over state policy, the many areas of overlap between men and women tended to offset many of the resulting dissimilarities.

This was so for two key reasons. First, like their male counterparts, female convicts were increasingly regarded as a bonded labour force, with the result that they too became subject to intensified servitude and to heightened discipline and punishment. Imperatives of class and coercion had come to the fore. Second, while family formation remained a key part of the system's ultimate aims, marriage, parenthood and domesticity became ever more difficult and drawn-out ambitions for convicts to achieve. Private and intimate relations increasingly became matters of public policy. Ensnared in a web of state regulations and constraints, relationships, families and households had become ever more central to the state's ability to control and discipline convicts. One result of this was that personal and supposedly private issues such as sex, childbirth and marriage were transformed into arenas of conflict and contestation, both between assigned servants and their employers and between convicts and the state. Convict courtship, sex and love had, in other words, become sites of class conflict. Thus, although the system had in some ways become less differentiated by gender, control of convict gender and sexual relations had nevertheless become increasingly central to the exercise of power.

Notes

1   On the rationale for sending Bigge to the settlements see: John Ritchie, *Punishment and profit: the reports of Commissioner John Bigge on the colonies of New South Wales and Van Diemen's Land, 1822–1823* (Melbourne: Heinemann, 1970).
2   On execution see: V.A.C Gatrell, *The hanging tree: execution and the English people* (Oxford: Oxford University Press, 1994); and J.A. Sharpe, *Judicial punishment in England* (London: Faber, 1990). On post-war crime rates see: V.A.C. Gatrell & T.B. Hadden, 'Criminal statistics and their interpretation', in E. A. Wrigley (ed.), *Nineteenth-century society* (Cambridge: Cambridge University Press, 1972), pp. 336–96.
3   Charles Bateson, *The convict ships* (Glasgow: Brown, Son & Ferguson, 1959), pp. 381–95.
4   Bathurst cited in Ritchie, *Punishment and profit*, p. 63.
5   Christopher Bayly, *Imperial meridian: the British Empire and the world* (London: Longman, 1989), pp. 160–2.
6   'Report of the Commissioner of Inquiry into the state of the colony of New South Wales', *BPP* XX (448), 1822, p. 157.
7   George Arthur, *Defence of transportation* (London: George Cowie, 1835), p. 106; *HRA* III, 7, p. 299.
8   Arthur, *Defence*, p. 36. See also: George Arthur, 'Select Committee on Transportation', *BPP* XIX (518), 1837, p. 285.
9   Arthur, *Defence*, p. 37.
10 Arthur, *BPP* XIX (518), 1837, pp. 286, 298.
11 *HRA* III, 8, p. 726.
12 'Despatch from Lieutenant Governor Sir J. Franklin October 1837 relative to the present system of convict discipline in Van Diemen's Land', *BPP* XLII (309), 1837–38, p. 109.
13 John Tosh, *A man's place: masculinity and the middle-class home in Victorian England* (New Haven, CT: Yale University Press, 1999), p. 29.
14 Anne McClintock, *Imperial leather: race, gender and sexuality in the colonial contest* (New York: Routledge, 1995), pp. 31, 34–5. Emphasis in original.
15 Jeremy Bentham, 'Panopticon versus New South Wales', in John Bowring (ed.), *The works of Jeremy Bentham* (Edinburgh: William Tait, 1843), Vol. IV, pp. 174–5.
16 Henry Phibbs Fry, *A letter to the householders of Hobarton, on the effects of transportation, and on the moral condition of the colony* (Hobart: John Moore, 1847), pp. 12–13.
17 AOT CSO 22/50, p. 355.
18 *Ibid.*, pp. 187–8.
19 Franklin, *BPP* XLII (309), 1837–38, p. 109.
20 *Ibid.*, p. 109.
21 *BPP* XX (448), 1822, p. 19; *HRA* III, 3, p. 274; *HRA* III, 4, p. 141.
22 *BPP* XX (448), 1822, p. 19; *HRA* III, 4, p. 141.
23 *BPP* XX (448), 1822, p. 15.
24 See, for example: Government Orders, *Hobart Town Gazette*, 16 August 1817, 3 January 1818, 28 March 1818, 4 July 1818, 29 August 1818, 10 October 10 1818, 1 May 1819, 1 July 1820, 6 January 1821 & 5 January 5 1822.
25 *BPP* XX (448), 1822, p. 171.

26 Bigge spent several months of his time in the Australian settlements visiting Van Diemen's Land. For the evidence gathered by him see: *HRA* III, 3, Section C and *HRA* III, 4, pp. 627–856.
27 *HRA* III, 3, p. 247.
28 *HRA* III, 3, p. 248.
29 See for example: *HRA* III, 3, pp. 358, 389–90, 404.
30 *BPP* XX (448), 1822, p. 43.
31 *HRA* III, 3, pp. 231–2; *BPP* XX (448), 1822, p. 42.
32 *HRA* III, 3, p. 219.
33 *Ibid.*, pp. 313–15.
34 *Ibid.*, p. 248. See also pp. 219, 350–1.
35 *Ibid.*, pp. 313–14.
36 *Ibid.*, pp. 220, 231–2; *BPP* XX (448), 1822, p. 42.
37 On the police see: Stefan Petrow, 'Policing in a penal colony: Governor Arthur's police system in Van Diemen's Land, 1826–1836', *Law & History Review*, 18:2 (2000), pp. 351–95.
38 *HRA* III, 6, pp. 366–7.
39 Franklin, *BPP* XLII (309), 1837–38, p. 109. On the benefits of summary jurisdiction see: Arthur to Bathurst, 26 March 1827, GO 25/3.
40 On the disciplinary role of penal stations see: Raymond Evans & William Thorpe, 'Power, punishment and penal labour: *Convict workers* and Moreton Bay', *Australian Historical Studies*, 25:98 (1992), pp. 90–111.
41 *Hobart Town Gazette*, 12 August 1826.
42 Appendix 1, *BPP* XIX (518), 1837, p. 4.
43 Hamish Maxwell-Stewart, '*Convict workers*, "penal labour" and Sarah Island: life at Macquarie Harbour, 1822–1834', in Ian Duffield and James Bradley (eds), *Representing convicts: new perspectives on convict forced labour migration* (London: Leicester University Press, 1995), p. 145.
44 Appendix 1, *BPP* XIX (518), 1837, p. 4.
45 *HRA* III, 4, p. 287.
46 On the impact of similar measures in New South Wales in this period see: W.M. Robbins, 'Spatial escape and the Hyde Park convict barracks', *Journal of Australian Colonial History*, 6:1 (2004), pp. 81–122.
47 *Hobart Town Gazette*, 7 October 1826; Appendix 1, *BPP* XIX (518), 1837, p. 18.
48 *BPP* XX (448), 1822, p. 168.
49 *Ibid.*, pp. 2–3.
50 *HRA* III, 5, pp. 128–9. *HRA* III, 6, pp. 126–7, 157–60.
51 Appendix 1, *BPP* XIX (518), 1837, p. 59.
52 *HRA* III, 2, p. 310.
53 *Ibid.*, p. 310.
54 'Select Committee on Transportation', *BPP* XXII (669), 1837–38, p. 311.
55 *HRA* III, 2, p. 273.
56 *Ibid.*, pp. 299–300, 485.
57 *HRA* III, 3, p. 408.
58 Government Order, *Hobart Town Gazette*, 1 July 1820. See also: Government Orders, *Hobart Town Gazette*, 3 January 1818 and 28 March 1818.
59 *HRA* III, 2, pp. 299–300, 485.
60 *HRA* III, 3, p. 9.
61 *HRA* III, 3, p. 37.
62 Information on assignment from the ship comes from: AOT GO 25/2; ML MM 33/6, MM 33/7; AOT CSO 1, CSO 5; ML TP 21 to 34; AOT CSO 19/5, pp. 16, 20; *Hobart Town Gazette*, September 2 1820, December 22 1821, April 21 1824. Lists and information regarding appropriation from the ship survive for thirty-three of the forty-seven female convict ships that arrived between 1820 and July 1843. On the distribution of all female convicts in the colony see: 'Muster of women convicts, 1822', NA HO 10/18; 'List of female convicts, October-November 1823', NA HO 10/45; 'Nominal return of women convicts for the year ending

31 December 1832', NA HO10/48; 'Return of female convicts shewing their distribution on 31 December 1833', AOT CSO 1/700/15322; 'Nominal return of female convicts for the year ending 31 December 1835', HO 10/50; 'Muster of female convicts 30 April 1842', HO 10/51. These figures and the data from musters hereafter are calculated as a percentage of all women listed on the muster who remained fully under sentence and therefore available for assignment. Excluded are the small numbers holding tickets of leave or pardons or whose sentences had expired and those listed as missing or dead as well as the few against whose name no details were recorded. A female convict muster also exists for 1820 (NA HO 10/44) but 30 per cent of the women listed on it are entered as unknown, making it a less than reliable source. For a fuller discussion of these shifting trends in female assignment see: Kirsty Reid, 'Setting women to work: the assignment system and female convict labour in Van Diemen's Land', *Australian Historical Studies*, 34:121 (2003), pp. 1–25.

63 NA HO 10/18, HO 10/45, HO 10/48, HO 10/50, HO 10/51; AOT CSO 1/700/15332.
64 See, for example: *HRA* III, 3, pp. 54, 65, 71.
65 *HRA* III, 3, p. 450. On the inadequate provision at George Town, see: *HRA* III, 3, pp. 401, 410.
66 *HRA* III, 3, pp. 286, 467. *HRA* III, 6, pp. 284–8.
67 *BPP* XX (448), 1822, p. 74.
68 *HRA* III, 3, p. 71.
69 From the 1830s these returns were published regularly, and often weekly, in the *Hobart Town Gazette*.
70 See, in particular: Paula Byrne, *Criminal law and colonial subject: New South Wales, 1810–1830* (Cambridge: Cambridge University Press, 1993), pp. 46–8, 50–1; and R.W. Connell & T.H. Irving, *Class structure in Australian history: documents, narrative and argument* (Melbourne: Longman Cheshire, 1980), pp. 56–7.
71 Kirsty Reid, '"Contumacious, ungovernable and incorrigible": convict women and workplace resistance, Van Diemen's Land, 1820–39', in Duffield and Bradley, *Representing convicts*, pp. 106–23.
72 The domestic nature of female convict service worked both ways, however: although it tended to confine women to the house, this meant that even minor protests brought tension, ill-will and conflict into the home, and this undoubtedly encouraged some employers to compromise for the sake of some domestic peace. The experience of assigned service for women also almost certainly varied with the class position of an employer. As the colonial authorities were all too aware, in some households convict women were allowed considerable liberty, others associated openly with lower-class, and particularly ex-convict, mistresses, and some of these women even went drinking with their servants during their leisure time. See, for example, AOT CSO 22/50, pp. 307–11, 321–2.
73 Henry Widowson, *The present state of Van Diemen's Land* (London: S. Robinson, 1829), p. 56.
74 Colonist John Russell, for example, considered masters who allowed their female convicts to sleep in the outhouses at night and who let their male and female servants 'do as they like' at night to be responsible for the 'ruin' of these women. According to Russell, most settlers locked their male convict servants out of the house at night in order to protect their families; *BPP* XXII (669), 1837–38, pp. 55, 57.
75 For a discussion see: Joy Damousi, *Depraved and disorderly: female convicts, sexuality and gender in colonial Australia* (Cambridge: Cambridge University Press, 1997), p. 85.
76 On male convict suffering see: Raymond Evans and Bill Thorpe, 'Commanding men: masculinities and the convict system', *Journal of Australian Studies*, 56 (1998), pp. 17–34.
77 Richard Davis, *The Tasmanian gallows: a study of capital punishment* (Hobart: Cat & Fiddle Press, 1974).

78 On contemporary ideas about femininity and reform see: Lucia Zedner, *Women, crime and custody in Victorian England* (Oxford: Clarendon Press, 1991); Gatrell, *Hanging tree*, pp. 339–70; and Martin Wiener, *Reconstructing the criminal: culture, law and policy in England, 1830–1914* (Cambridge: Cambridge University Press, 1990), pp. 129–31.

79 John Gregory, 'Select Committee of the House of Lords appointed to enquire into the execution of the criminal law, especially respecting juvenile offenders and transportation', *BPP* VII (534), 1847, p. 519.

80 See for example: Memorandum 16 May 1836, CSO 1/365/8341; AOT CSO 1/644/14486; *HRA* III, V, p. 676.

81 On the use of 'carrot' and 'stick' in the management of coerced labour see: Stefano Fenoaltea, 'Slavery and supervision in comparative perspective: a model', *Journal of Economic History*, 44:3 (1984), pp. 635–68.

82 Josiah Spode, *BPP* XLII (309), 1837–38, p. 32.

83 *HRA* III, 7, p. 639; Appendix C, *BPP* XXII (669), 1837–38, p. 225.

84 *HRA* III, 5, p. 669.

85 There is now a substantial literature on convict resistance. See, for example: Alan Atkinson, 'Four patterns of convict protest', *Labour History*, 37 (1979), pp. 28–51; Bruce Hindmarsh, 'Scorched earth: contested power and divided loyalties on Midlands properties, 1820–1840', in Peter Chapman *et al.* (eds), *Exiles of empire: convict experience and penal policy, 1788–1852* (Hobart: Tasmanian Historical Studies, 1999), pp. 63–80; and W. Nichol, 'Malingering and convict protest', *Labour History*, 47 (1984), pp. 18–27. As we will see in chapter five, the continued use of incentives was one of the criticisms levelled against assignment in the 1830s.

86 *BPP* XX (448), 1822, p. 104.

87 NA HO 10/18, HO 10/45, HO 10/48, HO 10/50, HO 10/51; AOT CSO 1/700/15332.

88 *Ibid.*

89 Arthur, *BPP* XIX (518), 1837, p. 312.

90 Government Order, *Hobart Town Gazette*, 26 September 1829.

91 David Kent & Norma Townsend, *The convicts of the Eleanor: protest in rural England, new lives in Australia* (London: Merlin, 2002), p. 213.

92 Appendix 1, *BPP* XIX (518), 1837, p. 18.

93 Sir Francis Forbes, *BPP* XIX (518), 1837, p. 6.

94 *BPP* XX (448), 1822, p. 104.

95 *Ibid.*, p. 104.

96 This was undoubtedly one motive for marriage. For a discussion see: Marian Aveling (now Quartly), 'She only married to be free: or Cleopatra vindicated', in Norma Grieve and Patricia Grimshaw (eds), *Australian women: feminist perspectives* (Melbourne: Oxford University Press, 1981), pp. 119–33.

97 *HRA* III, 3, p. 365.

98 *BPP* XX (448), 1822, p. 11.

99 Thomas McCulloch, 'Copy of a very interesting letter from Botany Bay', broadside, 1821, National Library of Scotland, LC Fol. 73(022).

100 *BPP* XX (448), 1822, p. 104.

101 *Ibid.*, p. 17.

102 *BPP* XX (448), 1822, p. 13.

103 *Ibid.*, pp. 16–18.

104 *Ibid.*, p. 13.

105 Historians disagree as to how the women lied. Ian Donnachie suggests many 'deliberately lied ... abandoning husbands at home' to 'enhance their marriage prospects in the colony'; Ian Donnachie, '"Utterly irreclaimable": Scottish convict women and Australia, 1787–1852', *Journal of Regional & Local Studies*, 8:2 (1988), p. 2. Atkinson, by comparison, argues that 'convict women were thought to be better married than single' with the result that women 'advised each other to say on arrival that they were already married, whether they were so or not'; Alan Atkinson, 'Convicts and courtship', in Patricia Grimshaw *et al.* (eds), *Families in colonial Australia* (Sydney: George Allen & Unwin, 1985), p. 21.

106 *BPP* XX (448), 1822, pp. 16–17.
107 *Ibid.*, p. 16.
108 *Ibid.*, pp. 13, 20, 156–7.
109 *Ibid.*, p. 49.
110 *Ibid.*
111 *Ibid.*, p. 167.
112 See, for example: AOT CSO 84, pp. 185, 189, 215.
113 *BPP* XX (448), 1822, pp. 11, 167.
114 AOT CSO 1/468/10380.
115 AOT CSO 1/180/4340.
116 *Bent's News*, 17 March 1838. Colonial opinion varied on these matters, however. Others complained of the cruelty of separating husband and wife.
117 AOT CSO 1/180/4340.
118 Arthur, *BPP* XIX (518), 1837, p. 312.
119 John Franklin, *A confidential despatch from Sir John Franklin on female convicts, Van Diemen's Land* (Hobart: Sullivan's Cove, 1996), p. 48.
120 Forbes, *BPP* XIX (518), 1837, p. 6.
121 On NSW see: Dianne Snow, 'Family policy and orphan schools in early colonial Australia', *Journal of Interdisciplinary History*, 22:2 (1991), pp. 255–84.
122 AOT CSO 1/216/5194; Arthur to Hay, 8 March 1828, GO 33/3.
123 On the development of welfare facilities in VDL see: Joan Brown, *Poverty is not a crime: social services in Tasmania, 1803–1900* (Hobart: Tasmanian Historical Research Association, 1972).
124 AOT CSO 84, p. 60.
125 *HRA* III, 7, p. 499.
126 AOT CSO 1/377/8578/31, pp. 1–6.
127 The informal nature of these arrangements means, of course, that they are rarely documented in the archives, but officials were aware of the practice. See, for example: AOT CSO 5/191/4635.
128 AOT CSO 1/378/8600. Emphasis in original.
129 AOT CSO 1/761/16330. CON 52/1, p. 179.
130 AOT CSO 1/761/16330. RGD 36/2/1835/3078.
131 A series of important works have begun to challenge these kinds of conceptual frameworks. See, in particular: Grace Karskens, *The Rocks: life in early Sydney* (Carlton, Victoria: Melbourne University Press, 1997); Kent and Townsend, *Convicts of the* Eleanor; Portia Robinson, *The women of Botany Bay* (Sydney: Macquarie Library, 1989); and Christina Picton Phillipps, 'Convicts, communication and authority: Britain and New South Wales, 1810–30' (PhD thesis, University of Edinburgh, 2002).
132 John Barnes, *BPP* XXII (669), 1837–38, p. 48.
133 Petition of George Bagshaw and Mary Sullivan, AOT CON 2/1.
134 Government Regulation, *Colonial Times*, 9 October 1829.
135 *Colonist*, 7 May 1833.
136 Soper and Kelly tried to get round this by faking a reference from Browne on their petition; AOT CSO 1/886/18785.
137 Peter Murdock, *BPP* XXII (669), 1837–38, p. 118.
138 Josiah Spode, Memorandum, 31 August 1837, AOT CSO 5/134/3210.
139 Arthur to Spode, 4 August 1829, AOT CSO 84, p. 465.
140 John Barnes, *BPP* XXII (669), 1837–38, pp. 46–7.
141 AOT CSO 1/378/8600.
142 W. D. Forsyth, *Governor Arthur's convict system. Van Diemen's Land 1824–1836: a study in colonisation* (Sydney: Sydney University Press, 1935), p. 77.
143 James Mudie, *BPP* XIX (518), 1837, p. 39.
144 *Ibid.*, p. 40.
145 *HRA* III, 3, p. 54. The reunion scheme survived in different forms until the 1870s. On its first phase see: Jennifer Parrott, 'Agents of industry and civilisation: the

British government emigration scheme for convicts' wives, Van Diemen's Land 1817–1840', *Tasmanian Historical Studies*, 4:2 (1994), pp. 25–30.

146 Sorell to Hay, 25 December 1821, AOT GO 25/1. See also: *HRA* III, 3, p. 54.
147 *HRA* III, 6, p. 401.
148 *Ibid.*, pp. 401–2.
149 AOT CSO 1/377/8578/31, pp. 53–4.
150 Despite his petition's failure, Hurst's family nevertheless slipped through the state's net, arriving on the *Mellish* in 1830; AOT CSO 1/377/8578. Emphasis in original.
151 Letter from William Archer, Longford, VDL, 15 December 1851, ML TP 39.
152 Arthur nevertheless offered to enter into a private arrangement by advancing part of the money to Barry if the latter agreed to pay a portion of the costs upfront; Petition of John Barry, AOT CSO 1/377/8578.
153 In many cases, applicants were, in addition, skilled or semi-skilled workers – men, in other words, whom colonial employers were keen to keep. Around seventy surviving petitions from the 1820s and 1830s are to be found in AOT CSO 1/377/8578/31.
154 AOT CSO 22/50, pp. 226–7.
155 William Denison, *Varieties of vice-regal life* (London: Longmans, Green & Co., 1870), Vol. 1, p. 31.
156 AOT CSO 22/50, pp. 226–7.
157 Trial of Eleanor Murphy, 3 June 1846, AOT LC 251.
158 Trial of Mary Lambert, 22 July 1833, ML TP 325.
159 AOT CSO 22/50, p. 228.
160 AOT CSO 1/377/8578/31, pp. 265–9.
161 Anne Summers, *Damned whores and God's police; the colonisation of women in Australia* (Middlesex: Penguin, 1975), p. 270.

CHAPTER FIVE

'A nation of Cyprians and Turks'[1]

Convict transportation, colonial reform and the imperial body politic

Whoever had devised the plan of transporting convicts to the Australian colonies, Archbishop Richard Whately declared, had 'set in motion a machine for the production of evil, which has for years been working with a continually increasing power, and a constantly accelerated velocity'. The results, he contended, were 'noxious and revolting'; the colonies had become like 'a foul ulcer . . . corroding the vitals' of the imperial body politic.[2] Corporeal images of sickness likewise sprang to Sir William Molesworth's mind: transportation had accumulated such vast quantities of 'moral filth' in one place that it had spread 'moral typhus, plague, pestilence, and all manner of hideous disease'.[3] The system's 'pernicious moral influence' was, moreover, steadily contaminating all those resident in the colonies and was now moving throughout the southern hemisphere, threatening the health of the empire as a whole.[4]

Images of corporeal debilitation and sickness were complemented by other naturalised discourses in which the Australian colonies figured variously as the noxious weeds and alien offspring of empire. The problem, critics agreed, lay in the concentration and reproduction of the wrong kind of seed and of too much bad stock. No virtuous empire, Sir Francis Bacon had warned several centuries before, ever sought to 'plant' with the 'scum of the people'.[5] The Australian colonies, James Mudie declared, were formed of 'branches lopped' for their 'rottenness from the tree of British freedom' and 'cast forth' with 'abhorrence' from the 'outraged soil of England'. Although the population was 'entirely British' in its 'numerical and physical construction', it was, as a result, entirely 'un-British in social and civilised spirit and in moral feeling and character'.[6] Convict transportation, Edward Gibbon Wakefield agreed, had enabled 'the English' to create 'from their own loins a nation of Cyprians and Turks'.[7]

[161]

These discourses of alien and demonic reproduction inevitably gave rise to familial and domestic metaphors in which the imperial state figured as a perverted parent and the empire as a mal-constructed house. 'Imagine', colonial commentator Samuel Hinds asked his readers:

> the case of a household most carefully made up of picked specimens from all the idle, mischievous and notoriously bad characters in the country! Surely the man who should be mad or wicked enough to bring together this monstrous family, and to keep up its number and character by continual fresh supplies, would be scouted from the society he so outraged – would be denounced as the author of a diabolical nuisance to his neighbourhood and his country, and would be proclaimed infamous for setting at nought all morality and decency.[8]

Nothing good could be expected of the Australian colonies, *The Times* agreed, given that their 'very brick and mortar' had been composed of 'sin and crime'.[9] To continue with transportation, Whately concluded, was to proceed with the 'misconstruction' of 'a house' in ways which placed it beyond repair and which would inevitably 'cause it to fall down by its own weight'.[10]

By the 1830s and 1840s, growing numbers of imperial theorists regarded the empire as a unitary state – a single body politic – and the colonies as integral components of a greater British nation. Older mercantilist views of imperial emigration as an unwelcome drain on population and thus as a debilitating loss were being displaced by a vision of the colonies as vital outlets for excess population, helping to restore national health by providing renewed balance at home while simultaneously reproducing the nation abroad.[11] Empire was reconceived as a means of expanding the national stock and of spreading its virtues and principles around the globe. The nation's boundaries were consequently considered culturally dynamic and elastic rather than geographically bound and fixed. The 'spirit of England', Herman Merivale asserted, 'lives in our language, our commerce, our industry, in all those channels of inter-communication by which we embrace and connect the vast multitude of states ... throughout the world'.[12] Empire, J.R. Seeley later explained, consisted of 'a great homogenous people, one in blood, language, religion and laws ... dispersed over a boundless space' but held together by 'strong moral' and natural ties.[13]

Organic and familial visions were particularly fundamental to the conceptual schemes of the Colonial Reformers – a group, or perhaps more accurately a network, of early to mid-nineteenth-century British politicians and thinkers who were dedicated to the reform of the empire and to the restructuring of imperial relations. Imperial endeavour, they argued, was an expression of national character, an outgrowth of the 'indomitable energy of our race'.[14] Properly organised, it therefore laid the basis for the endless reproduction of the self. Settlers took the 'language, the habits, and the manners of England' with them, establishing them in their new communities and transmitting them to each new generation. While these colonial children would, like their parents, 'find a country and a home' abroad, they would nevertheless always also look 'back to England as their origin and parent'. The colonies would, in turn, become 'nations to which Englishmen will go as to their own home'. Strong ties of natural affection obviated any need for force and coercion. Even colonial independence could be incorporated within this schema: self-government was deemed akin to a boy reaching adulthood, marrying and becoming the master of his own household, the father of his own family, but yet retaining strong bonds to his original parental home.[15] By creating communities of common character, habit and taste, colonialism also promised to enable the free market. 'Trade between people so intimately related is sure to arise', J.A. Roebuck explained, and 'needs no coercive laws to force it into being'.[16] A vision of empire as a naturally affectionate, tightly knit and enduring, if far-flung, family was thus integral to the Reformers' commitment to free trade and liberal democracy.

All this depended, however, on the colonies becoming mirror images of the mother country, an 'extension, though distant, of Britain itself'.[17] Colonies had to be formed in such a way that there would be 'little more in Van Diemen's Land, or in Canada revolting to the habits and feelings of an emigrant than if he had merely shifted his residence from Sussex to Cumberland or Devonshire'.[18] This act of seamless replication was crucial because the reformers considered character to be volatile and conditional rather than constant and fixed. 'Man – how often must it be repeated', Wakefield asserted, 'is the creature of circumstances'.[19] Although colonisation was imagined as a naturalised process of reproduction, it was nevertheless also deemed to require careful organisation. Far too much had previously been left to 'caprice and chance' with the result, the reformers argued, that the colonies were fast becoming 'new' societies rather than mirror images of the 'old' and that the settler was gradually 'ceasing to be an Englishman'.[20] It was simply not the case, John Stuart Mill advised, that 'civilisation has but one law and that a law of progressive advancement'.[21] This was amply proven by colonial experience: empire, Wakefield contended, had given birth to an entirely *New People*, a people whose characters and habits had originally been English but who were becoming progressively degraded with each new generation. 'The barbarism of new countries', he declared, 'is become my ruling idea'.[22]

To reproduce the nation, it was necessary to transplant the whole social body. 'All classes should migrate together', Molesworth explained, if 'new communities analogous to that of the parent state' were to be formed.[23] Britain had, however, previously sent out paupers, criminals and workers, alone creating 'colonies of the limbs without the belly and head' and fostering a 'want of resemblance' and 'congenial feeling'.[24] Balanced reproduction was therefore partly a question of establishing due social order and hierarchy. At the moment, Hinds contended, colonists were like 'creeping and climbing plants' without poles to 'entwine round': the plants inevitably became 'matted confusedly together' and were left 'scrambling on the ground in tangled heaps'. If, by contrast, representatives of the whole nation were exported, 'every new comer' to a colony would have 'his own class to fall into' and the other classes to relate to, and he would consequently immediately feel at home. The lower classes, in particular, would find a squire, a parson, a church and a school – all those 'natural' leaders and institutions that they had grown accustomed to since childhood but that were all too often absent in the colonies. These would provide the rich soil necessary to nourish a perfect British tree.[25]

Convict transportation was considered a major obstacle to this. It not only filled the colonies with social refuse but also blocked the emigration of properly independent and moral men. No man of a 'superior class' or with even 'common feelings of morality' would ever 'consent to become an inmate of one of these communities of felons', Molesworth asserted. 'Many of the free settlers' were, therefore, 'low and abandoned characters, as bad perhaps as the convicts'.[26] Consequently, the lower classes dominated the colonies and with wholly negative results. In 'old countries', Wakefield explained, the 'modes and manners' of the people 'flow downwards from the higher classes', but in 'new' countries the absence of sufficient numbers of civilised and educated men allowed the 'baser English appetites' to set the tone.[27] Australia, a place where 'pure English' had supposedly been abandoned in favour of thieves' cant, provided a prime example.[28] The 'most needy' classes in society, Hinds agreed, were those least fit 'to perpetuate our national character' and 'to become the fathers of a race whose habits of thinking and feeling' corresponded with those which 'we are cherishing at home'. This kind of colonisation had already ended badly: in the American colonies, he counselled, Britain had 'formed the embryo of a plebeian nation' by severing 'the humble from the nobles of our land'.[29] The Australian colonies presented a comparable spectre: if transportation did not end, Molesworth warned, Van Diemen's Land would eventually become 'a Red criminal republic, with liberty for crime, equality in infamy, and fraternity in vice'.[30]

The convict presence was considered equally to distort and inhibit the domestication of the colonies. By creating a marked preponderance of men, transportation had founded an unnatural society. The relative absence of women, considered as crucial instruments of morality, was destroying the civilising process. Nothing, however, could allegedly be done about this while transportation continued: no young, single women of 'respectable' character would, under current circumstances, go voluntarily to the colonies.[31] The convict presence similarly blocked family emigration. No 'respectable or virtuous man' who 'is or intends to become the father of a family' could consider Australia his prospective home, Molesworth declared.[32] Rather than creating spaces for the multiplication of home, the colonies were, instead, undermining and subverting familial and domestic order.

The programme of systematic colonisation propounded by the reformers was designed explicitly to reverse this: once transportation had ended, properly balanced emigration schemes could be implemented, designed to encourage the export of young men and women in equal numbers. The young would not only be most fertile, they also promised to be most adaptable – capable of applying already established English habits to a 'new climate' and to 'embrace new modes of cultivation'. They would also be driven by their familial ambitions to settle and civilise the land: 'having families to rear', Wakefield asserted, 'they would be more industrious' and 'more apt to save'.[33] The settlement of families across colonial space, moreover, would guarantee the nation's reproduction abroad, fostering a domesticated landscape which truly mirrored home and ensuring that the national character would continue to be passed, in secure and pristine form, down through each successive generation.

Properly ordered imperial expansion was considered equally crucial to the continued vitality of the mother country. 'If England does not train up her colonial children to be like her', one commentator observed, 'she will herself very probably decline into a miserable likeness of themselves. . . . A common fortune, like a common blood, must belong to parent and child'.[34] Economic instability and over-population were deemed to be progressively destroying Britain's physical, moral and political health, eating their way, at every turn, 'into the heart' of the nation and giving rise to political diseases and disorders which, by provoking government repression, threatened its liberties.[35] Poverty was also a powerful block to family formation. While many men and women were forced to delay marriage, others faced a prolonged and debilitating struggle to keep their families afloat. Commentators feared that this was subverting the 'natural' ties: that the father who struggled to feed his children would come inevitably to see them as 'his chief enemies'.[36] A family without love was like a world without order: decline of home prefigured decline of nation. Love of country, one observer explained, was an outgrowth of the 'domestic affections': 'a man's country was sacred to him' only in so far as it 'enlarged and multiplied' the 'image of his childhood's home'.[37] Emigration was heralded as a key remedy to this web of inter-related problems. Systematic colonisation promised to restore order by creating spaces for the physical and moral replenishment of British men and women, their re-establishment on an industrious and independent stage, thus allowing them to secure the conditions for the survival and reproduction of their families.[38]

By the 1830s, the Colonial Reformers had acquired a marked and growing influence. They had established numerous colonisation societies and companies designed to apply the principles of systematic colonisation to new colonies like South Australia and New Zealand, and by the later 1830s, with a weakened and fractured Whig government increasingly dependent upon the votes of Radical MPs, they had also acquired increased authority in the Commons.[39] Led by Molesworth, a new generation characterised by 'spirit' and 'energy' was, John Stuart Mill noted, fast redeeming the 'past errors' of the parliamentary Radicals by 'bombarding' government 'with good measures'.[40] This bombardment was primarily colonial in its focus: in 1836 the reformers gained the chair of the Select Committee on Colonial Lands; in 1837–38 they accompanied Lord Durham on his crucial mission to the Canadian colonies; and in early 1838 Molesworth moved a motion of no confidence in Lord Glenelg, Secretary of State for the Colonies.

Reared in the tenets of classical political economy and Enlightenment moral philosophy the reformers were also committed philosophic Radicals and the friends and fellow travellers of the likes of John Stuart Mill. They supported extensive political and franchise reform at home and were committed to building an empire based upon consensual relations, self-government, democratic exchange, free trade, free labour and free emigration.[41] Their opposition to convict transportation flowed inevitably from these principles, and in 1837, they pushed the government into establishing a Select Committee on Transportation with Sir William Molesworth in the chair.[42] This was their best chance to date to 'prove' that the current colonial system was creating a crisis of reproduction, and that in the Australian colonies, in particular, it was fostering a profound degradation of British manhood, producing deviant and disordered families and giving birth to gross and decidedly alien offspring.

* * *

Transportation, its critics proclaimed, had not only failed to reform convicts, it had made them immeasurably worse. The system degraded and brutalised its subjects and destroyed every last vestige of moral character. Its tendency, *The Times* declared, had been 'to make our criminals as bad as human nature could be made, and to change men into devils'.[43] These views were heavily dependent upon two key contentions: first, that convict labour was a form of slavery and that it was, as a result, directly antithetical to moral reform; second, that the system was overly reliant upon compulsion and that it depended, in particular, upon physical punishments that were irrational and extreme. Although opponents of the convict system were concerned about its impact upon women, it was the effects that it supposedly had upon men that most caught their attention. This was because their primary fears were grounded in a series of beliefs that equated ordered masculinity with self-discipline, independence, voluntary labour and the exercise of free but rationally informed choice. Civilised man, they contended, ought to be subject to no rule or mastery but his own: penal discipline should therefore seek to transform criminals into self-regulating individuals.[44] The convict system appeared, however, to be largely dependent upon external constraints: it seemed, in other words, to be designed to master men rather than to teach men to master themselves.

All sides in the debates over transportation agreed that convict assignment was a form of slavery. However, whereas its critics regarded this as an evil, supporters of transportation contended that forced labour was a wholly necessary and beneficial thing. In his *Defence of transportation*, Arthur argued that the compulsion to labour and the total loss of liberty were absolutely vital spurs to reform. Convicts, he explained, were constitutionally different to free men because they suffered from a profound 'dissoluteness of character' and an ingrained 'habit of idleness'.[45] Contemporaries considered that criminals suffered from an imbalance of appetite over discipline, body over mind: having succumbed to their passions, they were unwilling to work to fulfil their desires and had become incapable of delayed gratification. Even the 'many' who had been 'driven' to crime as a result of 'want' had, in Arthur's view, become mentally 'unreflecting' and morally 'desperate'. The 'main body of Convicts' were suffering 'under mental delirium', he explained; they 'see and appreciate every thing through a false medium'.[46] This meant that rational and 'ordinary inducements' to work like 'the stimulus of profit and self-respect' no longer had influence over them. The only way to make convicts work therefore was to subject them to coercion and the 'fear of pain': 'the man', Arthur concluded, 'must be compelled to labour'.[47] Surrounded by ex-convicts who were earning relatively good wages, the idea was that the convict would gradually learn to associate industry with reward, begin to value his assigned service as a moral and occupational apprenticeship and be inspired to work towards a ticket of leave. Assignment was designed to give a totally 'new direction' to convict minds by encouraging them to associate freedom with the self-discipline of regular labour.[48]

Critics of the convict system contended, by contrast, that slave labour was inherently unnatural because it failed to develop man's internal will to labour and destroyed his capacity for self-restraint. In developing their case they drew upon two influential and inter-connected bodies of thought: the theories of wage labour developed by the classical political economists from the mid-eighteenth century onwards and the intellectual legacies of anti-slavery. These theories suggested that it was man's innate or natural desire to accumulate and to consume that motivated him to work. 'Every thing in the world is purchased by labour', David Hume explained, 'and our passions are the only cause of labour'.[49] Higher wages and the allure of luxury consumption – previously condemned as a cause of idleness and vice – were consequently reconceived as spurs to industry and morality.[50] Commercial society, free wage labour and the market were considered the highest stage of human development because they gave free rein to man's *natural* desire to accumulate and so his willingness to labour. The link between labour and desire also enabled the free worker to associate present effort with future reward, thus stimulating his reputedly innate propensity for self-discipline, prudence and restraint. Civilised societies were founded upon the pursuit of man's 'natural' passions *and* his willingness to keep these passions in constant check.

Slavery was constructed as the polar opposite, the absolute antithesis, of free labour. Rather than stimulating man's innate desire to labour, it was condemned for degrading and destroying it. With no benefits to be gained from his work, no direct self-interest in it, the convict worker had, like the slave, an interest in being as idle as much and as often as was possible. He had always to be pushed into work. It was, the eighteenth-century philosopher John Millar explained, because the slave received 'no wages in return for his labour' that he failed 'to exert much vigour or activity in the exercise of any employment. He obtains a livelihood at any rate; and by his utmost assiduity he is able to procure no more. As he works merely in consequence of the terror in which he is held, it may be imagined that he will be idle as often as he can with impunity'.[51] Recipients of poor relief allegedly suffered a similar fate. 'As his subsistence does not depend on his exertions', the 1834 Poor Law Commissioners concluded, so 'he loses all that sweetens labour, its association with reward, and gets through his work, such as it is, with the reluctance of a slave'.[52] Drawing upon these ideas, opponents argued that the convict assignment system tended to undermine and destroy rather than promote and inculcate habits of industry. 'Like slavery', penal reformer Joseph Atkinson asserted, transportation had 'the effect of destroying all dignity in labour'.[53] It was, Sir Francis Forbes explained, simply impossible to get a convict to do a job with 'the same care, or . . . the same skill, as he would perform the same labour if he were employed as a free man'.[54]

Forced labour was denounced equally for destroying man's natural propensity for self-restraint. 'A person who can acquire no property', Adam Smith explained of the slave, 'can have no other interest but to eat as much, and to labour as little as possible'.[55] Convicts appeared to suffer from a similarly morally debilitating dependence. 'The practice of assigning convicts to masters who feed, clothe and lodge them, without casting on themselves the slightest care for their own maintenance, is', the penal reformer Alexander Maconochie declared, 'a bad preparation for their liberty when they obtain it'. 'It keeps them in a state of pupilage', he argued, made them 'careless, reckless and spendthrift accordingly' and caused them to acquire 'improvident, and frequently dissipated habits', which, because they would become engrained, would be virtually impossible for them 'to throw aside' upon gaining their freedom.[56]

The loss of independence contingent upon servitude was also condemned as the antithesis of a proper manly state. Rigorous restraint and supervision destroyed all the 'manly impulses', Maconochie contended. The convict system appeared, therefore, to have directly perverse effects: while the weakest and most 'pliable' men were able to bend and submit to the authority of another, the 'most sturdy', 'better principled' and more 'manly' writhed at this 'indignity' and were more likely to resist and to be punished until they had become 'universally degraded and demoralized'.[57] The humiliation of servitude also stimulated a loss of character. 'All fly to liquor, whenever they can obtain it, to drown humiliation and care', Maconochie commented.[58] Transportation, the exiled Tolpuddle Martyr George Loveless agreed, so degraded and humiliated convicts that, feeling that they had nothing left to lose, many became 'careless and regardless of consequences' and 'rush[ed] forward, plunging headlong into [the] abyss'.[59]

Slave labour was also thought to demoralise men because, in the absence of wages, masters were forced to turn to irrational stimuli and means of control. In the case of assignment, convicts appeared either to be unduly coaxed or excessively coerced into work. The use of incentives was believed to be systematic. Recognising that they would 'derive most profit from their servants by keeping them as much as possible in a cheerful and contented state', Richard Whately contended that settlers were willing to 'acquiesce in any thing short of the most gross idleness and extravagance' to get their convicts to work.[60] Most masters, Van Demonian settler John Russell agreed, went far beyond the government rations and gave their servants 'great quantities of animal food' as well as 'extra allowances of tobacco'.[61] Rum was 'the best stimulus to induce the convicts to labour', the ex-New South Wales settler James Mudie declared, and it had, in his view, become such a universal reward for work that 'every employer of convicts' could be 'considered a licensed seller of spirits'. The substitution of alcohol for wages had, moreover, apparently infected class relations more generally. According to Mudie, free and ticket-of-leave workers were also routinely paid in 'grog' and many spent their evenings getting 'glorious', often in the company of the convict workers assigned to the same estate.[62] The assignment system appeared, therefore, to contain a stimulus to immoral appetite at its very heart; convict labour was apparently being encouraged systematically to associate liberty with licence.

Coercion was regarded as the flipside of indulgence: what masters could not achieve by 'bribery', they allegedly sought to extract through 'terror'. In the eyes of the system's opponents, convicts laboured under a 'slave code': 'here', one critic asserted 'are . . . a long list of offences made expressly for the convict, which have neither end nor bounds to their meaning, and which range every where over the deeds of man from a mere nothing up to any thing short of capital . . . offences'.[63] Penalties for even minor offences were, in addition, allegedly 'severe' to the point of 'excessive cruelty'. Flogging and hard labour in chains, Maconochie asserted, were all too often 'lightly ordered for crimes' which were 'in themselves of no deep dye'.[64] Settlers were said to have developed a particular taste for flogging, because it ostensibly occasioned 'less interruption of work', with the result that the lash had become 'the great persuader to work and good order' in the colonies.[65] Coercion was condemned on the same grounds as indulgence: it, too, appealed to the body instead of the mind and therefore did little, if anything, to cultivate self-discipline and an internal will to labour. 'The essential difference between the slave and the free labourer', Sir George Grey, ex-Under Secretary of State for the Colonies and a member of the Molesworth Committee explained, 'is that the latter is induced to work by motives which act upon his reason, the former by the dread of bodily pain'.[66]

The application of excessive pain and the apparent extreme suffering experienced by convicts in the road and chain gangs and at the penal stations were condemned even more roundly. According to almost all the witnesses called before the Select Committee, convicts at these sites were subject to intense physical and mental deprivation. The men in the gangs were 'doomed' to work on 'hot and dust-hurling roads', 'loaded and cankering with heavy irons', until their 'flesh is burnt to copper' and their 'hair is scorched as yellow as the jaundice', the Reverend William Ullathorne, Vicar-General of the Australian colonies, declared. Those banished to the penal stations were reportedly being systematically brutalised, suffering 'unmitigated wretchedness', 'incessant and galling' labour and repeated floggings. Left without hope, they were driven to desperate mutinies and to murder-suicide pacts. It was, convict Robert Hepburne wrote to Ullathorne from Norfolk Island, like living in a hell upon earth.[67]

Contemporaries considered that suffering upon this scale unsettled the mind and destroyed the soul. Various eighteenth-century shifts including breakthroughs in anaesthesiology, the influence of moral sense philosophy, the rise of humanitarianism and the emphasis, particularly within Evangelicalism, upon the godly nature of 'feeling' and compassion for others had all helped to inspire a new respect for the body within reforming circles and to raise doubts about the moral utility of pain. Man was increasingly understood as a complex, unitary and sensitive being whose physical and mental capacities were intricately interwoven and delicately balanced.[68] These shifts in thinking had had a profound influence upon attitudes to criminals, helping to lay the basis for the broader contemporary transition from punishments that targeted the body to those that targeted the mind.[69] Although penal reformers did not reject the use of pain per se, they asserted that it could be inflicted only under carefully managed conditions and in strictly calibrated quantities for fear that *excessive* torment might desensitise the subject, destroy the capacity for moral feeling and rational thought, reduce men to purely physical and instinctual beings and thus eradicate all hope of self-discipline.[70]

Although condemned for its focus upon the body and its appeal to external force, extreme suffering was considered to have profound *internal* consequences upon convicts. The 'effect of the lash is not confined to the marks' on a man's 'back' but rather 'enters his soul', one-time colonist Charles Rowcroft contended.[71] 'The iron which cankers their heel, corrodes their heart', Ullathorne declared: convicts were systematically desensitised by their suffering. The 'feelings of the convict', he elaborated, 'are petrified by the hardness of every thing about him. He never feels the touch of kindness. Wonder not that his vital warmth dies, and he becomes a haggard, insensible thing'.[72] This loss of feeling was progressive: a man flogged for the first time was acutely sensible to his pain and humiliation, but with each successive infliction, he became physically and mentally hardened to his suffering and was rendered indifferent, unfeeling and heartless. 'The flogged man' was thus 'a worthless man'.[73] Chains had a similar effect: when first put on they 'chafe and gall the flesh and are burdensome', but 'in time', James Ross contended, 'the wearer will dance and run with agility, almost insensible, at least careless, of the trouble of carrying them'. The 'human frame', he argued, was uniquely 'pliant', and man was the product of circumstance. The more severely he was punished, the more likely it was that his 'spirit' would 'be broken' and that he would be transformed into an 'inert' and unfeeling 'animal'.[74]

Systems of extreme discipline were also deemed to render convicts 'dead to all sense of honest shame' and, as a consequence, increasingly 'careless' of wrongdoing and punishment.[75] Convicts subjected to the most extreme forms of discipline allegedly committed the most heinous colonial offences, driven to bushranging, indiscriminate plunder, rape, murder and cannibalism.[76] This thirst for retribution was further intensified because, in the eyes of the system's critics, convicts were invariably either unjustly punished or subjected to extreme sanctions for relatively minor offences. 'That offenders should object to punishment is natural', Alexander Cheyne, colonial official and critic of transportation, observed, 'but when unmerited, a sense of wrong is excited which in ill-ordered minds creates the fiercest passions. Revenge against the immediate object of its production, perhaps, induces fresh crime, which in its turn brings new punishment, and fuel is thus added to the flame'.[77] Finally, man's ability to think was deemed to be undermined progressively by extreme suffering and pain, his 'moral character' was consequently subverted, and his capacity for self-discipline destroyed.[78] As the 'dignity and independence of the mind is lost' so, Joseph Atkinson explained, 'mental prostration' occurred and 'active virtue' became 'all but impossible'.[79] Extreme pain enabled the body to conquer the mind and strengthened rather than undermined the rule of the passions. It reduced men to their bodies alone, made them slaves to instinct and caused them to respond like animals and 'savages' to all base and sensual temptations. 'A morbid, sickening sort of indifference . . . distempers the long punished convict', one observer commented, 'seeking merely to gratify his desires, now alas reduced to the lowest level of the sensual appetites, he will renew his depredations . . . with apathetic indifference of the very worst sort of catastrophe that can overtake him'.[80]

Critics of the system were confident that its reliance upon external forms of constraint meant that it was capable of stimulating limited and superficial reform at best. Even when 'the outward man' was transformed into a 'well-behaved subject', 'the inward man' was scarcely altered.[81] Assigned servants acquired 'the virtue of a slave' at most – the ability to be obedient to the commands of others. This kind of virtue was, however, considered 'no preparation' whatsoever 'for a state of comparative freedom'.[82] Control by others 'enfeebles character, makes it always seek to lean upon direction, and delivers it up hand-bound to subsequent temptation', Maconochie explained. Consequently, convicts in Van Diemen's Land had been reduced to a state of 'apathy' and 'deep demoralisation'.[83] The more coercive the discipline, the more destructive its effects were judged to be. Men banished to the gangs and to the penal stations became like 'useless machines', settler Peter Murdock alleged. They were 'so accustomed to be wound up as it were by machinery', he explained, that 'when they are unwound, they have not moral principle enough to resist anything; . . . they become useless and sink; . . . their physical force is gone by starvation, . . . their moral force is gone by discipline'.[84]

Although many convicts appeared to have reformed while they were under constraint, this was deemed superficial and short-lived: once released, most allegedly suffered a 'relapse'. This was the product of a faulty system of discipline, the Molesworth Committee asserted, one that relied 'solely upon the infliction of pain, without attempting to encourage and strengthen the moral feelings of a culprit'. This kind of system 'hardens and brutalizes' the convict, the Committee concluded:

> [it] renders him mentally incapable of looking beyond the present moment, and confines his ideas to the feelings of the next instant; by these feelings alone his will is determined and he indulges his vicious appetites, or refrains from gratifying them, in proportion as he expects their immediate results will be pain or pleasure. Not only is an offender, whose moral character is subverted by such punishments, incapable of moral restraint, but he only dreads punishment, and is acted upon by it when he sees the lash at hand, and suspended over his head; and prospective punishment has no effect in deterring him from the immediate gratification of his desires when exposed to temptation.[85]

A proper 'school of training' was one which sought, by contrast, to inculcate 'self-command and exertion' and to do so 'from the stimulus of distant hope' rather than 'present fear'. It was, Maconochie concluded, hopeless to seek to achieve by 'physical means' what 'is only valuable where obtained under the influence of moral motives'. To reform a prisoner, he explained, it was necessary to inoculate him with habits of 'self-guidance, self-denial and virtuous restraint' and to provide him with 'voluntary and even emulative labour'. 'Wages', Maconochie concluded, were 'the habitual stimulant to virtuous exertion in free life' and they must form some part of penal discipline if convicts were ever to reform.[86] These ideas informed the central components of the convict probation system, introduced into Van Diemen's Land from 1842: under this system, convicts were free, after an initial period of imprisonment, religious and moral education and government labour, to seek their own employment in the colony as passholder servants, and they were, in addition, entitled to work for wages.[87]

At all levels, then, the existing convict system appeared to its critics to stimulate and further disorder rather than genuinely discipline convicts. It enabled its subjects to satisfy and even expand their appetites and seemed to foster a descent into ever more 'savage' and 'vicious' tastes. At the same time, it reduced, and in the most extreme cases permanently destroyed, man's ability to resist temptation and thus his supposedly innate capacity for self-discipline and restraint. Released from their sentences, the vast majority of convicts allegedly reverted almost immediately to a life of sensual riot and revelry. In the eyes of the Molesworth Committee, ex-convicts were invariably 'incorrigible bad characters', persons of 'violent and uncontrollable passions' and 'insatiable appetites' who continued to prefer 'a life of idleness and debauchery' to one of 'honest industry'.[88] The consummate failure of the existing convict system, Maconochie declared, lay in its inability to 'train up free men'.[89]

*   *   *

The system's failings were allegedly most manifest in the disordered bodies, ungoverned passions and licentious sexual appetites of the convicts. This was supposedly most clearly expressed in widespread prostitution among the women and in a pronounced proclivity for sexual depravity and cruelty among the men. 'Unnatural' sexual practices were deemed particularly widespread: the men were alleged to have developed an insatiable and animalistic appetite for practices such as sodomy, bestiality and child rape. Determined to prove that these practices were rife, Molesworth, in particular, set about grooming witnesses and, on their appearance before the Committee, he subjected them to a series of leading questions.[90] Ullathorne, for one, remembered how Molesworth had arranged a 'private interview' with him in order to 'coach me up as to the best way of giving evidence', during which time he sought, in particular, to impress upon the Reverend that any refusal to testify openly about unnatural offences would have 'grave' consequences. Despite his misgivings, Ullathorne succumbed, providing a sustained and detailed account of the moral horrors that allegedly prevailed in the colonies.[91]

This kind of testimony served two key purposes. First, it undoubtedly enabled the Select Committee to produce a highly coloured account of the penal colonies which, given its sensationalist tone, ensured widespread and sustained attention for the abolitionist case. Much of the testimony was reported verbatim in *The Times* and from there it circulated across Britain and around the empire. The Molesworth Committee's account of colonial sexual disorder was destined, in turn, to achieve an enduring resonance, shaping literary and historical narratives about the penal colonies for decades thereafter.[92] Second, 'unnatural' offences, and sodomy in particular, served as a highly potent symbol of the absolute moral inversion suffered by convict men. Addiction to such practices was considered to signal the 'ultimate state of corruption' and the permanent and 'thorough breaking up of the moral man'.[93] Sodomy had served as an index of irredeemable character for centuries, interpreted as a symbol of the total dominion of the passions. The sodomite was, as a result, considered the absolute antithesis of moral, self-governing and civilised man.[94]

Witnesses oscillated between explanations that sought to account for the prevalence of unnatural sexualities by blaming it upon criminal man's innate inability to govern his appetite and those that stressed active brutalisation by the convict system. Same-sex relations were endemic among the men, Ullathorne contended, both because the system had so humiliated and destroyed them, reducing them to their bodies and to base and animalistic desires, and because, as their transportation for crime illustrated, they already lacked sufficient discipline to resist temptation. The men in the gangs, he declared, suffered intense 'degradation' from being forced to wear chains and a distinguishing and stigmatising dress with the result that they eventually became insensible to shame and lost all concern for their character. They were, however, also characterised by a pre-existing disposition to base passions. Consequently, they were equally polluted by the fact that the gangs congregated bad men together and provided them with facilities for 'mutual converse' and association that led inevitably to 'mutual corruption' and a levelling down of the best to the habits of the worst. Crowded together at night, it was almost inevitable that such men would become 'heated' and 'excited' and that this would lead to 'consequences ... of a very immoral kind'.[95]

Critics contended that this bad situation was made even worse by the ways in which transportation ruptured families and kept men unnaturally apart from female company for long periods at a time.

The separation of husbands and wives was considered an affront to 'the dictates of religion and pure morality'; it was unethical, critics contended, to seek to 'sever forever those whom "God had joined together"'.[96] By destroying these natural ties of affection and by sundering family bonds, transportation had, moreover, created 'a peasantry unlike any other in the world; a peasantry without domestic feelings or affections, without parents or relations, without wives, children or homes'.[97] The fact that convicts were, in addition, allegedly forced to live in intolerable conditions, in huts rather than homes, and in circumstances more fitting for animals than human beings, and with nothing but the fast-fading memory of lost loved ones to console them was also deemed destructive; undermining and degrading the emotions and the capacity for love, affection and compassion. Severed 'from all kindness and love', convicts learned to live by the senses alone, with the result that their personal and familial relationships became correspondingly callous, brutal and instrumental. Wives who followed their convict husbands out to the colonies allegedly found their once loving spouses totally changed. 'Poor woman', Ullathorne wrote of these wives generally, 'little did she suspect how transportation, and slavery . . . had hardened and brutalized that man's heart'.[98]

The unbalanced demographic ratio produced by transportation was equally condemned. The relative scarcity of women had caused colonial society to develop in a distorted fashion with moral consequences that made 'the blood curdle'.[99] Transportation, Maconochie contended, had created a 'fictitious and artificial . . . Society' that defied 'the laws of God and nature'. 'Nature', he explained:

> is uniform in her arrangements; and if we Seek to Stem her stream, we must bend all our efforts to elude her inherent tendencies. . . . Providence has placed Man in the Midst of Women and children in ordinary life and they . . . are there also beneficially made Subject to his influence and authority. . . . It is vain expecting improvement in the morals of this Colony except on a basis of families and the exercise of the relative domestic duties. On the great charities of life, that is, on the establishment of families, depends all morals. It is the law of Nature. The family . . . is the cradle of order and morality. A house full of unmarried men is the cradle of disorder and immorality.[100]

Consequently, contact between the sexes was considered crucial to reform. The company of women had 'a thousand Softening influences' upon men and vice versa, Maconochie argued. Both sexes, therefore, ought always to live alongside one another, even at the most remote sites of punishment like Norfolk Island.[101] These ideas were grounded in a view of human beings as quintessentially social creatures and of the family as the key site for the production of social virtues like sympathy, altruism and cooperation. 'Man', James Ross explained, 'is a social being, and if we are either to punish or reform him, we must bring his social powers and sensations into use'. The 'better qualities of man' were correspondingly considered to 'fall into decay in the midst of an assembly composed of any one sex constantly confined together'. The 'very presence of a female', Ross elaborated:

> has a soft and chastening influence in the company of the other sex, and so ... has that of a male amongst a number of women. As the separation is unnatural, so when persisted in for any length of time, nature itself must deteriorate – a new and melancholy catalogue of crimes springs up, and is perpetuated.[102]

The family, therefore, had crucial civilising functions, and those who lived apart from it were considered to descend to the level of the 'savage'. Given the scarcity of women, colonial conditions were deemed to have had a particularly deleterious effect upon men. One of the system's 'most demoralizing evils', Caroline Chisholm, a leading campaigner for free emigration, later explained, lay in the fact that it had doomed 'men to be for years incarcerated together ... like a menagerie of wild beasts, or to live a solitary hopeless life in the bush' and thus to 'undergo all the frightful and deteriorating effects' of a 'more than savage life'. Transportation, she declared, had for many men entailed the cruel and demoralising effects of compulsory 'bachelorism'.[103]

Those who demanded the abolition of transportation contended that these problems would be overcome only when it had been abandoned. Until then, attempts to redress the demoralising demographic ratios – either by assisted female emigration schemes or by increasing the numbers of female convicts – were doomed to failure. As evidence of this, commentators pointed to the alleged failure of the assisted female emigration schemes of the 1820s and 1830s. Critics argued that these schemes had, on the whole, simply increased colonial vice and enabled it to take more public and 'outrageous' forms.[104] While some contended that female emigrants had been dissolute and depraved before their departure, others argued that they had been fatally contaminated by colonial society and by their inevitable association with female convicts. The majority were 'decided prostitutes' before they left Britain, Murdock asserted, and it was this which explained why they had taken so 'readily to the trade' of prostitution on their arrival.[105] In Whately's view, by contrast, the women had been of originally 'good character' but any attempt to use them to 'purify the character of the colonial community' was simply akin to an attempt:

To pour, from time to time, portions of sound wine into a cask full of vinegar, in hopes of converting the vinegar back into wine ... The result has been, as might have been expected, that the new-comers, instead of disinfecting this moral lazar-house, for the most part become as deeply infected as the rest.[106]

Female convicts were considered to make even more inadequate wives. As with the convict men, abolitionists contended that assignment degraded and demoralised convict women. Female assignment was condemned as a system of prostitution, a charge with metaphorical as well as literal meaning. It was metaphorical in the sense that anti-slavery advocates had long associated the enslavement of women with the immoral commodification of the female body, and thus with systems of sexual trade and exchange such as prostitution.[107] It was literal in the sense that many of the women had supposedly been distributed for sexual purposes rather than as servants. Although claims that settlers applied for female convict servants in order to earn income by their prostitution were, in fact, few and far between, the Molesworth Committee nevertheless wove them into a coherent critique of female assignment, concluding on the basis of very scant evidence indeed that the overwhelming tendency of the system was to render the women 'still more profligate'.[108] As with the critiques of male convict assignment, the Select Committee tended, moreover, to downplay the evidence of those with sustained, first-hand experience of the convict system – such as Arthur, who testified that female convicts were sought as servants, that they made good servants on the whole and that their assignment had generally reformatory effects – and to prefer the more sensationalist evidence from witnesses who often had more limited knowledge.[109]

Much greater emphasis was placed than in abolitionist accounts of convict men upon the idea that the women were originally and even innately bad. 'What shall I say of the female convict', Ullathorne asked rhetorically, 'acknowledged to be worse, and far more difficult of reformation than the man? Her general character is immodesty, drunkenness, and the most horrible language'.[110] It was simply impossible for someone without first-hand experience of the colonies to imagine their 'depravity of character', Mudie asserted: convict women were without exception, morally intemperate and sexually 'incontinent' and 'worse than the men in all descriptions of vice'. No woman of a 'fair character' had ever been transported; rather, he claimed, all female convicts were, from the outset, decidedly 'bad subjects'.[111] These views were founded in contemporary understandings of female criminality. The criminal woman was considered the unnatural antithesis of moral femininity: she was, like the prostitute, 'a woman with half the woman gone, and that half containing all that elevates her nature leaving her a mere instrument of impurity . . . a social pest carrying contamination and foulness to every quarter'.[112] Convict women were deemed to have fallen further and harder than their male counterparts; 'when a woman is bad', Ullathorne helpfully explained, 'she is generally very bad'.[113]

Female convicts were allegedly so vice-ridden and morally repellent that 'respectable' mistresses kept their distance from them. Consequently they failed either to exert a chastening influence over them or to supervise them properly. The women were generally so awful, Murdock explained, that the settlers 'have no heart to treat them well'. Even a relatively 'well disposed' and 'modest' woman, intent on reform, would find herself 'despised and insulted by her mistress'. Isolated and victimised, in Murdock's view, she was inevitably driven to form liaisons with other convicts on the property. Desperate to find 'a protector' from these uncaring employers, most women, he told the Select Committee, endeavoured to form a relationship with a particular man. They inevitably became pregnant, were returned to the house of correction and later re-assigned elsewhere. The whole demoralising cycle then began all over again: 'a new place, a new lover, a fresh crime and then back to the penitentiary again'. This, Murdock agreed with the Select Committee, was the path which most convict women were forced repeatedly to take.[114] Although Murdock blamed this situation upon the harsh demeanour and indifferent attitude of the mistress, his narrative had nevertheless been subtly reworked by the time it reached the Select Committee's report. It was because the convict woman was surrounded by sex-starved colonial men, Molesworth concluded, who subjected her to 'constant pursuit and solicitation' that she was 'obliged to select one man, as a paramour, to defend her from the importunities of the rest'.[115] This version of the story almost certainly fitted better with the emphasis placed by the Colonial Reformers on the idea that male sexual rapacity was widespread in the colonies.[116]

Above all else, however, the sexual licentiousness of female convicts was deemed to be a product of their own moral weakness and inability to withstand temptation. Having just completed his account of female convict victimisation – in which it was supposedly 'the general fate' of the women to 'prostitute' themselves to a man in order to 'obtain a protector' – Murdock resorted immediately to a totally different explanation of convict immorality. It was, he alleged, simply impossible for even the most 'respectable' and proactive settlers to prevent the women from prostituting themselves to all the men on the estate. The lure of gain was simply too strong, the 'temptation . . . so constant and urgent' that not 'one woman in a thousand' had sufficient 'moral energy to resist'.[117] The temptations to vice were considered to be a product of the demographic imbalance; shortages of women meant that the rates for sex were relatively high. Convict women consequently had access to an abundance of stimulating and demoralising luxuries, including beer, rum, tobacco, sugar and tea.[118] Colonial temptation, therefore, confirmed the women in habits of vice. Transportation, Sir Francis Forbes asserted, tended to 'superadd ... intemperance and unchastity' to the crimes for which female convicts were originally sentenced.[119]

According to the critics, colonial conditions produced universally demoralised wives and mothers. Many female convicts, Ullathorne claimed, had become so morally reduced and debased by the experience of transportation and assignment that they scarcely even looked like women any longer. 'Filthy, swollen-faced wretches', he wrote, with 'something of the shape of woman in them' 'haunt' the streets and 'stagger with drunkenness, dissoluteness and debauchery'. 'What can I say of such women as mothers', he asked, 'but that their children are cradled in vice, are nursed at the bosom of profanity, and fed with the poison of ungodly lips, and that they drink in iniquity from their parent's example'.[120] Convicts sought to marry only in order to gain their liberty, witnesses contended. Their family relationships were, as a result, wholly instrumental and totally lacking in either love or warmth from the outset. Convict unions were based upon 'a slight' and 'often ... accidental acquaintance', Ullathorne asserted, 'affection unconsulted – disparity of age, of character, and of manners, thrown out of consideration – the possibility of a previous union in the mother country, unheeded – the known fact of such a prior engagement not rarely concealed – and they are married, to drag each other through a life of misery and mistrust'.[121] Some of his male convict servants, Mudie claimed, developing a similar theme, had even asked him to pick out a wife for them from the house of correction when he was in Sydney. The marriage of his convict servants never turned out well; 'I never allowed one to get married', he declared sweepingly, 'but I had cause to regret it'. Immediately they were married, convict husbands allegedly connived at the prostitution of their wives to all the other men on the property – 'they wink at it', he declared. Convict men, he concluded, 'are not particular'.[122] The prostitution of wives and children was thus depicted as a way of life in convict families. 'Mothers are not ashamed to sell their own daughters even before the young creatures know what chastity means', Wakefield asserted, and 'husbands make a market of their wives'.[123] Britain, Ullathorne concluded, had created 'a community without the feelings of

[180]

community, whose men are very wicked, whose women are very shameless, and whose children are very irreverent'; 'a people such as since the deluge, has not been'.[124]

*   *   *

Systems of forced labour were deemed to have even more destructive effects upon the character of the master. This critique was founded in the idea that slavery was rooted in the passions and, in particular, in the innate but irrational and demoralising desire to exercise power over others. 'The pride of man', Adam Smith commented, 'makes him love to domineer . . . Wherever the law allows it, and the nature of the work can afford it, therefore, he will generally prefer the service of slaves to that of freemen'.[125] Slavery, therefore, represented a giving way to the base passions, a deterioration of moral character and the destruction of sympathy. The everyday experience of slavery, the use of coercion and the feelings of hostility generated between slave and slave-master had a similar impact. 'The whole commerce between master and slave', Thomas Jefferson had explained, 'is a perpetual exercise of the most boisterous passions; the most unremitting despotism on the one part, and degrading submission on the other'.[126] The boundless authority which slavery gave one human being over another was also deemed unnatural, denying the sovereignty of the individual and the inviolability of the body, and these concerns had given rise to repeated images of sexual coercion and cruelty within anti-slavery propaganda. 'Incurable vices', Wilberforce concluded, 'will invariably exist wherever the power of man over man is unlimited'.[127]

Critics argued that assignment had similarly negative effects: settlers' 'hearts' had been 'hardened', 'their contentious feelings whetted', and their 'self-esteem elevated' as a result of the power they enjoyed over their convict servants.[128] The convict system had also encouraged settlers to develop an instrumental approach towards their servants with dehumanising consequences. The power that the master enjoyed over his assigned workers, Russell explained, 'blunts the man's feelings. He looks on a servant as a sort of slave almost; a tool that he is to get as much work out of as he can'.[129] The master's only 'object is profit', Ullathorne agreed, and 'his contention is to produce as much labour out of his slave, in as short a time, as possible'.[130] With 'no permanent property' in their convict servants, assignment was deemed even more demoralising to the master than slave systems else-where. 'The West Indian owner of negro slaves is as careful of his people as he is of his horses' but, Ullathorne explained, 'the owner of the convict slave has not the same cause for care. On receiving him, he pays the sum of One Pound for the clothes on his back, this is all. And when one is worked out, another may be easily had for the asking'.[131]

The constant stimulus that this power gave to the master's temper was thought to harden and debase settlers, destroying their capacity for human sympathy, inuring them to bad feelings, harshness and violence, and giving rise, in turn, to a range of base passions. The resulting decline of character was considered progressive. Settlers were deemed to have become addicted to cruel and degrading punishments like flogging. 'Where a master in England finds fault', Ullathorne declared:

> the master in Australia threatens the lash; where the master here grows angry, the master there swears, and invokes the lash; where here he talks of turning away, there he procures the infliction of the lash: for idleness, the lash; for carelessness, the lash; for insolence, the lash; for drunkenness, the lash; for disobedience, the lash; wherever there is reason, and wherever there is not reason, the lash. Ever on the master's tongue, and ever in the prisoner's ear ... sounds the lash! – the lash! – the lash![132]

Violence, particularly of an interpersonal nature, was read as a loss of the self-discipline and control that supposedly characterised 'civilised' man and it was increasingly associated in this period with unmanly conduct and masculine dishonour.[133] Sympathy was considered a crucial component of 'civilised' societies, but prolonged exposure to human suffering and violence – regarded as characteristics of the primitive – was deemed to progressively erode and ultimately destroy it. 'The civilised conscience', historian Randall McGowen notes, was considered 'a fragile instrument, civilised to the extent that it was sensitive to social feelings, but susceptible of being overwhelmed or destroyed'.[134] These concerns reflected broader anxieties about the stability of masculinity and, in turn, 'civilised' society. As Martin Wiener notes, for all their celebration of the manly powers of self-command, contemporaries feared that unbridled and illicit desires, an inner savage, lurked just beneath the surface of even the most 'respectable' man.[135]

In the penal colonies, if the Molesworth Committee was to be believed, this inner savage had been unleashed. Surrounded by the constant and very public spectacle of punishment, critics contended that colonists were rendered insensible and incapable of compassion for others. 'Every kind and gentle feeling of human nature is constantly outraged', Molesworth asserted, 'by the perpetual spectacle of punishment and misery, by the frequent infliction of the lash, by the horrid details of the penal settlements, till the heart of the emigrant is gradually deadened to the sufferings of others, and he becomes at last as cruel as the other gaolers of these vast prisons'.[136] Settlers who had become most addicted to violent practices such as flogging were depicted as men of bad habits more generally, supposedly revelling in the base delights of the body, and in immoral practices such as drinking, fighting, prostitution and swearing.[137] These ideas underpinned contemporary depictions of the Australian colonists as intemperate and demoralised demons. Settlers, critics contended, had 'sordid hearts'; they were men 'devoid of feeling', 'bloated profligates', who relished the idea of keeping other human beings in a state of 'hopeless servitude' and whose only ambition was to make money 'even though it should be out of the blood of their fellow man'.[138]

Accusations that the convict system was a form of slavery also generated anxiety about the economic foundations of Australian society, and this formed one component of a much broader critique of settler wealth. Civilised societies were deemed to be those in which private gain stimulated public good. Slavery, by subjugating the interests of one human being to that of another, clearly contravened this.[139] Transportation also appeared to have fostered a direct conflict between colonial interests and the British public good, placing a strain upon imperial relations. Instead of reading colonial economic development as a sign of progress, critics denounced it as the product of a demoralising dependence upon convict labour. The colonists, Wakefield asserted, owed practically 'everything . . . to the wickedness of the people of England'; this he concluded, was 'an ill wind which blows no good', because for colonial growth to be sustained, crime in Britain would have to 'keep pace with the spread of colonization'.[140] 'Every employer of labour', he explained, 'longs with the most selfish recesses of his heart, for an increase in . . . transportation, and loudly expresses his dread lest the parent Government should disgorge its criminals on any shore but this. Can human nature be so base?'[141] Colonial development, therefore, supposedly contravened the 'natural' rule that increases in national wealth should go hand in hand with increases in national morality, making a descent into 'savagery' inevitable. 'The *Antipodes*', Whately declared, 'are [a] people among whom every thing is *reversed*', the 'mode of civilization practiced is of a piece with the rest'.[142]

The nature of colonial wealth making was also considered to challenge conventional beliefs about the civilising nature of capital accumulation. Colonists 'must have been well-conducted to have amassed . . . fortunes', the Select Committee asked Mudie. 'Quite the reverse', he replied. Clearly perplexed by this, Committee members set about interrogating him. 'How', they repeatedly demanded to know, 'can a man beginning with nothing acquire £20,000 a year, without being an industrious, well-conducted man?' A 'great deal', Mudie continually asserted, 'was done from trick and depravity'.[143] The accumulation of property, the Reverend John Dunmore Lang agreed, was a 'very questionable' test of character in the colonies. Emancipist (ex-convict) wealth in particular had frequently been acquired in 'so questionable a way' that it allegedly inevitably failed to 'excite' the convicts 'to habits of industry and good conduct'.[144] Money-lending at extortionate terms, profiteering from the sale of demoralising consumables like spirits and tobacco, and running gambling dens were among the key sources of colonial wealth, Mudie and other witnesses claimed. Openly criminal practices including squatting, bribery, smuggling, corruption, embezzlement, cattle theft and receiving also allegedly played central roles. The economy, moreover, was allegedly in the hands of a 'sort of masonry' composed of convicts and ex-convicts who preferred to trade and deal exclusively with one another, and this 'masonry' dominated and distorted the market, eroding its civilising potential.[145]

Even when colonial wealth was accumulated by more honest means, critics were still concerned about its impact. Although the reformers regarded commerce as a civilising force, they nevertheless rejected the idea that the pursuit of wealth *alone* was positive. The 'ascendancy of mere wealth' was instead considered an obstacle to 'improvement'; it 'degrades and brutalizes the intellects and morality of the people', John Stuart Mill asserted, corrupting 'the measures of our statesmen, the doctrines of our philosophers, and harden[ing] the minds of our people so as to make it almost hopeless to inspire them with any elevation either of intellect or soul'.[146] This obsession with wealth was said to have had equally deleterious effects upon the colonies. Colonial society was 'in a barbarous condition', Wakefield asserted; 'money-making' was the 'universal object'. Colonists had consequently become a people who, despite their economic advances, had made 'no progress in the art of living'.[147] The de-civilising effects of colonial wealth accumulation similarly concerned the Select Committee. Witnesses were, as a result, repeatedly questioned as to how 'new' men of wealth spent their money. 'Does the man in possession of £20,000 a year go on accumulating his wealth, or does he spend it liberally', Molesworth asked. 'Do the arts flourish, and are there painters?' 'Is there', he continued, 'a considerable degree of refinement in the manners of that class of society, the persons who have such a command of all the luxuries and elegancies of life?' The responses were disconcerting. 'I do not know of any man in the colony who lives as a gentleman would do, who possesses that income in England', Mudie explained.[148] Colonists, Dunmore Lang agreed, were so intent on

[184]

becoming wealthy that they 'bent the whole energy of mind and body to money making'. Colonial wealth consequently appeared to be 'accumulating faster' than the 'means of employing it in a liberal and refined manner'.[149]

Clearly discomfited by the apparent speed with which some colonists had made money, a number of commentators turned to the image of the fast-moving, horse-drawn carriage to express their anxieties. Mudie, for one, clearly felt outpaced by some of his colonial competitors. Questioned as to whether there was any evidence of 'improved' civilisation in Australia, his immediate resort was to the subject of carriages. 'A great portion of the present carriages . . . belong to the emancipists', he replied, as if this told the Select Committee all it needed to know. The 'first alteration' emancipists made to their lifestyle on making their 'fortune' was to 'get some description of carriage and horses'. This ambition was so universal among emancipists that 'two or three' such vehicles could be seen 'passing at a time' with decidedly unsettling results; he regularly ran the risk of 'being run down in the streets', Mudie complained.[150] Colonial carriages equally fascinated Wakefield. Keeping a carriage was, he noted, a test of 'respectability' in Britain but in the colonies, its message was decidedly ambiguous. 'A dashing English landau' (a four-wheeled carriage) has 'just passed my window', Wakefield wrote, 'it contains a 'lady' who married a poor half-pay lieutenant' but 'who now drinks tea that would cost in England twenty shillings the pound'. The couple had recently emigrated so their wealth was wholly 'new'. How, Wakefield asked, 'did she get that carriage?' By crime in Britain was the answer. Even the 'coat of arms' on her carriage was deceptive; apparently a badge of 'respectability' and established class status, it had, in fact, been invented by the Heralds' College in return for a payment out of those same convict-derived profits.[151]

These sentiments were undoubtedly partly inspired by crude class snobbery and by fear and resentment at the prospect of being 'run down' by those who were supposed to be socially inferior. The success of lower-class colonists, and of ex-convicts in particular, undercut the belief of men like Mudie in the established social hierarchy, challenging their decidedly exclusivist and conservative world views. These kinds of critiques were, however, equally nourished and sustained by liberal claims about the destabilising effects of colonial society on the balance between body and mind. In Wakefield's view, the body all too often dominated and governed the settler. This was partly a product of their predominantly lower-class origins: 'emigrants', he asserted, were overwhelmingly 'of the gormandising and guzzling classes', people who delighted in 'goose, sausages and pork chops'. They came to the colonies 'to live not to enjoy; to eat and drink, not to refine; to "settle" – that is, to roll in a gross plenty for the body, but to starve their minds'.[152] Colonial conditions further strengthened these tendencies, producing bodies that were stronger and healthier, taller and even more beautiful in their youth than their metropolitan counterparts, but providing next to no intellectual conversation or stimuli correspondingly to develop and strengthen the mind. Endless over-indulgence eventually took its toll: the settlers gradually became fat and acquired bad teeth. These were the outward manifestations of a profound deterioration of the British self. 'The face is the mirror of the mind', the 'form' an 'index of the habits', Wakefield wrote. Bad teeth and fat were therefore certain signs that it was the destiny of a 'new people' to become 'rotten before they are ripe'.[153]

Colonial conditions had equally unsettled the broader body politic. Wakefield's fictional settler reported that he had brought John, his 'own man' with him, a servant 'who had served me for eight years in England' and who 'had often sworn that he would go the wide world over with me, seeing that I was the best of masters'. John, however, had deserted him even before they reached their new colonial home, exchanging stable Old World loyalties and hierarchical social affiliations for a historically immature and volatile social, cultural and political egalitarianism. Investing his money in some land of his own, John quickly became 'one of the most consequential persons in the Colony', and his class-based irrationality and indiscipline rapidly shone through. John had 'grown enormously fat', Wakefield reported; he 'feeds upon greasy dainties' and 'drinks oceans of bottled porter and port wine'.[154] John's appetite for politics was deemed equally irrational: he 'damns the Governor and swears by all his gods, Jupiter, Jingo and Old Harry, that this Colony must soon be independent'.[155] This, Wakefield declared, was the kind of 'democratic spirit which *must* exist, where every man possesses a little wealth and a little knowledge, but no man' possesses 'much of either'. Like the Americans before them, he contended, the Australians were in danger of 'growing up ... ignorant and democratical' and would eventually 'govern, or rather misgovern themselves'.[156] Self-government, Wakefield asserted, was inevitable and, in principle, welcome, but colonists had to be educated and prepared for it: their minds had to be systematically cultivated. These views reflected fears about the unbalanced character of colonial class structure: the preponderance of lower-class settlers was deemed to have created a society without a head. Only by using 'a mixture of all classes of society' to colonise, Wakefield noted, would it be possible to maintain proper habits of 'regularity and subordination'.[157]

Finally, the reformers condemned the colonial economic system on the grounds that it stimulated an unnatural and demoralising reliance upon government. Dependence in men was considered both morally and physically enervating: the 'best mode of developing' the 'bold, energetic and self-relying' manliness which empire required was, Molesworth contended, not to 'coddle and fondle' men nor to 'tie them to a mother's apron' but to 'throw them upon their own resources and let them rough it and battle it with the world'. Imperial mis-government, he claimed, was achieving the exact opposite: London's failure to allow colonists to govern their own affairs had transformed them into 'weak, puling infants, ever crying to their mother for assistance and emptying her purse'.[158] Although Molesworth considered these features to be evident throughout the empire, he argued that they were particularly pronounced in the Australian colonies because settlers there were unduly reliant, as a result of the convict system, upon government contracts and public spending. Rather than devel-oping their own independent resources they had instead allegedly become dependent upon the state and formed part of a 'noxious race', a 'jobbing and peculating tribe' who 'made, or expect to make, large gains by contracts, jobs, and . . . innumerable other modes of robbing the mother country'.[159]

Habits such as these were considered destructive of proper manli-ness *and* of British character. Dependence upon the state had created 'listlessness and unmanly apathy' within the colonial community, Anthony Trollope asserted on a visit to Van Diemen's Land some years later. 'Men', he explained, 'learn to regard the government as babies regard the nurse – and are like the big calf which can only be kept from its overwrought mother's dugs by some process of disagree-able expulsion. Personal enterprise and national enterprise are equally destroyed by it'.[160] Heavy state spending was also considered a certain sign of 'Old Corruption': radicals believed that the strength of illiberal government was founded in the corruption of men by patronage and bribery, and these arguments had formed part of their critique of the unreformed British state for decades. Imperial expenditure was interpreted as a sign of 'Old Corruption' abroad, apparent evidence that the colonies were becoming bastions of aristocracy, privilege and tyranny.[161] Reformers argued that growing numbers of colonists were, as a result, losing their attachment to the principles of the constitution. They had, in Molesworth's view, become 'unworthy Anglo-Saxons', men 'who in their hearts, prefer Colonial Office despotism, with huge imperial expenditure, to the freest institutions with imperial economy'.[162]

This situation was allegedly made worse by the undemocratic nature of colonial government and by the feelings of social caste that reformers believed slavery invariably aroused. Combined, these were deemed to have created a profoundly illiberal and irrational colonial public sphere. Settlers, Maconochie contended, were rarely given the chance to think for themselves for colonial government was characterised by 'discretionary authority' and despotic habits of 'command'. Arthur's propensity for centralised government and his 'strong love of power' were particularly condemned: 'he sought to make obedient, well con-ducted slaves', Maconochie asserted, 'not to give a moral development to the community under him'. In Maconochie's view, the colonial state had a crucial tutelary role to play and thus a fundamental respon-sibility to govern in ways that would help fashion moral, rational and self-governing subjects. Van Diemen's Land required 'a constitution' which:

> will *compel* its Government to *reason* with the people, and *bear* and *forbear*; not merely *command*, in dealing with them. This of itself would soon cure every evil. The intelligence of the people, stimulated by intelligence and confidence on the part of the Government, would soon remove misconceptions on both sides; and passion, and its exciting causes, would go to sleep together.[163]

In the eyes of the reformers, such a constitution, although desirable, was, nevertheless, impossible while transportation continued. Political rights were to be exercised by rational, morally sensible, self-governing men. Liberty was to be extended to colonists on the same basis as the franchise would be expanded to include workers at home: as they matured and developed manly habits of independence, intelligence, 'industry' and 'prudence'.[164] Thus, although the Colonial Reformers considered self-government and the political emancipation of the colonies to be an ultimate good they argued that the timing and char-acter of this process would inevitably vary. 'The form of government which a colony should possess must depend', Molesworth explained, 'upon the special circumstances of the case'. Only a tiny handful of colonies, he contended, were as yet ready 'to try the experiment of pure democracy'.[165]

The penal colonies were deemed insufficiently mature both because they contained large populations of convicts and because slavery was considered to have generated irrationality and a 'prejudice of caste' among the settlers.[166] The reformers contended that the latter fact, in particular, had created a volatile and irrational colonial public sphere and had fostered illiberal and un-British political sentiments. In Molesworth's view, the existence of the 'exclusives', a faction that sought to prevent ex-convicts from regaining the 'constitutional privileges of Englishmen' provided compelling evidence of the ill effects of the convict system upon settler character. These men, he concluded, were:

> persons upon whose characters and dispositions the domestic slavery and penal nature of the colony has had the worst possible effect, by rendering them harsh, peremptory and overbearing, and by converting them into cruel and hard-hearted slave-owners, with feelings of hatred, suspicion and ill-disguised contempt for all who have had the misfortune of incurring the displeasure of the criminal tribunals of their country.[167]

Although the Select Committee rejected exclusivist claims, concerned that civil disabilities would create a permanent 'stigma' upon a whole class of colonial men, it was anxious, nevertheless, about the dangers of extending political liberties to the penal colonies.[168] Free institutions, Judge William Westbrook Burton averred, might be the birthright, the 'pride and the boast', of Englishmen, but it was questionable whether they could be safely extended to New South Wales and Van Diemen's Land. In his view, the influence of 'bad men' would almost certainly lead to the 'total corruption' of such institutions.[169] These views appeared to be confirmed by a host of witnesses who claimed that ex-convicts were addicted to practices such as 'false swearing' in court and that they could not be trusted to play an impartial role on a jury. The value of principles such as freedom of the press was also called into question. Contemporaries considered that newspapers played a key role in the creation of a rational and educated public, but that this was distorted in the colonies where convicts and ex-convicts allegedly largely controlled them.[170] In Wakefield's view, for example, the colonial press contained nothing 'but the miserable party politics of this speck upon the globe, reports of crime and punishment, and low-lived slang and flash'.[171] All this tended to confirm fears that British liberties could not be extended to the colonies while transportation continued.

* * *

The disorder and demoralisation pervading the colonial public sphere was allegedly reflected in the aberrant character and deviant state of the settler family. This was profoundly worrying because contemporaries regarded the family as the basic building block of a good society. The separation of public and private spheres supposedly served to guarantee this: the home provided a moral haven and a bulwark against the pollution and disorder of the wider world.[172] In the penal colonies, however, the convict system appeared to have invaded the

[189]

private sphere, bringing not only the world but also its most demor-alised and criminal aspects into the home. Assignment was con-sequently not only denounced as a form of slavery but more crucially as a system of '*domestic* slavery'.[173] Every settler, Whately declared, 'is, as far as his own household is concerned, the keeper of *a house of correction*'.[174] The presence of coercion and force within the domestic sphere was considered a sign of savagery and historical backwardness. The slave, the concubine and the harem woman were deployed repeatedly in this period as symbols of the de-civilising habits of cruelty and force which supposedly invaded the intimate relations and domestic spaces of 'other' nations and races. Families were properly based upon love and consent; coercion and force had no place within the home. These ideas were grounded in Enlightenment and liberal discourses, which regarded companionate and consensual relations within the private sphere as the mirror image of a rational and partici-patory civil society.[175]

Contemporaries regarded the home as a crucible of sympathy and social affection. Consideration and kindness were vital *social* virtues, Sarah Stickney Ellis, one of the key architects of early Victorian domestic ideology asserted, but they were acquired and inculcated at home. The ordered home was a site of 'natural' affection and thus an antidote to the competitive and individualistic spirit that perme-ated the male public sphere. 'Fireside comforts' and a wife's good character had the power to draw a man away from the 'snares of the world' and, in particular, the single-minded and selfish pursuit of 'mammon'.[176] The family also served as a model for social union. 'Where the female members of a family are considerate', Ellis advised, 'there is a secret spring of sympathy linking all hearts together, as if they were moved by a simultaneous impulse of kindness on one side and gratitude on the other'.[177] This model could be applied fruitfully to the world beyond the home and to class relationships, in particular. Servants, Ellis urged, should never be treated as 'a sort of household machinery' but as 'individuals, possessing hearts as susceptible of certain kinds of feeling, as those of the more privileged beings'. Nothing 'softens and ennobles, subdues and exalts' so much as 'gratitude', she advised.[178] The well-ordered and affectionate family was also a model for the empire. The 'noble daring of Britain has sent forth her adven-turous sons' to 'every point of danger on the habitable globe', Ellis commented. 'They have borne along with them a generosity, a dis-interestedness and a moral courage, derived ... from the female influence of their native country'. In common with other liberal and reforming thinkers, Ellis believed that moral femininity and properly ordered domesticity were powerful forces for imperial reform.[179]

The Australian family was, however, perceived as a site of coercion and conflict and thus as a potent source of social disunion. The presence of convict slaves within the home had filled 'domestic life' with 'discord', 'fretfulness of temper', 'suspicion and violent invective'. The 'habit of enforcing obedience by mere compulsion' had, moreover, led to 'a total disuse of moral motives in the domestic relations of life'. A 'harsh, peremptory and overbearing character' supposedly characterised colonial family life, and this, in turn, pervaded the 'whole intercourse of society'. The volatile and divisive character of colonial politics and the inflammatory tone of the press were allegedly grounded in these facts. 'The habit which most of the free contract, of thinking and speaking of, and treating the convicts contemptuously' had, Maconochie declared, fostered a culture in which 'every difference of opinion constitutes a ground of quarrel'. 'Every man' in Van Diemen's Land 'appears to be armed against his fellow', Cheyne concurred. Colonial society was characterised by feelings of 'envy, hatred' and 'uncharitableness' and by a marked absence of public spirit. A culture of rank individualism, 'suspicion' and 'disunion' allegedly 'without precedent in civilised life' supposedly prevailed.[180]

Colonial femininity was also deemed to have failed in the task of softening and morally replenishing men upon their return home from the hardening, individualistic and competitive domain of the market. Domesticated, moral women and an ordered and loving family life were supposed to draw men away from the ruthless habits that were fostered by the market. There was, however, an allegedly limited correlation between colonial wealth and proper standards of domesticity. The wives of some of the wealthiest colonial men were tainted and debased and consequently incapable of playing a softening and 'civilising' role. Many of the wealthiest men lived with female convicts, often out of wedlock, Mudie alleged. They, therefore, allowed 'women of the lowest grade to take the head of their table'. One such man, he elaborated, emphasising the alien and deviant character of colonial domesticity, was married to an ex-convict 'by the name of Tambourine Sal' who 'used to beat the tambourine about the streets of London with the hurdy-gurdy people' and was 'very much like a gipsy'. She 'could not talk, Mudie recounted, 'without swearing in the coarsest way'. Power relations within these households were distorted and inverted; all too often, Mudie claimed, these 'ladies' were allowed to 'rule the roost'. No attempts were made to educate and civilise the children in such households, with the result that most grew up 'ignorant', hardly 'able to read and write' and knowing little of moral propriety. Their daughters dress 'in a sort of showy, tawdry stuff', Mudie alleged, and they had become so devoid of feminine sensibilities that they were happy to 'look on' while their brothers indulged in cruel and irrational pastimes like badger baiting, cock and dog fighting, bull baiting and boxing.[181]

The perceived effects of the convict system upon colonial children particularly exercised critics. The settler had at least benefited from a British upbringing, and the fact that his character was 'already formed' before he arrived in the colonies provided some grounds for hoping that contact with the system might not '*wholly* subvert' him. His children, by contrast, were 'reared in the midst of it', their 'habits and dispositions' supposedly completely determined by convict society. Where adults acquired capricious and tyrannical *tendencies*, the children developed a *full-blown* capacity for 'cruel, imperious and haughty' behaviour.[182] They 'imbibe' feelings of scorn towards convicts from 'their infancy', Van Demonian author Caroline Leakey explained; 'it grows with their growth and strengthens with strength at rapid paces'. Inured to cruelty from an early age, Charlie, one of several children in Leakey's novel *Broad arrow*, has consequently become insensible to suffering. Unlike his cousin Bridget who, recently arrived from England, still 'trembles' with suitably innocent pity at the sight of men in chains, Charlie is wholly unperturbed. Convicts have become such a normal part of his everyday life that their presence no longer elicits even a 'shudder' from this 'lovely specimen of infant Tasmania'.[183]

Contact with convict servants was, in addition, considered to morally contaminate the rising generation. Colonial children were, as a result, considered undisciplined and contemptuous of authority: under convict influence, they had allegedly developed habits of disrespect and were deemed to lack that 'spirit of reverence' for 'superior authority' so routinely found among their counterparts in the mother country. For those like the Colonial Reformers, who regarded the family as a model of ordered imperial relations, the 'insolence of feeling and of bearing' which colonial children had allegedly developed 'towards their elders' did not bode well. Children were also deemed to have acquired morally dissipated and corrupt characters: 'there is', Ullathorne asserted, 'a great deal of dissoluteness of language amongst the children at a very early age'. Too few of them, he contended, were given the chance to develop sufficiently 'their moral powers' before they came into contact with convicts. Instead, the majority were 'taught' crime at an age when their 'animal spirits' were still dominant and before they were old enough to judge right from wrong.[184] Although little more than an infant, Charlie had therefore lost his 'innocence', acquired a vocabulary of slang and 'bad' words, and had become complicit with the secret immoralities of his family's convict servants. He was able to navigate the 'low' back streets and demoralised sexual and drinking 'dens' of Hobart with frightening ease and was repeatedly drawn to the spectacle of convict wrongdoing. His 'moral sensibilities' have been 'imperceptibly weakened' by his 'daily contact with crime'.[185]

Sexual knowingness was regarded as the ultimate sign of this process of systematic degradation, not least because it signalled the total moral destruction of the child. Female convict servants, because so many of them associated closely with their employers' children, were regarded inevitably with suspicion. There was, Murdock asserted, nothing 'more injurious to the character of the rising generation' than 'to be under the charge of such people'. 'Horrible cases', he declared, had 'occurred ... to the younger members of a family, arising from association with these depraved females'.[186] These kinds of accounts led repeatedly, and almost inevitably, to sensationalist tales of seduction. 'I know of a melancholy instance', John Russell claimed, 'where three girls ... were left in the society of a convict servant maid by their mother'. 'These children', he elaborated, 'were used as spies' for the convict woman's 'paramour, and were often witnesses of her intrigues, and, I believe, absolutely of her connexion with the man'. It was, in Russell's mind, but a small step from this passive, but illicit, spectatorship to active participation: having 'watched' their convict maid, these three girls quickly became pregnant 'by a connexion of their own'.[187]

For all the emphasis that historians have placed upon the idea that convict women were perceived as the ultimate source of moral pollution, assigned female servants mostly played subordinate roles in these seduction narratives. Male convicts, by comparison, were constructed as figures of outright danger and as a compelling sexual threat. There had, colonist John Barnes asserted, been 'many instances' of 'improper intercourse ... between a prisoner and the female branches of a family'. Although male convicts in positions of trust – particularly those employed in families as tutors and schoolmasters – came under particular suspicion, Barnes was convinced that the problem was even more widespread. Regaling the Select Committee with the details of several cases, he claimed that the daughters of some 'respectable' settlers had also formed sexual liaisons with convict men in the road gangs and even the 'common farm servants'. In only one of these cases was Barnes actually able to furnish anything approaching hard evidence, however – the young women concerned were infected with venereal disease. The other cases he cited were, by contrast, almost wholly based upon colonial gossip, rumour and repute.[188]

Much of the other testimony about the seduction of children delivered to the Select Committee was similarly impressionistic and anecdotal in nature. Witnesses repeatedly made sweeping claims on the basis of a tiny number of cases. 'I remember being very much shocked' by cases in which convict men had 'attempted to violate children of very tender years', Ullathorne testified. When pressed he could, however, only recall two such instances.[189] Russell also sought – at the express invitation of the Select Committee – to substantiate wide-ranging claims that male 'convict servants contaminated the rising generation' by providing an extremely detailed account of just *one* child rape trial.[190] While carnal knowledge and child rape cases certainly occurred, there was little to sustain claims that they were endemic, or that they were more prevalent than in Britain.[191] The shocking and sensationalist details of a handful of individual cases nevertheless provided the basis for sweeping generalisations, enabling critics to depict the colonies as places of extreme cruelty and depravity. Convict men, Molesworth concluded – as if it happened every day – had forced their 'brutal caresses' upon even the most 'tender infants'.[192] These views predated the Select Committee's enquiries, and they had circulated among the Colonial Reformers, in particular, for some time. 'Every female child in this colony', Wakefield had, for example, proclaimed as early as 1829 (and despite the fact that he had never been in the Australian colonies), 'is sure to be hunted by a dozen roaring lions, and her destruction is almost inevitable'.[193]

Witnesses contended that it was impossible for even the most vigilant of parents completely to protect their children.[194] Constant contact between children and convict servants meant that families faced an uphill struggle to counteract the convict 'poison' with the 'antidote' of good parenting. The lessons that a child received 'with reverence on the mother's lap or father's knee' were, Leakey argued, endlessly being 'contradicted by the practices of convict life'. To believe that it was possible to 'shield' a child from convict influence was akin to imagining that a 'lily' might 'grow up . . . among thorns'.[195] Allegations of child rape served to dramatise and thoroughly moralise the question of convict labour for they begged the question of why colonial parents continued to hire convicts as household servants. In Dunmore Lang's view the answer lay in the thoroughly deficient character of colonial parenthood. 'The moral sense of many parents . . . is sufficiently obtuse', he asserted, 'to lead them to prefer the service of the convict who can be obtained on easy terms, to that of the free man, for whom a respectable salary would be required'. 'Do you mean', Molesworth asked, 'that the pecuniary advantage which they would acquire by engaging the service of a convict gets the better of their apprehension of the immoral influence likely to be created on the mind of a child?' 'Decidedly so', Dunmore Lang replied.[196]

Public forms of 'fatherhood' were deemed to have been equally fatally impaired. Settlers were allegedly so distracted by the selfish pursuit of material gain and by their claims to 'superior distinction and consideration' that they had forsaken their 'relative duties' for the moral welfare of their lower-class brothers. Consequently a social chasm had opened up with the result that a 'settled antipathy nearly amounting to hatred' allegedly prevailed between the classes.[197] Long after their sentences had been served, convicts supposedly turned their backs on the free, forming entrenched anti-communities of their own, which were inevitably devoid of the beneficial moral leadership that ought to have been supplied by properly ordered middle-class men. The constant and inevitable association with convicts was, moreover, systematically demoralising and debasing every other group of lower-class colonial men, creating drunken and dissipated free labourers and ill-disciplined and depraved soldiers.[198] 'There is', Dunmore Lang proclaimed, 'an action and reaction ... perpetually going on between the classes of society originally depraved' – the convicts – 'and those which have, ostensibly at least, a better character'.[199]

The failure of colonial 'fatherhood' was considered to have had equally baneful effects upon 'helpless' groups like women and Aborigines who ought, of course, in a 'civilised' society, to have been proper subjects of paternalistic protection. Violence against these groups, and sexual violence in particular, was instead allegedly widespread.[200] Prostitution and rape were, for example, deemed to govern settler–Aboriginal relations, the diseased and violated body of the Aboriginal woman providing a potent sign that the European presence was not only incapable of civilising 'savages' but was instead dragging them backwards through time. 'The naked savage', Ullathorne asserted, 'knew of nothing monstrous in crime ... until England schooled him in horrors'.[201] Allegations of miscegenation once again raised the spectre of alien offspring. Illicit sexual relations between convict men and Aboriginal women were ostensibly creating a 'fringe ... of half-castes' all around the southern hemisphere, Whately declared. These societies had mixed 'the blood of the most debased of savages, with that of the more refined and intelligent scoundrels of civilised society' and they were consequently already 'exhibiting ... a curious specimen of the worst possible form of human nature'.[202]

* * *

The narratives of colonial disorder produced by the Molesworth Committee and a host of other critics of convict transportation were thoroughly grounded in a set of idealised notions of gender, family and domesticity. For liberal and humanitarian opponents of the system, its apparent reliance upon slave labour was antithetical to the self-governing and independent masculinity that they deemed to be both natural and desirable. The de-civilising effects of the convict system, upon settlers as well as convicts, were considered, in turn, to have fostered deviant, immoral and even 'unnatural' sexual propensities and profoundly disordered families. The physical effects were disastrous: the system was denounced as a disease and a pollutant, spreading poison through the individual body as well as infecting and contaminating the wider body politic. In the eyes of the Colonial Reformers, in particular, these conditions had created a crisis of reproduction: generating a race of increasingly 'savage' offspring in the colonies, provoking a profound deterioration of British character, and turning otherwise potentially productive and healthy imperial spaces into alien nations.

The solution, the reformers contended, lay in the creation of a new type of colonial productive and reproductive order: a putatively natural system in which the self-commanding and self-regulating independent male wage labourer would be conjoined to an equally natural and ordered domestic sphere. These conditions were designed to lay the foundations for the reconfiguration of imperial power more generally. Capable of governing himself, the colonial man would, in time, require no more than the disinterested oversight of the imperial state. Redesigned in ways that would allow them to reproduce and thus mirror the metropole, the colonies would be able to take their natural place within the consensual and companionate order that was the idealised imperial family.

The kind of colonial society that the reformers desired to build was, of course, no more or less 'natural' than the one they sought to replace. The idea that wage labour was innate and thus more inclined to enable the emergence of virtuous and self-regulating men was, as historian Thomas Holt explains, bound up with a set of views that tended 'almost by sleight of hand' to transform 'market-governed social relations' into *'natural* phenomena'.[203] The naturalised models of family to which the reformers appealed were equally social, political and cultural productions, designed to foster freedom, on the one hand, but also to contain and control, on the other. Nowhere was this more evident than in the notion of the colonies as children, developing but yet still apparently lacking that maturity which manly independence and self-government allegedly required.

Notes

1   Edward Gibbon Wakefield, *A letter from Sydney*, in M.F. Lloyd Pritchard (ed.), *The collected works of Edward Gibbon Wakefield* (London: Collins, 1968), p. 139.

2 Richard Whately, *Thoughts on secondary punishments* (London: B. Fellowes, 1832), p. 155; William Molesworth, *Report from the Select Committee of the House of Commons on transportation together with a letter from the Archbishop of Dublin on the same subject; and notes* (London: Henry Hooper, 1838), pp. 51–2.

3 Hugh Egerton (ed.), *Selected speeches of Sir William Molesworth on questions relating to colonial policy* (London: John Murray, 1903), p. 254.

4 *Ibid.*, p. 122. On the impact upon the empire see also: 'Select Committee on Transportation', *BPP* XXII (669), 1837–38, Appendix 10, pp. 262–3, 271; and Molesworth, *Report*, p. 50.

5 Francis Bacon, 'Of plantations', in *Essays of Francis Bacon* (Harmondsworth: Penguin, 1985), p. 162.

6 James Mudie, *The felonry of New South Wales* (London: Whaley & Co, 1837), pp. 13–14.

7 Wakefield, *Letter*, p. 139.

8 Hinds, cited in Whately, *Thoughts*, pp. 201–2.

9 *The Times*, 24 February 1849.

10 Richard Whately, *Remarks on transportation* (London: B. Fellowes, 1834), p. 26.

11 Klaus Knorr, *British colonial theories, 1570–1850* (Toronto: University of Toronto Press, 1944), especially chapters 3 and 7.

12 Herman Merivale, *Lectures on colonization and colonies* (London: Longman, Orme, Brown, Green and Longmans, 1841), Vol. 1, p. 134.

13 J.R. Seeley, *The expansion of England* (London: Macmillan, 1883), p. 159.

14 William Molesworth, *On colonial expenditure and government* (London: Financial Tract Association, 1882), p. 8. Originally published in 1849.

15 J.A. Roebuck, *The colonies of England* (London: John Parker, 1849), pp. 3, 170–1, 174.

16 Roebuck, *Colonies*, p. 14. See also: Molesworth, *Colonial expenditure*, p. 13; William Molesworth, *State of the nation: condition of the people* (London: Henry Hetherington, 1840), pp. 7–8.

17 Wakefield, *Letter*, p. 166.

18 Hinds cited in Whately, *Thoughts*, pp. 197–8.

19 Wakefield, *Letter*, p. 115.

20 Roebuck, *Colonies*, p. 1. Wakefield, *Letter*, p. 165.

21 Francis Mineka (ed.), *The earlier letters of John Stuart Mill 1812–1848* (Toronto: University of Toronto Press, 1963), p. 37.

22 Wakefield, *Letter*, pp. 120, 151. Emphasis in original.

23 Molesworth, *Colonial expenditure*, p. 14.

24 Hinds cited in Whately, *Thoughts*, pp. 190, 195.

25 *Ibid.*, pp. 190–1.

26 Molesworth, *Report*, p. 35. Egerton, *Selected speeches*, p. 139.

27 Wakefield, *Letter*, pp. 148–50.

28 *Ibid.*, pp. 137–8.

29 Hinds cited in Whately, *Thoughts*, pp. 190, 195.

30 Egerton, *Selected speeches*, p. 149.

31 *Ibid.*, p. 121.

32 *Ibid.*, p. 139.

33 Wakefield, *Letter*, pp. 164–5.

34 'Colonization', *Edinburgh Review*, CLXXXIII, 1850, pp. 36–7.

35 *Ibid.*, p. 54.

36 *Ibid.*, p. 4.

37 *Ibid.*, pp. 6–7.

38 For a fuller discussion see: Kirsty Reid, 'Family matters: masculinity, domesticity and power in early nineteenth-century Britain and Australia', unpublished paper presented to the 'British World' conference, Melbourne, July 2004. Available from the author.

39 On their influence in Parliament see Miles Taylor, *The decline of British radicalism, 1847–1860* (Oxford: Clarendon Press, 1995).

40 Ann Robson and John Robson (eds), *Newspaper writings by John Stuart Mill* (Toronto: University of Toronto Press, 1986), *Mill collected works*, Vol. XXIV, p. 791.

41 On the Colonial Reformers see: Bernard Semmel, *The rise of free trade imperialism: classical political economy, the empire of free trade and imperialism* (London: Cambridge University Press, 1970); Alan Mark Thornton, *The Philosophic Radicals, their influence on emigration and the evolution of responsible government for the colonies* (California: Pomona College, 1975); Miles Taylor, 'Imperium et libertas? Rethinking the radical critique of imperialism during the nineteenth century', *Journal of Imperial and Commonwealth History*, 19:1 (1991), pp. 1–23.

42 The Select Committee contained a range of individuals sympathetic to colonial reform, including Molesworth, Charles Buller, Henry Ward, Benjamin Hawes and Henry Temple Leader. While, as John Ritchie observes, there were also several leading Whigs and Tories on the committee, the Colonial Reformers attended most regularly and, led by Molesworth, they asked the most questions. There seems little doubt that they dominated proceedings. On the Molesworth Committee see: John Ritchie, 'Towards ending an unclean thing: the Molesworth Committee and the abolition of transportation to New South Wales, 1837–40', *Historical Studies*, 17:67 (1976), pp. 144–64; Norma Townsend, '"The clamour of inconsistent persons": attitudes to transportation within New South Wales in the 1830s', *Australian Journal of Politics and History*, 25:3 (1979), pp. 345–57; and Norma Townsend, 'A "mere lottery": the convict system in New South Wales through the eyes of the Molesworth Committee', *Push from the Bush*, 21 (1985), pp. 58–86.

43 *The Times*, 7 March 1847.

44 Martin Wiener, *Reconstructing the criminal: culture, law and policy in England, 1830–1914* (Cambridge: Cambridge University Press, 1990), pp. 11–12.

45 George Arthur, *Defence of transportation* (London: George Cowie, 1835), pp. 20–1.

46 George Arthur, 'Select Committee on Transportation', *BPP* XIX (518), 1837, p. 290; Arthur, *Defence*, p. 128.

47 Arthur, *Defence*, pp. 20–1.

48 *Ibid.*, pp. 103–4; Arthur, *BPP* XIX (518), 1837, p. 296; Sir Francis Forbes, *BPP* XIX (518), 1837, p. 84.

49 Hume cited in Anthony Brewer, 'Luxury and economic development: David Hume and Adam Smith', *Scottish Journal of Political Economy*, 41:1 (1998), p. 81.

50 On shifting attitudes to labour see: Brewer, 'Luxury'; A.W. Coats, 'Changing attitudes to labour in the mid-eighteenth century', *Economic History Review*, 11:1 (1958), pp. 33–51; and M.G. Marshall, 'Luxury, economic development and work motivation: David Hume, Adam Smith and J.R. McCulloch', *History of Political Economy*, 32:3 (2000), pp. 631–48.

51 John Millar, *The origin of the distinction of ranks: or, an inquiry into the circumstances which gave rise to influence and authority in the different members of society* (Bristol: Thoemmes, 1990), p. 250.

52 Poor Law Commission, Great Britain, *Copy of the report made in 1834 by the Commissioners for Inquiring into the administration and practical operation of the Poor Laws* (London: HMSO, 1905), I.3.3.

53 Joseph Atkinson, *Penal settlements and their evils* (London: Charles Gilpin, 1847), p. 36. For a similar view, see also: *BPP* XIX (518), 1837, p. 37 & *BPP* XXII (669), 1837–38, p. 70.

54 Forbes, *BPP* XIX (518), 1837, p. 79.

55 Atkinson, *Penal settlements*, p. 63.

56 Alexander Maconochie, 'Despatch from Lieutenant Governor Sir J. Franklin October 1837 relative to the present system of convict discipline in Van Diemen's Land', *BPP* XLII (309), 1837–38, p. 9.

57 *Ibid.*, p. 17; Alexander Maconochie, *Report on the state of prison discipline in Van Diemen's Land* (London: W. Clowes, 1838), p. 6.

58 Maconochie, *Report*, p. 5.
59 George Loveless, *The victims of Whiggery; being a statement of persecution experienced by the Dorchester labourers; their trial; banishment & c. Also reflections upon the present system of transportation; with an account of Van Diemen's Land, its customs, laws, climate, produce and inhabitants* (London: Cleave, 1838), p. 42.
60 Whately, *Remarks*, pp. 30–1.
61 John Russell, *BPP* XXII (669), 1837–38, p. 55.
62 James Mudie, *BPP* XIX (518), 1837, pp. 32–3.
63 William Ullathorne, *The horrors of transportation briefly unfolded to the people* (Dublin: Richard Coyne, 1838), p. 9. For a similar view see: Forbes, *BPP* XIX (518), 1837, p. 90.
64 Alexander Maconochie, *BPP* XLII (309), 1837–38, p. 6.
65 Molesworth, *Report*, p. 15; Ullathorne, *Horrors*, p. 19. The views of the abolitionists long dominated the record, shaping both literary and historical depictions of the Australian colonies. It seems more likely, as Nicholas and Shergold suggest, that employers had a disincentive to flog, given the physical injuries involved; Stephen Nicholas & Peter Shergold, 'Unshackling the past', in Stephen Nicholas (ed.), *Convict workers: Reinterpreting Australia's past* (Cambridge: Cambridge University Press, 1988), p. 11. Shaw's work supports this and suggests, additionally, that rates of flogging were lower in Van Diemen's Land than in New South Wales; A.G.L. Shaw, *Convicts and the colonies* (London: Faber & Faber, 1966), p. 201.
66 Sir George Grey cited in Thomas Holt, *The promise of freedom: race, labor, and politics in Jamaica and Britain, 1832–1938* (Baltimore, MD: Johns Hopkins University Press, 1992), p. 47.
67 Forbes, *BPP* XIX (518), 1837, pp. 86–7; William Ullathorne, *BPP* XXII (669), 1837–38, p. 27; Molesworth, *Report*, pp. 16–17; Ullathorne, *Horrors*, p. 10; Robert Hepburne, *BPP* XXII (669), 1837–38, pp. 58–9.
68 On the body and pain see: G.J. Barker-Benfield, *The culture of sensibility: sex and society in eighteenth-century Britain* (London: University of Chicago Press, 1992); Steven Bruhm, *Gothic bodies: the politics of pain in Romantic fiction* (Philadelphia, PA: University of Pennsylvania Press, 1994); Thomas Laqueur, 'Bodies, details, and the humanitarian narrative', in Lynn Hunt (ed.), *The new cultural history* (Berkeley, CA: University of California Press, 1989), pp. 176–204. On flogging see: J.R. Dinwiddy, 'The early nineteenth-century campaign against flogging in the army', *English Historical Review*, 97:383 (1982), pp. 308–31; and Myra Glenn, 'The naval reform campaign against flogging: a case study in changing attitudes towards corporal punishment, 1830–1850', *American Quarterly*, 35:4 (1983), pp. 408–25.
69 See, in particular: Michel Foucault, *Discipline and punish: the birth of the prison* (London: Allen Lane, 1977); Michael Ignatieff, *A just measure of pain: the penitentiary in the Industrial Revolution, 1750–1850* (London: Macmillan, 1978); and Randall McGowen, 'The body and punishment in eighteenth-century England', *Journal of Modern History*, 59:4 (1987), pp. 651–79.
70 On the continued use of pain see Wiener, *Reconstructing the criminal*, pp. 111–13, 123–4.
71 Charles Rowcroft, *Tales of the colonies or, the adventures of an emigrant edited by a late colonial magistrate* (London: Saunders & Otley, 1843), Vol. 2, p. 281. On contemporary depictions of the Australian colonies as places of indiscriminate flogging, see: J.B. Hirst, *Convict society and its enemies: a history of early New South Wales* (Sydney: George Allen & Unwin, 1983).
72 Ullathorne, *BPP* XXII (669), 1837–38, p. 21; William Ullathorne, *The Catholic mission in Australasia* (Liverpool: Rockliff & Duckworth, 1837), pp. iv, 18.
73 Ullathorne, *Catholic mission*, p. 24.
74 James Ross, *An essay on prison discipline in which is detailed the system pursued in Van Diemen's Land* (Hobart: James Ross, 1833), pp. 17–18. Ross was not opposed

to transportation but he nevertheless shared contemporary concerns about the dehumanising and demoralising effects of severe penal discipline.

75 Russell, *BPP* XXII (669), 1837–38, p. 51.
76 Ullathorne, *BPP* XXII (669), 1837–38, p. 31; John Barnes, *BPP* XXII (669), 1837–38, p. 38.
77 Alexander Cheyne, *BPP* XLII (309), 1837–38, pp. 55–6.
78 Molesworth, *Report*, p. 23.
79 Atkinson, *Penal settlements*, p. 15.
80 Ross, *Essay*, pp. 12–13. Ross was here speaking of severe punishment as it was inflicted in Britain, but the broader point remains the same.
81 Matthew Forster, *BPP* XLII (309), 1837–38, p. 65. See also Forbes, *BPP* XIX (518), 1837, pp. 84–5.
82 Maconochie, *BPP* XLII (309), 1837–38, p. 17.
83 Alexander Maconochie, *On punishment* (London: Mitchell & Son, 1857), pp. 7–8; Alexander Maconochie, *Secondary punishment: the mark system of prison discipline* (London: John Ollivier, 1848), pp. 3–4.
84 Peter Murdock, *BPP* XXII (669), 1837–38, p. 124.
85 Molesworth, *Report*, p. 23.
86 Maconochie, *BPP* XLII (309), 1837–38, p. 74.
87 Ian Brand, *The convict probation system: Van Diemen's Land 1839–1854* (Hobart: Blubber Head Press, 1990).
88 Molesworth, *Report*, p. 33.
89 *BPP* XLII (309), 1837–38, p. 16.
90 Few brought the matter up voluntarily but eleven of the fourteen witnesses who had first-hand experience of the colonies were questioned on these matters and several had clearly been prepared in advance. Sir Edward Parry, for example, noted that his attention had been drawn to the subject 'two or three days' prior to his appearance; Parry, *BPP* XXII (669), 1837–38, p. 66.
91 William Ullathorne, *The Devil is a jackass being the dying words of the autobiographer William Bernard Ullathorne* (Bath: Downside Abbey Publications, 1995), p. 163; Ullathorne, *BPP* XXII (669), 1837–38, pp. 21, 24–6. See also Ernest Augustus Slade, *BPP* XIX (518), 1837, pp. 66–70.
92 See, for example, Price Warung, *Tales of the convict system* (St Lucia, Queensland: University of Queensland Press, 1975), especially pp. 113–67.
93 Ullathorne, *Catholic mission*, p. 32; Ullathorne, *BPP* XXII (669), 1837–38, p. 24.
94 Alan Bray, 'Homosexuality and the signs of male friendship in Elizabethan England', *History Workshop Journal*, 29 (1990), pp. 1–19; Harry Cocks, *Nameless offences: homosexual desire in the nineteenth century* (London: I.B. Tauris, 2003).
95 Ullathorne, *BPP* XXII (669), 1837–38, p. 21. These ideas about criminal appetite were grounded in broader discourses depicting working-class men and women as heated, governed by appetite and likely to succumb to temptation. See Francoise Barret-Ducrocq, *Love in the time of Victoria: sexuality, class and gender in nineteenth-century London* (London: Verso, 1991).
96 Caroline Chisholm, *Emigration and transportation relatively considered* (London: John Ollivier, 1847), p. 16. See also: Loveless, *Victims*, p. 23.
97 Molesworth, *Report*, p. 33.
98 Ullathorne, *Horrors*, pp. 14–15, 26–7.
99 *BPP* XLII (309) 1837–38, p. 83.
100 *HRA* I, 20, pp. 539–41.
101 *Ibid.*, p. 540; Maconochie, *Report*, p. 10. These ideas formed the second key strand of Maconochie's Mark System, which he also notably referred to as his Social System.
102 Ross, *Essay*, pp. 25–6, 33. Ross was critiquing the contemporary emphasis on separating the sexes. He considered that the assignment system, by placing men and women together, overcame this.
103 Chisholm, *Emigration*, pp. 16, 20.

104 Dunmore Lang, *BPP* XIX (518), 1837, pp. 254–5. See also: *BPP* XIX (518), 1837, pp. 153–4.
105 Murdock, *BPP* XXII (669), 1837–38, p. 120. On emigration see: Robin Haines, *Emigration and the labouring poor: Australian recruitment in Britain and Ireland, 1831–60* (Basingstoke: Macmillan, 1997); and Jan Gothard, *Blue China: single female migration to colonial Australia* (Carlton, Victoria: Melbourne University Press, 2001).
106 Whately cited in Molesworth, *Report*, p. 51. Emigration officials contended that the emigrants had been of 'unblemished character' prior to departure and that if they had become dissolute it was as a result of colonial corruption. See: *BPP* XXII (669), 1837–38, pp. 88–101, 105–13.
107 See, for example: Diana Paton, 'Decency, dependence and the lash: gender and the British debate over slave emancipation, 1830–34', *Slavery and Abolition*, 17:3 (1996), pp. 163–84; and Marcus Wood, *Slavery, empathy and pornography* (Oxford: Oxford University Press, 2002).
108 Molesworth, *Report*, p. 12. Mudie and Slade alone testified that female convicts were sought by *some* settlers to work as prostitutes. The Committee nevertheless concluded that this was widespread. See: *BPP* XIX (518), 1837, pp. 46, 63.
109 Arthur, *BPP* XIX (518), 1837, pp. 311–12.
110 Ullathorne, *Catholic mission*, p. 26.
111 Mudie, *BPP* XIX (518), 1837, pp. 38, 102.
112 William Acton, *Prostitution* (London: MacGibbon & Kee, 1968), p. 119. On femininity and deviance in the period see: Lynda Nead, *Myths of sexuality: representations of women in Victorian Britain* (Oxford: Basil Blackwell, 1988); and Lucia Zedner, *Women, crime and custody in Victorian England* (Oxford: Clarendon Press, 1991).
113 Ullathorne, *BPP* XXII (669), 1837–38, p. 21.
114 Murdock, *BPP* XXII (669), 1837–38, p. 118.
115 Molesworth, *Report*, p. 12.
116 Wakefield, *Letter*, p. 138.
117 Murdock, *BPP* XXII (669), 1837–38, pp. 118–19.
118 *BPP* XIX (518), 1837, pp. 40, 64.
119 Forbes, *BPP* XIX (518), 1837, p. 92.
120 Ullathorne, *Catholic mission*, p. 29.
121 *Ibid.*, p. 27.
122 Mudie, *BPP* XIX (518), 1837, pp. 40–1. See also Mudie, *Felonry*, pp. 195–9.
123 Wakefield, *Letter*, p. 138; Slade, *BPP* XXII (669), 1837–38, pp. 62–3.
124 Ullathorne, *Catholic mission*, p. v.
125 Adam Smith, *An inquiry into the nature and causes of the wealth of nations* (London: Methuen and Co., 1904), III.2.10.
126 Thomas Jefferson cited in William Wilberforce, *Negro slavery; or a view of some of the more prominent features of that state of society, as it exists in the United States of America and in the colonies of the West Indies, especially in Jamaica* (New York: Greenwood, 1969), pp. 23–4.
127 William Wilberforce, *An appeal to the religion, justice and humanity of the inhabitants of the British empire in behalf of the Negro slaves in the West Indies* (London: J. Hatchard, 1823), p. 4.
128 Maconochie, *Report*, p. 8.
129 Russell, *BPP* XXII (669), 1837–38, p. 57.
130 Ullathorne, *Catholic mission*, p. 22.
131 Maconochie, *Report*, p. 6; Ullathorne, *Horrors*, p. 17.
132 Ullathorne, *Catholic mission*, pp. 22–3.
133 Robert Shoemaker, 'Male honour and the decline of public violence in eighteenth-century London', *Social History*, 26:2 (2001), pp. 190–208.
134 Randall McGowen, 'Civilising punishment: the end of the public execution in England', *Journal of British Studies*, 33:3 (1994), p. 263.

135 Wiener, *Reconstructing the criminal*, pp. 26–8.
136 Molesworth, *Report*, p. 36.
137 See, for example: *BPP* XXII (669), 1837–38, pp. 57, 123.
138 William Ashton, *A lecture on the evils of emigration and transportation* (Sheffield: J. Lingard, 1838), pp. 4, 6, 9; Saxe Bannister, *On abolishing transportation and on reforming the Colonial Office* (London: Effingham Wilson, 1837), pp. 5, 38.
139 G.R. Searle, *Morality and the market in Victorian Britain* (Oxford: Clarendon Press, 1998).
140 Wakefield, *Letter*, pp. 125–7.
141 *Ibid.*, p. 139.
142 Whately, *Remarks*, p. 38. Emphasis in original. See also: Richard Whately, *Introductory lectures on political economy* (London: B. Fellowes, 1832), VIII.8.
143 Mudie, *BPP* XIX (518), 1837, pp. 103–4.
144 Lang, *BPP* XIX (518), 1837, p. 258.
145 Mudie, *BPP* XIX (518), 1837, pp. 103, 106. See also: pp. 219–20, 254.
146 Mineka, *Earlier letters*, pp. 36–7, 48.
147 Wakefield, *Letter*, pp. 119, 151–2.
148 Mudie, *BPP* XIX (518), 1837, p. 101.
149 Lang, *BPP* XIX (518), 1837, p. 256; Mudie, *BPP* XIX (518), 1837, p. 103.
150 Mudie, *BPP* XIX (518), 1837, p. 107.
151 Wakefield, *Letter*, pp. 118, 126.
152 *Ibid.*, pp. 115, 148–50.
153 *Ibid.*, pp. 148, 152. On the health, physical strength and beauty of colonists see: *ibid.*, pp. 101, 146–49. On the supposed absence of 'intellectual society': *ibid.*, pp. 114, 118–19.
154 *Ibid.*, p. 105.
155 *Ibid.*, p. 105.
156 *Ibid.*, p. 124. Emphasis in original.
157 Cited in *ibid.*, p. 100.
158 Egerton, *Selected speeches*, p. 277; Molesworth, *State of the nation*, p. 9.
159 Egerton, *Selected speeches*, pp. 288–9.
160 Anthony Trollope, *Australia and New Zealand* (London: Dawsons of Pall Mall, 1968), Vol. 2, pp. 5–6.
161 See, for example: Egerton, *Selected speeches*, p. 11. On the radical critique of imperial spending see: Miles Taylor, 'Empire and parliamentary reform: the 1832 Reform Act revisited', in Arthur Burns and Joanna Innes (eds), *Rethinking the Age of Reform* (Cambridge: Cambridge University Press, 2003), especially pp. 303–5.
162 Egerton, *Selected speeches*, p. 288.
163 Alexander Maconochie, *On Colonel Arthur's general character and government* (Adelaide: Nag's Head Press, 1989), pp. 18–19, 21–2.
164 Molesworth, *State of the nation*, pp. 11, 14–15; William Molesworth, *Southwark election speech* (London: Charles Westerton, 1852), p. 9.
165 Egerton, *Selected speeches*, p. 13.
166 Cheyne, *BPP* XLII (309), 1837–38, p. 63. In Molesworth's view, NSW had reached the point by the late 1830s when it was mature enough for political rights; Egerton, *Selected speeches*, pp. 27–8.
167 Molesworth, *Report*, p. 31.
168 *BPP* XXII (669), 1837–38, p. 271.
169 Judge Burton cited in *BPP* XIX (518), 1837, p. 78.
170 Slade, *BPP* XIX (518), 1837, pp. 58–9, 62. On the press and the influence of educated convicts see also: *BPP* XIX (518), 1837, pp. 21–2, 235–40.
171 Wakefield, *Letter*, p. 105.
172 Catherine Hall, 'The early formation of Victorian domestic ideology', in Sandra Burman (ed.), *Fit work for women* (London: Croom Helm, 1979), pp. 15–32.
173 Maconochie, *Report*, p. 9. Emphasis in original.
174 Whately, *Remarks*, p. 35. Emphasis in original.

175 John Tosh, *A man's place: masculinity and the middle-class home in Victorian England* (New Haven, CT: Yale University Press, 1999), p. 29. On ideas about the harem – zenana – see, for example: Antoinette Burton, 'Contesting the zenana: the mission to make "Lady Doctors for India", 1874–85', *Journal of British Studies,* 35:3 (1996), pp. 368–97.

176 Sarah Stickney Ellis, *The women of England, their social duties and domestic habits* (London: Fisher, Son & Co., 1839), pp. 52–3.

177 *Ibid,*, p. 188.

178 *Ibid.*, pp. 86, 179. Penal reformers similarly extolled the virtue of familial models and the value of disinterested kindness. See: Randall McGowen, 'A powerful sympathy: terror, the prison and humanitarian reform in early nineteenth-century Britain', *Journal of British Studies,* 25:3 (1986), pp. 312–34.

179 Ellis, *Women of England*, p. 54.

180 *BPP* XLII (309), 1837–38, pp. 7, 63; Maconochie, *Report*, p. 6.

181 Mudie, *BPP* XIX (518), 1837, pp. 101–3, 107–10.

182 Molesworth, *Report*, p. 36. Emphasis added.

183 Caroline Leakey, *Broad arrow: being passages from the history of Maida Gwynnham, a lifer* (London: Richard Bentley, 1859), www.blackmask.com/ books13c/broadarleak.htm, pp. 31–3 (accessed 9 October 2002).

184 Ullathorne, *BPP* XXII (669), 1837–38, p. 23.

185 Leakey, *Broad arrow*, pp. 31–4, 50–1, 62–3, 66–7, 93.

186 Murdock, *BPP* XXII (669), 1837–38, p. 119. For similar views, see: Russell, *BPP* XXII (669), 1837–38, p. 56; Ullathorne, *Catholic mission*, p. 28; Molesworth, *Report*, p. 36.

187 See also: Barnes, *BPP* XXII (669), 1837–38, p. 47; Ullathorne, *BPP* XXII (669), 1837–38, p. 24.

188 Barnes, *BPP* XXII (669), 1837–38, p. 47.

189 Ullathorne, *BPP* XXII (669), 1837–38, p. 24.

190 Russell, *BPP* XXII (669), 1837–38, pp. 55–6.

191 Slade, *BPP* XIX (518), 1837, p. 67. Between 1824 and 1838 the VDL Supreme Court convicted *just* eleven men of carnal knowledge, of ravishment or of the intent to commit these offences; AOT SC 41.

192 Molesworth, *Report*, p. 36.

193 Wakefield, *Letter*, p. 138.

194 See, for example, Russell, *BPP* XXII (669), 1837–38, p. 57.

195 Leakey, *Broad arrow*, pp. 30–1.

196 Lang, *BPP* XIX (518), 1837, p. 257.

197 *BPP* XLII (309), 1837–38, p. 55.

198 See, for example, William Henry Breton, *BPP* XIX (518), 1837, pp. 135–42.

199 Lang, *BPP* XIX (518), 1837, p. 234.

200 See: Bannister, *Abolishing*, p. 7; and *BPP* XIX (518), 1837, pp. 23–4, 27, 48, 66, 151.

201 Ullathorne, *Catholic mission*, p. v. These views had already been well established and popularised, not least by the 1836–37 British Parliamentary Select Committee on Aborigines: 'Select Committee on Aborigines in British Settlements', *BPP* VIII (538), 1836 and *BPP* VII (425), 1837.

202 Whately, *Thoughts*, p. 96.

203 Holt, *The promise*, p. xix. Emphasis in original.

CHAPTER SIX

Sodomy and self-government

Convict transportation and colonial independence

On 11 November 1846, Michael Lyons was executed at Hobart, having been convicted before the colony's Supreme Court of an 'unnatural crime'.[1] Aged just nineteen, Lyons had been transported from Ireland some fifteen months before. Three other convicts – William Bryant, George Bowden and Alexander McKay – testified that they had discovered him having sex with a goat. Insisting that he was innocent of the charge, Lyons claimed that Bryant, Bowden and McKay were engaged in a conspiracy against him and that they had warned him on several occasions that they would get him into trouble. They regarded him as a traitor, he argued, and had determined to exact revenge upon him for informing on a number of other convicts in a previous case involving stolen blankets. Concerned both by the safety of the conviction and the severity of the sentence, Catholic chaplain William Hall repeatedly sought clemency. Surely, Hall appealed to the colonial government, it was always better 'that twenty guilty escape than one innocent man be sacrificed'.[2]

Lyons's fate had been all but sealed, however, by the arrival of a despatch from London shortly before his trial announcing the summary dismissal of Governor John Eardley Wilmot. Accusations about the prevalence of 'unnatural' crimes in the colony and claims about his own personal sexual immorality were central to Eardley Wilmot's abrupt removal and consequent disgrace. The despatch accused the Governor of allowing a state of affairs to exist in which 'crime' in 'some of its very worst and most revolting excesses' enjoyed an 'extensive and undisputed reign'. A private communication accompanied it, from William Gladstone, then Under-Secretary of State, informing Eardley Wilmot that he would not be re-appointed to a government position until he cleared his name of 'rumours' relating to his private life. Despite the Governor's appeals, Gladstone steadfastly refused to furnish information as to the sources or details of these 'rumours', making it practically impossible for Eardley Wilmot to defend himself. The result, the ex-Governor argued, was that after a lifetime of public service defending the 'rule of law' he now found himself 'in the un-English position of a man charged with unknown acts' and so below the position of even the 'meanest criminal'.[3] He was, he noted, the victim of the 'most shameful conspiracy that has ever destroyed an English gentleman'.[4]

A whispering campaign against Eardley Wilmot had begun almost immediately he had taken up office. Campaigns of 'misrepresentation and detraction' were common in Van Diemen's Land, the ex-Governor claimed. Colonial interest groups had long been in the habit of spreading 'fabrications and calumnies respecting the private and public conduct of such persons as are opposed to them'. Their intention in his case, he argued, was to destroy the convict system.[5] In Eardley Wilmot's eyes, overtly political objectives lay behind the rumours that he had been guilty of an affair with 'a young lady' and, more sensationally still, that he had invited convict women to his parties and even had them 'dressed for the occasion'.[6] Not content with colonial rumour mongering, the opposition had also spread allegations in the British press.[7] Since he was thousands of miles away, it was virtually impossible for Eardley Wilmot to refute such claims. This, of course, was what gave the claims such power. Within days of receiving Gladstone's despatch, Eardley Wilmot had been forced to hand over power to Charles Joseph La Trobe, sent from Melbourne with orders to institute an interim administration until a new governor arrived. Eardley Wilmot died in Hobart shortly thereafter from 'a complete exhaustion of the frame', his public career in tatters, his private reputation in ruins. Although news of his death prompted a parliamentary inquiry, the subsequent exoneration came far too late.[8]

The decision to execute Michael Lyons was powerfully influenced by these events. Placed on trial just ten days after Eardley Wilmot's dismissal, the judge explicitly exhorted the jury to take the 'increase of crime of this description' into account.[9] The Executive Council's deliberations as to whether to proceed with sentence of death also occurred in the shadow of Eardley Wilmot's disgrace. Noting that bestiality had not been punished capitally in the colony for some years, the Colonial Secretary and the Colonial Treasurer both argued that sending Lyons to the gallows would be an injustice. The majority opinion nevertheless favoured death. It was the past failure to punish these offences properly that had enabled the natural 'horror' of them to diminish and their incidence among the convicts to increase, the Chief Police officer and the colony's leading magistrates agreed. The colony's peculiarity, they argued – particularly its demoralised convict population and relative lack of women – also made capital punishment necessary in all such cases even although it was now rarely used for these offences in Britain. Signing the death warrant, La Trobe agreed that a merciless judicial regime was crucial in a society where 'the most painful evidence of the existence of unnatural crime' was 'to be met with on every hand' and yet was treated 'with indifference' by the convict population.[10]

Ironically, it had been Eardley Wilmot who initially had done most to raise concerns about 'unnatural' sexual offences among the convicts. Within weeks of his arrival in Van Diemen's Land in 1843 he had sent a detailed 'confidential' report to Lord Stanley in an effort to draw the latter's 'attention' to the prevalence of these 'enormities'.[11] When Stanley finally replied to this, some two years later, his approach was fairly lackadaisical. Although concerned by the reports of 'unnatural' vice, he concluded that there was no particular evidence to suggest that the convict system had 'afforded peculiar temptations or facilities for the perpetration of such offences'. Concluding that there therefore were no grounds for radical changes to the system, Stanley's only advice was that a few alterations be made to convict sleeping arrangements and that Eardley Wilmot look to the clergy for help in providing convicts with extra religious instruction and thus additional moral fibre.[12]

Eardley Wilmot, by contrast, had tackled the issue of 'unnatural' offences with energy and determination. He had, he reported, used 'every means' available to him 'of suppressing or lessening this evil'. Extra police had been appointed, hundreds of additional separate cells and sleeping apartments for convicts had been built, boards had been placed between the beds of men in dormitories, night lamps had been installed, watchmen had been instructed to keep a constant eye on sleeping men through specially made apertures in the doors and walls, and officers had been ordered to make 'frequent and unexpected visits' to sleeping quarters throughout the night.[13] In addition, from late 1845 onwards, convict men confined to the penal stations and the probation gangs were – despite their protests and attempts to resist – regularly required to assemble, strip naked and undergo intimate medical examinations designed to identify and isolate those whose bodies appeared to bear signs of sexual disease and 'vice'. These initiatives, Eardley Wilmot claimed, had produced a marked reduction in the practice of 'nameless' crimes.[14] *His* actions must therefore be compared with London's systematic *in*action: for, the sacked Governor claimed, the Colonial Office had '*never answered*' his despatches on these matters and had issued him with absolutely no instructions or advice on how to proceed. It was then Gladstone rather than he who had 'failed in his duty', Eardley Wilmot alleged, but instead of admitting this, 'atrocious falsehoods' against his character had been used as a cover-up.[15]

The unprecedented haste with which the Governor was removed from office – before his successor had even arrived – almost certainly reflected the imperial government's sense that a scandal about 'unnatural' offences was about to break.[16] This, in turn – as Eardley Wilmot had suggested – was the product of a deliberate, increasingly vocal and, in many ways, brilliantly executed, colonial campaign against convict transportation. From 1844 onwards, growing numbers of colonists began to put pressure on London to abolish the convict system and to grant colonial self-government. Protest meetings were called, petitions were sent to London, and a string of letters purportedly detailing the state of the colony were published in *The Times*. Throughout this same period, a steady stream of influential colonists met with government ministers, including Lord Stanley, Earl Grey and Gladstone, and with Sir James Stephen, the powerful Permanent Under-Secretary at the Colonial Office. These lobbying efforts were formalised in early 1846 when a group of settlers established the London Agency Association of Van Diemen's Land and sent John Alexander Jackson, a prominent colonist, to London to represent their interests. Approaches were also made to the radical MP Joseph Hume to act as the colony's unofficial parliamentary representative.[17]

Colonists used these interventions to insist that Van Diemen's Land faced imminent disaster. The 'moral condition of the colony' was 'daily becoming worse and worse', one petition asserted. If transportation did not end, Van Diemen's Land would soon 'exhibit a spectacle of vice and infamy such as the history of the world cannot parallel'.[18] Those who met privately with government related similarly sensationalist stories. 'Such a picture of vice and degradation I never yet contemplated of any human society', Sir James Stephen noted in his diary after one such meeting.[19] 'The public opinion of the colonial community affirms the moral inefficiency of the system', he remarked in a letter shortly thereafter. Although these 'unofficial accounts' painted a picture 'directly opposite to that of the official reports' they had nevertheless 'convinced Mr Gladstone' that the 'system' was 'lifeless and inert for the purposes of good' and, Stephen asserted, that it had reduced convicts to a state of 'advanced depravity' by 'effacing every remaining trace of virtuous sentiment or habit'.[20]

Backed into an embarrassingly public moral corner, the imperial government was now forced to accept that 'immediate and vigorous efforts' for the 'effectual reform' of the convict system had to be made.[21] London, nevertheless, remained committed at this stage not only to transportation but also to the idea that Van Diemen's Land remained the most suitable destination for convicts. Thus, rather than blaming the system per se, the Secretary of State instead argued that the current problems were rooted in the temporary colonial depression of the early to mid-1840s – which had caused widespread unemployment and large numbers of convict men to be congregated together in an ostensibly demoralising fashion in the gangs – and by the inferior quality and 'inexperience' of many of its Convict Department and colonial government personnel, which had, among other things, allegedly created a 'want of zeal'.[22] The solution, Earl Grey advised William Denison, Eardley Wilmot's successor as governor, was to suspend transportation for two years while the convict system was reorganised. During this interim period, he explained, new overseers and superintendents would be appointed, buildings extended and improved, and preparations made to subject all convicts to an initial period of solitary confinement, followed by a period under the silent system, before they were released to work for settlers.

Grey considered that the two-year suspension would also enable sexual order to be restored. During this time, he advised, it would be possible to clear the gangs of all the men who were currently in them, including the large numbers who allegedly had become addicted to 'unnatural' offences. In Grey's view, something also had to be done urgently about 'the great disproportion between the sexes'. Unless more women were sent to Van Diemen's Land, he advised, 'unnatural' offences inevitably would 'appear on a yet wider scale, and in forms (if that be possible) of still greater malignity'.[23] The temporary cessation of transportation was, as a result, to apply to *male* convicts only. Consequently, throughout 1847 and early 1848 – and for the only time in the history of transportation – the numbers of convict women arriving outstripped the numbers of men.[24] A shift in female convict management was also advised. The separate system was to be fully instituted among the women and 'the most assiduous attention' paid to 'their moral and religious instruction' in order that they might become 'in some measure fitted' for a future role as the 'wives and mothers of families'. The 'subject' of convict women becomes 'of much importance', Grey noted:

> when it is considered that the tendency to unnatural crime, fostered as it must be when numbers of one sex are congregated together, though checked by material obstacles will in all probability break out when the convict is released from controul [sic] and seeks indulgence, unless some opportunity be afforded for legitimate sexual intercourse.[25]

'Every inducement' was, as a result, 'to be held out' to convict women to form 'legitimate unions' with unmarried male convicts at the end of their sentence. Measures were also to be adopted to reinstate the scheme – abandoned in 1842 on the grounds of cost – to bring the wives and families of male convicts to the colony.[26]

Grey believed that these measures would not only help to stifle 'unnatural' offences among the convicts but that they might also lay the basis for a much broader reform of colonial order. Villages could be built across the colony, he suggested to Denison, composed of one to two hundred cottages – each with 'a well fenced garden of a quarter of an acre' attached – a church, a school, a resident clergyman and a schoolmaster. The population would be made up of a mixture of ex-convict and emigrant labourers – the latter designed to provide 'an infusion of wholesome blood' – and each man would live in a cottage with his wife and family. The cottages would be rented to the house-holder by government to encourage the men to seek work for wages and thus to develop steady and industrious habits. By building roads and clearing land their labour might, in turn, attract more 'emigrant agriculturists with capital' – men capable of moral and social leadership – to the colony. On the whole, however, these labourers were to be encouraged to gain their own subsistence by working 'the land attached to the garden'. They would, as a result, enjoy all the basic 'human wants' but have a limited access to demoralising luxuries.[27]

Grey's vision of a blissfully domesticated and hierarchical social order was, however, rapidly rendered redundant by events. Eardley Wilmot's removal had done little to placate colonial opposition to the convict system, and petitions, complaints and protests from Van Diemen's Land continued to arrive. To add to this pressure, details of a convict revolt – at Norfolk Island penal station in July 1846 – began to come in. Almost from the outset, this event was reported in ways that ensured that it would become linked indelibly to the allegations about 'unnatural' male sexuality. Norfolk Island's public reputation as a hell upon earth had already been firmly established as a result of the sensationalist publicity surrounding the 1837–38 Select Committee on Transportation. In 1843, the island's administration had been transferred from Sydney to Hobart, with the result that, upon leaving the station, convicts from there were now transferred to Van Diemen's Land. The island quickly acquired mythical status among colonists, and convicts arriving from there were regarded as one of *the* most potent streams of pollution. 'We cannot be said to indulge in idle or morbid fears', the Bishop of Tasmania asserted of the men from Norfolk Island, 'when we look with horror to the hour that shall bring these monsters to our shores, with the prospect of being gradually drafted into the mass of our moral population'.[28]

The July uprising appeared to confirm claims that widespread convict immorality would, sooner rather than later, result in total colonial destruction. Two reports about Norfolk Island, submitted to government in late 1846, appeared to confirm this. According to the first, written by Visiting-Magistrate Robert Pringle Stewart, indiscipline and sexual immorality prevailed.[29] According to the second, written by the Reverend Thomas Naylor, chaplain at Norfolk Island until September 1845, the whole station had become a 'plague-spot', making it impossible for the convicts to avoid contamination. Naylor finished with a prescient warning: 'an outbreak that would astonish the civilised world' had become almost inevitable, he asserted, because convict immorality was like a 'volcano' waiting to 'burst forth'.[30] These claims gained a degree of official sanction when, in January 1847, acting Governor La Trobe wrote to Grey claiming – with next to no evidence – that the mutiny had been sparked by attempts to check 'the gratification of the degraded passions of the convicts'.[31]

The continuing pressure undoubtedly forced Grey's hand: in September 1846, upon receipt of these reports, he ordered Denison to close Norfolk Island down. The following February, he again wrote to the Governor, this time noting that the mutiny had been 'the natural fruit' of a 'radically vicious' 'system of convict management' and announcing that, in light of this, transportation to Van Diemen's Land would now cease.[32] A relatively short if sustained bout of colonial campaigning appeared to have borne fruit. The imperial government was, however, about to engage in what appeared to colonists as a total U-turn, announcing in 1847 that transportation to Van Diemen's Land would once again resume. Failure to find alternative destinations for convicts had played a key role in this reversal: all the British colonies – with the exception of Western Australia – had refused to accept convicts.[33] In June 1847, a Select Committee of the House of Lords nevertheless reported that transportation could not 'safely be abandoned' because it contained 'Terrors for Offenders' that no other punishment 'short of Death' could match.[34] The revival of Chartism, and fears of large-scale public disorder, provided additional pressure.[35] Severe financial problems gave government strictly limited room for manoeuvre. Against this backdrop, the fact that a well-established penal infrastructure already existed in Van Diemen's Land made the resumption of transportation to the colony almost a foregone conclusion.

Not surprisingly, colonists opposed to transportation regarded Grey's about-turn as 'a monstrous breach of public faith'.[36] News that convicts were also to be transported to the Cape, and that ex-convicts, or exiles, were – after a period of imprisonment in British penitentiaries – to be sent to a range of the other Australian colonies, including New South Wales and Port Phillip (soon to be Victoria), further inflamed passions, stimulating an unprecedented wave of protest and civil disobedience across the empire and laying the basis for an organised trans-colonial opposition that united settlers across the Australian colonies with their counterparts in New Zealand and South Africa.[37] In the Antipodes, anti-transportation sentiment led to the formation, in 1851, of the first-ever inter-colonial political organisation in the form of the Australasian League.[38] Imperial protests notably coincided with the re-launch, in late 1845 and early 1846, of mass campaigning by the Chartists for the repatriation of transported political offenders. This, combined with the anger that followed the decision to transport yet more prominent radicals from Britain and Ireland in the wake of the disturbances of 1848, helped to ensure that the question of convict transportation would also stimulate intense political debate and continued popular protest at home.[39] Faced by widespread and implacable opposition, government succumbed: London announced that self-governing institutions and a colonial constitution were in the offing, and in 1852, transportation to Van Diemen's Land ceased.

Colonial opposition to convict transportation was waged in the language of extreme moral outrage. Abolitionists deployed a highly charged, sensationalising and explicitly sexualised discourse of bodily excess, corporeal degradation and moral devastation. Accusations about 'unnatural' sexualities – and about sodomy in particular – lay at the core of the campaign. These claims were, in turn, woven into an extremely potent narrative of colonial sexual danger: child rape scares, the corruption of settler youth and images of Van Diemen's Land being engulfed by corruption and disease all played their role. Colonists repeatedly asserted their right to speak as parents, and particularly as fathers, and they claimed to be engaged in a heroic defence of home and family. The language of abolitionism was increasingly apocalyptic: if transportation continued, campaigners asserted, the colony would, like Sodom and Gomorrah, be struck down by a righteous divine vengeance. The words of one anti-transportation poem encapsulates much of the breadth and scale of the perceived threat:

Hail, sons of Freedom, hail!
Who dwell in Tasman's isle;
O'erwhelm'd by streams corrupt, impure –
The *refuse* and the *vile*.

Say, shall these streams yet flow
Thro' our adopted land;
Engend'ring death, disease and woe,
With *an unsparing hand*?

[211]

Shall crime and vice still pout
Their floods upon our soil;
Destroy, with unrelenting power,
The *parents' care and toil*?

Shall fathers weep and mourn
To see a lovely son
Debas'd, demoraliz'd, deform'd
By Britain's *filth and scum*?

Shall mothers heave the sigh,
To see a daughter fair
Debauch'd and sunk in infamy
By *those imported here*?

. . . .

Shall Tasman's Isle so fam'd,
So lovely and so fair,
From other nations be estrang'd –
The *name of Sodom bear*?

Till Nature's God, provok'd,
Stretch forth His mighty arm;
And, in relentless fury, pour
His *righteous judgments down.*

Arise, then, Freemen – rise:
Secure your liberty;
Ne'er rest till Transportation dies;
And Tasman's Isle be FREE.[40]

*   *   *

The growth of colonial opposition to convict transportation can, at one level, be accounted for relatively easily. Most colonists had angrily rejected the conclusions of the 1837–38 Select Committee and had continued to support convict transportation and assignment.[41] It was only in the early 1840s that many began to shift sides, a change in sentiment occasioned by reform of the convict system. The abolition of transportation to New South Wales in 1840 had resulted in a huge increase in the numbers of convicts being sent to Van Diemen's Land, causing some colonists to complain that the free population was being swamped and that the colony was being turned into a giant gaol.[42] Assignment was also abandoned and, unlike its predecessor, the probation system did not supply colonists with free labour but rather required them to pay wages to convict servants. The link between settler self-interest and convict transportation had thus been weakened substantially.[43]

The fact that these changes coincided with the severe economic crisis of the early to mid-1840s was also important. Although demand for female convict labour continued to be relatively stable, many of the growing numbers of male convicts were unable to find work.[44] The numbers confined to the probation gangs grew precipitously as a result, increasing settler fears about the threat to morality, property and security supposedly posed by congregating large numbers of convicts.[45] The fact that some of the gangs were employed in agricultural labour designed to supply the Convict Department with food also caused resentment, as it made it harder than in the past for colonists to secure government contracts.[46] Faced with rising unemployment, free labourers also became increasingly vocal in their opposition to convict passholder servants, whom they considered – because they were employed at lower wage-rates – to be unfair competition.[47]

Although campaigners accepted that the economic crisis was part of a broader Australian phenomenon, they nevertheless blamed the convict system for the fact that Van Diemen's Land was slower than the other colonies to recover. Abolitionists asserted that colonial investment had been affected negatively because those settlers who could afford to do so were leaving the colony in droves and disinvesting their capital. Neither was any new capital arriving. The convict presence was also blamed for the exodus of free labourers from the colony and for the fact that emigration had come to a virtual halt, increasing the dependence of settlers on convict labour.[48] Campaigners claimed that the colony had suffered a catastrophic turn-around in fortunes as a result.

Fears about the colony's economic future also became embroiled with growing resentment over the absence of substantive political change. Although the abolition of transportation had brought a degree of reform to New South Wales, Van Diemen's Land had only been granted a partially nominated legislative assembly, and it continued to be denied self-governing institutions because it remained a penal colony. An already tense situation was inflamed further when the government in London endeavoured to force the colonists to pay a greater share of the cost of the Convict Department, the police force and the civil establishment. These changes provoked a political crisis: in 1845, the six nominated members of the Legislative Assembly refused to sanction the colonial budget and withdrew from the Assembly. These men, who became known as the 'Patriotic Six', would head a popular protest movement insisting that there would be 'No taxation without Representation'.[49] The campaign for the abolition of transportation had thus become linked increasingly to the movement for colonial self-government.

While this complex of economic and political issues does much to explain the rise of widespread opposition to convict transportation, it fails to account either for the campaign's profoundly moralising tenor or for its deployment of a systematically sexualised rhetoric. Abolitionists claimed that 'unnatural' sexual offences had reached the level of a plague and that, contaminated by their time in the gangs, convicts presented a universal sexual and moral threat. There was, however, limited evidence to support such claims. As in 1837–38, abolitionist allegations about the widespread sexual assault of children were once again based on a handful of cases: in the decade after 1840 only around a dozen men were convicted of the carnal knowledge or ravishment of a child or of assault with intent to commit these offences by the colony's higher courts.[50] Despite attempts in the early 1840s to make 'unnatural' sexual offences easier to prosecute, the increased state surveillance of convict men and the inflamed character of public opinion, the numbers of men convicted of sodomy, bestiality and buggery also remained remarkably low. Thirty-seven men were convicted either of these acts or of assault with intent to commit them during the course of the decade.[51]

Repeated enquiries by the colonial state and the Convict Department also failed to support abolitionist claims. Although some of these enquiries concluded that 'unnatural' sexual practices were indeed widespread, these claims were often based upon anecdotal and impressionistic evidence. Statements from Convict Department officers with first-hand experience of convicts were, moreover, frequently contradictory. While a few argued that 'unnatural' offences were widespread, the majority of officers believed that the opposite was true. Thus, for example, the vast majority of Convict Department surgeons concluded on the basis of the regular medical examinations of the convict men in their charge that 'unnatural' sexual acts were relatively rare. Many officers believed, in addition – and probably with some justice – that the extraordinarily close and punitive regime of surveillance and regulation that had been imposed upon male convicts by the late 1840s had crushed what little space there was for same-sex practices and relationships to flourish.[52]

The abolitionist focus upon 'unnatural' crimes undoubtedly served a range of mobilising and propagandising purposes. Sexual acts such as sodomy and bestiality were considered 'unspeakable' by the nineteenth century. These were crimes, as one colonial newspaper explained, that it was simply 'not lawful for Christians to name'.[53] Even the discussion of these acts supposedly threatened to corrupt and infect. Abolitionists were able to exploit these conventions by arguing that the situation in the colony was now so bad that they had been left with no choice but to speak out. 'Nothing', the Bishop of Tasmania assured the Colonial Office:

> but an imperative sense of duty would induce me to notice . . . a subject so revolting, so abhorrent to all our social and Christian feeling . . . We cannot shut our eyes and ears to what is passing around us [but] are compelled to regard the rapid extension of that evil atmosphere in which we, and all dear to us, are constrained to live.[54]

These were excellent shock tactics, helping to establish and to reinforce repeatedly the idea of an extreme colonial crisis. 'The moral and social interests of the colony are in imminent peril', the *Launceston Examiner* asserted; 'all that can render this island desirable as a residence or field of enterprise for men of family is in jeopardy'. 'In such circumstances', the paper declared, 'silence would be criminal'.[55] By the same token, abolitionists were able to construct an image of themselves as men of duty and so of sound character. This was reinforced by repeated emphasis upon the idea that they had come to this battle as moral family men engaged in a life-and-death struggle to defend their homes and communities. 'We, who are husbands and fathers – we, who have so deep a stake in the moral, social and spiritual welfare of the colony – dare no longer be silent', the Bishop of Tasmania explained.[56]

Despite arguing that it was their duty to speak openly and truthfully, campaigners in fact adopted the literary conventions of the unspeakable to dramatise and sensationalise their texts. No moral man either could or would describe the depths to which convicts had fallen: convict immorality was literally 'beyond the power of imagination to conceive'.[57] 'It is impossible', the *Launceston Examiner* asserted, 'to describe in language sufficiently plain not to be revolting, the degradation that exists at penal stations'.[58] The scenes among the convict men were so 'fearful', the 'horror' so great, the 'evil' so 'enormous', the Reverend Henry Phibbs Fry agreed, that they 'cannot be written'.[59] The situation in Van Diemen's Land was without 'parallel in the history of human beings'; the colony was beset by 'unheard-of-crime', Robert Pitcairn, a leading spokesman against the convict system, concluded.[60] Indeed, these acts were so unheard of and unknown that they suggested the colony lay outside the boundaries of the imperial nation. The men, the Bishop of Tasmania remarked, 'have acquired . . . habits here, which they had not – could not have had – in English society'.[61]

In the absence of a suitable language of sex, abolitionists repeatedly resorted to allusion, allegory, metaphor and code. These strategies enabled abolitionist texts to reinforce notions of strangeness and unheard-of monstrosities while simultaneously drawing readers in by references to the known. The deployment of biblical texts, in particular, enabled campaigners to locate themselves within a broader imperial community of religious belief and to interweave the unknown and the allegedly unimaginable with the familiar by deploying a common language and a shared moral and imaginative code. 'The private accounts which I have just received from Van Diemen's Land would shock and horrify your moral readers, could I narrate them in direct and unpalliative language', but James Smith informed *The Times*:

> they are too repulsive to moral feeling to be fully given; I may be allowed to state that crimes which drew down upon two memorable cities of antiquity the vengeance of an offended God are now of common occurrence at all the probation gangs in Van Diemen's Land.[62]

Campaigners also deployed textual elisions and strategically placed asterisks for fear, as the Reverend Naylor explained, that they might 'pollute these pages' by an over-abundant account of this 'awful' crime.[63] Unwittingly or not, these kinds of devices served to highlight the salacious, voyeuristic and even titillating potential of the abolitionist case. Given the market in early nineteenth-century Britain for sensationalist and scandalous literature, anti-transportation narratives quickly gained a life of their own. Their dramatic and compelling nature meant, importantly, that they were not only able to gain but also to hold the attention of the British and imperial press. The more prosaic conclusions of government investigations that 'unnatural' crime was 'much more talked of than committed' were destined, by contrast, to gain a more limited hearing.[64]

Reliance upon sensationalist and allegorical narratives also enabled campaigners to play fast and loose with the truth. Isolated events and individual cases regularly formed the basis for wild and apocryphal claims about endemic 'pollution'. The convict coal mines – near Port Arthur – provided a particularly fertile imaginative site, and the December 1845 trial and execution of Job Harris and William Collier, convict men stationed at the mines, for the rape of David Boyd did much to spark the initial moral panic. The case became a source of alarmist accusation, laying the basis, for example, of Robert Pitcairn's first letters to the Colonial Office. In Pitcairn's opinion, the trial proved that 'unnatural' crimes were 'of constant, almost universal occurrence' among the men at Port Arthur. Pitcairn backed these allegations up by arguing that Dr Motherwell, surgeon at the coal mines, recently had had three hundred men under his care suffering from 'a particular disease ... caused by this crime'.[65] Motherwell's inquiries had, in fact, revealed just twenty men 'labouring under' this 'disease' (anal gonorrhoea), and medical investigations elsewhere suggested that 'out of 1,200 prisoners' at Port Arthur 'only one' was so 'diseased'.[66] This did little to silence Pitcairn who refused to take up Colonial Secretary Bicheno's offer for him to examine the official documents. 'Humanity' was being 'outraged', he asserted; the convict system was so successful in diffusing 'vices' throughout 'the Australian colonies' that it was doing 'the work of hell efficiently and completely'. It was his duty, he informed Bicheno – who considered Pitcairn to be 'fanatical' – 'to make' this 'known throughout the empire'.[67]

The 'secret' and 'unknowable' character of convict sexual practices almost certainly formed part of their appeal for abolitionists, making it difficult, if not impossible, for the state to refute their claims decisively. Thus, even had the government been able totally to suppress same-sex acts among the convicts, it seems unlikely that this would have quelled the campaign because it was, as one Convict Department official noted, 'impossible to prove a negative'. [68] This was an issue, then, with extraordinary propagandising scope and with the potential to run and run. When official enquiries concluded that 'unnatural' sexual offences were widespread, abolitionists seized upon them as evidence that they were right. When investigations reached the opposite conclusion, campaigners contended that Convict Department officials, surrounded by constant immorality and brutality, had become as indifferent to 'vice' as the men and that they were, in addition, so dependent on government 'favour' that it was in their interest to 'hush up' the facts.[69] Others argued that there was anyway no need to provide detailed facts to substantiate their case; 'on such a subject', one group of campaigners declared, even 'bare suspicion' warrants 'the expression of belief'.[70] 'Hearsay evidence', Eardley Wilmot commented, 'is not the best or the most infallible test of the truth'.[71] While that may have been true for government purposes, gossip, speculation and exaggeration nevertheless served the abolitionists well. 'Rumour', as one civil servant in the Colonial Office remarked of the Van Diemen's Land case, 'has a hundred tongues'.[72]

The idea that 'unnatural' sexual offences were at the level of a contagion enabled abolitionists to depict themselves as soldiers in a great moral battle and to deploy a simplified and melodramatic narrative of good versus evil, light versus dark. The spectre of child rape, in particular, left no room for compromise. 'No middle course is open' to colonists, campaigners asserted. 'To tamper for terms is to surrender their children, their interests, their independence, to the direful influence of all the future crime of Great Britain', the Australasian League declared.[73] These melodramatic declarations not only helped to provide the movement with a powerful unifying theme, they also enabled abolitionists to draw a firm moral line between themselves and colonists who continued to support transportation. Those who campaigned against transportation were the 'respectable people' of the colony, 'the real colonists', and they had 'true hearts' and 'virtuous principles'; God was on their side.[74] *In Hoc Signo Vinces* was the motto of the Australasian League: 'by this sign [the cross] thou wilt conquer'. The stars emblazoned upon the Australasian League's flag were 'signs taken from the heavens', leading abolitionist spokesman Thomas Gregson declared, as he explained to campaigners that it was 'to Heaven we must look for our deliverance from the convict curse'.[75]

Colonial character was, of course, in urgent need of restoration having been seriously damaged by the conclusions of the 1837–38 Select Committee that settlers were tyrannical and unfeeling slave masters, that their moral capacity had been profoundly injured by the constant association with convicts and that they were, as a result, becoming progressively less British. In the wake of the Molesworth Committee, colonists had struggled to re-assert their claims to moral equality within the empire and to declare their affinity with British moral and humanitarian sentiments, sending petitions and protests to London. The character of the free population, one petition asserted, easily bore comparison with Her Majesty's subjects elsewhere 'whether as to humanity, as to good morals, or as to their attention to the ordinances of religion'. 'Their whole aspect', the petition concluded, was that 'of a moral, religious, intelligent, active and industrious community of Britons'.[76]

These kinds of assertions had, however, gained an at best limited hearing in the political atmosphere of the late 1830s. The idea of settler sin had become increasingly well established within Britain by the end of the decade, a product not only of anti-transportation sentiment but also of broader concerns with the colonial treatment of indigenous peoples.[77] The melodramatic and moral focus of the movement to abolish convict transportation presented colonists with a powerful means of rebutting this negative image. 'The strenuous resistance of transportation had cleared the character of the colonists', the Reverend John West, editor of the *Launceston Examiner* and one of the key leaders of the campaign, declared.[78] 'The efforts of the Tasmanian people to cast off the convict yoke' had 'excited unbounded admiration', the Australasian League agreed, revealing them to be 'wise, earnest and patriotic men' as well as 'tender parents and Christian citizens'.[79]

The willingness of settlers opposed to transportation to forego convict labour formed a central aspect of these claims to virtuous character. Colonists had for too long been misunderstood by 'the world', the

Australasian League asserted, and had been denounced unjustly by their critics as 'mercenary and insincere' for their reliance upon the convict system and their apparent willingness to 'ring a petty profit from the degradation of a brother'.[80] A colonial boycott of convict labour, launched in 1848–49, became an important mobilising tactic for abolitionists, binding those who opposed transportation into a more unified community by requiring them to make common and – given the shortages of colonial labour – often genuine sacrifices in pursuit of principle. Colonists who supported the boycott were required to sign a 'pledge', a tactic borrowed from the early nineteenth-century temperance movement and a well-understood contemporary sign of moral self-restraint. The pledge served as a public symbol that abolitionists were men who put morals before money, thus helping to refute the Molesworth Committee's allegations that colonists were driven by a demoralising obsession with wealth.

Like the earlier generation of anti-transportationists, the abolitionists of the 1840s interpreted colonial reliance upon convict labour as a de-civilising and demoralising force. The promise of material gain from convict labour was like 'the glitter of a cesspool'.[81] Those who continued to support the convict system were depicted as men with no sense of public interest or commitment to the public good. 'They run over criminal calendars to ascertain their prospects', the Australasian League declared, 'and when patriots are ashamed, and mourn at the swollen list, they rejoice exceedingly as one that hath found great spoil'.[82] The continued use of convict labour was considered compelling evidence of their lack of moral character. 'Of course, 'there is a want of labour in Van Diemen's Land', the *Launceston Examiner* exclaimed, 'but none, except men whose moral perceptions are wholly blunted, would choose to fill the vacuum by the labour of the off-scourings of Britain's felon population'.[83] Those who supported the continuation of transportation on the grounds that it provided the colony with 'cheap labour' were consequently condemned as 'unreasoning men' whose 'mental vision' and 'moral perception' had been fatally 'impaired' by their residence in a penal colony.[84] They were men 'who valued their own selfish ends above the moral interests of the community' and who had forgotten that there 'were 20,000 youth in this island under 20 years'.[85] 'Immoral', 'dishonest' and 'dissipated', their continued support for transportation, despite the moral horrors it threatened to unleash upon colonial society, revealed these men to be 'pollutionists'.[86]

The unspeakable nature of 'unnatural' offences helped further to underpin claims by campaigners that they were men of virtue and self-sacrifice engaged in a righteous cause. The decision to speak out about the devastating moral effects of the convict system was interpreted as the product of a profound internal struggle and of the ultimate victory of conscience. 'I have sat down a hundred times to my present ungracious task', the Reverend Naylor declared, 'and have as often risen from it in disgust'. 'Forgive me', he proceeded, 'if I at length feel that I ought not to remain silent. I should justly be blamed by others, and worse than all, I should be tormented by self-reproach, if I were any longer to shrink from the task'.[87] Some of those who had argued for abolition during the 1830s had represented themselves in similar ways. 'I have gone through a great deal of pain and torture of mind in consequence of the horrors which I have witnessed in the colonies', Ullathorne declared. The experience of being told about 'unnatural' offences by the men had, he explained, 'completely harrowed my soul'; 'I have suffered their sorrows in my own heart, and have felt the crushing load of their degradation as if it were my own'.[88]

The greater the system's horrors were, the more the campaigners suffered. In Ullathorne's eyes, the penal colonies were akin to Hell. 'Suffer me to weep a little my sorrow; for I shall go and shall not return, to a land of misery and of darkness, where is the shadow of death, and no order, but eternal horror dwelleth', read the extract from the Book of Job with which Ullathorne began one of his accounts of convict life.[89] Like the Old Testament Job – forced to endure a series of painful and terrible challenges – Ullathorne's struggle to overcome the convict system could be interpreted as a profound test of his personal faith and moral strength. Anti-transportation might thus be read as an act of self-making. 'Struggle, thou art better for the strife, the very energy will hearten thee', the *Launceston Examiner* declared, in an article praising the sacrifices and exertions of colonists opposed to transportation. 'Suffering brings gratitude, suffering blossoms into beauty and forms into fruit, and the path of the just, though it be tearful and troubled, is yet a shining path, bearing a joyful certainty of progression to the perfect day'.[90] Lesser men were deemed to have balked at the 'painful and revolting' nature of this challenge. The convict system was so 'horrible', 'nauseous', 'disgusting and unutterably indecent' that, Whately declared, men had previously:

> turned aside and shut their eyes, with a vague hope that things were not so bad as had been represented. ... thus the very enormity and loathsomeness of the evil helped to perpetuate it; as that noxious kind of vermin, the American pole-cat, called the skunk, is said to escape from its pursuers by its intolerably fetid odour.[91]

Willingness to resist the convict system was interpreted as a sign of 'wise and manly virtue' and of the 'spirited' nature of colonial character.[92] 'Few persons', the Reverend Henry Phibbs Fry asserted, could 'appreciate the perseverance and moral courage' that the campaign 'required'. Abolitionists had 'battled on' nevertheless and resisted the 'odium of government' because they had been 'impelled by humanity to denounce the moral and physical pollution of the unhappy convicts'.[93]

Despite these enunciations of horror and disgust, expressions of sympathy and compassion repeatedly structured and informed abolitionist narratives: the convict was a fallen brother and an 'object of pity'.[94] What man, James Syme asked, could fail to be affected by the sight of convicts 'manacled in chains' or to 'feel deeply for the degradation' of these 'sadly debased fellow creatures'? The condition of the convict was, he declared, 'deserving of the attention and exertions of the Christian, the philanthropist, the moralist, and the ameliorist of the human family'.[95] Likewise, Fry had been inspired to act by 'Christian love for the distressed' and 'sympathy for suffering humanity'. He thus began his account of convict life with a passage from Psalms, asking his readers to 'let the sighing of the prisoner come before thee'.[96] 'Humanitarianism', historian Andrew Porter notes, 'had become a vital component of Britain's national or Imperial identity' by the 1840s.[97] By denouncing the colonists as cruel and tyrannical, the Molesworth Committee had placed the Van Demonian settlers beyond the pale of this compassionate nation. By evoking convict suffering, colonial abolitionists were able to re-assert their claims to belong. Their expressions of empathy with convicts provided a dramatic illustration that colonists, like all true Britons, embodied humanitarian and progressive principles.

Consequently, abolitionist pleas were directed at the heart of the nation; campaigners repeatedly begged for the support of 'British Justice and Humanity' and they sought to enlist the support of the 'generous, humane and moral British public', appealing explicitly to its record for 'assisting the oppressed, both at home and abroad'.[98] Campaigners consolidated these claims to belong by citing their humanitarian credentials, providing details of colonial support, not just for convicts but for progressive causes more generally, including charities, schools, hospitals, churches, public libraries, and literary and scientific societies. He had, C.G. Stevens declared on behalf of the Van Diemen's Land Anti-Transportation Committee, never lived in a community that 'spends larger voluntary sums for the purposes of literature, philanthropy and religion'.[99] These claims were much more than mere rhetoric: as historian Michael Roe noted many years ago, sections of colonial society in Van Diemen's Land had long taken pride in their involvement in a range of educated, literary, scientific and charitable causes, their cultural associations and endeavours inspired by an amalgam of 'Romantic, Protestant and liberal attitudes' which he describes as 'moral enlightenment'.[100] These activities were considered proof of the educated and enlightened nature of colonial society and in the hands of the abolitionists they consequently became a political weapon.

However, the abolitionist appeal to the nation was not only made on behalf of convicts. The opposition to transportation was equally heralded as a sign that colonists ought rightly to be re-incorporated within the political nation. 'Tasmania' was suffering from 'cruel wrongs' and 'ministerial oppression' and campaigners appealed to 'the liberal press of the nation' for help and asked the British people 'to lift' their 'all-powerful voice in universal condemnation'.[101] The continued imposition of convicts upon Van Diemen's Land despite colonial opposition provided compelling evidence of the arbitrary and despotic nature of colonial government. This was the people's 'monster-grievance', Stevens explained, a 'social, political and moral wrong' on such a scale that its 'malignant sublimity dwarfs every other grievance, not only of theirs but of any free people in any country, and in any age'.[102] To underscore these claims to colonial political rights, abolitionists returned to the allegedly disordered and demoralised bodies of male convicts. In so doing, they would develop a dualistic image of the convict – as a victim of the system and so a legitimate subject of pity, and as a monstrous and diseased threat and thus as an object of horror, revulsion and detestation.

* * *

Abolitionists contended that the prevalence of 'unnatural' sexual practices among the convicts was integral rather than incidental to the convict system. Transportation, therefore, led almost inevitably to physical degradation and moral pollution. The system was conducted upon wholly 'unsound and perverted' principles, the Reverend Fry declared, and it exercised an 'unmitigated evil influence' which no human being had the power to 'resist'. It changed 'men ... into monsters' and even the very worst of the convicts – those confined to the solitary cells as punishment for 'unnatural' sexual offences – were to be considered its 'victims'. 'Who can tell', he asked of these men, 'what compulsory pollution, what engrossing vice they may have endured, beholding all that is execrable, breathing air tainted with corruption, and surrounded with fiends whose delight it is to drag all near them into the same abyss of wickedness?'[103] The 'Balance of Evil over Good', the Bishop of Tasmania agreed, was an 'essential and inherent' feature of the probation system.[104] Critics considered the use of gangs to be one of the system's most radical defects. It was condemned as archaic and reactionary and as marking the return to an unenlightened system of penal discipline. The ostensibly contaminating and polluting effects of congregating large numbers of criminals had formed a central aspect of penal reform thought since the eighteenth century. Classification, separation and segregation had been promoted as solutions, promising to reform offenders – by creating new environments characterised by order and silence – in which prisoners might begin to reflect and become alive again to conscience.[105]

The probation system appeared to turn these principles upon their head. Men were 'herded' together like animals, abolitionists declared, with no attempt made to classify and separate them by character. The results were wholly negative. When relatively innocent men were 'forced to herd with the most profligate Beings on the Face of the Earth', 'moral and spiritual Contamination' was simply unavoidable, the Bishop of Tasmania asserted. Under such circumstances, it was 'not much to be wondered at' if even the best of the men began 'a downward Progress'.[106] On Norfolk Island, Naylor likewise alleged, 'the comparatively innocent and the thoroughly degraded are . . . thrown together' and 'novices are . . . initiated into . . . the mysteries of crime'. The 'English farm labourer, the tempted and fallen mechanic, the suspected but innocent victims of perjury or mistake' were forced to associate with 'scoundrels'. 'With them', he proceeded to explain, conjuring up images of racial as well as moral pandemonium, 'are mixed Chinamen from Hong Kong, the aborigines of New Holland, West Indian blacks, Greeks, Caffres, and Malays; soldiers for desertion; idiots, madmen, pig-stealers and pickpockets'. The system, therefore, turned the men into a single 'pestilential mass', fostering 'moral pollution' on a scale that 'was painful to contemplate'.[107]

Campaigners also condemned the system's apparently excessive reliance upon external force, arguing that cruelty and suffering tended to reduce man to the level of the beast. The penal stations, West declared, were places of 'inexpressible depravity, degradation and woe . . . sacred to the genius of torture'. 'There', he concluded, 'man lost the aspect, and the heart of man!'[108] The violent and harsh character of penal discipline was deemed to break the men down. Critics were particularly exercised by the impact of flogging, believing that it tended to destroy man, undermine his self-respect, erode his manly sensibilities and deliver him to the sway of the base passions. 'The flagellator', West declared, 'extinguished the last feeling of the man, and roused the temper of the demon', inciting him to 'crimes of savage violence'.[109] As we saw in chapter five, these ideas were founded upon the belief that unregulated pain disturbed the mind–body balance and stripped its victim of the capacity for rational self-command. 'Unnatural' sexual practices were considered the most extreme manifestation of this state of radical demoralisation.

While these denunciations of convict suffering were partly informed by Enlightenment and liberal thought, they were also the product of deeply held Christian beliefs. Several of the foremost colonial abolitionists were, notably, ministers of religion, and the Bible provided them with an enduring belief in the redeeming power of love and compassion. 'Seek first the Kingdom of God and his righteousness and all other things shall be added unto you', Naylor reminded government. A properly ordered convict system, therefore, ought always to seek 'the good of man' as its primary aim and to 'give hope and exertion to the penitent'; 'the rest', Naylor advised, 'will follow'. A system of 'gentleness', and not one governed by 'vindictive' instincts, ought, therefore, to be established; only by such means might convict men be restored to society. Even the most degraded and debased of the convicts – 'human beings whom I can scarcely call men' – ought not to be pronounced 'hopelessly lost', Naylor declared, because there were no limits to 'the power or mercy of God'.[110] Religious criticism of the convict system was partly inspired by a belief in man's shared humanity before God. The convict, Ullathorne declared, was no 'mere stomach for the passage of bread and meat' for he had 'a mind to be fed with pleasant feelings and an immortal soul to be fed with truth and light, and happiness'.[111]

The conviction that man had the right to communicate freely with God and to express his conscience without constraint was equally important, again fostering an emphasis upon the rights of the individual. The men had 'Souls to be saved as well as Bodies to be punished', the Bishop of Tasmania explained: earthly forms of justice were rightly to be limited.[112] Conditions in the convict gangs, in particular, defied this. As men were herded together and forced to associate with others who had been reduced to devils and demons there was little space for them to repent and reform. The 'vices and Iniquities constantly practised in those probationary Gangs are', the Bishop asserted:

> of such a Character, and carried on to such an Extent, that it is next to impossible for a Man, however strongly he may be convinced of the Sinfulness of his Course of Life, boldly to speak of or to act upon his Convictions; he dares not show any Sign of Repentance or Reformation when surrounded by his ungodly Companions.[113]

Under such conditions, even the most talented and devoted of the religious instructors allegedly stood next to no chance of affecting

[224]

any 'permanent Good'.[114] Thus, the chaplain at the coal mines reportedly felt so powerless that he believed he was preaching the convicts into Hell.[115] The suffering inflicted upon convicts by transportation was, as a result, 'far greater' than government had ever contemplated, for they were 'deprived' of God's love and compassion *and* of 'the Power of Repentance'. 'In good Truth', the Bishop of Tasmania informed the 1847 Select Committee of the House of Lords, 'you punish the Soul as well as the Body, and you virtually stretch your penal Code beyond this World into Eternity itself'.[116] The penal settlements, John West agreed, had too often 'been the theatres of great iniquity and oppression', places where commandants had 'dared injustice which no supreme authority would venture'.[117]

The convict system was also represented as a very earthly form of tyranny. Nineteenth-century penal reformers considered suffering to be legitimate only in so far as it served as a moral curative and as a necessary deterrent to crime. These views reflected the influence of new ideas about the relationship between the individual, the state and society. As historian Randall McGowen explains, reformers 'viewed the body' of the criminal 'differently because they valued the individual in a new way'. Their shifting concerns reflected a transition from notions of the 'body treated metaphorically within a language of the social body to a concern for the fate of the individual body'. While older models of punishment had relied upon organic metaphors to express and symbolise social hierarchy, conceiving of crime and other disorders as diseased limbs or organs to be judicially excised from the body politic through punishments like execution or transportation, reforming models considered each individual to be a coherent and separate entity in his or her own right.[118] Punishment was justified only in so far as it sought to deter the offender from crime and to reincorporate him within the community. The state consequently had no right to destroy the criminal or to sacrifice his or her individual rights in the name of society. Rather, progressive systems of penal discipline sought to inflict 'more terror than pain and more pain than permanent mischief such as the degrading, hardening, and corrupting of offenders, and of others'. 'A judicious legislator', Whately advised, aimed 'to inflict the least possible amount of pain that is necessary for wholesome terror, and he is even far more tender of doing mischief than of giving pain'.[119]

Critics had long argued that transportation, by inflicting dispro-portionate and undue pain, breached these boundaries. The suffering of convicts was deemed to have a strictly limited deterrent value because distance undermined spectacle. Transportation to the Antipo-des was doomed to failure, Jeremy Bentham had asserted as early as

1802, because it made punishment as remote as was possible from that 'mass of individuals, on whose minds it is wished that the impression should be made'.[120] It was, Ullathorne likewise advised, simply impossible 'to keep 'the horrors of transportation . . . long before the minds of the people'. 'Remoteness of space as well as remoteness of time tends very much to diminish impressions', he observed.[121] Reformers believed that these problems had led to ever greater levels of pain and suffering being inflicted upon convicts in an effort to maintain transportation's deterrent value at home. The system was, as a result, deemed to produce 'much more pain than terror' and so 'incomparably more mischief than pain'.[122] Convict suffering, therefore, appeared to signal a return to an earlier and less enlightened age. Progress had been inverted; the convict system marked a historical retrogression. To journey to Australia was thus to travel backwards through time to an 'age of darkness and barbarism'.[123] Convict suffering, the Molesworth Committee had agreed, was akin to the irrational and barbaric cruelties of a now supposedly long-past feudal age.[124]

The image of the suffering convict served to turn the notion of impe-rial civilising mission upon its head. Transportation, the *Launceston Examiner* asserted, was 'a system that reflects eternal disgrace upon a civilised nation and an eternal scandal upon a Christian people'.[125] Unlike the British government, however, colonists opposed to the convict system had become alive to these evils. 'There was a time', the Australasian League declared, when the cries of 'tortured white men' had filled the colony, when the spectacle of violent punishment had been everywhere, and when the lash had served as the chief currency of labour. The 'colonial conscience' had at that time been 'benumbed', with the result that men had 'submitted to be actors in scenes, at the remembrance of which they now shudder'. 'Those days are for ever passed', the League declared; a new and 'estimable class' had appeared, composed of men who were determined to occupy 'higher ground' and 'who looked forward . . . with faith in the eternal laws of providence, in their country, and in mankind'.[126] The rise of anti-transportation sentiment could be interpreted as a sign of the colony's advance towards civilisation and enlightenment, a progress achieved despite Van Diemen's Land's subjection to the reactionary and tyrannical misrule of the British state.

Of equal concern was the belief that distance rendered the system opaque, inhibiting the ability to detect and check abuses of power. The 'characteristic feature' of the 'colonizing-transportation system', Bentham had asserted, was its 'radical incapacity of being combined with any efficient system of inspection'.[127] The further the site of punishment from the seat of government and the eye of the people the greater the abuses of power were thought to be. The 'extreme isolation' of Norfolk Island, for example, meant that the men there were totally cut off from the world, with the result, Naylor alleged, that 'years of anguish may have been endured; the eye and every sense may have been outraged by exhibitions of vice' and still the convicts might be forced 'to suffer without the chance or possibility of escape from the horrors' that were 'being inflicted upon them'. The men had next to no legal means of righting wrongs. 'Not a soul', Naylor explained:

> is allowed to land on the island except its officials; not a letter can the prisoner write; not a complaint can he utter; not a single step can he take towards his extrication, without the consent of the authorities about him, and how difficult it is to obtain this ... almost insuperable objects are placed in the prisoner's way.[128]

In Naylor's view, Norfolk Island even lacked a proper criminal court, leading to further deviations 'from constitutional practice'. The officers were allegedly virtually free to do what they liked. This was made worse, Naylor asserted, by the fact that government was not always careful to appoint men capable of 'so great a personal responsibility'. 'Interest' and 'patronage' all too frequently informed the selection process, with the result that men of 'narrow and selfish views' who were prone to 'chuckle at their own evasions' and to indulge in 'the most flagrant violations' of the regulations were appointed as commandants.[129] Intolerable suffering, others agreed, was inflicted upon convicts at the remotest penal stations because the commandants there enjoyed a 'despotic power'.[130]

Convict sodomy – and the spectre of male rape in particular – armed abolitionists with a powerful symbol of this despotism and thus with a trenchant and compelling critique of the system. Man's ability to control his own body was considered the fundamental prerequisite of liberal systems of governance. Systems of power and authority that impinged upon the corporeal integrity of the individual subject were, by contrast, associated with an effeminising dependence and degradation. If self-rule was the precondition of liberty, the unjust dominion of one man over another represented the negation of manly self-command and was associated routinely in this period with bodily excess, sexual cruelty and corporeal subjection. There was no more compelling evidence of the absence of self-government than man's inability to command his own body. Self-possession and self-command were thus deemed the antithesis of the physically and morally reduced condition produced by systems like aristocracy, tyranny and slavery. Drawing upon these ideas, abolitionists linked the alleged epidemic

[227]

of 'unnatural' acts to the despotic, and thus profoundly unmanly, character of the convict system.

Critics contended that the sexual immorality that supposedly prevailed among the men was deeply embedded within the system's power structures. The most depraved and criminal of the convicts had allegedly risen to the top of the system, dominating its informal *and* formal lines of command. 'There are flash men on the island who keep it in awe and who beard the Commandant himself', Naylor declared of Norfolk Island.[131] These men forced the others to submit to immoral and 'unnatural' practices. Many had even gained official power. The overseers, critics contended, were frequently selected from among the very worst of the convict men. Some had committed 'detestable' crimes, the Reverend Willson, Roman Catholic Bishop of Van Diemen's Land, declared, and 'ought not to have been permitted to walk upon the Ground . . . with Christians' never mind to manage men.[132] Once appointed as overseers, John West agreed, these men either stood by while already 'vile' and 'hardened' men took their pleasures upon newly arrived 'innocents' or themselves abused their power for their own immoral gratification.[133]

Campaigners returned repeatedly to the fate of boy convicts and of newly arrived and allegedly relatively innocent men, in particular, emphasising their consumption and destruction at the hands of the depraved. 'Youths are seized upon and ******', Naylor asserted. The barracks had been transformed into 'dens' of the devil, the 'High Capitals of Satan and his peers'. Men newly arrived on Norfolk Island entered these buildings on their first night with a visible 'agony of mind', and he would, Naylor reported, 'as long as I live . . . never lose the impression made upon me by the horror I have seen expressed' on their 'countenances' when they were let out the next morning. The 'old hands' had become tyrants, he declared, men whose 'fiendish satisfaction' it was to degrade the better convicts until they too became addicted to the 'abominations' that had made 'this penal settlement a bye-word in language and a curse in morals'.[134] Officers at other settlements alleged a similar pattern of violent coercion and proactive demoralisation. Thus, the chaplain at the convict coal mines reported that the new men would come to him the day after their arrival 'with tears to state that they had been compelled by the rest to submit to their evil practices'.[135]

Equally, convict suffering and oppression were symbolised by the physical destruction of the men. Convicts were generally 'lively' and 'fresh-looking' upon their arrival, Ullathorne had declared, but their features quickly became 'stagnant', 'sluggish' and 'slovenly', and their previously active demeanour was replaced with a 'downward head' and a 'drowsy ox-like movement of feet and shoulders'. These, Ullathorne had concluded, were the inevitable characteristics of the man 'who has felt his bondage'; tyranny had reduced the convicts to 'wretched', 'shrunken' and 'spectral' forms.[136] Ten years on from the Molesworth Committee, the Reverend Naylor developed similar themes: the convicts on Norfolk Island were enslaved and they soon developed the 'indolent and listless' characteristics, the idleness of 'mind and body' that was 'the very essence of slavery'. This was made worse by the fact that the men survived on 'miserable' rations and were forced to perform hard labour under a 'semi-tropical sun . . . much too warm for English prisoners'. 'I am no mawkish sentimentalist', Naylor informed Earl Grey, 'I know that these men are undergoing punishment', but 'I am not ashamed to confess that it has excited my strongest compassion to see the ravages this fare has made on strong and hearty Englishmen. You can scarcely recognise the same men within a few weeks after their arrival'.[137]

Flogging was once again deemed to have particularly powerful debilitating effects. 'Man even in his debased state is proud and jealous of his free agency', one commentator explained, and 'his spirit, however, much corrupted, yet revolts at being driven into a corner'.[138] By reducing its victims to a state of extreme and unnatural powerlessness, flogging defied this ostensibly natural propensity for masculine independence. The convicts, colonist John Barnes remarked, consequently considered flogging 'a most unmanly kind of punishment', and feeling that they had suffered a total and degrading loss of self, some men sought out death in its aftermath, by deliberately committing crimes that would take them to the gallows.[139] The lash also represented a very real violation of the individual's rights to corporeal integrity. Numerous accounts, including those produced by convicts themselves, dwelt heavily upon the injuries that were inflicted. 'The wiry cords suck and eat their fill of the flesh and gore of the wretched man', Ullathorne remarked; 'the scourge drinks the blood of their flesh' and 'devours the spirit of their manhood'.[140] If the lash destroyed man's mind, subverting his soul and undermining his ability for self-command, it equally emasculated him by literally consuming his body.

The struggle between the flagellator and the convict was, like the tyranny exercised in the gangs, deemed akin to a battle between two opposing forms of masculinity: the one naturally independent, rational, energetic, self-possessing and moral, the other unnaturally dependent, irrational, sensual, physically diminished and demonic. Abolitionists once again turned to male rape to dramatise and symbolise this struggle. 'Think of miscreants stained with every crime placed in the position of sub-overseers', the *Launceston Examiner* asked its readers; 'think of the prisoner refusing to submit to their unnatural purpose, hearing the response: "Please God I shall see your backbones before long – I will prefer a charge which will subject you to the lash"'.[141] Flogging, the exiled Chartist leader John Frost similarly declared, was a 'contest' between the flogger, a man who 'felt a gratification in inflicting and witnessing human misery', and the man who still retained his natural feelings of pride and self-respect. 'Unprincipled' men with 'no sense of debasement' were able to adjust to the convict system and even to thrive under it, but 'men of spirit' balked at the utter submission and rule by others that it demanded. 'The flogger', Frost declared, was determined to use 'every means in his power to break [this] spirit', with the result that it was the better men who were targeted and eventually 'broken down by suffering'.[142] The 'mode' in which the convicts 'are treated drives them to desperation', Frost explained, and 'the very worst passions then become excited'. 'Injustice and cruelty', he elaborated, 'destroy the reflecting faculties and leave no thought or wish but for the immediate gratification of the sensual. In such cases no moral feelings can restrain men from the commission of the very worst acts'.[143]

In Frost's eyes, the physical and spiritual destruction of the convict was a symbol of the unnatural and insatiable appetite for total power and subjection fostered by aristocratic government. 'Every reader of history', Frost told the mass audiences that gathered to greet him upon his return to Britain:

> must be well aware that the aristocracy of the British Isles were, and are, a curse to the world. The power of the lawgiver, in their hands has been used for purposes destructive of everything which virtuous men would prize. . . . Insatiable and mean in the pursuit of wealth, the aristocracy were a raging lion, seeking whom it might devour.[144]

In Van Diemen's Land, he declared, the British state had created a tyrannical code 'not equalled in severity in any part of the civilised world'. Convicts were consequently flogged routinely for breaches of regulations so minute that they were impossible for any man to remember and obey. Only a 'tyrant', Frost concluded, could punish a man for being *unable* to obey. Since 1788, he declared, the British government had 'destroyed thousands, and probably scores of thousands, of the bodies and souls of [the] men and women placed in their charge'. Flogging represented a form of human 'sacrifice' to the 'ferocious spirit of those who rule'; sodomy was what happened when 'irresponsible power' was placed 'in the hands of vicious men'. The 'state of things' in Van Diemen's Land, he concluded, 'shows, too clearly, what men possessed of power are capable of when subject to no restraint' and 'when far removed from public observation and censure'.[145]

While Frost's analysis was partly informed by the ideas of the colonial abolitionists – he had observed and taken part in their debates during his time in the colony – it also drew fulsomely upon the gendered ideological framework of British popular radicalism. Radicals had long counterposed their own claims to a virile and virtuous masculinity against an image of the aristocracy as an effeminate and debauched 'other'. Those in power, such critiques claimed, lacked the necessary self-discipline and restraint which idealised forms of manly authority and citizenship were supposed to entail. The aristocrat – like the slave-master – enjoyed an unnatural dominion over others and was thus free to exercise his temper and indulge his passions. These ideas repeatedly stimulated tales of ruling-class sexual excess. The image of the aristocratic libertine seducing and debauching the poor but virtuous moral maiden was, historian Anna Clark tells us, a recurring theme within both radical discourse and popular culture: figuring not only in political tracts and critiques but also in chapbooks, theatre, ballads and other cultural forms.[146] The popularity of these kinds of seduction narratives reflected the idea that sexual danger and rapacity were inevitable consequences of political misrule, an idea that prevailed throughout the nineteenth century. To nineteenth-century audiences sodomy was thus an easily interpretable 'sign', a readily recognisable symbol of tyranny's inevitable excess.

The idea that the penal colonies represented an unnatural and un-British form of slavery and tyranny had been nourished and sustained within popular culture and radical discourse for decades. Broadside ballads about convict transportation were, for example, replete with images of Britons being enslaved.[147] Radical denunciations of the Australian colonies had long pursued similar themes. As early as the 1790s, George Dyer, one of the leading English radicals of his generation, had lambasted Botany Bay as an infamous site of 'slavery and famine' and a product of aristocratic tyranny.[148] Slavery was deemed alien and antithetical to British liberties in this period. 'Freedom', the transported radical Maurice Margarot declared, was 'the common Birthright of Britons'. The system of slavery instituted in the Australian settlements was therefore 'unknown to our Laws and directly contrary to the British Constitution as it was established at the Revolution of 1688'.[149] Bentham expressed similar fears: the system of military despotism and legislative authority established in early Australia was, he declared, 'a wound in the vitals' of the English 'constitution'. The absence of a colonial charter meant that the settlements must either be condemned as illegal or that Magna Charta [*sic*] must be dismissed as just so much 'waste paper'.[150]

Many of these critics also raised the idea that colonial enslavement, once established, would inevitably rebound at home: 'every Briton' was threatened, Margarot declared, for 'if the Executive power can make One slave it may make all so'.[151] It was all too possible, Bentham likewise warned, that the seed of 'military despotism' that had been planted in Australian soil might eventually be transplanted and flourish in Britain.[152] These kinds of fears had inspired some leading British radicals to keep a close eye on colonial conditions over the decades. Thus, Joseph Hume, for example, received petitions from convict men at penal settlements like Macquarie Harbour, and he regularly tried to intervene on their behalf as well as raising questions in Parliament about the state of the convict settlements more generally.[153] Others declared that colonial oppression and cruelty were, in fact, the inevitable outgrowths of undemocratic and aristocratic government at home. Van Diemen's Land, the political offender William Ashton told public meetings on his return to England in the late 1830s, was the product of an already illiberal and 'blood-stained' British state. 'Look at the annals of' this 'country', he counselled:

> keep in mind the Manchester massacre [Peterloo] . . . the butcherings at Derby and other places . . . bear in mind . . . the disgusting, cruel and deliberate sacrifice of life under the *New Poor Law Bill*, and then say are there not Englishmen to be found . . . to perpetrate any act that the fiendish heart of man can devise? . . . even English laws at home are not sufficient to protect the poor and weak from the tyrannical despotism of oppressors.[154]

Radical denunciations of the penal colonies had, not surprisingly, been kept alive over the decades by the regular and continued deportations of thousands of social and political protesters, not only from Britain and Ireland but also from other parts of the empire.[155] Waves of protests, petitions and mass demonstrations had greeted the deportation of men like the Glasgow Cotton Spinners, the Dorchester Labourers (or Tolpuddle Martyrs) and the Newport rebels. Many of these transported political offenders had produced accounts of colonial cruelty and oppression that had circulated both in the British radical and liberal press and as ballads, broadsides and cheap pamphlets. Some had gained a mass audience: 12,000 copies of the first edition of George Loveless's *Victims of Whiggery* had, for example, sold out within four months.[156] These high-profile cases had also inspired action in Parliament, particularly on the part of Radical MPs. Thus it was Sir William Molesworth's opposition to the transportation of the

Dorchester men – his belief that their deportation defied the rule of law – that had initially sparked his interest in the convict colonies.[157] Anxieties about the threat which transportation posed to British liberty were more broadly espoused: George Cruikshank's cartoon, 'The Freeborn Englishman', published in 1819 in the wake of Peterloo, and in the midst of the repressive Six Acts, vividly expresses these kinds of fears. It depicts the once freeborn Englishman with his lips padlocked, standing in convict chains, the Transportation Act in his hands, the Bill of Rights trampled under his feet.

By focusing upon the figure of the enslaved and suffering convict, colonial campaigners were able to immerse themselves within these broader radical–liberal traditions and thus to connect with a series of empire-wide debates about political rights. The fact that colonial campaigning coincided with the resumption of Chartist mass petitioning and public meetings demanding the return of transported political offenders further reinforced these links. The predicament faced by convicts served as a metaphor for the broader condition and oppression of the colonists. The free population of Van Diemen's Land were also in chains, 'chains of degradation', campaigners declared, and they were waiting 'with intense but pardonable anxiety for . . . their moral and political manumission'.[158] Liberty, campaigners sought to remind their audiences, was a part of their natural birthright as Britons, and settlers had, despite their distance from the metropole, retained a profound attachment to these inalienable rights.[159] 'I have', C.G. Stevens asserted:

> travelled through, and sojourned in, many dependencies of the British crown [and] have resided some years in Van Diemen's Land, but have never met, in other Colonies, nor in any provincial population of England of equal dimensions, a body of men more intelligent, high-minded, loyal and liberal, and more attached to the English constitution than the Colonists of Van Diemen's Land.[160]

Images of an enslaved Van Diemen's Land formed the basis of a patriotic appeal to the nation. Appealing directly to the British people's recent record of fighting slavery, one colonial campaigner asserted that 'he had too much confidence in the character of the British people to think that while they are ready to succour the oppressed of every land . . . they would allow any ministry to destroy a whole community of their own countrymen'.[161] Just as the convicts had been forced to submit to the unnatural despotism of the convict system, so too, campaigners argued, colonists had been subjected to the degrading and unmanly tyranny of the imperial state. The settlers were 'political bondsmen' and, John West

George Cruikshank, 'The freeborn Englishman' (1819)

asserted, they had been 'conveyed from hand to hand' as if they were 'the property of others'.[162] The health and the strength of the colonists were suffering as a result: their once virtuous energy was becoming diminished and enfeebled by enslavement and oppression.[163] Van Diemen's Land, West explained, was like 'the man who languishes in disease'.[164] The continued convict presence was the most palpable sign of this affliction; threatening to 'poison' the colony's 'social blood'.[165] Transportation, one campaigner declared, was 'like a cancer' and the longer that it remained in the colonial body, the 'more difficult' it would be 'to get rid of it'.[166] Abolitionists returned repeatedly to metaphors of sickness and disease to condemn transportation: the convict presence was variously a 'festering virus', a 'pestilence' and a 'plague'.[167] Corrupted in the gangs, the supposed addiction of convict men to 'unnatural' vices and the spread of disease among them allegedly threatened widespread colonial pollution.

Yet for all that the convict presence was constructed as a highly contagious disease, abolitionists were proof positive that it was possible to resist this infection. 'The Colonists', Stevens asserted, 'do not complain that they are personally depraved by convictism'. 'They are generally men of robust intellect, virtue and enterprise', he explained. 'They repel the daring calumny' but 'plead for the prisoners and tremble for their children'.[168] Contemporaries considered slavery to be as much a state of mind as a system of exploitation and oppression. As one radical poem of the period explained 'the tyrant's chains are only strong, while slaves submit to wear them'.[169] The ability to overcome enslavement was partly a matter of one's strength of character. Thus, if expressions of empathy with convict suffering enabled colonists to identify their struggle for political rights with the battle against the despotic and demoralising convict system, the idea that the free community was also enslaved equally enabled abolitionists to differentiate themselves from convicts. Unlike convict men, who had apparently succumbed en masse to the system's moral disease, free settlers were distinguished by their ability to resist. Convicts were ostensibly the passive victims of imperial misrule; free settlers had moral agency and thus the courage and capacity to fight back.

This strength was interpreted as a manifestation of the settlers' innately British virtue. 'We are not the less Britons for being colonists', one campaigner explained, 'there is a doggedness, a sort of never say die spirit, inherent in every Briton', and it was this, he declared, that would see the free population through, making them 'intrinsically and inherently strong' and enabling them to free themselves from misgovernment, to 'discard the Government go-cart, wherein we have so long been bolstered and dragged' and to 'advance . . . on our own stalwart limbs'.[170] These claims of innate strength were further nourished by the idea that colonisation was itself a heroic endeavour, affirming, consolidating and further extending British virtue and character. Settler masculinity, in particular, was constructed around notions of stoicism, courage and self-discipline and upon the idea that colonial settlement demanded a dual conquest of nature: the command of one's own nature and the simultaneous subjugation of the natural world.[171]

Campaigners deployed these two complementary strands of thinking about nature to further distance themselves from convicts. Convicts were – by virtue of their conviction and transportation – already morally suspect. Crime was a sign of unregulated appetite and of the unmanly rule of the passions, and consequently it was associated with bodily excess and thus with the victory of 'nature' over 'culture'. While the convict's descent into sexual vice was partly considered an inevitable product of the system's tyranny, it was also interpreted as a sign of this already deficient self-command. Observers intertwined these two ideas, denouncing the compulsory pollution of the gangs as the offspring of a coercive and violent despotism, while at the same time attributing the prevalence of 'unnatural' sexual practices to 'nature'. The climate, the Colonial Treasurer explained, undoubtedly exacerbated the demoralising effects of crowding men together in gangs. The fact that, in his view, 'the Men' were 'well fed and lightly worked' also had 'unnatural' sexual consequences, stimulating their physical energy and appetite and thus further distorting the balance of body over mind.[172]

Observers considered that the degenerative effects of 'unnatural' sexual practices were, moreover, permanent. Sodomy marked a point of no return; it signalled the 'thorough breaking up of the moral man'.[173] Once reduced to this state the convict man was rendered incapable of self-restraint and thus a total slave to 'nature'. Sodomy, bestiality and child rape were simply the different manifestations of this process. 'When a bad man is under the dominion of a passion of that kind he will', Ullathorne declared, 'gratify that passion in any manner that suggests itself to his imagination'.[174] Convicts also ostensibly underwent a lasting *physical* transformation as a result of their moral degradation. The 'unnatural lust' in which the prisoners indulged, one colonial doctor reported, led to 'an unnatural appearance of the parts'. This corporeal transformation was accompanied by a total reversal of gender identity: 'many' of these men had become 'commonly known and recognised amongst their fellow prisoners as females or colonial women', he explained.[175] Physiognomy, the belief that the face provided an external map or an index to the inner self, also served to

[236]

link sexual demoralisation with bodily degeneration and racial difference. Thus, the Reverend Fry had no need to hear the convict men speak in order to confirm their addiction to 'unnatural' vice because he believed he could see the telltale marks upon their faces.[176] Convicts 'guilty' of 'abominable acts', another campaigner declared, presented identifiable 'signs ... in their features'.[177]

Images of the convict man as a moral and physical 'other' were most potently and sensationally expressed in abolitionist allegations about cannibalism. 'Unnatural assaults', the leading colonial campaigner Dr Matthias Gaunt declared, were but one aspect of the 'monstrous effects' produced by the convict system. He proceeded to narrate a tale about a convict named Cripps who, escaping from his gang, had also enticed 'away with him a boy' who, like Cripps, was 'notoriously addicted to unnatural practices'.[178] Although Cripps was eventually apprehended, his companion was nowhere to be found, but a 'bag' containing 'pieces of flesh' *was* discovered, 'secreted' about Cripps's person. In Gaunt's view, this proved that 'this Monster in human shape' had 'used the boy for his unnatural purposes' and had 'afterwards killed him for food'. 'I could', Gaunt claimed, making wild allegations about the cannibalistic threat which convicts posed upon the basis of one, partly fictionalised, story, 'adduce many instances where Men of most brutal propensities have thus been let loose upon us'.[179]

Cannibalism had been associated with sexual excess and racial difference for centuries and, by the 1800s, it was a well-established and powerful signifier of savagery.[180] Abolitionist allegations about cannibalism, therefore, enabled campaigners to draw links between 'unnatural' sexual vices and the idea that convicts were racially different, thus helping to construct the convict sodomite as the alien, repulsive and 'savage' antithesis of 'civilised' and self-governing settler manhood.[181] Cannibalism spoke additionally to abolitionist fears that the convict presence would eventually entirely consume and eradicate the settler self. As H.L. Malchow notes, the cannibal was not merely 'the photographic negative' of 'civilized man' but a creature who threatened 'literally to eradicate boundaries: by incorporating others within himself'. The cannibal, he tells us, presents:

> [an] image of chaos beyond the structured world of personality, sub-ordination and hierarchy ... The cannibal transforms his objects of desire by eradicating their separateness ... the transgression of taboo evokes an essentially gothic unnaturalness – a crossing of lines, a contamination, and an obscenity – not merely an 'otherness'.[182]

Fears that transportation would engulf the free community were likewise expressed through the deployment of images in which convicts figured as the uncontrollable forces of nature. They were variously constructed as a 'volcano' of vice waiting to erupt, a 'moral lava which consumes whatever it touches', 'an overwhelming torrent', and as 'streams corrupt' and 'impure' that threatened to 'overwhelm . . . Tasman's isle'.[183] Settlers were deemed to have conquered nature: their powers of self-command had enabled them to transform Van Diemen's Land from a 'savage wilderness' into a 'charming, thriving and social residence for civilised man'.[184] The convict presence threatened to undo all this by once again unleashing the natural world.

Campaigners counterposed the destructive effects of convictism against the natural and bounteous beauty of Van Diemen's Land. The colony was a 'paradise', James Syme contended, a land littered with 'enchanting views', 'the brightest verdure' and 'the greatest fertility'.[185] 'Nature', the Australasian League similarly declared, had bestowed great favours upon Van Diemen's Land, creating a 'teeming land and a brilliant sky'; 'no country on this side the line', the League concluded, 'affords so fair a sphere for the development of civilised man'.[186] 'The contrast between the natural beauties' of the colony, its potential for human perfection and 'the moral turpitude' of its inhabitants could not, however, have been greater. The comparison 'tempts us', Syme declared, 'to exclaim with the poet, "Strange that where nature loves to trace, As if for gods a dwelling place; There man, enamoured of distress, Should mar it into wilderness"'.[187]

These kinds of images of Van Diemen's Land as an Eden were partly tied up with agrarian discourses and thus, in turn, with roman-ticised notions of a lost golden age, with critiques of industrialising Britain and of aristocracy.[188] For some, the colony's attractiveness was bound up with the way in which it appeared to create liberating spaces enabling both independent manhood and family formation. 'In a new world, and in a new life', Charles Rowcroft wrote of Van Diemen's Land:

> a man may till his own land, and work in his own fields with his own hands, and neither feel it to be a degradation in his own eyes, nor in the eyes of those around him. . . . In his new state, his new mind, so lately bowed down by care and anxiety, recovers its natural independence. He stands on his own land, the source of certain subsistence, and of almost certain wealth, for himself and for his children. Above is the light of God's sky, of which no assessed tax debars him. He is not driven to obsequious fawning on the rich or great for countenance or patronage. He has to pray to no man 'to give him leave to toil'.[189]

Van Diemen's Land was a 'land of promise', colonist William Jackson agreed, 'a beautiful island' with a 'most fertile' soil and a 'climate . . . peculiarly congenial to the English constitution'. Were it not for the convict presence, it would consequently have attracted Englishmen in droves, particularly those who were now struggling as a result of overcrowding and industrial manufacturing. Under different circumstances, he asserted, it might have become 'a home for 'honourable misfortune and persevering energy', but the colony was instead, under Earl Grey's dominion, becoming an 'unproductive and useless ... prison-house'.[190]

Transportation not only served as a block to the impoverished but virtuous emigrant; it was also supposedly eradicating the hopes of those who had already settled in the colony. Campaigners asserted that convict labour threatened to destroy the small farmer, in particular, and to replace him with a new colonial-bred aristocracy. Although the anti-transportation movement, in fact, brought together a broad social coalition – and a number of wealthy individuals from the large landowning class played key roles as its leaders and spokesmen – abolitionists nevertheless at times adopted a populist, and even class-based, discourse, declaring that their fight was primarily that of the ordinary but industrious and independent smallholder. Thus the 'honest yeoman who drives his own plough' was deemed least likely to employ convict labour or to:

> permit his family to be exposed to the violence of bushrangers, that somebody else may grow corn for sixpence for a bushel less than himself. The cottage farmer, who with his sons cultivates his limited fields, would disdain to own a slave; bond wages, all about him, reduce the value of his labor, and the labor of his sons. The effect is to expose his little property to the depredations of the rich man's gang – to expose his children to their example – too often to their violence.[191]

Van Diemen's Land, West concurred, had the potential to become a 'rich and great' country but only through the labour of the hardworking, industrious and 'respectable ... Tasmanian Yeoman'. It was with men such as this that Tasmania's future lay, not with those wealthy landowners who depended upon the demoralising labour of slaves.[192]

Images of the colony as a land of great bounty and beauty were interwoven, in turn, with naturalised discourses of family. Van Diemen's Land figured repeatedly as a natural site for home. 'The physical character of this country', West remarked, 'is all a parent could desire'. 'Nature', he explained:

> seems to approve his choice, and pours its bounty in endless variety at his feet. It is a land of corn and wine, and springs of water, of butter and honey; its soft light atmosphere, its brilliant days and glorious starlight; its hills and dales, its rivers and downs – all conspire to perfect its claim to pre-eminence among desirable lands.[193]

[239]

The abolitionist struggle was conceived as a profoundly familial and domestic drama. Transportation, West asserted, was a question to which every 'patriot and parent' must devote 'most anxious thought'; 'this is a question which comes home – it is domestic – it affects every man; his estate, his children and their posterity'. 'Parents of Van Diemen's Land', he demanded to know, 'can you hesitate?' 'Let the timid and sordid doubt – let them reckon the farthing they may lose; let the official men guard the system on which they live – they watch for their own interests; yours are immeasurably more valuable!'[194] Colonists opposed to transportation had been driven to act as the 'fathers of families', one campaigner explained, and because they were determined to 'ward off pollution from their own homes and hearths'.[195] 'Every commendable feeling in their individual character' as 'husbands, fathers or brothers' had, John Alexander Jackson agreed, been 'enlisted' against the continuation of transportation.[196]

Abolitionists also repeatedly laid emphasis upon the fact that their decision to leave Britain had been governed largely by familial concerns. They had come to the colony, they stressed, primarily in order to create a place where 'their children' might still 'be around them when they die' and to found 'a country' that they might 'bequeath' to them.[197] The oppression of the imperial government had, however, reduced these hopes to naught. The convict presence was transforming Van Diemen's Land into a moral and economic wasteland from which free settlers and their families must flee. 'For his part', one colonial father declared at an anti-transportation public meeting, 'he was ready to do anything and to risk anything to be free', but should their campaign eventually prove unsuccessful, he would take his 'young wife and young family, cast himself upon the world, and go where his children would not be sold'.[198] Others contended that transportation was forcibly dividing their families. 'He was not a rich man', another colonist announced, 'but he was a father, and had six sons – a qualification which entitled him to speak'. 'He wished transportation to cease', he explained, 'because he wished his children to live in this colony. His eldest son had already gone away and another had been offered a situation in a distant land'.[199] There was no longer 'anything like domestic safety, comfort or enjoyment in the colony', colonist William Crooke agreed. 'Our homes', he remarked, are 'dismembered by the departure of our children' to 'other lands', 'our household ties ... dissevered by the fell influence of convictism'.[200]

Images of beleaguered domesticity – which were, notably, also an increasingly important part of British radical discourse in this period – found their most intense form in the repeated discussions about child rape, a threat which was, despite the absence of hard facts to support this moral panic, considered increasingly all-encompassing.[201] Transportation, one abolitionist announced, was 'a system fraught ... with dreadful peril' because convict men presented a 'danger ... to every little girl in the community'.[202] 'As he was walking to the meeting', another colonist explained at an anti-transportation rally in Launceston, he had 'looked at the countenance of a beautiful and innocent child who crossed his path, and that sight determined him'. 'Whilst he had a voice to raise, a hand to use, and a foot to move, he would never rest until the curse of convictism was removed'.[203] Convicts equally threatened to pollute the bodies and the minds of male children. 'Shall fathers weep and mourn', abolitionists asked, 'to see a lovely son Debas'd, demoraliz'd, deform'd, by Britain's *filth and scum*?'[204] Claims about child rape were notably interwoven with narratives of class. Convict men 'guilty of ... abominable acts' were, James Aikenhead announced, indiscriminately mixed with the free population and allowed by government to enter 'private service' where their inevitable association with children all too often produced 'painfully apparent' results. If this could happen in the better and more 'respectable' households, what, he asked Earl Grey, must be the fate of those children 'whose parents are poor' and who were 'infinitely more exposed to the machinations' of these 'degraded wretches'?[205]

This focus upon the family took real as well as figurative form within the anti-transportation movement. Abolitionists stressed the urgency of involving children as well as parents, wives as well as husbands, in the struggle. Consequently, although men often dominated the campaign, the voices of women, and even of children, were nevertheless to be heard. It was, for example, a woman who was chosen to open the Australasian League's juvenile fete in 1853, and she used her address to remind the children present that 'the battle of anti-transportation is fought by their parents, chiefly on their account'. 'When ladies' are 'enlisted in the cause of purity', the *Launceston Examiner* reported approvingly, 'pollution may be expected to retire'.[206] When the flag of the Australasian League was hand-sewn in silk by the women of Launceston, John West was likewise impressed. Australia's future glory, he proclaimed, would be achieved by a 'moral force as fine as the spotless border which surrounds the Standard' that these women had sewn.[207] Female activism played its role in a range of other ways, too, including the organisation of an exclusively female petition designed to appeal directly to Queen Victoria on the grounds that she was, like them, a wife and a mother.[208] Other events were likewise designed with their symbolic charge in mind. A League regatta was, for example, the scene for the triumphal adulation of the manly stature and energetic physique of native-born colonial youth.[209]

Campaigners also repeatedly returned to domestic and familial discourses in order to negotiate and explore their relationship with the imperial government *and* the British nation. Van Diemen's Land was still in its infancy, they remarked repeatedly: Britain was the 'mother country', one petition declared, 'the illustrious nation which gave them birth', the colonies her 'feeble and dependent . . . offspring'. Allegations about the sexual threat which convicts supposedly presented to children were therefore analogous to the ways in which the imperial state preyed on colonists, continuing to import convicts, despite the fact that they brought 'horror', 'social depravity, degradation and wretchedness' in their wake. The petitioners concluded by uniting 'in solemn appeal to those eternal principles, which should . . . restrain a parent state from thus injuring its offspring'.[210] Here then was an unnatural 'family', one where the parent actively failed to nurture the child.

These allegations were interwoven, in turn, with a broader critique of government which contended that settlers – like the convicts –were suffering both as a result of the inevitably despotic tendencies of government at a distance and from the tendency of the aristocratic 'faction' that was in power in London to rely upon nepotism and patronage to appoint men to office regardless of their ability. 'We are in reality mere slaves', the *Launceston Examiner* proclaimed, 'subject to the caprice of governors, sent from home . . . [who are] too frequently very bad and very incapable men'.[211] Colonial officials, campaigners declared, were not only incapable of good government but, concerned to keep their jobs, they also had a vested interest in continued colonial misrule. Thus both the Governor and the Comptroller-General of Convicts were denounced as 'gentlemen who thrive on the ruins, material and moral, of the colony'.[212] The colonial state, abolitionists repeatedly alleged, was staffed by base, false men; 'stipendiaries of a 'foul system' with only 'sinister, self-interested purposes to serve' they necessarily sent 'defective and partial' reports to London.[213] The system ostensibly bred concealment and duplicity rather than the transparency and public accountability which liberal and Enlightenment theories of the state demanded. The imperial government was depicted in similarly bleak terms. The Secretary of State, campaigners declared, 'excelled' only in 'baseness and falsehood'; he was a man content to allow convicts to 'carry on their customary atrocities . . . with impunity'.[214] Given that the 1832 Reform Act had systematically reconstituted claims to political power around notions of masculine independence and morality – and that its provisions had not only excluded large constituencies in Britain from the franchise but also

[242]

throughout the empire – these kinds of allegations had a powerful purchase and heightened resonance in these years.[215]

Through such means, campaigners were also able to raise a series of wider questions about the nature and legitimacy of the current system of imperial power. Given that the empire was conceived of repeatedly as a 'family' in this period, questions of moral masculinity and of a properly constituted fatherhood, in particular, came to the fore almost inevitably. While abolitionists depicted themselves as independent, moral and virtuous heads of household, preparing to do anything to shelter their children and protect their homes, the same, they argued, could not be said of those who staffed the colonial and imperial states. Governor Denison, the *Launceston Examiner* declared, was like a grotesque and effeminate 'man midwife', donning petticoats and nightcap, to prepare the cradle for the 'unnatural' offspring of the convict state.[216] The imperial government, meanwhile, was busy converting 'convicts into demons' and planting 'the germs of a race' in the southern hemisphere 'to which, in moral turpitude, the annals of past history will furnish no parallel'.[217]

Building on these kinds of ideas, abolitionists argued that their continued oppression at the hands of the imperial government was forcing them to break their once tight bonds of familial loyalty and affection. Transportation, they explained, was 'rapidly weaning the affections of the colonists from the parent state' and destroying that natural connection with Britain which had 'hitherto been their pride and boast' by forcing them to 'seek refuge' from the 'heartless tyranny and oppression' of government 'in national independence'.[218] It was 'all very well to talk about our loyalty to the mother country', one colonist asserted, 'but loyalty', he proceeded to explain, 'is like filial duty':

> it must depend upon the education we receive. If one child is made the slave and drudge of the whole family – if it receives nothing but blows and abuse, its sense of the duty it owes to its parents will be very slight. So it is with us: if we are kicked and cuffed, and made to do all the dirty work of the empire, we shall begin to lose respect for the mother country and become downright democrats.[219]

Another colonist asked: What sort of a father was the imperial government? By resuming transportation, it had broken its pledges and gone back on its word. 'Can any of us ... doubt', he asked the audience at one public meeting:

> that the violation of such solemn pledges were not calculated to destroy that feeling of confidence in the honesty and integrity of our rulers and snap the bonds of an affection which naturally exist between ourselves

[243]

and the mother country? Were a parent to promise in like manner an indulgence to his child and neglect to perform it, what would the child think of the neglect and apathy which led to the violation of his parent's promise? And if these promises were made repeatedly, and as often repudiated, would not the filial tie be stretched to the most extreme point of separation, if not dissevered between them? Would it not lessen the love, the confidence, and the respect the child formerly entertained, and has not the violation of the pledge made to the colonists already sowed seeds of distrust and dislike, which, if not speedily eradicated, will produce crops of bitter strife?[220]

The solution was two-fold: to stay within the empire, as a mature and thus independent member of the British family but simultaneously to demand independence in order to remove the colony from under the rule of the imperial government. This juggling act was partly achieved through the body of the Queen. While abolitionists turned their back on the aristocratic 'faction' that ruled the British state – its tyrannical fatherhood – they nevertheless continued to express their affinities with, and love of, Victoria. Emphasising the feminine qualities of the young Queen, abolitionists appealed to her as a 'princess whose empire girdles the world'; a figure upon whose maternal assistance and 'natural' familial sentiments they might surely rely.[221] Her allegedly open and democratic ways presented, in turn, a powerful contrast to the secrecy and duplicity of government by 'faction'. The monarchy was 'the fountain of honour, truth and justice', campaigners declared, and Victoria was 'the type of all these virtues'.[222] Earl Grey's breach of faith in reversing his decision to end transportation was as much an affront to the Queen as to her colonists for government had become so debased as to 'barter the honour and dignity of their Royal Mistress for the purpose of clinging to places, patronage and power'.[223] These assertions of loyalty to Victoria were backed up by declarations of ongoing affection for, and kinship with, the nation. The colonists' 'one desire', the Australasian League explained, was 'to cultivate the love and to share the glories of the British people'.[224] It was by virtue of their common blood and heritage, one campaigner explained, that Van Diemen's Land now demanded her emancipation. The colonists, he explained, were Britons and thus a 'part and parcel' of the 'common stock, transplanted from the mother country' but 'identified by the same lineage, religion and impulses as herself'. Convicts, by contrast, were foreign 'blood', whose presence could only pollute, degrade and debase.[225]

Finally, campaigners also appealed to, and began to situate themselves within, an incipient notion of a new Australian family. Asking that the colonists of Australia and New Zealand rise together against transportation, the Launceston anti-transportation association reminded its audience of the new community, or family, of interests that was Australasia. 'The arm of oppression . . . has smitten' Van Diemen's Land 'with desolation', the association noted, and it would, in turn, inevitably 'strike at' the 'social well-being' of the Australian colonists as a whole.[226] The system of 'imperial despotism' that had devastated Van Diemen's Land, another campaigner remarked, was already 'practising' its 'arts on the young' settlement of 'Victoria'.[227] Van Diemen's Land was but one part of a broader colonial community that was, despite its geographical expanse, 'allied by blood, language and commerce'. Abolitionists were consequently confident that the colony would not 'long suffer alone'.[228] When, another campaigner declared, 'the voice of a whole people is raised in a righteous cause it will be omnipotent, and like the power of the mighty ocean when it puts forth its strength, sweep away from before it all paltry opposition'.[229] Within these proclamations was a developing vision of a young, virile and independent colonial society that had now entirely outgrown the imperial state. The 'past belongs to the Parent state', one group of petitioners asserted, 'the future belongs to [us] and among the bright visions of the future, there is not one more cheering than that which exhibits these Colonies as the grateful refuge and pleasant home of millions of industrious and honest men'.[230]

*　*　*

In a recent study of settler discourse within the British empire, the historical geographer Alan Lester contends that, in the face of a 'critique elaborated by British humanitarians', settlers were forced to redefine themselves radically in these decades. Using two case-studies – colonial debates over the rights of indigenous peoples and the campaign for the abolition of convict transportation – Lester concludes that this struggle became a site not only for the redefinition of the imperial project but also of the very 'nature of Britishness itself'. 'With their denunciations of settler brutality and degradation', Lester writes, 'humanitarians threatened a rupture between bourgeois metropolitan Britishness and colonial Britishness. If settlers were to resist being cast as aberrant Britons, or not Britons at all, then they had to reinvent and popularise a new conception of trans-imperial Britishness'.[231]

They did so, he argues, by developing a critique not just of 'specific humanitarian individuals' but of 'the humanitarian complex as a whole'. In the process, settlers both connected with, and contributed to, the development of a much more exclusive and 'reactionary discourse' of Britishness, one which was 'premised on the notion of deeply inscribed differences between social categories', or human

[245]

beings, and which constructed both indigenous peoples and the metropolitan working class, in particular, as 'savage', thereby placing both groups beyond the pale of civilisation.[232] On this basis, settlers were able to appeal to the British bourgeoisie whose face was also hardening to its own subordinate groups in the wake of parliamentary reform and in the face of the Chartist challenge. The reconstitution of settler discourse consequently enabled 'middle-class metropolitan Britons and bourgeois colonial settlers' to 'be understood within the same frame of reference as intrinsically racially superior' and as 'the means for the diffusion of an appropriate form of civilisation around the world'.[233] The ground was thus laid, Lester concludes, for the response to the Morant Bay rebellion in Jamaica of 1865 and for the final defeat of early nineteenth-century humanitarianism in the ensuing controversies over the Governor Eyre case.[234]

The evidence from Van Diemen's Land presents a rather different picture: at the hub of the empire-wide movement against transportation, sections of the settler community there developed a case against the convict system and for colonial political rights that was grounded in radical, liberal and humanitarian discourses. In so doing they not only sought to make gains for themselves but also contributed to wider critiques of the illiberal and 'aristocratic' nature of the current system of imperial government. The focus upon the disordered bodies of male convicts within colonial abolitionism was founded in two overlapping belief systems: first, an undoubted compassion for, and humanitarian sympathy with, the plight of the suffering convict, which drew, among other things, upon deeply held Christian convictions about the shared brotherhood of man; second, a belief that corporeal integrity was integral to male political rights and to liberal democracy. A focus upon manly self-command lay at the heart of liberal conceptions of the subject – and thus of political rights – in this period. As the antithesis of self-government, sodomy figured both as a powerful condemnation of tyranny and as a symbol of man's potential for 'savagery'. The developing emphases upon convicts as morally diseased, racially different and sexually monstrous were as much the logical extension of these humanitarian and liberal beliefs as any reactionary or conservative deviation from them.

Notes

1 Supreme Court, 20 October 1846, AOT SC 41/5. Judges' reports on capital cases, AOT CSO 20/17.
2 William Hall to Charles Joseph La Trobe, 8 October 1846, CSO 20/17.
3 'Correspondence relative to the recall of Sir Eardley Wilmot from the government of Van Diemen's Land', *BPP* XXXVIII (262), 1847, Part 1, pp. 3–4, 6.

4   John Eardley Wilmot to Robert Lathrop Murray, 21 December 1846, AOT NS 1010/2.
5   *BPP* XXXVIII (262), 1847, Part 2, p. 2.
6   *Ibid.*, p. 7.
7   *Ibid.*
8   See: *The Times*, 26 March 1847, 8 April 1847, 3 June 1847, 8–9 June 1847 and 17 July 1847.
9   *Colonial Times*, 23 October 1846.
10 CO 280/197.
11 Eardley Wilmot to Gladstone, 10 July 1846, 'Correspondence on the subject of convict discipline and transportation', *BPP* XLVIII (785), 1847, p. 101.
12 Stanley to Eardley Wilmot, September 1845, 'Copies or extracts of correspondence between the Secretary of State for the Colonies and the Lieutenant Governor of Van Diemen's Land on the subject of convict discipline and reports from the Comptroller-General of Convicts in Van Diemen's Land', *BPP* XXIX (402), 1846, pp. 3–13.
13 For details of some of these changes see: *BPP* XLVIII (785), 1847, pp. 47, 113–16.
14 See, for example, 'Medical returns on unnatural crimes, December 1845', *BPP* XLVIII (785), 1847, pp. 48–56. In some instances, Edward Swarbreck Hall, surgeon at Deloraine Probation Station reported, 'men have refused to submit to this examination, or have endeavoured to evade it, and have been punished for so doing, on my charge before the Visiting-Magistrate'; *ibid.*, p. 51; Eardley Wilmot to Gladstone, 10 July 1846, *BPP* XLVIII (785), 1847, p. 101.
15 AOT NS 1010/2.
16 The decision to sack Eardley Wilmot was undoubtedly more complex, however, and at least partly motivated by London's longer-term dissatisfaction with his administrative and money-handling skills. See: Ian Brand, *The convict probation system: Van Diemen's Land 1839–1854* (Hobart: Blubber Head Press, 1990), pp. 24–50; and Kathleen Fitzpatrick, 'Mr. Gladstone and the Governor: the recall of Sir John Eardley-Wilmot from Van Diemen's Land, 1846', *Historical Studies: Australia & New Zealand*, 1:1 (1940), pp. 31–45.
17 *Launceston Examiner*, 31 January 1846.
18 *BPP* XXIX (402), 1846, pp. 36–40.
19 Stephen cited in Brand, *Convict probation system*, p. 36.
20 *BPP* XLVIII (785), 1847, p. 9.
21 *Ibid.*
22 *Ibid.*, p. 57.
23 *BPP* XLVIII (785), 1847, pp. 57–8.
24 The proportion of female to male convicts remained high thereafter. See: Charles Bateson, *The convict ships* (Glasgow: Brown, Son & Ferguson, 1959), pp. 391–4.
25 *BPP* XLVIII (785), 1847, pp. 65–6.
26 *Ibid.*, p. 66.
27 *Ibid.*, p. 59.
28 Bishop of Tasmania, 'Notes on transportation and prison discipline as applied to Van Diemen's Land', *BPP* XXXVIII (741), 1847, p. 4.
29 For Pringle Stewart's report see: *BPP* XLVIII (785), 1847, pp. 77–97.
30 Report of the Reverend Naylor, *BPP* XLVIII (785), 1847, pp. 73, 76.
31 'Further correspondence on the subject of convict discipline and transportation', *BPP* XLVIII [811], 1847, p. 43.
32 *BPP* XLVIII (785), 1847, p. 193.
33 For an account of the final stages of transportation to VDL and the various alternatives explored see: Leon Radzinowicz, *A history of English criminal law and its administration from 1750 Vol. 5: The emergence of penal policy* (London, Stevens & sons, 1986); and A.G.L. Shaw, *Convicts and the colonies* (London: Faber & Faber, 1971), pp. 295–360.
34 'Second report from the Select Committee of the House of Lords appointed to inquire into the execution of the criminal law, especially respecting, juvenile offenders and transportation', *BPP* VII (534), 1847, pp. 3–4.

35 On the broader context see: Miles Taylor, 'The 1848 Revolutions and the British empire', *Past & Present*, 166 (2000), pp. 146–80.

36 Australasian League, *The League tracts* (Launceston: Henry Dowling, 1851), Tract 1, p. 3.

37 On the protests elsewhere see: A.F. Hattersley, *Convict crisis and the growth of unity: resistance to transportation in South Africa and Australia, 1848–53* (Pietermaritzburg: University of Natal Press, 1965); Kirsten McKenzie, *Scandal in the colonies: Sydney & Cape Town, 1820–1850* (Carlton, Victoria: Melbourne University Press, 2004); and Gregory Picker, 'A state of infancy: the anti-transportation movement in New Zealand, 1848–52', *New Zealand Journal of History*, 34:2 (2000), pp. 226–40.

38 Charles Blackton, 'The Australasian League, 1851–54', *Pacific Historical Review*, 8:4 (1939), pp. 385–400.

39 On the re-launch of this campaign see, for example: *Northern Star*, 3 January 1846.

40 James Syme, *Nine years in Van Diemen's Land: comprising an account of its discovery, possession, settlement, progress, population, value of land, herds, flocks, &c.; an essay on prison discipline; and the results of the working of the probation system; with anecdotes of bushrangers* (Perth: James Dewar, 1848), p. 200. Emphasis in original.

41 On continued support for the assignment system in the late 1830s and early 1840s see: *BPP* XLV (280), 1851, pp. 15–16. Despite the take-off of anti-transportation sentiment, local opinion remained firmly divided. See: Anne McLaughlin, 'Against the League: fighting the "Hated Stain"', *Tasmanian Historical Research Association*, 5:1 (1995–6), pp. 76–104.

42 For figures see: Bateson, *Convict ships*, pp. 381–95.

43 Brand, *Convict probation system*.

44 'There was more Market for the Labour of the Women than for the Labour of the Men in private Service', one official explained, 'because their Numbers were much fewer. Females were employed in a greater Proportion than Males relatively to their Numbers'; A.C. Stonor, *BPP* VII (534), 1847, p. 498. On demand for convict labour during this period see: David Meredith and Deborah Oxley, 'Contracting convicts: the convict labour market in Van Diemen's Land 1840–1857', *Australian Economic History Review*, 45:1 (2005), pp. 45–72.

45 Letter from 'A Van Diemen's Land Colonist', *The Times*, 11 April 1846; J.S., *The moral and pecuniary evils which the free colonists of Van Diemen's Land are suffering from the conversion of that island into the chief receptacle of British convicts* (London: privately circulated pamphlet, 1846), pp. 8–9.

46 J.S., *Moral and pecuniary evils*, p. 6; John Bisdee, *BPP* VII (534), 1847, p. 509.

47 For these protests see: 'Petitions on convict discipline and transportation delivered to the House of Commons from Australia or Van Diemen's Land since 1838', *BPP* XLV (130), 1851, pp. 22–3, 27; 'Petitions on convict discipline and transportation presented to the House of Commons from Australia or Van Diemen's Land since 1838', *BPP* XLV (280), 1851, p. 29; 'Petitions on convict discipline and transportation presented to the House of Commons from Australia or Van Diemen's Land since 1838', *BPP* XLV (262), 1851, p. 30.

48 J.S., *Moral and pecuniary evils*, pp. 5–7.

49 The conflict in Van Diemen's Land was one part of a wider wave of protest across the empire, sparked by London's attempts to resolve its financial problems by making the colonies absorb a greater share of the costs of empire. See: Taylor, '1848 Revolutions'.

50 Others were charged, but their cases either failed to proceed from lack of evidence or they were found not guilty. See: 'Returns of offences, Supreme Court of Van Diemen's Land', *BPP* XLVIII (785), 1847, pp. 41–2; 'List of cases tried before Quarter Sessions', AOT SGD 14; 'Register of prisoners tried in criminal proceedings', AOT SC 41. Carnal knowledge cases involved children under the age of twelve; cases involving females above this age were tried as rape.

51 AOT SGD 14, SC 41. On the attempts to change the law see: AOT CSO 22/83/1805. While the absolute number of convictions for 'unnatural' sexual crimes grew during the 1840s, so too did the male convict population: any relative increase in rates of conviction was almost certainly quite small. The Supreme Court convicted three men of sodomy or bestiality and six on carnal knowledge charges during the 1830s. During the 1840s, fifteen men were convicted by the Supreme Court of sodomy, bestiality or buggery and eight on charges relating to child sexual assault; AOT SC 41. Criminal statistics, of course, only really reveal policing and prosecution trends and tell us little about the actual occurrence of a crime because an unknown quantity of incidents go undetected or unreported. This is particularly the case with sex crimes, given their often private and even secret character. Given the increased attempts to police and regulate male convict sexual behaviour and the public hysteria, we might, however, have expected a peak in prosecution and conviction patterns for offences such as sodomy and bestiality.

52 See for example: *BPP* XLVIII (785), 1847, p. 51.

53 *Hobart Town Courier*, 4 February 1846. On this tradition in early nineteenth-century Britain see: H.G. Cocks, *Nameless offences: homosexual desire in the nineteenth century* (London: I.B. Tauris, 2003).

54 *BPP* XXXVIII (741), 1847, pp. 3–4.

55 *Launceston Examiner*, 5 December 1846.

56 *BPP* XXXVIII (741), 1847, p. 4.

57 *The Times*, 4 March 1847.

58 *Launceston Examiner*, 31 January 1846.

59 *BPP* XLVIII (785), 1847, p. 188.

60 *Ibid.*, p. 39.

61 *BPP* XXXVIII (741), 1847, p. 3.

62 *The Times*, 11 May 1846. See also J.S., *Moral and pecuniary evils*.

63 *BPP* XLVIII (785), 1847, p. 69.

64 Mr E. Smith, Superintendent of the Coal Mines to Matthew Forster, 9 November 1845, CON 1/4323.

65 *BPP* XLVIII (785), 1847, p. 39.

66 *Ibid.*, p. 48.

67 *Ibid.*, pp. 37, 39.

68 Comptroller-General Hampton to Governor William Denison, 10 January 1849, GO 46/1, p. 252.

69 Syme, *Nine years*, p. 203; Henry Phibbs Fry, *A system of penal discipline with a report on the treatment of prisoners in Great Britain and Van Diemen's Land* (London: Longmans, Brown, Green & Longmans, 1850), pp. 156, 162.

70 *BPP* XLV (280), 1851, p. 27.

71 *BPP* XLVIII (785), 1847, p. 186.

72 Stafford Northcote cited in Brand, *Convict probation system*, p. 45. As Michael Sturma notes, critiques of the convict system often bordered upon 'a subtle form of pornography'; Michael Sturma, *Vice in a vicious society: crime and convicts in mid-nineteenth century New South Wales* (St Lucia: University of Queensland Press, 1983), p. 3.

73 Australasian League, *League tracts*, Tract 1, p. 3.

74 J.A. Jackson to Earl Grey, 'Further correspondence on convict discipline and transportation', *BPP* XLV (1361), 1851, p. 66; Henry Anstey, 'Address to the electors', *Launceston Examiner*, 1 January 1853.

75 *Launceston Examiner*, 25 January 1853.

76 *BPP* XLV (130), 1851, pp. 20–1.

77 See: Elizabeth Elbourne, 'The sin of the settler: the 1835–36 Select Committee on aborigines and debates over virtue and conquest in the early nineteenth-century British white settler empire', *Journal of Colonialism and Colonial History*, 4:3 (2003), pp. 1–49; Alan Lester, 'British settler discourse and the circuits of empire', *History Workshop Journal*, 54:1 (2002), pp. 24–48; and Alan Lester,

'Obtaining the "due observance of justice": the geographies of colonial humanitarianism', *Environment and Planning: D: Society and Space*, 20:3 (2002), pp. 277–93.

78 West cited in Patricia Fitzgerald Ratcliff (ed.), *John West's Union of the Colonies: essays on federation published under the pseudonym of John Adams in 1854* (Launceston: Queen Victoria Museum and Art Gallery, 2000), p. 18. On West see: Patricia Fitzgerald Ratcliff, *The usefulness of John West: dissent and difference in the Australian colonies* (Launceston: The Albernian Press, 2003).

79 Australasian League, *League tracts*, Tract 3, p. 1.

80 *Ibid.*

81 W. Crooke, *BPP* XLV (1361), 1851, p. 85.

82 Australasian League, *League tracts*, Tract 3, p. 2.

83 *Launceston Examiner*, 8 January 1853.

84 *Ibid.*, 15 January 1853.

85 *Ibid.*, 4 September 1852.

86 *Ibid.*, 6 and 8 January 1853.

87 *BPP* XLVIII (785), 1847, p. 71.

88 William Ullathorne, 'Select Committee on Transportation', *BPP* XXII (669), 1837–38, pp. 16, 24–5; William Ullathorne, *The horrors of transportation* (Dublin: Richard Coyne, 1838), p. 6.

89 William Ullathorne, *The Catholic mission in Australasia* (Liverpool: Rockliff & Duckworth, 1837), frontispiece.

90 *Launceston Examiner*, 13 August 1853.

91 Richard Whately, cited in William Molesworth, *Report from the Select Committee of the House of Commons on Transportation together with a Letter from the Archbishop of Dublin on the same subject; and notes* (London: Henry Hooper, 1838), p. 52.

92 *The Times*, 15 February 1850; C.G. Stevens, *An appeal from Earl Grey and Sir W. Denison to British justice and humanity, against the proposed continuance of transportation to Van Diemen's Land* (London: John Snow, 1851), p. 12.

93 Fry, *System of penal discipline*, pp. 153–4.

94 *Ibid.*, p. 173.

95 Syme, *Nine years*, pp. iv, 13.

96 Fry, *System of penal discipline*, title page.

97 Andrew Porter, 'Trusteeship, anti-slavery and humanitarianism', in Andrew Porter (ed.), *The Oxford history of the British Empire* (Oxford: Oxford University Press, 1999), Vol. 3, p. 198.

98 Stevens, *Appeal from Earl Grey*; J.S., *The Times*, 11 May 1846; 'A Tasmanian', *The Times*, 22 January 1846.

99 Stevens, *Appeal from Earl Grey*, p. 17.

100 Michael Roe, *Quest for authority in eastern Australia, 1835–1851* (Parkville, Victoria: Melbourne University Press, 1965), p. 6.

101 Stevens, *Appeal from Earl Grey*; *BPP* XLV (1361), 1851, p. 62; J.S., *The Times*, 11 May 1846.

102 Stevens, *Appeal from Earl Grey*, p. 3. *BPP* XLV (1361), 1851, p. 66.

103 Fry, *System of penal discipline*, pp. 173–5.

104 *BPP* VII (534), 1847, p. 473.

105 Michael Ignatieff, *A just measure of pain: the penitentiary in the Industrial Revolution, 1750–1850* (London: Macmillan, 1978); W.J. Forsythe, *The reform of prisoners, 1830–1900* (London: Croom Helm, 1987), Martin Wiener, *Reconstructing the criminal: culture, law and policy in England* (Cambridge: Cambridge University Press, 1990).

106 *BPP* VII (534), 1847, p. 234.

107 *BPP* XLVIII (785), 1847, pp. 69–70, 72–3.

108 John West, *The history of Tasmania* (Launceston: Henry Dowling, 1852), Vol. 2, pp. 181–2.

109 *Ibid.*, p. 257.

110 *BPP* XLVIII (785), 1847, pp. 69, 76.
111 Ullathorne, *Horrors*, p. 26.
112 *BPP* VII (534), 1847, p. 240.
113 *Ibid.*, p. 488.
114 *Ibid.*, p. 234.
115 Fry, *System of penal discipline*, p. 177.
116 Bishop of Tasmania, *BPP* VII (534), 1847, p. 488.
117 West, *History*, Vol. 2. p. 165.
118 Randall McGowen, 'The body and punishment in eighteenth-century England', *Journal of Modern History*, 59:4 (1987), pp. 654–5.
119 Whately cited in Molesworth, *Report*, p. 50.
120 Jeremy Bentham, 'Panopticon versus New South Wales', in John Bowring (ed.), *The works of Jeremy Bentham* (Edinburgh: William Tait, 1843), Vol. IV, p. 174.
121 Ullathorne, *BPP* XXII (669), 1837–38, p. 33.
122 Whately cited in Molesworth, *Report*, p. 50.
123 Ullathorne, *Catholic mission*, pp. 9, 32.
124 Molesworth, *Report*, p. 16.
125 *Launceston Examiner*, 8 January 1853.
126 Australasian League, *League tracts*, Tract 3, p. 4.
127 Bentham, 'Panopticon', pp. 175, 177. Emphasis in original.
128 *BPP* XLVIII (785), 1847, p. 69.
129 *BPP* XLVIII (785), 1847, p. 68.
130 *BPP* XXII (669), 1837–38, p. 52.
131 *BPP* XLVIII (785), 1847, p. 69.
132 Reverend Willson, *BPP* VII (534), 1847, p. 542.
133 West, *History*, Vol. 2, pp. 296–7.
134 *BPP* XLVIII (785), 1847, pp. 69, 71, 74.
135 Fry, *System of penal discipline*, p. 178.
136 Ullathorne, *Catholic mission*, pp. 21, 55.
137 *BPP* XLVIII (785), 1847, pp. 68, 73–4.
138 James Ross, *An essay on prison discipline in which is detailed the system pursued in Van Diemen's Land* (Hobart: James Ross, 1833), p. 30.
139 John Barnes, *BPP* XXII (669), 1837–38, p. 38.
140 Ullathorne, *Catholic mission*, pp. iv, 24.
141 *Launceston Examiner* cited in Dan Huon, 'By moral means only: the origins of the Launceston anti-transportation leagues, 1847–49', *Tasmanian Historical Research Association*, 44:2 (1997), p. 105.
142 John Frost, *The horrors of convict life* (Hobart: Sullivan's Cove, 1973), pp. 9, 30.
143 *Ibid.*, pp. 34, 55.
144 *Ibid.*, p. 12.
145 *Ibid.*, pp. 43, 45; John Frost, *A letter to the people of Great Britain and Ireland showing the effects of irresponsible power on the physical and moral conditions of convicts* (London: Holyoake, 1857), pp. 1, 6, 8–9.
146 Anna Clark, *The struggle for the breeches: gender and the making of the British working class* (Berkeley, CA: University of California Press, 1995).
147 For a fuller discussion see Kirsty Reid, 'Convict ballads, empire and popular culture in nineteenth-century Britain', unpublished paper presented at the Economic and Social Research Council 'Colonial Possessions' workshop, University of Warwick, December 2005. Available from the author.
148 George Thompson, *Slavery and famine: punishments for sedition or an account of the miseries and starvation at Botany Bay with some preliminary remarks by George Dyer* (London: J. Ridgway, 1794). Dyer wrote his pamphlet to protest about the transportation of the 'Scottish Martyrs' in the 1790s. On the Martyrs, see: Frank Clune, *The Scottish Martyrs: their trials and transportation to Botany Bay* (Sydney: Angus & Robertson, 1969).
149 *HRA* I, 5, pp. 536–7.

150 Jeremy Bentham, 'A Plea for the Constitution', in John Bowring (ed.), *The works of Jeremy Bentham* (Edinburgh: William Tait, 1843), Vol. IV, pp. 254, 269.

151 *HRA* I, 5, pp. 536–7.

152 Bentham, 'Panopticon', p. 211.

153 See, for example: *HRA* III, 8, pp. 610, 617–18. Hume was interested in issues of colonial misrule more broadly. See: Miles Taylor, 'Joseph Hume and the reformation of India, 1819–33', in G. Burgess and M. Festenstein (eds), *Radicalism in English political thought, 1550–1850* (Cambridge: Cambridge University Press, forthcoming). My thanks to Professor Taylor for allowing me to see this paper before it was published.

154 William Ashton, *A lecture on the evils of emigration and transportation* (Sheffield: J. Lingard, 1839), p. 7. Emphasis in original.

155 George Rudé, *Protest and punishment: the story of the social and political protesters transported to Australia, 1788–1868* (Oxford: Clarendon, 1978).

156 George Loveless, *The victims of Whiggery; being a statement of persecution experienced by the Dorchester labourers; their trial; banishment & c: also reflections upon the present system of transportation; with an account of Van Diemen's Land, its customs, laws, climate, produce and inhabitants* (London: Cleave, 1838), p. 11.

157 Millicent Garrett Fawcett, *Life of the Right Honourable Sir William Molesworth* (London: Macmillan, 1901), pp. 85–6.

158 Stevens, *Appeal from Earl Grey*, p. 6.

159 *Launceston Examiner*, 4 September 1852.

160 Stevens, *Appeal from Earl Grey*, p. 17.

161 *BPP* XLV (1361), 1851, p. 74.

162 Jacob Lackland, *Common sense: an enquiry into the influence of transportation on the colony of Van Diemen's Land* (Launceston: Henry Dowling, 1847), pp. 3–4. Lackland was a pseudonym for John West.

163 Zachary Pearce Pocock, *Transportation and convict discipline considered* (London: Simmonds & Co., London, 1847), p. 3; Letter from 'A Van Diemen's Land Colonist', *The Times*, 11 April 1846; Fitzgerald Ratcliff, *John West's Union*, p. 3.

164 Lackland, *Common sense*, p. 10.

165 C.H.M., *The Times*, 2 January 1852.

166 *BPP* XLV (1361), 1851, p. 67.

167 *Launceston Examiner*, 1 January 1853.

168 Stevens, *Appeal from Earl Grey*, p. 18.

169 Charles Cole, 'The strength of tyranny', *Northern Star*, 9 May 1846. On the varied deployment of slavery in contemporary political discourse see: Kelly Mays, 'Slaves in Heaven, laborers in Hell: Chartist poets' ambivalent identification with the (black) slave', *Victorian Poetry*, 39:2 (2001), pp. 137–63.

170 John Best, *A review of the letter addressed to the householders of Hobart Town by the Reverend H. P. Fry, by a member of the medical profession* (Hobart: Advertiser Office, 1847), pp. 6–7.

171 For a more detailed discussion see: Kirsty Reid, 'Family matters: masculinity, domesticity and power in early nineteenth-century Britain and Australia', unpublished paper presented to the 'British World' conference, Melbourne, July 2004. Available from the author.

172 *BPP* VII (534), 1847, p. 525.

173 Ullathorne, *Catholic mission*, p. 32. Ullathorne, *BPP* XXII (669), 1837–38, p. 24.

174 Ullathorne, *BPP* XXII (669), 1837–38, p. 26.

175 Dr Motherwell, 'Reports from the medical officers of every male convict station in Van Diemen's Land as to the existence, or otherwise, of unnatural crime amongst the convicts', CO 280/216. Similar claims about altered anatomy as a result of 'unnatural' practices were also made about convict women. See: Kay Daniels, *Convict women* (St Leonards, NSW: Allen & Unwin, 1998), pp. 165–7.

176 *BPP* XLVIII (785), 1847, pp. 188.

177 James Aikenhead to Grey, GO 33/65.

178 Dr Matthias Gaunt to Grey, GO 33/68, pp. 942–61.
179 Although Gaunt's version of Cripps's story drew upon a number of verifiable facts, the case had, in fact, taken place over a decade before and had involved not a 'boy', a claim which Gaunt made much of, but a man of twenty-three; 'Memorandum on Cripps', GO 33/68, pp. 962–5. Transmitting Gaunt's letter to London, Denison noted that it contained 'the usual tissue of garbled statements calculated to mislead Your Lordship'; Denison to Grey, 12 December 1849, GO 33/68. The most famous convict 'cannibal', then as now, was Alexander Pearce, whose narrative achieved widespread attention in Britain and Australia, and who had also attracted the interest of the Molesworth Committee. See: BPP XXII (669), 1837–38, Appendix I, p. 316. On Pearce see: Dan Sprod, Alexander Pearce of Macquarie Harbour: convict, bushranger, cannibal (Hobart: Cat & Fiddle Press, 1977); and Paul Collins, Hell's gates: the terrible journey of Alexander Pearce, Van Diemen's Land cannibal (South Yarra, Melbourne: Hardie Grant Books, 2002).
180 'Cannibalism', Jennifer Morgan argues, was 'an absolute indicator of savagery and distance from European norms', and it had been linked with images of 'female sexual insatiability' since at least the sixteenth and seventeenth centuries; Jennifer Morgan, '"Some could suckle over their shoulder": male travellers, female bodies and the gendering of racial ideology, 1550–1770', William & Mary Quarterly, 54:1 (1997), p. 173.
181 Narratives about convict cannibalism had already been in circulation for several decades with the result, H.L. Malchow suggests, that the transported convict was fast becoming the stock character in 'white' cannibal tales; H.L. Malchow, Gothic images of race in nineteenth-century Britain (Stanford, CA: Stanford University Press, 1996), especially pp. 60–1, 96–9.
182 Ibid., p. 44.
183 BPP XLVIII (785), 1847, p. 73; Launceston Examiner, 31 January 1846; Pocock, Transportation, p. 3; Syme, Nine years, p. 200.
184 David Burn, A picture of Van Diemen's Land (Hobart: Cat & Fiddle Press, 1973), p. 44.
185 Syme, Nine years, pp. 141–4.
186 Australasian League, League tracts, Tract 3, p. 1.
187 Syme, Nine years, p. 144. The extract is from Byron's poem 'The Giaour'.
188 Part of the 'attraction of Australia' in this period, historian David Goodman notes, was 'that it was a new land which could be made free from the political corruption and aristocratic domination of the old'; David Goodman, 'Gold fields/golden fields: the language of agrarianism and the Victorian gold rush', Australian Historical Studies, 23:90 (1988), p. 34. On radical agrarianism in Britain see: Malcolm Chase, The people's farm: English radical agrarianism, 1775–1840 (Oxford: Clarendon, 1988).
189 Charles Rowcroft, Tales of the colonies or, the adventures of an emigrant edited by a late colonial magistrate (London: Saunders & Otley, 1843), Vol. 1, pp. xi–xii. On the application of these ideas to Van Diemen's Land see: Reid, 'Family matters'.
190 BPP XLV (1361), 1851, pp. 65–6.
191 Australasian League, League tracts, Tract 3, p. 3.
192 Lackland, Common sense, p. 16.
193 Ibid., p. 21.
194 Ibid., pp. 3, 21.
195 Best, Review, p. 8.
196 J. A. Jackson, Correspondence with the Colonial department on transportation to Van Diemen's Land, April and May 1848 (London: Richards, 1848), pp. 12–13.
197 Australasian League, League tracts, Tract 3, p. 1.
198 BPP XLV (1361), 1851, p. 73.
199 Ibid., pp. 69–70.
200 Ibid., p. 85.

201 On domesticity and British radical discourse see: Clark, *Struggle for the breeches*; and Anna Clark, 'The rhetoric of Chartist domesticity: gender, language and class in the 1830s and 1840s', *Journal of British Studies*, 31:1 (1992), pp. 62–88.
202 *BPP* XLV (1361), 1851, p. 66.
203 *Ibid.*, p. 85.
204 Syme, *Nine years*, p. 200. Emphasis in original.
205 Aikenhead to Grey, GO 33/65.
206 *Launceston Examiner*, 3 February 1853.
207 Fitzgerald Ratcliff, *John West's Union*, p. 9.
208 *The Times*, 10 May 1851.
209 *Launceston Examiner*, 25 January 1853.
210 'Petition of the inhabitants of the Australasian Colonies of New South Wales, Victoria, Van Diemen's Land, South Australia and New Zealand', in *A collection of printed and autographed material prepared in the Launceston District to further the cause of the Australasian League*, Item 5, Tasmaniana Library, State Library of Tasmania.
211 *Launceston Examiner*, 8 January 1853.
212 Stevens, *Appeal from Earl Grey*, p. 7.
213 *Launceston Examiner*, 1 and 8 January 1853. Aikenhead to Grey, GO 33/65.
214 *Launceston Examiner*, 8 January 1853.
215 See: Catherine Hall, 'The rule of difference: gender, class and empire in the making of the 1832 Reform Act', in Ida Blom, Karen Hagemann and Catherine Hall (eds), *Gendered nations: nationalism and gender order in the long nineteenth century* (New York: New York University Press, 2000), pp. 107–35; Miles Taylor, 'Empire and parliamentary reform: the 1832 reform act revisited', in Arthur Burns and Joanna Innes (eds), *Rethinking the age of reform: Britain, 1780–1850* (Cambridge: Cambridge University Press, 2003, pp. 295–311; and Miles Taylor, 'Colonial representation at Westminster, c. 1800–65', in Julian Hoppit (ed.), *Parliaments, nations and identities in Britain and Ireland, 1660–1850* (Manchester: Manchester University Press, 2003), pp. 206–20.
216 *Launceston Examiner*, 23 January 1853.
217 J.S., *The Times*, 11 May 1846.
218 Australasian League, *Sessional papers & c. of the Australasian League conference, held in Hobart Town and Launceston, Van Diemen's Land, in the months of April and May, 1852* (Launceston: 1852), pp. 14, 28.
219 *BPP* XLV (1361), 1851, p. 72.
220 *BPP* XLV (1361), 1851, p. 81.
221 *Launceston Examiner*, 11 January 1853. On contemporary images of Victoria as an imperial mother see: Randi Davenport, 'Thomas Malthus and maternal bodies politic: gender, race and empire', *Women's History Review*, 4:4 (1995), pp. 415–39.
222 *BPP* XLV (1361), 1851, p. 83. For an example of these arguments, see: *Launceston Examiner*, 11 January 1853.
223 *BPP* XLV (1361), 1851, p. 81.
224 Australasian League, *Sessional papers*, pp. 14, 28.
225 C.H.M., *The Times*, 2 January 1852.
226 *BPP* XLV (1361), 1851, p. 90.
227 *Ibid.*, p. 93.
228 *Ibid.*, p. 91.
229 *Ibid.*, p. 84.
230 Stevens, *Appeal from Earl Grey*, p. 21.
231 Lester, 'British settler discourse', pp. 25, 44.
232 *Ibid.*, pp. 34, 42.
233 *Ibid.*, p. 44.
234 On the Morant Bay rebellion and the Governor Eyre case see: Catherine Hall, *White, male and middle-class: explorations in feminism and history* (Cambridge: Polity, 1992); and Gad Heuman, *The killing time: the Morant Bay rebellion in Jamaica* (London: Macmillan, 1994).

Conclusion

Throughout the first half-century of colonisation the family – and with it particular configurations of gender and sexual relations – had assumed diverse functions and taken different forms. It had been something from which the transported had been deliberately torn – the fragmentation and forcible disruption of this supposedly natural order an integral part of the sentence imposed upon convicts by the state – and a place to which many would dream of making their return. For others – free colonists as well as convicts – it had almost certainly been a source of conflict, oppression and burdensome obligation – from which, through empire, they had sought to run. In the colony itself, the family had, from the outset, been imagined explicitly as a site of discipline and a channel for power. Initially at least, convicts were trusted to run their own households and thus to experience the 'transforming' power of the domestic sphere, and of the work required to support and maintain it, in a relatively independent fashion. From the late 1810s on, the settler family was, however, reconceived as a prison house and as a site, through the exploitation of convict coerced labour, for class domination and capital accumulation. Against this backdrop, convict hopes of family formation or reunion, of sexual and intimate relations and of a private life were destined not only to become more tenuous and fragile but increasingly also matters of class conflict and contestation. While – as numerous historical studies have shown – relations between male and female convicts were undoubtedly characterised at times by violence, force, coercion and bids for male domination, the shared experience of transportation, and of forced labour in particular, brought convict men and women together as much as these other practices and forces tended to push them apart.

If attachment to the family form was bound up integrally with the material and ideological production of social difference and thus with the creation of hierarchies of class, it was also always associated with prescriptive ideas about sexual morality and gender roles and so with the belief that men and women belonged in particular places and spaces. Family and state power were associated, in particular, with the expression of masculine authority. Although repeatedly imagined as natural, state strategies and imperial and colonial anxieties reflected the extent to which this masculine mode was not only socially and culturally manufactured, and as often imposed as willingly embraced, but also a site for discussion, debate and dissent. Just as the state often did not trust settlers to run their households in an ordered enough fashion without government surveillance and regulation, so too settlers deployed notions of proper fatherhood and moral masculinity to scrutinise and lambast the state. These tensions expressed themselves in different ways in different contexts and periods, but they came to a head during the late 1830s and 1840s, when reformers, intent on the refashioning of empire, turned their attention not only to the alien nature of the tyranny and slavery which they believed to characterise the Australian colonies but also to the reputedly disordered nature of colonial domesticity and to the deviant, foreign and savage character of convict and settler masculinities. In giving voice to these fears, these reformers imagined a different order, one that they regarded as unproblematically natural, and in which a multitude of independent and self-governing men formed the lynchpin of a liberal and self-governing empire. But, for all that the reformers of the 1830s, and the colonial campaigners of the 1840s, imagined the family as a vehicle of emancipation and freedom, hierarchies of class and gender, and the notions of due discipline and coercion which tended to go with them, remained powerfully embedded within their plans.

Throughout August and September 1853, Van Diemen's Land celebrated its liberation. A series of jubilee parades and ceremonials were staged across the island and these events were designed explicitly to focus upon the future in the form of the colony's children and native-born youth. At Longford, in the north, the children processed to the church and were given pieces of 'demonstration cake', while at Sorell, in the south, children's games were organised, cakes and ginger beer distributed to the young, and a special lunch prepared for the ladies. At the River Forth, there was a children's banquet, at Oatlands 'long tables in the open air' were arranged 'for their special accommodation' and 'loaded with cakes and other good things', and at Evandale, five hundred of 'the native youth of all ages and both sexes mustered' to lead off the parade. Throughout the colony, those who marched were asked to dress in symbolic colours, all were to wear white (the sign of unblemished virtue), and the native born were asked, in addition, to attach light-blue ribbons to their left breasts, in order to mark them out for special admiration and appreciation.[1] In the aftermath of abolition, the colony was figuratively reborn, renamed Tasmania in a conscious bid to cast off the 'convict stain'.[2] This 'stain' would nevertheless prove stubborn, and it would appear, at times, to be almost indelible. Its effects were felt, in particular, within the homes and families of those who had been convicts, or who were descended from them, many of whom were forced to retreat into decades of shame-ridden silence about the past and to fashion new stories about their origins and descent.[3]

As colonists, or at least those who had opposed transportation, gathered to celebrate their freedom in the early 1850s, many were already looking ahead. In the absence of convicts it was hoped that a new, and less polluting stream of population and labour would spring forth, in the form of increased free emigration. With this prospect before them, observers began to imagine new ways of fashioning colonial order. In doing so, some turned, once again, to the household and to the family. In the Reverend John West's eyes, convicts and ex-convicts had an at best limited, and progressively diminishing, part to play. 'They die childless', he wrote in an obvious flight of fantasy about ex-convict men, 'melt from the earth ... and pass away like a mournful dream'. Settlers, by contrast, with their naturally self-commanding, virtuous and healthy bodies, would become the fathers of a new race, capable of domesticating the colony, and thus of staking full claim to it, by covering it with well-ordered families and homes.[4] Others, in addition, had already begun to explore the family's future potential as a disciplining and regulatory force for labour. The women and children of the emigrant labourers who would now come to the colony would be positive assets, the Australasian League declared, because, it explained, they would act as 'hostages for the honest fulfilment' of agreements to work by the men.[5]

Notes

1 *Launceston Examiner*, 16, 23 and 25 August 1853, 3, 13 and 17 September 1853.
2 See: Henry Reynolds, 'That Hated Stain: the aftermath of transportation in Tasmania', *Historical Studies*, 14:35 (1969), pp. 19–31.
3 This silence only really began to be broken in the late twentieth century when many Australians became interested in family history and genealogy. On the interesting concatenation of identities of class, gender, nation and race which has partially given rise to this upsurge of interest in the convict past and to the aspirations among some groups to uncover a convict ancestor see: Ronald Lambert, 'Reclaiming the ancestral past: narrative, rhetoric and the "convict stain"', *Journal of Sociology*, 38:2 (2002), pp. 111–27; and Bruce Tranter and Jed Donoghue, 'Convict ancestry: a neglected aspect of Australian identity', *Nations and Nationalism*, 9:4 (2003), pp. 555–77.

4 John West, *The history of Tasmania* (Launceston: Henry Dowling, 1852), Vol. 2, p. 330.
5 Australasian League, *The League tracts* (Launceston: Henry Dowling, 1851), Tract 3, p. 3.

Select bibliography

Archival and manuscript collections

Archives Office of Tasmania, Hobart

Non-state records
Bayles, Robert, Diary, NS 395/1.
Eardley Wilmot, John, letter, NS 1010/2.
Laing, Alexander, Reminiscences of Alexander Laing, District Constable, Pittwater, Tasmania, 1819–38, NS 1116/1.
Withers, Peter, convict, letters, NS 887.

Colonial Secretary's Office
CSO 1 General correspondence records, 1824–36.
CSO 2 Register of general correspondence, 1824–36.
CSO 3 Index to the general correspondence records, 1824–36.
CSO 4 Index to the general correspondence records, 1836–7.
CSO 5 General correspondence records, 1837–41.
CSO 7 Index to general correspondence, 1837–41.
CSO 19 Miscellaneous papers transferred from the Private Secretary's Office 1820–46.
CSO 20/17 Judges' reports on capital cases.
CSO 22 Correspondence records, Legal Branch, 1841–47.
CSO 22/50 'Report and evidence of a committee enquiring into female convict discipline, 1841–1843'.
CSO 73 Correspondence from the Principal Superintendent of Convicts, 1838–41.
CSO 76 Correspondence records relating to convict matters, 1839–41.
CSO 84 Letterbook of memoranda addressed to the Principal Superintendent of Convicts, 1828–29.
CSO 88 Letterbook of memoranda and correspondence addressed to the Board of Assignment, 1830–41.

Colonial Office
CO 280 Colonial Office, Tasmania, original correspondence, despatches.

SELECT BIBLIOGRAPHY

Convict Department
CON 1 General correspondence records, 1844–67.
CON 2 Miscellaneous correspondence and associated documents, Van Diemen's Land, 1831–68.
CON 27 Convict appropriation lists, Van Diemen's Land.
CON 44 Convict memorials for indulgences, Van Diemen's Land, September 1833–October 1834.
CON 45/1 Alphabetical registers of convicts' applications for indulgences, Van Diemen's Land.
CON 77 Miscellaneous convict documents, Van Diemen's Land, 1833–1860.

Governor's Office
GO 25 Letterbook of despatches to the Secretary of State.
GO 29 Letterbook of despatches addressed to the Under-Secretary and Secretary of State and to the Commissioners of the Navy.
GO 33 Duplicate dispatches received by the Colonial Office 1825–55.
GO 46 Reports of the Comptroller General of Convicts.

Lower courts
LC 251 Record of cases against women heard in petty sessions, 1846–54, Hobart.

Police Office records
POL 211 Miscellaneous petitions returned to the Morven Police Office from the Lieutenant Governor c.1840–c.1850.

Supreme Court
SC 41 Register of persons tried in criminal cases.
SGD 14 Register of prisoners tried in criminal proceedings.

National Archives, Kew, London
HO 10 Returns of convicts, Van Diemen's Land.

National Library of Australia, Canberra
Diary of John Ward, convict, 1841–42, MS 3275.
Journal of Lady Jane Franklin, MS 248/84–96.

Mitchell Library, State Library of New South Wales, Sydney
MM 33 Convict indents and appropriation lists, Van Diemen's Land.
TP Tasmanian Papers.

State Library of Tasmania, Hobart
Australasian League, 'A collection of printed and autographed material prepared in the Launceston District to further the cause of the Australasian League', Tasmaniana Library.
Australasian League, 'Leaflet', 29 September 1852, Tasmaniana Library.

Royal Society of Tasmania Archives, University of Tasmania Library
James Belbin, Pocket Book, RS 90/1.

Printed primary sources

Historical Records of Australia
Watson, Frederick (ed.), *Historical Records of Australia. Series 1: Governor's despatches to and from England* (Sydney: the Library Committee of the Commonwealth Parliament, 1914–25), Volumes 1–26.
Watson, Frederick (ed.), *Historical Records of Australia. Series 3: Despatches and papers relating to the settlement of the states* (Sydney: the Library Committee of the Commonwealth Parliament, 1914–25), Volumes 1–6.
Chapman, Peter (ed.), *Historical Records of Australia. Resumed series 3: Despatches and papers relating to the settlement of the states* (Canberra: Australian Government Publishing Service, 1997), Volume 7.
Chapman, Peter (ed.), *Historical Records of Australia. Resumed series 3: Despatches and papers relating to the settlement of the states* (Melbourne: Melbourne University Press, 2003), Volume 8.

British Parliamentary Papers
'Select Committee on Transportation', *British Parliamentary Papers*, II (341), 1812.
'Papers relating to H.M. settlements at New South Wales 1811–1814', *British Parliamentary Papers*, XVIII (450), 1816.
'Select Committee on the state and description of gaols and other places of confinement, and into the best method for providing for the reformation as well as the safe custody and punishment of offenders', *British Parliamentary Papers*, VII (579), 1819.
'Report of the Commissioner of Inquiry into the state of the colony of New South Wales', *British Parliamentary Papers*, XX (448), 1822.
'Select Committee on secondary punishments', *British Parliamentary Papers*, VII (276), 1831.
'Select Committee on transportation', *British Parliamentary Papers*, XIX (518), 1837.
'Select Committee on transportation', *British Parliamentary Papers*, XXII (669), 1837–38.
'Despatches from the Governor of New South Wales and the Lieutenant Governor of Van Diemen's Land relative to the transportation and assignment of convicts', *British Parliamentary Papers*, XXXIV (76), 1837–38.
'Despatch from Lieutenant Governor Sir J. Franklin October 1837 relative to the present system of convict discipline in Van Diemen's Land', *British Parliamentary Papers*, XLII (309), 1837–38.
'Notes on transportation and secondary punishment', *British Parliamentary Papers*, XXXVIII (582), 1839.
'Papers relative to the transportation and assignment of convicts', *British Parliamentary Papers*, XXXVIII (582), 1839.

'Correspondence on convict discipline, 1843–46', *British Parliamentary Papers*, XLII (158–59), 1843.

'Copies or extracts of correspondence between the Secretary of State for the colonies and the Lieutenant Governor of Van Diemen's Land on the subject of convict discipline and Reports from the Comptroller General of Convicts in Van Diemen's Land', *British Parliamentary Papers*, XXIX (402), 1846.

'Correspondence relative to the recall of Sir Eardley Wilmot from the government of Van Diemen's Land', *British Parliamentary Papers*, XXXVIII (262), 1847.

'Correspondence on the subject of convict discipline and transportation', *British Parliamentary* Papers, XLVIII (785), 1847.

'Further correspondence on the subject of convict discipline and transportation', *British Parliamentary Papers*, XLVIII (800), 1847.

'Select Committee of the House of Lords appointed to enquire into the execution of the criminal law, especially respecting juvenile offenders and transportation', *British Parliamentary Papers*, VII (534), 1847.

'Correspondence on the subject of convict discipline and transportation', *British Parliamentary Papers*, LII (941), 1847–48.

'Further correspondence on the subject of convict discipline and transportation', *British Parliamentary Papers* XLVIII [811], 1847.

Bishop of Tasmania, 'Notes on transportation and prison discipline as applied to Van Diemen's Land', *British Parliamentary* Papers, XXXVIII (741), 1847.

'Further correspondence on convict discipline and transportation', *British Parliamentary Papers*, XLV (1361), 1851.

'Petitions on convict discipline and transportation delivered to the House of Commons from Australia or Van Diemen's Land since 1838', *British Parliamentary Papers*, XLV (130), 1851.

'Petitions on convict discipline and transportation presented to the House of Commons from Australia or Van Diemen's Land since 1838', *British Parliamentary Papers*, XLV (280), 1851.

'Petitions on convict discipline and transportation presented to the House of Commons from Australia or Van Diemen's Land since 1838', *British Parliamentary Papers*, XLV (262), 1851.

'Second report from the Select Committee on transportation', *British Parliamentary Papers*, XVII (296), 1856.

Published sources and contemporary works

Anon, *The farmers, or, tales for the times: addressed to the yeomanry of England* (London: C. & J. Rivington, 1823).

Anon, *An earnest and respectful appeal to the British and Foreign Bible Society, by its South African Auxiliary, on behalf of the injured colony of the Cape of Good Hope* (Cape Town: Saul Solomon, 1849).

Arthur, George, *Defence of transportation, in reply to the remarks of the Archbishop of Dublin in his second letter to Earl Grey* (London: George Cowie, 1835).

Ashton, William, *A lecture on the evils of emigration and transportation, delivered at the town-hall, Sheffield, on July 23, 1838* (Sheffield: J. Lingard, 1839).

Australasian League, *Sessional papers & c. of the Australasian League conference, held in Hobart Town and Launceston, Van Diemen's Land, in the months of April and May, 1852* (Launceston: 1852).

Australasian League, *The League tracts* (Launceston: Henry Dowling, 1851).

Bannister, Saxe, *On abolishing transportation; and on reforming the Colonial Office, in a letter to Lord John Russell* (London: Effingham Wilson, 1837).

Bensley, Benjamin (ed.), *Lost and found; or light in the prison: a narrative with original letters, of a convict, condemned for forgery* (London: W. Wells Gardner, 1859).

Best, John, *A review of the letter addressed to the householders of Hobart Town by the Reverend H. P. Fry, by a member of the medical profession* (Hobart: Advertiser Office, 1847).

Burn, David, *A picture of Van Diemen's Land* (Hobart: Cat & Fiddle Press, 1973).

Button, Henry, *Flotsam and jetsam: floating fragments of life in England and Tasmania, an autobiographical sketch with an outline of the introduction of responsible government* (Launceston: A.W. Birchall & Sons, 1909).

Chisholm, Caroline, *Emigration and transportation relatively considered; in a letter, dedicated, by permission, to Earl Grey* (London: John Ollivier, 1847).

Collins, David, *An account of the English colony in New South Wales: with remarks on the dispositions, customs, manners & c. of the native inhabitants of that country. To which are added some particulars of New Zealand; compiled, by permission, from the Mss. of Lieutenant-Governor King, by David Collins Esquire, late Judge Advocate and Secretary of the colony. Illustrated by engravings* (London: T. Cadell & W. Davies, 1798), 2 volumes.

Currey, John (ed.), *An account of the settlement at Sullivan Bay, Port Phillip, 1803 by William Pascoe Crook* (Melbourne: The Colony Press, 1983).

Currey, John (ed.), *Records of the Port Phillip expedition* (Melbourne: The Colony Press, 1990).

Denison, William, *Varieties of vice-regal life* (London: Longmans, Green & Co., 1870), 2 volumes.

Dyer, George, *Slavery and famine: punishments for sedition or an account of the miseries and starvation at Botany Bay by George Thompson who sailed in the Royal Admiral, May 1792, with some preliminary remarks by George Dyer* (Sydney: D.S. Ford, 1947).

Egerton, Hugh Edward (ed.), *Selected speeches of Sir William Molesworth on questions relating to colonial policy* (London: John Murray, 1903).

Ellis, Sarah Stickney, *The women of England, their social duties and domestic habits* (London: Fisher, Son & Co., 1839).

Fawcett, Millicent Garrett, *Life of the Right Honourable Sir William Molesworth* (London: Macmillan, 1901).

Franklin, John, *A confidential despatch from Sir John Franklin on female convicts, Van Diemen's Land* (Hobart: Sullivan's Cove, 1996).

Frost, John, *A letter to the people of Great Britain and Ireland showing the effects of irresponsible power on the physical and moral conditions of convicts, by John Frost, late of Van Diemen's Land* (London: Holyoake, 1857).

Frost, John, *The horrors of convict life* (Hobart: Sullivan's Cove, 1973).

Frost, Lucy, *A face in the glass: the journal and life of Annie Baxter Dawbin* (Melbourne: Heinemann, 1992).

Fry, Henry Phibbs, *A letter to the householders of Hobarton, on the effects of transportation, and on the moral condition of the colony* (Hobart: John Moore, 1847).

Fry, Henry Phibbs, *A system of penal discipline with a report on the treatment of prisoners in Great Britain and Van Diemen's Land* (London: Longman, Brown, Green & Longman, 1850).

Godwin, *Emigrants' guide to Van Diemen's Land* (London: Sherwood, Jones & Co., 1823).

Hamilton-Arnold, Barbara (ed.), *Letters of G.P. Harris, 1803–1812* (Sorrento, Victoria: Arden Press, 1994).

Ingleton, Geoffrey Chapman, *True patriots all or news from early Australia as told in a collection of broadsides* (Sydney: Angus & Robertson, 1952).

Isbister, Alexander, *A proposal for a new penal settlement, in connexion with the colonization of the uninhabited districts of British North America* (London: Trelawney Saunders, 1850).

Jackson, J.A., *Correspondence with the Colonial Department on transportation to Van Diemen's Land, April and May 1848* (London: Richards, 1848).

Lackland, Jacob, *Common sense: an enquiry into the influence of transportation on the colony of Van Diemen's Land* (Launceston: Henry Dowling, 1847).

Lloyd, George Thomas, *Thirty-three years in Tasmania and Victoria* (London: Houston & Wright, 1862).

Loveless, George, *The victims of Whiggery; being a statement of persecution experienced by the Dorchester Labourers; their trial; banishment & c: also reflections upon the present system of transportation; with an account of Van Diemen's Land, its customs, laws, climate, produce and inhabitants* (London: Cleave, 1838).

McKay, Anne (ed.), *Journals of the land commissioners for Van Diemen's Land 1826–28* (Hobart: Tasmanian Historical Research Association, 1962).

Maconochie, Alexander, *Report on the state of prison discipline in Van Diemen's Land* (London: W. Clowes, 1838).

Maconochie, Alexander, *Secondary punishment: the mark system of prison discipline* (London: John Ollivier, 1848).

Maconochie, Alexander, *On Colonel Arthur's general character and government* (Adelaide: Nag's Head Press, 1989). Originally published in 1849.

Maconochie, Alexander, *On punishment* (London: Mitchell & Son, 1857).

Marriott, Fitzherbert Adams, *Is a penal colony reconcilable with God's constitution of human society and the laws of Christ's Kingdom?* (Hobart: William Gore Elliston, 1847).

Melville, Henry, *The history of the island of Van Diemen's Land, from the year 1824 to 1835 inclusive, to which is added a few words on prison discipline* (London: Smith & Elder, 1835).

Melville, Henry, *Australasia and prison discipline* (London: Effingham Wilson, 1851).

Meredith, Louisa, *Notes and sketches of New South Wales* (London: Murray, 1844).

Meredith, Louisa, *My home in Tasmania* (London: Murray, 1852), 2 volumes.

Mereweather, John Davies, *Diary of a working clergyman in Australia and Tasmania: kept during the years 1850–53; including his return to England by way of Java, Singapore, Ceylon and Egypt* (London: Hatchard, 1859).

Merivale, Herman, *Lectures on colonization and colonies* (London: Longman, Orme, Brown, Green & Longmans, 1841), 2 volumes.

Millar, John, *The origin of the distinction of ranks: or, an inquiry into the circumstances which gave rise to influence and authority in the different members of society* (Bristol: Thoemmes, 1990).

Mineka, Francis (ed.), *The earlier letters of John Stuart Mill 1812–1848* (Toronto: University of Toronto Press, 1963).

Molesworth, William, *Report from the Select Committee of the House of Commons on transportation; together with a letter from the Archbishop of Dublin on the same subject; and notes by Sir Willam Molesworth, Bart., Chairman of the Committee* (London: Henry Hooper, 1838).

Molesworth, William, *State of the nation: condition of the people* (London: Henry Hetherington, 1840).

Molesworth, William, *On colonial expenditure and government* (Liverpool: Financial Reform Tracts, 1882).

Molesworth, William, *Speech on the discontinuance of transportation to Van Diemen's Land* (London: Richards, 1851).

Molesworth, William, *Southwark election speech* (London: Charles Westerton, 1852).

Molesworth, William, *Speech on the ballot* (London: B.D. Cousins, 1854).

Mudie, James, *The felonry of New South Wales, being a faithful picture of the real romance of life in Botany Bay, with anecdotes of Botany Bay society, and a plan of Sydney, by James Mudie of Castle Forbes, and late a Magistrate for the territory of New South Wales* (London: Whaley & Co., 1837).

Nicholls, Mary (ed.), *The diary of the Reverend Robert Knopwood, 1803–1838* (Hobart: Tasmanian Historical Research Association, 1977).

Phillip, Arthur, *The voyage of Governor Phillip to Botany Bay with an account of the establishment of the colonies of Port Jackson and Norfolk Island* (London: John Stockdale, 1789).

Pocock, Zachary Pearce, *Transportation and convict discipline considered in a letter to the Right Honourable Earl Grey, Her Majesty's Principal Secretary for the Colonial Department showing the evils attendant upon the system pursued in Van Diemen's Land, and the remedy for those evils; with suggestions for the profitable employment of convict labour, and for*

[265]

rendering it a source of wealth and prosperity to the colony and the mother country (London: Simmonds & Co., 1847).

Pocock, Zachary Pearce, *Emigration and colonisation, in a letter to the Right Honourable Earl Grey, Her Majesty's Principal Secretary of State for the Colonial Department, showing them to be a means of affording profitable employment for convict labour; of promoting the success and happiness of emigrants, as individuals, and the prosperity and comfort of England and her colonies* (London: Simmonds & Co., London, 1847).

Poor Law Commission, Great Britain, *Copy of the report made in 1834 by the Commissioners for inquiring into the administration and practical operation of the Poor Laws* (London: HMSO, 1905).

Pritchard, M.F. Lloyd (ed.), *The collected works of Edward Gibbon Wakefield* (London: Collins, 1968).

Ratcliff, Patricia Fitzgerald (ed.), *John West's Union of the Colonies: essays on federation published under the pseudonym of John Adams in 1854* (Launceston: Queen Victoria Museum and Art Gallery, 2000).

Roebuck, John Arthur, *The colonies of England: a plan for the government of some portion of our colonial possessions* (London: Dawsons, 1968).

Ross, James, *An essay on prison discipline in which is detailed the system pursued in Van Diemen's Land* (Hobart: James Ross, 1833).

Ross, James, *The settler in Van Diemen's Land* (Melbourne: Marsh Walsh Publishing, 1975).

Rowcroft, Charles, *Tales of the colonies or, the adventures of an emigrant edited by a late colonial magistrate* (London: Saunders & Otley, 1843), 2 volumes.

Schaffer, Irene (ed.), *Land musters, stock returns and lists: Van Diemen's Land, 1803–1822* (Hobart: St David's Park Publishing, 1991).

Seeley, J.R., *The expansion of England: two courses of lectures* (London: Macmillan, 1883).

S., J., *The moral and pecuniary evils which the free colonists of Van Diemen's Land are suffering from the conversion of that island into the chief receptacle of British convicts* (London: privately circulated pamphlet, 1846).

Statistical returns of Van Diemen's Land from 1824 to 1839 (Hobart: William Gore Elliston, 1839).

Statistical returns of Van Diemen's Land or Tasmania from the date of its first occupation by the British nation in 1804 to the end of the year 1823 (Hobart: James Barnard, 1856).

Stevens, C.G., *An appeal from Earl Grey and Sir William Denison, to British justice and humanity, against the proposed continuance of transportation to Van Diemen's Land, in a letter to the liberal press of the nation* (London: John Snow, 1851).

Syme, James, *Nine years in Van Diemen's Land: comprising an account of its discovery, possession, settlement, progress, population, value of lands, herds, flocks & c; an essay on prison discipline; and the results of the working of the probation system; with anecdotes of bushrangers* (Perth: James Dewar, 1848).

Tardif, Phillip, *Notorious strumpets and dangerous girls. Convict women in Van Diemen's Land, 1803–1829* (Sydney: Angus & Robertson, 1990).

Tench, Watkin, *A complete account of the settlement at Port Jackson* (Melbourne: Text Publishing Company, 1996).

Tennant, Charles, *A letter to the Right Hon Sir George Murray on systematic colonisation* (London: James Ridgway, 1830).

Torrens, Robert, *Transportation considered as a punishment and as a mode of founding colonies* (London: William Ridgway, 1863).

Trollope, Anthony, *Australia and New Zealand* (London: Dawsons, 1968), 2 volumes.

Tuckey, James, *A voyage to establish a colony at Port Philip on Bass's Strait on the south coast of New South Wales, in His Majesty's Ship Calcutta, in the years 1802–3–4* (London: Longman, Hurst, Rees & Orme, 1805).

Ullathorne, William, *The Catholic mission in Australia* (Liverpool: Rockliff & Duckworth, 1837).

Ullathorne, William, *The horrors of transportation briefly unfolded to the people* (Dublin: Richard Coyne, 1838).

Ullathorne, William, *The Devil is a jackass being the dying words of the autobiographer William Bernard Ullathorne* (Bath: Downside Abbey Publications, 1995).

Warung, Price, *Tales of the convict system* (St Lucia, Queensland: University of Queensland Press, 1975).

West, John, *The history of Tasmania* (Launceston: Henry Dowling, 1852), 2 volumes.

Whately, Richard, *Introductory lectures on political economy* (London: B. Fellowes, 1832).

Whately, Richard, *Thoughts on secondary punishments, in a letter to Earl Grey* (London: B. Fellowes, 1832).

Whately, Richard, *Remarks on transportation, and on a recent defence of the system in a second letter to Earl Grey* (London: B. Fellowes, 1834).

Whately, Richard, *Substance of a speech on transportation, delivered in the House of Lords, on the 19th May 1840* (London: B. Fellowes, 1840).

Widowson, Henry, *The present state of Van Diemen's Land* (London: S. Robinson, 1829).

Wilberforce, William, *An appeal to the religion, justice and humanity of the inhabitants of the British empire in behalf of the Negro slaves in the West Indies* (London: J. Hatchard, 1823).

Wilberforce, William, *Negro slavery; or a view of some of the more prominent features of that state of society, as it exists in the United States of America and in the colonies of the West Indies, especially in Jamaica* (New York: Greenwood, 1969).

Wood, William, *An answer to the calumnies of the English press: being the testimony of the Lieutenant-Governor, and of the resident Ministers of the various communions of Van Diemen's Land, upon the moral and religious character of the free population of that colony* (Launceston: H. Dowling, 1839).

Worgan, George, *Journal of a First Fleet surgeon* (Sydney: Library Council of New South Wales/Library of Australian History, 1978).

Newspapers and periodicals

Van Diemen's Land

Bent's News
Colonial Times
Colonist
Cornwall Chronicle
Cornwall Press
Derwent Star
Hobart Town Courier
Hobart Town Gazette
Launceston Advertiser
Launceston Examiner
Launceston Independent
Tasmanian & Austral-Asiatic Review
Tasmanian & Port Dalrymple Advertiser
True Colonist

Britain

Edinburgh Review
Northern Star
The Times

Secondary books and articles

Adburgham, Alison, *A radical aristocrat: the Right Honourable Sir William Molesworth* (Padstow: Tabb House, 1990).

Alford, Katrina, *Production or reproduction? An economic history of women in Australia, 1788–1850* (Melbourne: Oxford University Press, 1984).

Alford, Katrina, 'The drover's wife and her friends: women in rural society and primary production in Australia, 1850–1900', *Australian National University Working Papers in Economic History*, no. 75 (November 1986).

Altink, Henrice, '"An outrage on all decency": abolitionist reactions to flogging Jamaican slave women, 1780–1834', *Slavery & Abolition*, 23:2 (2002), pp. 107–24.

Atkinson, Alan, 'Four patterns of convict protest', *Labour History*, 37 (1979), pp. 28–51.

Atkinson, Alan, 'Marriage and distance in the convict colonies, 1838', *Push from the Bush*, 16 (1983), pp. 61–70.

Atkinson, Alan, 'Convicts and courtship', in Patricia Grimshaw, Chris McConville and Ellen McEwen (eds), *Families in colonial Australia* (Sydney: George Allen & Unwin, 1985), pp. 19–31.

Atkinson, Alan, 'Time, place and paternalism: early conservative thinking in New South Wales', *Australian Historical Studies*, 23:90 (1988), pp. 1–18.

Atkinson, Alan, *Camden: farm and village life in early New South Wales* (Melbourne: Oxford University Press, 1988).

Atkinson, Alan, 'The first plans for governing New South Wales, 1786–87', *Australian Historical Studies*, 24:94 (1990), pp. 22–40.

Atkinson, Alan, 'The freeborn Englishman transported: convict rights as a measure of eighteenth-century Empire', *Past & Present*, 144 (1994), pp. 88–115.

Atkinson, Alan, *The Europeans in Australia* (Melbourne: Oxford University Press, 1997 & 2005), 2 volumes.

Aveling, Marian (now Quartly), 'She only married to be free: or Cleopatra vindicated', in Norma Grieve and Patricia Grimshaw (eds), *Australian women: feminist perspectives* (Melbourne: Oxford University Press, 1981), pp. 119–33.

Aveling, Marian (now Quartly), 'Gender in early New South Wales society', *Push from the Bush*, 24 (1987), pp. 31–41.

Aveling, Marian (now Quartly), 'Imagining New South Wales as a gendered society, 1783–1821', *Australian Historical Studies*, 25:98 (1992), pp. 1–12.

Aveling, Marian (now Quartly), 'Bending the bars: convict women and the state', in Kay Saunders and Raymond Evans (eds), *Gender relations in Australia: domination and negotiation* (Sydney: Harcourt Brace Jovanovich, 1994), pp. 144–57.

Barker-Benfield, G.J., *The culture of sensibility: sex and society in eighteenth-century Britain* (London: University of Chicago Press, 1992).

Bateson, Charles, *The convict ships, 1788–1868* (Sydney: A.H. & A.W. Reed, 1974).

Bayly, Christopher, *Imperial meridian: the British Empire and the world* (London: Longman, 1989).

Blackton, Charles, 'The Australasian League, 1851–54', *Pacific Historical Review*, 8:4 (1939), pp. 385–400.

Bolton, G.C., 'The idea of a colonial gentry', *Historical Studies*, 13:51 (1968), pp. 307–28.

Bowring, John (ed.), *The Works of Jeremy Bentham* (Edinburgh: William Tait, 1843), Volume IV.

Brand, Ian, *The convict probation system: Van Diemen's Land 1839–1854* (Hobart: Blubber Head Press, 1990).

Bray, Alan, 'Homosexuality and the signs of male friendship in Elizabethan England', *History Workshop Journal*, 29 (1990), pp. 1–19.

Breen, Shayne, 'Land and Power in the District of Deloraine: 1825–1875', *Tasmanian Historical Research Association*, 37:1 (1990), pp. 23–33.

Breen, Shayne, *Contested places: Tasmania's northern districts from ancient times to 1900* (Hobart: Centre for Tasmanian Historical Studies, 2001).

Brewer, Anthony, 'Luxury and economic development: David Hume and Adam Smith', *Scottish Journal of Political Economy*, 41:1 (1998), pp. 78–98.

Bruhm, Steven, *Gothic bodies: the politics of pain in Romantic fiction* (Philadelphia, PA: University of Pennsylvania Press, 1994).

Byrne, Paula-Jane, 'Women and the criminal law: Sydney, 1810–1821', *Push from the Bush*, 21 (1985), pp. 2–19.

[269]

SELECT BIBLIOGRAPHY

Byrne, Paula-Jane, *Criminal law and colonial subject: New South Wales, 1810–1830* (Cambridge: Cambridge University Press, 1993).

Byrne, Paula-Jane, 'A colonial female economy', *Social History*, 24:3 (1999), pp. 287–93.

Chase, Malcolm, *The people's farm: English radical agrarianism, 1775–1840* (Oxford: Clarendon, 1988).

Clark, Anna, 'The rhetoric of Chartist domesticity: gender, language and class in the 1830s and 1840s', *Journal of British Studies*, 31:1 (1992), pp. 62–88.

Clark, Anna, *The struggle for the breeches: gender and the making of the British working class* (Berkeley, CA: University of California Press, 1995).

Clarke, C.M.H., 'The origins of the convicts transported to Eastern Australia, 1787–1852', *Historical Studies: Australia & New Zealand*, 7:26–27 (1956), pp. 121–35; pp. 314–27.

Clarke, Patricia and Spender, Dale (eds), *Lifelines: Australian women's letters and diaries, 1788–1840* (Sydney: Allen & Unwin, 1992).

Coats, A.W., 'Changing attitudes to labour in the mid-eighteenth century', *Economic History Review*, 11:1 (1958), pp. 33–51.

Cocks, Harry, *Nameless offences: homosexual desire in the nineteenth century* (London: I.B. Tauris, 2003).

Connell, R. W. and Irving, T. H., *Class structure in Australian history* (Melbourne: Longman Cheshire, 1980).

Cotton, Frances, 'Home life in Van Diemen's Land', *Tasmanian Historical Research Association*, 21:4 (1974), pp. 175–80.

Cubit, Simon, 'Squatters and opportunists: occupation of lands to the westward to 1830', *Tasmanian Historical Research Association*, 34:1 (1987), pp. 7–14.

Currey, John, *David Collins, a colonial life* (Melbourne: Melbourne University Press, 2000).

Curthoys, Ann, 'Identity crisis: colonialism, nation and gender in Australian history', *Gender & History*, 5:2 (1993), pp. 165–76.

Damousi, Joy, *Depraved and disorderly: female convicts, sexuality and gender in colonial Australia* (Cambridge: Cambridge University Press, 1997).

Daniels, Kay, 'The flash mob: rebellion, rough culture and sexuality in the Female Factories of Van Diemen's Land', *Australian Feminist Studies*, 18 (1993), pp. 133–50.

Daniels, Kay, *Convict Women* (St Leonards, NSW: Allen & Unwin, 1998).

Daniels, Kay (ed.), *So much hard work: women and prostitution in Australian history* (Sydney: Fontana/Collins, 1984).

Davidson, Alastair, *The invisible state: the formation of the Australian State, 1788–1901* (Cambridge: Cambridge University Press, 1991).

Davis, David Brion, *The problem of slavery in Western culture* (Ithaca, NY: Cornell University Press, 1966).

Dinwiddy, J.R., 'The early nineteenth-century campaign against flogging in the army', *English Historical Review*, 97:383 (1982), pp. 308–31.

Dixson, Miriam, *The real Matilda: woman and identity in Australia, 1788–1975* (Ringwood, Australia: Penguin, 1976).

Duffield, Ian and Bradley, James (eds), *Representing convicts: new perspectives on convict forced labour migration* (London: Leicester University Press, 1997).

Duffield, Ian and Maxwell-Stewart, Hamish, 'Skin deep devotions: religious tattoos and convict transportation to Australia', in Jane Caplan (ed.), *Written on the body: the tattoo in European and American history* (London: Reaktion, 2000), pp. 118–35.

Duffy, Michael, *Man of honour: John Macarthur – duellist, rebel, founding father* (Sydney: Pan Macmillan Australia, 2003).

Dyster, Barrie, 'Transported workers: the case of Mayhew versus Mayhew', *Labour History*, 60 (1991), pp. 84–92.

Elbourne, Elizabeth, 'The sin of the settler: the 1835–36 Select Committee on aborigines and debates over virtue and conquest in the early nineteenth-century British white settler empire', *Journal of Colonialism and Colonial History*, 4:3 (2003), pp. 1–49.

Emsley, Clive, *Crime and society in England, 1750–1900* (London: Longman, 1987).

Evans, Raymond and Thorpe, William, 'Power, punishment and penal labour: Convict Workers and Moreton Bay', *Australian Historical Studies*, 25:98 (1992), pp. 90–111.

Evans, Raymond and Thorpe, Bill, 'The last days of Moreton Bay: power, sexuality and the misrule of law', *Journal of Australian Studies*, 53 (1997), pp. 59–77.

Evans, Raymond and Thorpe, Bill, 'Commanding men: masculinities and the convict system', *Journal of Australian Studies*, 56 (1998), pp. 17–34.

Evans, Raymond and Saunders, Kay (eds), *Gender relations in Australia: domination and negotiation* (Sydney: Harcourt Brace Jovanovich, 1992).

Evatt, H.V., *Rum rebellion: a study of the overthrow of Governor Bligh* (Sydney: Angus & Robertson, 1938).

Fenoaltea, Stefano, 'Slavery and supervision in comparative perspective: a model', *Journal of Economic History*, 44: 3 (1984), pp. 635–68.

Field, Michele and Millett, Timothy (eds), *Convict love tokens: the leaden hearts the convicts left behind* (Kent Town, South Australia: Wakefield Press, 1998).

Fitzpatrick, Kathleen, 'Mr. Gladstone and the Governor: the recall of Sir John Eardley Wilmot from Van Diemen's Land, 1846', *Historical Studies: Australia & New Zealand*, 1:1 (1940), pp. 31–45.

Fitzpatrick, Kathleen, *Sir John Franklin in Tasmania, 1837–1843* (Carlton, Victoria: Melbourne University Press, 1949).

Forsyth, W. D., *Governor Arthur's convict system. Van Diemen's Land 1824–36* (London: Longman, Green & Co., 1935).

Forsythe, W.J., *The reform of prisoners, 1830–1900* (London: Croom Helm, 1987).

Foster, S.G., 'Convict assignment in New South Wales in the 1830s', *Push from the Bush*, 15 (1983), pp. 35–80.

Foucault, Michel, *Discipline and punish: the birth of the prison* (London: Allen Lane, 1977).

Friends of the Turnbull Library (ed.), *Edward Gibbon Wakefield and the colonial dream: a reconsideration* (Wellington, New Zealand: G.P. Publications, 1997).

Frost, Lucy and Maxwell-Stewart, Hamish (eds), *Chain letters: narrating convict lives* (Carlton, Victoria: Melbourne University Press, 2001).

Gallagher, Catherine, *The industrial reformation of English fiction. Social discourse and narrative form, 1832–1867* (Chicago, IL: University of Chicago Press, 1980).

Gascoigne, John, *The Enlightenment and the origins of European Australia* (Cambridge: Cambridge University Press, 2002).

Gatrell, V.A.C., *The hanging tree: execution and the English people 1770–1868* (Oxford: Oxford University Press, 1994).

Glenn, Myra, 'The naval reform campaign against flogging: a case study in changing attitudes towards corporal punishment, 1830–1850', *American Quarterly*, 35:4 (1983), pp. 408–25.

Gothard, Jan, *Blue china: single female migration to Australia* (Carlton, Victoria: Melbourne University Press, 2001).

Grimshaw, Patricia, 'Women and the family in Australian history', in Elizabeth Windschuttle (ed.), *Women, class and history: feminist perspectives on Australia, 1788–1978* (Melbourne: Fontana/Collins, 1980), pp. 37–52.

Grimshaw, Patricia and Willett, Graham, 'Women's history and family history: an exploration of colonial family structure', in Norma Grieve and Patricia Grimshaw (eds), *Australian women: feminist perspectives* (Melbourne: Oxford University Press, 1981), pp. 134–55.

Haines, Robin, *Emigration and the labouring poor: Australian recruitment in Britain and Ireland, 1831–60* (Basingstoke: Macmillan, 1997).

Hall, Catherine 'The early formation of Victorian domestic ideology', in Sandra Burman (ed.), *Fit work for women* (London: Croom Helm, 1979), pp. 15–32.

Hall, Catherine, *White, male and middle class: explorations in feminism and history* (Cambridge: Polity, 1992).

Hall, Catherine, 'The rule of difference: gender, class and empire in the making of the 1832 Reform Act', in Ida Blom, Karen Hagemann and Catherine Hall (eds), *Gendered nations: nationalism and gender order in the long nineteenth century* (New York: New York University Press, 2000), pp. 107–35.

Hall, Catherine, *Civilising subjects: metropole and colony in the English imagination, 1830–1867* (Cambridge: Polity, 2002).

Halttunen, Karen 'Humanitarianism and the pornography of pain in Anglo-American culture', *American Historical Review*, 100:2 (1995), pp. 303–34.

Hartwell, R.M., *The economic development of Van Diemen's Land 1820–1850* (Carlton, Victoria: Melbourne University Press, 1954).

Hattersley, A.F., *Convict crisis and the growth of unity: resistance to transportation in South Africa and Australia, 1848–53* (Pietermaritzburg: University of Natal Press, 1965).

Heath, Laurel, 'A safe and salutary discipline: the dark cells at the Parramatta Female Factory, 1838', *Push from the Bush*, 9 (1981), pp. 20–9.

Heuman, Gad, *The killing time: the Morant Bay rebellion in Jamaica* (London: Macmillan, 1994).

Hilton, Boyd, *The age of atonement: the influence of Evangelicalism on social and economic thought, 1795–1865* (Oxford: Clarendon Press, 1988).

Hindmarsh, Bruce, 'Scorched earth: contested power and divided loyalties on Midlands properties, 1820–1840', in Peter Chapman (ed.), *Exiles of empire: convict experience and penal policy, 1788–1852* (Hobart: Tasmanian Historical Studies, 1999), pp. 63–80.

Hirst, J.B., *Convict society and its enemies: a history of early New South Wales* (Sydney: George Allen & Unwin, 1983).

Hollis, Patricia, 'Anti-slavery and British working-class radicalism in the years of reform', in Christine Bolt and Seymour Drescher (eds), *Anti-Slavery, religion, and reform: essays in memory of Roger Anstey* (Folkstone: Dawson, 1980), pp. 294–315.

Holt, Thomas, *The promise of freedom: race, labor, and politics in Jamaica and Britain, 1832–1938* (Baltimore: Johns Hopkins University Press, 1992).

Hughes, Robert, *The fatal shore: a history of the transportation of convicts to Australia, 1787–1868* (London: Pan, 1988).

Huon, Dan 'By moral means only: the origins of the Launceston anti-transportation leagues, 1847–49', *Tasmanian Historical Research Association* 44:2 (1997), pp. 92–119.

Hutchinson, R.C., 'Mrs Hutchinson and the Female Factories of early Australia', *Tasmanian Historical Research Association*, 11:2 (1963), pp. 50–67.

Ignatieff, Michael, *A just measure of pain: the penitentiary in the Industrial Revolution* (New York: Columbia University Press, 1978).

Karskens, Grace, *The Rocks: life in early Sydney* (Carlton, Vic.: Melbourne University Press, 1997).

Kent, David, 'Decorative bodies: the significance of convicts' tattoos', *Journal of Australian Studies*, 53 (1997), pp. 78–88.

Kent, David, and Townsend, Norma, *The convicts of the* Eleanor*: protest in rural England, new lives in Australia* (London: Merlin, 2001).

Kercher, Bruce, 'Perish or prosper: the law and convict transportation in the British Empire, 1700–1850', *Law & History Review*, 21:3 (2003), pp. 527–84.

Knorr, Klaus, *British colonial theories, 1570–1850* (Toronto: University of Toronto Press, 1944).

Lake, Marilyn, 'Helpmeet, slave, housewife: women in rural families, 1870–1930', in Grimshaw, Patricia, McConville, Chris and McEwen, Ellen (eds), *Families in Colonial Australia* (Sydney: George Allen & Unwin, 1985), pp. 173–85.

Lake, Marilyn, 'Convict women as objects of male vision: an historiographical review', *Bulletin of the Centre for Tasmanian Historical Studies*, 2:1 (1988), pp. 40–8.

Lambert, Ronald, 'Reclaiming the ancestral past: narrative, rhetoric and the 'convict stain'', *Journal of Sociology*, 38:2 (2002), pp. 111–27.

Lansbury, Coral, *Arcady in Australia: the evocation of Australia in nineteenth-century English literature* (Melbourne: Melbourne University Press, 1970).

Laqueur, Thomas, 'Bodies, details, and the humanitarian narrative', in Lynn Hunt (ed.), *The new cultural history* (Berkeley, CA: University of California Press, 1989), pp. 176–204.

Lester, Alan, 'British settler discourse and the circuits of empire', *History Workshop Journal*, 54:1 (2002), pp. 24–48.

Lester, Alan, 'Obtaining the "due observance of justice": the geographies of colonial humanitarianism', *Environment and Planning: D: Society and Space*, 20:3 (2002), pp. 277–93.

McClintock, Anne, *Imperial leather: race, gender and sexuality in the colonial contest* (London: Routledge, 1995).

MacFie, Peter, *Stock thieves and golfers: a history of Kangaroo Bay and Rosny Farm, Tasmania, 1803–1998* (Rosny Park, Tasmania: Clarence City Council, 2002).

McGowen, Randall, 'A powerful sympathy: terror, the prison and humanitarian reform in early nineteenth-century Britain', *Journal of British Studies*, 25:3 (1986), pp. 312–34.

McGowen, Randall, 'The body and punishment in eighteenth-century England', *Journal of Modern History*, 59:4 (1987), pp. 651–79.

McGowen, Randall, 'Civilising punishment: the end of the public execution in England', *Journal of British Studies*, 33:3 (1994), pp. 257–82.

McGrath, Anne, 'The white man's looking glass: aboriginal-colonial gender relations at Port Jackson', *Australian Historical Studies*, 24:95 (1990), pp. 634–52.

McKenzie, Kirsten, 'Women's talk and the colonial state: the Wylde scandal, 1831–1833', *Gender & History*, 11:1, 1999, pp. 30–53.

McKenzie, Kirsten, *Scandal in the colonies: Sydney and Cape Town, 1820–1850* (Carlton, Victoria: Melbourne University Press, 2004).

McLaughlin, Anne, 'Against the League: fighting the "Hated Stain"', *Tasmanian Historical Research Association*, 5:1 (1995–96), pp. 76–104.

MacNab, Ken and Ward, Russel, 'The nature and nurture of the first generation of native-born Australians', *Historical Studies: Australia & New Zealand*, 10:39 (1962), pp. 289–308.

Malchow, H.L., *Gothic images of race in nineteenth-century Britain* (Stanford, CA: Stanford University Press, 1996).

Marshall, M.G., 'Luxury, economic development and work motivation: David Hume, Adam Smith and J.R. McCulloch', *History of Political Economy*, 32:3 (2000), pp. 631–48.

Maxwell-Stewart, Hamish, 'I could not blame the rangers: Tasmanian bushranging, convicts and convict management', *Tasmanian Historical Research Association*, 42:3 (1995), pp. 109–26.

Maxwell-Stewart, Hamish, 'Convict workers, penal labour and Sarah Island: life at Macquarie Harbour, 1822–1834', in Ian Duffield and James Bradley (eds), *Representing convicts: new perspectives on convict forced labour migration* (London: Leicester University Press, 1997), pp. 142–62.

Maxwell-Stewart, Hamish, 'The rise and fall of John Longworth: work and punishment in early Port Arthur', *Tasmanian Historical Studies*, 6:2 (1999), pp. 96–114.

Mays, Kelly, 'Slaves in Heaven, laborers in Hell: Chartist poets' ambivalent identification with the (black) slave', *Victorian Poetry*, 39:2 (2001), pp. 137–63.

Meredith, David and Oxley, Deborah, 'Contracting convicts: the convict labour market in Van Diemen's Land 1840–1857', *Australian Economic History Review*, 45:1 (2005), pp. 45–72.

Midgley, Clare (ed.), *Gender and imperialism* (Manchester: Manchester University Press, 1998).

Morgan, Sharon, 'George and Mary Meredith: the role of the colonial wife', *Tasmanian Historical Research Association*, 36:3 (1989), pp. 125–9.

Morgan, Sharon, *Land settlement in early Tasmania: creating an antipodean England* (Melbourne: Cambridge University Press, 1992).

Nead, Lynda, *Myths of sexuality: representations of women in Victorian Britain* (Oxford: Basil Blackwell, 1988).

Neal, David, *The rule of law in a penal colony: law and power in early New South Wales* (Cambridge: Cambridge University Press, 1991).

Nichol, W., 'Malingering and convict protest', *Labour History*, 47 (1984), pp. 18–27.

Nichol, W, 'Ideology and the convict system in New South Wales, 1788–1820', *Historical Studies*, 22:86 (1986), pp. 1–20.

Nicholas, Stephen (ed.), *Convict workers: reinterpreting Australia's past* (Cambridge: Cambridge University Press, 1988).

O'Connor, Tamsin, 'Buckley's chance: freedom and hope at the penal settlements of Newcastle and Moreton Bay', *Tasmanian Historical Studies*, 6:2 (1999), pp. 115–28.

Oldfield, J.R., *Popular politics and British anti-slavery* (Manchester: Manchester University Press, 1995).

Oxley, Deborah, *Convict maids: the forced migration of women to Australia* (Cambridge: Cambridge University Press, 1996).

Parrott, Jennifer, 'Agents of industry and civilisation: the British government emigration scheme for convicts' wives, Van Diemen's Land 1817–1840', *Tasmanian Historical Studies*, 4:2 (1994), pp. 25–30.

Pateman, Carole, *The sexual contract* (Oxford: Polity, 1988).

Paton, Diana, 'Decency, dependence and the lash: gender and the British debate over slave emancipation, 1830–34', *Slavery and Abolition*, 17:3 (1996), pp. 163–84.

Perrott, Monica, *'A tolerable good success': economic opportunities for women in New South Wales, 1788–1830* (Sydney: Hale & Ironmonger, 1983).

Perry, Adele, 'The state of empire: reproducing colonialism in British Columbia, 1849–1871', *Journal of Colonialism and Colonial History*, 2:2 (2001).

Petrow, Stefan, 'Policing in a penal colony: Governor Arthur's police system in Van Diemen's Land, 1826–1836', *Law & History Review*, 18:2 (2000), pp. 351–95.

Philips, David, *Crime and authority in Victorian England: the Black Country, 1835–1860* (London: Croom Helm, 1977).

Picker, Gregory, 'A state of infancy: the anti-transportation movement in New Zealand, 1848–52', *New Zealand Journal of History*, 34:2 (2000), pp. 226–40.

Porter, Andrew, 'Trusteeship, anti-slavery and humanitarianism', in Andrew Porter (ed.), *The Oxford History of the British Empire, Volume 3: The nineteenth century* (Oxford: Oxford University Press, 1999), pp. 198–221.

Radzinowicz, Leon, *A history of English criminal law and its administration from 1750. Volume V: Grappling for control* (London: Stevens, 1968).

Ratcliff, Patricia Fitzgerald, *The usefulness of John West: dissent and difference in the Australian colonies* (Launceston: Albernian Press, 2003).

Rayner, Tony, *Historical survey of the Female Factory historic site, Cascades, Hobart* (Hobart: National Parks & Wildlife Service, 1981).

Reid, Kirsty, '"Contumacious, ungovernable and incorrigible": convict women and workplace resistance, Van Diemen's Land, 1820–39', in Ian Duffield and James Bradley (eds), *Representing convicts: new perspectives on convict forced labour migration* (London: Leicester University Press, 1997), pp. 106–23.

Reid, Kirsty, 'Setting women to work: the assignment system and female convict labour in Van Diemen's Land', *Australian Historical Studies*, 34:121 (2003), pp. 1–25.

Reynolds, Henry, 'That Hated Stain: the aftermath of transportation in Tasmania', *Historical Studies*, 14:35 (1969), pp. 19–31.

Ritchie, John, *Punishment and profit: the reports of Commissioner John Bigge on the colonies of New South Wales and Van Diemen's Land, 1822–1823* (Melbourne: Heinemann, 1970).

Ritchie, John, 'Towards ending an unclean thing: the Molesworth Committee and the abolition of transportation to New South Wales, 1837–40', *Historical Studies*, 17 (1976), pp. 144–64.

Ritchie, John, *Lachlan Macquarie: a biography* (Melbourne: Melbourne University Press, 1986).

Robbins, W.M., 'Spatial escape and the Hyde Park convict barracks', *Journal of Australian Colonial History*, 6:1 (2004), pp. 81–122.

Robbins, W.M., 'The supervision of convict gangs in New South Wales, 1788–1830', *Australian Economic History Review*, 44:1 (2004), pp. 80–100.

Robinson, Portia, *The hatch and brood of time: a study of the first generation of native-born white Australians, 1788–1828* (Melbourne: Oxford University Press, 1985).

Robinson, Portia, *The women of Botany Bay* (Sydney: The Macquarie Library, 1988).

Robson, Ann and Robson, John (eds), *Newspaper writings by John Stuart Mill* (Toronto: University of Toronto Press, 1986).

Robson, Lloyd, *The convict settlers of Australia: an enquiry into the origins and character of the convicts transported to New South Wales and Van Diemen's Land 1788–1852* (Carlton, Victoria: Melbourne University Press, 1965).

Robson, Lloyd, *A history of Tasmania. Volume 1: Van Diemen's Land from the earliest times to 1855* (Melbourne: Oxford University Press, 1983).

Roe, Michael, *The quest for authority in Eastern Australia, 1787–1852* (Carlton, Victoria: Melbourne University Press, 1965).

[276]

Rudé, George, *Protest and punishment: the story of the social and political protesters transported to Australia, 1788–1868* (Oxford: Clarendon, 1978).

Rudé, George, *Criminal and victim: crime and society in early nineteenth-century England* (Oxford: Clarendon Press, 1985).

Russell, Penny, *'A wish of distinction': colonial gentility and femininity* (Melbourne: Melbourne University Press, 1994).

Salt, Annette, *These outcast women: the Parramatta Female Factory, 1821–1848* (Sydney: Hale & Ironmonger, 1984).

Saunders, Kay and Evans, Raymond (eds), *Gender relations in Australia: domination and negotiation* (Sydney: Harcourt Brace Jovanovich, 1994).

Schedvin, M.B. and Schedvin, C.B., 'The nomadic tribes of urban Britain: a prelude to Botany Bay', *Historical Studies*, 18:7 (1978–79), pp. 254–76.

Schochet, Gordon, *The authoritarian family and political attitudes in seventeenth-century England* (London: Transaction Books, 1975).

Scott, James C., *Domination and the arts of resistance: hidden transcripts* (New Haven, CT: Yale University Press, 1990).

Searle, G.R., *Morality and the market in Victorian Britain* (Oxford: Clarendon Press, 1998).

Semmel, Bernard, *The rise of free trade imperialism: classical political economy, the empire of free trade and imperialism, 1750–1850* (Cambridge: Cambridge University Press, 1970).

Shakespeare, Nicholas, *In Tasmania* (London: The Harvill Press, 2004).

Shaw, A.G.L., *Convicts and the colonies: a study of penal transportation from Great Britain and Ireland to Australia and other parts of the British Empire* (London: Faber & Faber, 1966).

Shaw, A.G.L., *Sir George Arthur, Bart 1784–1854: Superintendent of British Honduras, Lieutenant-Governor of Van Diemen's Land and of Upper Canada, Governor of the Bombay Presidency* (Carlton, Victoria: Melbourne University Press, 1980).

Shoemaker, Robert, 'Male honour and the decline of public violence in eighteenth-century London', *Social History*, 26:2 (2001), pp. 190–208.

Sinha, Mrinalini, *Colonial masculinity: the 'manly Englishman' and the 'effeminate Bengali' in the late nineteenth century* (Manchester: Manchester University Press, 1995).

Smith, Babette, *A cargo of women: Susannah Watson and the convicts of the Princess Royal* (Kensington, NSW: New South Wales University Press, 1988).

Snow, Dianne, 'Family policy and orphan schools in early colonial Australia', *Journal of Interdisciplinary History*, 22:2 (1991), pp. 255–84.

Stoler, Ann, 'Making empire respectable: the politics of race and sexual morality in twentieth-century colonial cultures', *American Ethnologist*, 16:4 (1989), pp. 634–52.

Strobel, Margaret, 'Gender and race in the nineteenth and twentieth-century British empire', in Renate Bridenthal, Claudia Koonz and Susan Stuard (eds), *Becoming visible: women in European history* (Boston: Houghlon Mifflin, 1977), pp. 375–94.

Sturma, Michael, 'Eye of the beholder: the stereotype of women convicts', *Labour History*, 34 (1978), pp. 3–10.

Sturma, Michael, *Vice in a vicious society: crime and convicts in mid nineteenth-century New South Wales* (St Lucia: University of Queensland Press, 1983).

Summers, Anne, *Damned whores and God's police: the colonisation of women in Australia* (Ringwood, Victoria: Penguin, 1975).

Taylor, Miles, 'Imperium et libertas? Rethinking the radical critique of imperialism during the nineteenth century', *Journal of Imperial and Commonwealth History*, 19:1 (1991), pp. 1–23.

Taylor, Miles, *The decline of British radicalism, 1847–1860* (Oxford: Clarendon Press, 1995).

Taylor, Miles, 'The 1848 Revolutions and the British empire', *Past & Present*, 166 (2000), pp. 146–80.

Taylor, Miles, 'Colonial representation at Westminster, c. 1800–65', in Julian Hoppit (ed.), *Parliaments, nations and identities in Britain and Ireland, 1660–1850* (Manchester: Manchester University Press, 2003), pp. 206–20.

Taylor, Miles, 'Empire and parliamentary reform: the 1832 Reform Act revisited', in Arthur Burns and Joanna Innes (ed.), *Rethinking the Age of Reform* (Cambridge: Cambridge University Press, 2003), pp. 295–311.

Thornton, Alan Mark, *The Philosophic Radicals, their influence on emigration and the evolution of responsible government for the colonies* (Claremont, CA: Pomona College, 1975).

Tipping, Marjorie, *Convicts unbound: the story of the Calcutta convicts and their settlement in Australia* (Victoria: Viking O'Neil, 1988).

Tosh, John, *A man's place: masculinity and the middle-class home in Victorian England* (New Haven CT: Yale University Press, 1999).

Townsend, Norma, '"The clamour of inconsistent persons": attitudes to transportation within New South Wales in the 1830s', *Australian Journal of Politics and History*, 25:3 (1979), pp. 345–57.

Townsend, Norma, 'A "mere lottery": the convict system in New South Wales through the eyes of the Molesworth Committee', *Push from the Bush*, 21 (1985), pp. 58–86.

Tranter, Bruce and Donoghue, Jed, 'Convict ancestry: a neglected aspect of Australian identity', *Nations and Nationalism*, 9:4 (2003), pp. 555–77.

Weatherburn, Hilary, 'The Female Factory', in Judy Mackinolty and Heather Radi (eds), *In pursuit of justice: Australian women and the law, 1788–1979* (Sydney: Hale & Ironmonger, 1979), pp. 18–30.

Wiener, Martin J., *Reconstructing the criminal: culture, law and policy in England 1830–1914* (Cambridge: Cambridge University Press, 1990).

Wilson, Kathleen (ed.), *A new imperial history: culture, identity and modernity in Britain and the empire, 1660–1840* (Cambridge: Cambridge University Press, 2004).

Wood, Marcus, *Blind memory: visual representations of slavery in England and America* (Manchester: Manchester University Press, 2000).

Wood, Marcus, *Slavery, empathy, and pornography* (Oxford: Oxford University Press, 2002).

Zedner, Lucia, *Women, crime and custody in Victorian England* (Oxford: Clarendon Press, 1991).

Unpublished materials

Alexander, Alison, 'The public role of women in Tasmania, 1803–1914' (PhD dissertation, University of Tasmania, 1989).

Gilchrist, Catie, 'Male convict sexuality in the penal colonies of Australia, 1820–1850' (PhD dissertation, University of Sydney, 2004).

Hindmarsh, Bruce, 'Yoked to the plough: male convict labour, culture and resistance in rural Van Diemen's Land, 1820–40' (PhD dissertation, University of Edinburgh, 2002).

McKay, Anne, 'The assignment system of convict labour in Van Diemen's Land, 1824–42' (MA dissertation, University of Tasmania, 1958).

Maxwell-Stewart, Hamish, 'The bushrangers and the convict system of Van Diemen's Land, 1803–1846' (PhD dissertation, University of Edinburgh, 1990).

O'Connor, Tamsin, 'Power and punishment: the limits of resistance: the Moreton Bay penal settlement, 1824–1842' (BA dissertation, University of Queensland, 1994).

Picton Phillipps, Christina, 'Convicts, communication and authority: Britain and New South Wales, 1810–1830' (PhD dissertation, University of Edinburgh, 2002).

Reid, Kirsty, 'Work, sexuality and resistance: the convict women of Van Diemen's Land, 1820–1839' (PhD dissertation, University of Edinburgh, 1995).

Reynolds, John, 'Notes of a lecture on anti-transportation to the Royal Society of Tasmania' (Crowther Library, State Library of Tasmania).

Taylor, Miles, 'Joseph Hume and the reformation of India, 1819–33', in G. Burgess and M. Festenstein (eds), *Radicalism in English political thought, 1550–1850* (Cambridge: Cambridge University Press, forthcoming).

Electronic sources

Leakey, Caroline, *Broad arrow: being passages from the history of Maida Gwynnham, a lifer* (London: Richard Bentley, 1859), www.blackmask.com/books13c/broadarleak.htm.

Macquarie, Lachlan, *Journal to and from Van Diemen's Land to Sydney in New South Wales*, www.lib.mq.edu/all/journeys/1811/1811.html.

The trial of Thomas Picton, 24 February 1806, in *The Newgate Calendar*, www.exclassics.com/newgate/ng477.htm.

INDEX

Lightning Source UK Ltd.
Milton Keynes UK
UKOW01f1907041117
312152UK00006B/464/P